THE PUBLIC PRINTS

THE
PUBLIC PRINTS

The Newspaper
in Anglo-American Culture,
1665–1740

CHARLES E. CLARK

New York   Oxford
OXFORD UNIVERSITY PRESS
1994

Oxford University Press

Oxford   New York   Toronto
Delhi   Bombay   Calcutta   Madras   Karachi
Kuala Lumpur   Singapore   Hong Kong   Tokyo
Nairobi   Dar es Salaam   Cape Town
Melbourne   Auckland   Madrid

and associated companies in
Berlin   Ibadan

Copyright © 1994 by Charles E. Clark

Published by Oxford University Press, Inc.
200 Madison Avenue, New York, New York 10016

Oxford is a registered trademark of Oxford University Press

Library of Congress Cataloging-in-Publication Data
Clark, Charles E., 1929–
The public prints : the newspaper in Anglo-American culture,
1665–1740 / Charles E. Clark.
p.   cm.   Includes bibliographical references and index.
ISBN 0–19–508233–8
1. American newspapers—History. 2. British newspapers—History.
3. United States—Civilization—To 1783. I. Title.
PN4855.C53 1994   307.23'22'0942—dc20   93–2834

I gratefully acknowledge the American Antiquarian Society for permission to reprint from "The News-papers of Provincial America," *Proceedings*, Vol. 100, Part 2 (1990): 367–89; the Centre for Extra-Mural Studies, Birkbeck College, University of London, for permission to reprint from "Metropolis and Province in Eighteenth-Century Press Relations: The Case of Boston," *Journal of Newspaper and Periodical History*, 5 (Autumn 1989): 1–16; and the New England Quarterly Incorporated for permission to reprint from "Boston and the Nurturing of Newspapers: Dimensions of the Cradle, 1690–1741," *New England Quarterly*, 64:243–71.

2 4 6 8 9 7 5 3 1

Printed in the United States of America
on acid-free paper

*For Marilyn, Douglas, Jonathan, and David,
 who came of age (and then some) while this book
 was in the making,
and again for Margery:
 "Love is patient. . . ."*

Acknowledgments

To take a long view of the matter, this book probably started to germinate more than half a century ago. I lived in a New England mill town when there were still mills in New England. Occasionally I accompanied my father on his weekly visit to our only job printing office. His mission there, in his role as a minister, was to look after the coming Sunday's printing needs of the South Congregational Church. Mine was to experience exhilarating sights, sounds, and smells and to be moved, for reasons I could not have explained, by the notions of power and of community that were incorporated in my vision of identical copies of whatever little items were coming off the presses soon finding their way into the hands of hundreds of readers. The printers published a weekly newspaper, bearing the unlikely title of *Argus-Champion*. For me no part of the busy scene was more compelling than the big flatbed newpaper press duplicating again and again the words that had been written at a rolltop desk in the front office overlooking Main Street. If pressed, I probably would not have denied that the soul of the community, if anywhere, was down at the end of the street in my father's church. But here in the newspaper and printing office, I believed, was its heart and its nervous system.

And so I thank those small-town printers and publishers, now certainly dead, for stimulating those first inchoate ideas about news, print, and community. For a time I was so entranced with it all that I prepared to spend my life as a journalist—part-time reporting as a teenager, school and college newpapers, the august Columbia Graduate School of Journalism,

and a hard six-year apprenticeship with the Providence newspapers—
before finding my real niche in life as a student and teacher of early
American history. All those experiences, as must be obvious, have influenced this book, even though the decision to write it came quite a lot later.

Even taking a shorter view, I have been at this project for a distressingly
long time, and the specific debts I have accumulated are correspondingly
many.

I have been aided by grants from the American Council of Learned
Societies, the National Endowment for the Humanities, and several
funds, programs, and offices of my home institution, the University of
New Hampshire. These include the Central University Research Fund,
the Faculty Scholar Program, the Humanities Program, and the College of
Liberal Arts.

I have held valuable fellowships which combined financial support with
the use of wonderful facilities and the enjoyment of equally wonderful
company from the Henry E. Huntington Library and Art Gallery, the
American Antiquarian Society on two occasions, and the Commonwealth
Center for the Study of American Culture at the College of William and
Mary. The project really began at the Huntington Library many summers
ago and took coherent shape during two extended periods at the American
Antiquarian Society, where I did the bulk of my reading in the American
newspapers, the book's core source. The Antiquarian Society has sustained me in other ways as well; I have been fortunate to be included in
certain aspects of its Program in the History of the Book in American
Culture headed by David Hall, and in 1990 I was a lecturer in "Three
Hundred Years of the American Newspaper," the Society's important
observance, supported by the Gannett Foundation, of the tricentennial of
Publick Occurrences. My time at Williamsburg in the fall of 1990 came at a
crucial point because it was then, with financial support from the Commonwealth Center and daily encouragement from the staff of the Institute
of Early American History and Culture, where I was physically en-
sconced, that I recovered from a discouragingly unproductive period and
finished the first complete draft of the text while profiting from stimulating
new ideas.

The individuals who contributed to the fruitfulness of my times in
Worcester and in Williamsburg are far too numerous for a complete list,
but chief among them are John Hench, Nancy Burkett, Joyce Tracy,
Dennis Laurie, Keith Arbour, and Joanne Chaison at the Antiquarian
Society, and Thad Tate, Mike McGiffert, Fredrika Teute, and Bob Gross
in Williamsburg.

I have also made use of a number of other libraries and institutions
whose resources and staffs have helped make this book. The list must
begin with the University of New Hampshire's Dimond Library. It also
includes the Massachusetts Historical Society, Boston Athenaeum,
Widener Library at Harvard, Beineke Library at Yale, New-York Histori-

cal Society, New York Public Library, Library Company of Philadelphia, Pennsylvania Historical Society, Library of Congress, British Library, Institute of Historical Research of the University of London, Bristol Research Library, Cambridge University Library, and the libraries of the History Faculty and of Gonville and Caius College at Cambridge.

I learned something of the mechanics of printing in the summer of 1973 in the printing workshop led by Homer Martin and Richard Flint during the 26th annual Seminars on American Culture sponsored by the New York State Historical Association in Cooperstown. In the summer of 1986, my poor skills as a compositor were refreshed while I was introduced by Willie Parker and his associates to the workings of an eighteenth-century wooden printing press during a week as a costumed apprentice at the printing office of Colonial Williamsburg. I am grateful to the Colonial Williamsburg Foundation for making that experience possible and also for providing permission to use the photographs on pp. 195–98, which show Peter Stively setting type, Tim McMahon inking the form, and Williamsburg's master printer Willie Parker manning the press.

I am also grateful for the contributions to this project that have come from involvement in various programs of the New Hampshire Humanities Council, and specifically for the help and friendship of Charles Bickford.

I have received essential encouragement and counsel from many colleagues and friends at my own university, including Dean Stuart Palmer of the College of Liberal Arts and a succession of history department chairs beginning with the late Don Wilcox and proceeding through Hans Heilbronner, John Voll, and Jeff Diefendorf. I am grateful to them and to Warren Brown, who was similarly encouraging in practical ways during his term as coordinator of the Humanities Program. Other colleagues who have helped include especially Bill Harris, Laurel Ulrich, Lige Gould, and Cathy Frierson. Jeanne Mitchell, History Department secretary for many years, has been a faithful supporter and aide. I have been nourished in many ways by a succession of graduate students, usually in seminars related in some manner to the topic of this book. Some of these seminars have profited from the cooperation of the Portsmouth Atheneaum and its staff, but especially of one of its principal officers, Richard Candee. To name but a few of the many students whose work and conversation have contributed somehow to this project—apart from Ryan Madden, who did yeoman service as a research assistant one summer—would be to ignore others unjustly. A few of them, whose work I have used directly, are cited in the notes. However, there is one who cannot remain unmentioned here. The single recent student to whom I owe the greatest thanks is Preston (Tuck) Shea, both for his own arresting scholarship and for his help with mine.

"Recent" because Chuck Wetherell was once a student in my department as well, though I have nearly always thought of him as a collaborator and colleague instead. Our work together has enriched this book and, I think, helped to validate some of what it says. So has his own work on American printers and so have his reactions to an early version of this text.

Several of the persons mentioned above have read all or part of the manuscript at one stage or another and made valuable suggestions. Others who have performed the same service include Eldon Turner and my wise and talented friend of many years, Don Murray. Though it goes without saying, convention and morality nevertheless require me to say that even had I followed all their suggestions, which I have not, all blunders and shortcomings would remain, as they are, my responsibility alone.

Finally, a word about Margery, one of the five extraordinary persons to whom this book is dedicated. She has served this project as my closest confidante, my constant companion, and my best friend. She has waited for this part far too long.

Durham, New Hampshire   C. E. C.
April 1993

A Note about Dates

The treatment of dates presents a somewhat more delicate problem in this book than in most monographs whose subject, like this one, precedes the British adoption of the Gregorian calendar in 1752. Printed dates are a prime element in the identification of the very sources on which the book is mainly based, but writers and publishers in this period were not consistent. Some were treating January 1 as the beginning of the new year even though they were still numbering the days of the months according to the Julian calendar. Others were retaining the March 25 new year, and still others were using double year designations between January 1 and March 25. In the text, I have consistently rendered dates, even the dates of newspapers, as if the new year began on January 1 without regard to how a date was actually printed. In the reference notes, I have tried to keep the needs of the researcher foremost in mind. My aim there has been to provide the simplest identification possible consistent with clarity. I have, therefore, provided either double year designations or other clarification only when I have thought it necessary to avoid ambiguity—or, in a few cases, to *indicate* ambiguity.

Apart from the question of the calendar, most newspapers of the period printed not one but two dates on each number—for example, "Monday, April 5 to Monday, April 12," indicating the period ostensibly covered. I have identified such individual papers by the second date only, which was presumably the date of issue.

Contents

PART III   AMERICA: STRUCTURES AND
TRANSITION

THE PUBLIC PRINTS

Introduction

The Artifact

In his entry for April 24, 1704, that grave Puritan councilor, man-about-Boston, and inveterate diary keeper Samuel Sewall recorded one of the many hundreds of such events to which he attributed both private and public significance. He gave to President Samuel Willard of Harvard "the first News-Letter that ever was carried over the River. He shew'd it the Fellows."[1]

It mattered to Sewall personally that he was on intimate terms with yet another Massachusetts personage, the president of Harvard, and that he should have been the instrument of transmission over the Charles River ferry—that he was the bearer of news. Most of the "news" that he bore in his mercurial mission from Boston to Cambridge was actually rather old, much of it dating from the previous December and none of it of a nature that could have made any urgent difference to the conduct of affairs at Harvard, unless it was to provide materials for the president's daily prayers.

But the tiny episode had public significance as well for Sewall because the *Boston News-Letter* itself was news. Fourteen years earlier, Benjamin Harris had incurred immediate and decisive official displeasure with his abortive and clearly premature *Publick Occurrences*. Now for the first time since then, an American printing press had produced a systematic report, intended for continuation in successive numbers, of certain events taking place in Europe and British America. The copy that Sewall took to Willard was one of 250 that the *News-Letter*'s proprietor, Postmaster John Campbell, had, with official sanction, "published"—that is, made public—to an audience far larger than the handful of leading citizens who heretofore had had regular access to official information and to the "publick prints," as they were usually called, of London. This audience, small as it was, was also far larger than the few readers whose immediate daily work and personal concerns were any more dependent upon information such as this than those of the president of Harvard.

Clearly, however, publisher and readers alike recognized the demand for "news" and the value of publishing it. And governmental approval implied some vision of abstract social good. For Samuel Sewall, the beginning of the newspaper era in America was an event of great importance, and he was pleased to be a small agent of that event by being the first to carry the news of that beginning beyond Boston. He was, in fact, an agent in the enlargement of what Jürgen Habermas has called the "public sphere," a realm distinct from both state and private life, where private men formed a "public" for the discussion and expression of mutual concerns and, ultimately, the creation of a depersonalized public opinion.[2] Such a "public," centered in coffee houses, clubs, and, above all, in the medium of print, had been forming in London and in some of the larger provincial centers of England for perhaps a decade, and in the *salons* of Paris even longer. Unless one counts the church, the three colonial colleges, and various ritualized social practices of the Chesapeake gentry, no such "public" institutions had been, up to then, very far advanced in British America. The publication and distribution of the *Boston News-Letter* was a primitive step, heavy with implications for the decades ahead, in that direction.

The little public sphere that Samuel Sewall's friends in Cambridge entered on that April 24 was one in which the actual transmission of information, unless it was the news of the paper's existence, was of secondary importance. The *News-Letter* contained little of immediate relevance to the practical affairs of anyone in New England. But as James Carey's recent work on communications allows us to understand, the *News-Letter* was more than just a transmitter of information, and the news it contained more than intelligence alone. Communication, Carey has observed helpfully, can be understood as "ritual" as well as "transmission."[3] In reading of possible new papist dangers to England in the form of an incipient new Jacobite uprising in Scotland, actually scanning the words of their Queen's address to Parliament the previous December, and even seeing the words *London Flying-Post* and *London Gazette*, the named sources of most of the *News-Letter*'s news, the President and Fellows of Havard College, in company with Samuel Sewall, affirmed and celebrated their common identity as provincial Britons.

At this moment the *Boston News-Letter* served this tiny portion of the New England community, as it was doing simultaneously in other corners of greater Boston, as "ritual"—directed, as Carey suggests, "not toward the extension of messages in space but toward the maintenance of society in time," toward "the representation of shared beliefs."[4] In the end, it would be this function of the American newspaper that would mean the most in provincial culture.

This book is about newspapers. The main focus will be on the formative era of newspaper publishing in America. The story begins, however, in England, where the making of newspapers spread beyond London into English provincial centers on both sides of the Atlantic. This book explores how it was that information once designed mainly for private transmission became public, and how oral communications of certain kinds became supplemented and then supplanted by the printed word. Because its subject is the special printed medium that was adopted after 1665 as the main vehicle of public information, it moves rather quickly to the invention and early development of that medium, the newspaper. The genre itself soon transcended its function as incidental transmitter of its contents and acquired a meaning and a logic of its own.

It is neither surprising nor coincidental that changes in our own communications culture are being accompanied by a new scholarly sensitivity to the place of the printed word in history. It was Elizabeth Eisenstein, prompted in part by Marshall McLuhan's impish pronouncement in 1962 that the age of Gutenberg had now ended, who first articulated in a comprehensive way "the printing press as an agent of change," in her book of the same title.[5] More than a decade before the appearance of Eisenstein's important work in 1979, however, French historians were laying the foundations of what has since become a major scholarly industry, *histoire du livre*, or "the history of the book." This interdisciplinary attempt to understand the production, distribution, and use of printed materials in relation to the total human environment soon spread to the rest of western Europe and to America.[6] Here "the history of the book" within its American context flourishes in organized form in centers and programs at the Library of Congress and the American Antiquarian Society, while American historians explore in a wide variety of ways such topics as reading, the uses of print, the diffusion of information, publishing strategies, the relationship between government and press, the printed word and popular religion, and the social history of the early American printing trade.[7]

Although this new interest in books and printing has included a healthy emphasis upon the period of American history before the Revolution, only a small part of that emphasis up to now has focused upon newspapers. This is neither a deliberate slighting nor an inadvertent oversight. Modern historians of print communications are nothing if not catholic in their definition of "the book." It is only that, with a few important exceptions,[8] that obvious item on the scholarly agenda has not yet received the same kind of attention from the most recent historians of early America that has been devoted to other aspects of the print culture in that period.

On the English side, which needs to be understood if the newspapers of colonial America are to be seen in their whole context, scholars have been quite active in examining the early newspaper press.[9] Part of the aim of this book is to contribute not only to the "history of the book" in colonial America but also to our increasing awareness of the cultural relationships between Britain and her American colonies in the eighteenth century. To study what is sometimes called "Anglo-America" without adequate attention to the part before the hyphen is to create a distortion. In the case of the newspapers, as in many other cultural phenomena, the American versions were, literally, copies of the English models. They took their place in communities that differed from the outlying cities of the home island in size and in distance from London but, in most important respects, can be understood as English towns that shared with Bath, Bristol, Yarmouth, and Norwich a provincial relationship with the metropolitan capital of the empire. This relationship will here be examined through the use of the newspapers as one of many possible cultural artifacts that could serve this purpose.

Anglo-American culture, however, with emphasis on the part *after* the hyphen, underwent a process of development over time that was distinct. Concepts such as "anglicization" or a more complete developmental model such as "simplification-elaboration-replication" have helped clarify the process.[10] American newspapers, while derived and copied from their English models, also developed within their American context as their publishers struggled toward an appropriate role for their genre and their readers came to accept it as a necessary instrument for carrying on communal life. Like other commodities, the newspaper in its American setting underwent a period of diversification and experimentation, as it did earlier in London. By the middle of the eighteenth century, this process had yielded a quite standardized product that, at least for a time, seems to have been well suited to its milieu. "Americanization," therefore, as well as "anglicization," will be a theme of this book—using, again, the newspaper as the central artifact.

Although the first news to be printed in English was apparently produced in Amsterdam for export to England in 1620, the English-language newspaper, as we shall understand it here, began in England. If we accept a particular definition of "newspaper," we can date the event with precision: November 16, 1665.[11] The genre flourished first in London (though the first twenty-three semi-weekly numbers of what may be accepted as the first English-language "newspaper" were printed in Oxford before publication moved to London), spread to the more important provincial cities of England after a delay of some few decades, and appeared very soon after that in the English colonies in America.

By the end of the reign of George II, not quite a century after the birth of the *Oxford Gazette*, newspapers had become a vital element in the political, commercial, and even literary life of England and her American colonies as well. In London, close to fifteen weeklies, semi-weeklies, tri-weeklies, and dailies were sold on the city streets, delivered to coffee houses, and scoured avidly by both courtier and parliamentarian in Westminster and by both merchant and tradesman in the City. They were put in the post for the edification and entertainment of country squires and to provide fodder for the printers of provincial newspapers. And they were collected by the parcel by agents, factors, and captains to be sent to the colonies whenever a ship sailed for America. In towns and cities such as Norwich, Bristol, Bath, Liverpool, and York, some forty local and regional weekly papers copied the news from London and collected and printed their own "provincial" news and comment, frequently in efficient and lively style. In the American colonies, first from Boston to Philadelphia and later from Halifax to Charleston and the West Indies, steadily increasing numbers of weekly (and occasionally semi-weekly) newspapers were enriching the conversation and trade of each seaport while, at the same time, contributing to a growing sense of American community and identity. Each paper was designed primarily to be read in the town and province in which it was printed, but it also served as an important commodity of exchange among printers and postmasters throughout the colonies. Between 1720 and 1760, American newspapers grew in number from three to nearly twenty, not counting those with short lives or the flourishing German-language press in Pennsylvania.[12]

These newspapers were almost always printed on folio leaves varying in size between the $7\frac{1}{2}$ by $9\frac{1}{2}$ inches of the *Boston Weekly Post-Boy* and the early *St. James's Post* (a little smaller than our standard sheet of typing paper) to about 10 by $13\frac{1}{2}$ or 14 inches, the size of London's *Weekly Register* and of Benjamin Franklin's and David Hall's *Pennsylvania Gazette*— roughly the size of the modern tabloid. The contents were arranged in vertical columns, either two or three to a page, with the title of the paper in large type, sometimes elaborated with one or two woodcut "ears" (a modern term) or other such embellishment spread across the top of page one. A typical newspaper of the middle of the eighteenth century consisted of four pages, two of which were printed on each side of a full sheet of paper. The sheet was then folded to produce a folio of two leaves, a page of type on each side. Some publishers, however, printed frequent numbers of as few as two and as many as six pages. Illustrations were few. Some printers liked to use decorative initial letters called "factotums"; some varied the size of type with some consistency and used italics to set off blocks of type as well as for the more usual stylistic purpose of designating proper names and quotations; and a few used woodcuts to illustrate advertisements with stock figures of a ship, a book, or a black slave on the run. Unlike today's reader, the consumer of printed news and opinion in the eighteenth century could not easily pick and choose his reading by placement and headline. One started, or at least was intended to start, at the top of the left-hand column of page one and worked through the paper column by column and page by page. A modern reader can accomplish that in less time than it takes to read the "Op-Ed" page of today's *New York Times*. The main content of most papers was straight, unvarnished—indeed, usually unexplained—information about recent events from local ship arrivals to European battles. Often a sentence or two about each event or bit of gossip was all the reader got. But the newspapers also contained political and religious propaganda in the form of letters, essays, and slanted news— though neither the name nor the idea of "editorial" (or its English equiva- lent, "leader") had been invented. In addition, most of them occasionally and some very frequently carried articles and essays for entertainment, instruction, or the improvement of morals. Much of this sort of thing was uninspired and routine, but a few of these pieces were worthy of the place they have long since earned with the best literature of the day. Finally, the newspapers contained advertising, which can give us clues to the different audiences in England and America that advertisers intended to reach and to the importance of newspaper advertising to the respective systems of marketing that were used on the two sides of the Atlantic.

In neither content nor form was the evolution of the newspaper by any means finished in the eighteenth century. Publishers and printers experi- mented with features, type, and layout. Occasionally they did this too boldly for public acceptance. Most changes, however, occurred only grad- ually, resulting in very few significant variations from what became stan- dard format and content throughout the century. What did vary were the neatness and precision with which these standard forms were executed. By the standards of any subsequent period the eighteenth-century newspaper was crude and imperfect, in both content and form. But in the newspaper, imperfect as it was, the English-speaking peoples on both sides of the Atlantic had found an instrument of commerce, politics, literature, and awareness of themselves and the world, and by the middle of the eigh- teenth century it occupied an accepted and essential niche in the social ecology of both Britain and British America.

To study the origin and early development of the English-language newspaper is to instruct ourselves most usefully about the world it re- flected and the world it served. The evidence is various. The newspaper, in the first place, is a physical object. Like any artifact studied by the archaeologist, it is the product of certain technologies combined in such a way as to reflect its makers' ideas about design and about function as well as their tools and habits of work. Like any such artifact, it is also the product of a certain economic activity, and holds a place in a larger eco- nomic system.

But the newspaper is more than an archaeological artifact. It is also a document. Many of the questions that an archaeologist asks of his mate- rials (his attempt to date the object, for example) are answered at once by the printed information that the newspaper contains and therefore do not present a difficult problem. On the other hand, to use the newspaper as a piece of cultural evidence is to go beyond—but not to ignore—its size, shape, design, and technological and economic significance, and consider the "symbols," as a communications theorist might call them, that are printed on its pages.[13] The contents of the newspaper, and its arrangement, reflect the world as it was perceived by the writers and readers of the period and illustrate assumptions about the nature of news and history, the practice of certain literary styles, the political and commercial structure of communities, the communication links across the ocean and among the seaboard towns of America, and the larger process by which culture is transmitted and transformed.

The task of approaching an understanding of a culture through a single but central piece of evidence such as the newspaper is not complete until we have learned as much as possible about the people who produced this product and those who consumed it. We also want to know what these readers wanted to read in their newspapers and why they found it interesting, and we should like to know how these interests influenced, if they did, the contents of the newspapers. Finally, in the provincial culture of the eighteenth century, did the newspapers make a difference? And what can they inform us as modern visitors to their time about that culture? Certainly the readership side of the equation is the most difficult side to address when dealing with readers who are out of reach of modern methods of audience research. But we must make an attempt to consider all these questions with whatever tools are at hand.

Part I of the book, "English Backgrounds," deals first with the ancestry or "genealogy" of the English-language newspaper. The family tree turns out to have many roots, and the eighteenth-century fruit is an appropriately mixed breed of intelligencer, gazette, propagandist, advertiser, and literary journal all in one. That part next explores the metropolitan context within which the first English newspapers after the *Gazette* came to life and flourished in the two or three decades following the end of legislative restrictions on printing in 1694. The London journals of that era provided the models for the papers of the provinces. The final chapter of Part I explores the provincial world of William and Mary's England, concentrating especially on Norwich and Bristol, where newspapers were printed beginning respectively in 1701 and 1702. By deliberation choice, because it is important to one purpose of this book to emphasize the commonality of provincial newspaper publishing on both sides of the English Atlantic, that chapter ends by examining the context of publishing in Boston in the Province of Massachusetts Bay.

In Part II, five chapters, ordered roughly chronologically, narrate the evolution of American newspaper publishing from the pioneer efforts of the Boston postmaster John Campbell in 1704 to the rather standardized product being published almost exclusively by printers by the 1740s. Because Boston was by far the earliest and most prolific of the American publishing towns before 1740, and because nearly all of the experimentation took place there, the newspapers of that community command much of the attention in this part. The other two multi-newspaper towns of Philadelphia and New York, however, come in for their share of discussion. The two single-newspaper towns of Williamsburg and Charleston, which happen also to have been the only southern American communities publishing newpapers in 1740, receive less attention than their larger— and, as it happens, northern—counterparts, although they are mentioned occasionally for purposes of illustration and comparison. Neither the German-language newspaper of Germantown, Pennsylvania, nor the two British West Indian newspapers figure significantly in the discussion, nor do the short-lived initial efforts at newspaper publishing in Annapolis and Newport, where the *Maryland Gazette* and *Rhode-Island Gazette* lasted from 1727 to 1734 and from 1732 to 1733 respectively.

Part II traces two parallel evolutionary processes. There was in the first place an evolution in *publishing*, an evolution that took place in Boston as it did in a different way in London, but nowhere else. The tendency throughout this process was toward both ownership and control by the newspapers' *printers*, a tendency that carried with it a progressively clearer focus on commercial profit as the main purpose of newspaper publishing. This was an evolution that with but one exception was complete by 1741.

There was also an evolution in the nature of the product—an evolution in newspaper *content*. Generally, there was a movement somewhat, but only somewhat, away from the overwhelming dominance of European news in the American newspapers with which the *Boston News-Letter* began in 1704. Generally, as the number of American publishing towns modestly multiplied, the newspaper or newspapers of a given colony tended over the first half of the century to give their readers gradually larger and more frequent glimpses of life and concerns of other colonies—a force for what I shall call the partial "Americanization" of a New England or a New York or a Virginia consciousness. Finally, there was generally a movement over the course of this period away from the *Boston News-Letter*'s almost total dependence upon hard news and obsession with chronological continuity and toward a mixture of content that combined news reports with learned essays, political statements, letters of opinion, light and serious verse, and (in most cases) an ever-expanding and more varied diet of advertising.

These were not, however, straight-line developments. A self-consciously "literary" phase in the 1720s and '30s served at least two functions. On the one hand, it helped stimulate the production and consumption of a locally produced version of the literary culture of England and, thus, served as an agent of "anglicization" that complemented the "Americanizing" function of a broadening colonial newspaper press. On the other hand, it acted as a catalyst in the transformation of the newspaper into an instrument of purpose and content that had become nearly universal in the colonial publishing towns by 1740.

Part III discards a mainly narrative format in favor of a discussion of structures and meanings. Its subjects include the business of publishing a newspaper under a printer's ownership, which was standard by about 1740; the assumptions and values, even the "world view," that was shared by all the American newspapers of the period and communicated to their readers; the cultural significance of the newspaper in provincial America; and finally the transition in American newspaper content that came with the coincidence in 1739 of the outbreak of the War of Jenkins's Ear with Spain and the first American tour of George Whitefield.

I argue that despite individual variations in emphasis, disagreements on details of policy, and discernible divisions in partisan attachments of various kinds, the English-language newspapers of the eighteenth century, wherever they were printed, presented their readers with a remarkably unified and coherent vision of the world. This consensual world view covered a range of perceptions and attitudes extending from matters as fundamental as space and time to virtually unquestioned assumptions about religion, nationality, and the natural world, not to mention that triune scholarly shibboleth of our own day, race, class, and gender. It was the world view, by and large, of the upper-class, cultivated, ethnocentric, and fiercely patriotic Protestant English male.

I also offer an understanding of the newspapers' role in provincial culture that emphasizes their embodiment and diffusion to a broader population of this originally elite perception of things—the ritual, as it were, taking the form of a message. By broadening access to current information and by dignifying in print the familiar concerns of everyday life, the newspapers offered a kind of open communion; ordinary readers were invited to share with a previously privileged circle in the ritual of communal identity in which one participated by reading the news. At the same time, because newspapers as literature linked the world of ordinary affairs with that of formal learning, a broadened readership became exposed to a richer cultural world than they had previously known. Besides enjoying the obvious advantages of such exposure, newspaper readers were also drawn into the system of shared beliefs in which news and literature alike were almost universally embedded.

It is through the artifact of the newspaper, with whatever supplementary evidence seems relevent and useful, that we shall try to comprehend the culture of which it was an element. The first step is to understand the process by which seventeenth-century England came to produce this artifact in the form that very soon became standard in the English-speaking world.

Part I

ENGLISH BACKGROUNDS

Chapter 1

Genealogy

The English-language newspapers of the eighteenth century evolved not from one ancestor but from several. Put another way, the newspaper developed in England within several literary, technological, and political contexts; one must take account of all of them to see the evolutionary process as a whole. The origin and early development of the newspaper took place during a remarkable era of change in communications, but the change did not result from any new technologies.[1] Instead, existing technologies, examples, and traditions were adapted and combined in such a way as to meet new opportunities and new needs.

The existing components (besides the printing press, the European invention of which in the 1450s was almost as far removed from 1700 as 1700 is from us) were the tradition of the manuscript newsletter for communicating intelligence; the political pamphleteering of the Civil War, Interregnum, and Restoration that passed for news reporting in the so-called "newsbooks"; and the methods of book printing and organization of the printing trade.

The new needs were at first political and administrative as the Restoration government sought devices to unify the country and urge compliance with the new regime. The national appetite for political information and discussion soared with the crises and conflicts surrounding the Glorious Revolution and for diplomatic and military news with the wars of Louis XIV and the English diplomatic revolution that had accompanied the political one. With the end of the official licensing of printing in 1694, there came almost unlimited opportunities for newspaper enterprise and experimentation. At the same time, the commercial development of England and the burgeoning literary community of the Restoration and Augustan periods imposed demands for organs of communication and expression that the infant newspaper makers rushed to meet.

The social and economic changes that characterize this period were beginning to modify what was still fundamentally an oral culture.[2] The assumed vehicle for conducting all the necessary relationships in society was the spoken language, and such relationships involved direct personal contact. The written or printed page came to intervene in the process at this stage only as a supplement to word of mouth or as a necessary substitute when personal contact was not possible. The handwritten newsletters to be discussed below, for example, were necessary only because the recipient was removed physically from direct access to the source of intelligence. This was still the assumption that governed that part of the practice of printed journalism that was derived from the newsletter tradition. Newspaper advertising in early eighteenth-century London provides another example. This form of marketing was at first only a small, almost idiosyncratic supplement to the traditional methods by which the trade of the City was carried on, adopted to meet the special needs of the new book-buying public and the need for anonymity that was served by advertisements for medical cures, especially for venereal disease. But the change was under way, from a culture transmitted primarily by word of mouth to one that relied mainly on print, and the newspapers played their own part in bringing it about.

In order to think clearly about any given instance of communication, it is helpful first to consider what the originator wants to accomplish. This question of "intent" leads us to some important distinctions in thinking about the ancestry of the newspaper.

The Newsletter Tradition

Information is, in the first place, intelligence. And the first English newspapers were or were purported to be "intelligencers," to use a popular newsbook and newspaper title of both the Interregnum and the Restoration. In adopting the persona of intelligencer, the writers of these journals were acting in the oldest of the several traditions of written communication.

The collector and disseminator of intelligence is neither a disinterested observer of the passing scene nor a moral or philosophical commentator—those are the personae of the literary journalist, who appears later; nor is he, if he is true to his craft, a propagandist—which is not to say that a propagandist could not and did not often masquerade as an intelligencer. The intelligencer, in contrast to both these other types, is either allied with or in the service of his reader, and the interests of both writer and reader are presumed to be shared. Europeans had been selling and exchanging written intelligence for about five hundred years before the newspaper came to England, and the vehicle for this information had been the news-letter, written in hand by personal correspondent or professional scribe. The trade and politics of medieval and early modern Europe had required reliable information. Information itself, therefore, had become a commod-ity of value to be sold and exchanged.

Actual organized services for the transmission of news and messages appeared in the twelfth century, and by the fourteenth and fifteenth centu-ries town clerks in the German empire were receiving communications of current political events from other towns. Such a report was called a *Zeitung* (the modern German word for newspaper), meaning events or occurrences happening at the time.[3] By the time of the Reformation, these exchanges had become much more systematized, and in the case of the European community of scholars, reformers, and humanists had become a regular part of carrying on the frenzied intellectual life of the day. Philip Melanchthon, Luther's most important associate, acted as a sort of one-man news bureau by collecting current intelligence from his many con-tacts throughout northern Europe and supplying it in turn to his friends and a number of German princes. By the second half of the sixteenth century, one finds this kind of news agency organized as a formal business in Venice, Rome, and several German towns.[4] Before 1600 *scrittori d'avvisi* were making their livings by distributing the news in this way in Naples, and *novellanti* or *gazettanti* were doing the same thing in Rome. Slightly later, some French noblemen retained *nouvellistes* to keep them supplied regularly with news. In seventeenth- and eighteenth-century England— well overlapping the introduction of the printed newsbook and news-paper—newswriters were performing the same service for rural peers who needed to be kept abreast of the affairs of London and of Court.[5] In fact, the ban that the House of Commons placed in 1660 on printing its proceed-ings gave a boon to the writers of newsletters, since they supplied a de-mand that the newsbooks of the period could not meet because they were forbidden to do so.[6]

At the other extreme of organizational sophistication, one finds the elaborate intelligence networks of the German merchant House of Fugger at the end of the sixteenth century and, several decades later, those of the Restoration secretaries of state in England.[7] Networks similar to these, formally or informally organized, continued to feed the best London news-papers of the eighteenth century; the difference was that once in print, news originally reported from Russia, Turkey, or Flanders entered upon a much longer life of repetition and transmission than had once been the case. However elaborate the collection apparatus, and whether the report was addressed to one person or intended to be copied and distributed to many, the vehicle of information was the handwritten newsletter. The subject in every case was timely information that it was presumed was in the recipient's interest to know.

In England, the newsletter had achieved a high level of standardization, resulting in an accepted style for reporting the news. Once newspapers appeared on the scene, they adopted the newsletter style. It is simple but incorrect to assume that the transition from newsletter to newspaper tells pretty much the whole story—that to print a newspaper was only to take the obvious step of adapting the newsletter to the printing press. The process was more complicated than that, and, in fact, the manuscript newsletter continued to flourish alongside the newspaper for much of the eighteenth century. But the newsletter tradition did contribute not only the notion of intelligence but also strong influences of style and format. It will be useful to pick apart an especially instructive example of the genre, produced not in seventeenth-century England but in eighteenth-century Virginia.

In July 1778, Thomas Jefferson, home at Monticello between sessions of the Virginia House of Delegates and awaiting the imminent birth of his third daughter, was hungry for news of the outside world. So, apparently, were some of his neighbors. A servant of his was bound on an errand to Williamsburg, still the center of government and news for the Commonwealth, so Jefferson sent along with him a request for newspapers to Alexander Purdie, founder and printer of the third *Virginia Gazette*. As postmaster and printer for the government, Purdie would have been well known to the conspicuous young legislator. But the printer had run short of "last Week's Gazette," he said in his reply of July 27. There were not enough to furnish one to everyone in Jefferson's neighborhood who had asked for one, but even so, Purdie sent along a copy for Jefferson and one for Dr. George Gilman, another delegate from Albemarle County. Purdie had run so short of the Friday, July 24, *Gazette*, in fact, that none of that date or of the previous Friday survives to our day. What does survive is the remarkable letter with which the Scottish-born printer replied to Jefferson's request, apparently to atone both for the short supply of the *Gazette* and for the fact that, in any case, "there was no News of any Consequence in it."

"Since our last," Purdie began, "we have a Confirmation of Capt. Jones's taking the Drake 20 Gun ship and carrying her into Brest, also of his setting fire to some Vessels at Whitehaven, where 50 of his Sailors landed privately, at Night, and picked up several Cannon, to secure their Retreat, which they did, in the Bustle, about 4 in the Morning." The paragraph concludes with the remaining element of John Paul Jones's reputation-making expedition in command of the *Ranger* in April and May of 1778, the raid on the Earl of Selkirk's house at Kircudbright on the Scottish coast.

From the exploits of a new naval hero, Purdie moved to the latest news of Washington's army, this time with a dateline: "Philadelphia, July 16th.

General Washington, with the Army under his Command, was at Paramus last Sunday, within 21 miles of King's Ferry, where they were to cross the North Lines. General Clinton's, with his Army, pitched their Tents the same Day on Staten Island." Several similar paragraphs follow, one dated "Baltimore, July 21," a few consisting of only a sentence each. Two of these short paragraphs, mixed with items relating to the world at large, discussed Purdie's personal business with Jefferson. Purdie's last entry concerns the court-martial then in progress of Major General Charles Lee for his conduct at the Battle of Monmouth the previous May. For the first time, Purdie introduced a judgmental tone into his news: "His Behaviour and Deportment at the Battle were unaccountable, and rendered him odious to the whole Army."

Immediately then, Purdie wrote the customary complimentary closing of his day: "I am, sir, Your ob hum sert., A. Purdie."[8]

As printer of an important American newspaper during the War for Independence, Purdie stood at the end of several centuries of evolution of the business of collecting, processing, and distributing news. He also served in his own day as one of many equally vital links in a network of communications that reached throughout most of the known world. In this letter, he was engaged in the private communication of useful intelligence. To do the job, he used a style, a format, assumptions about the nature of his information, and knowledge of his reader that were much the same as the style, the format, and assumptions that he and the other publishers of newspapers in his era habitually used in compiling their weekly printed reports.[9]

What is more remarkable, however, is that in none of these particulars does Purdie disclose himself in this private newsletter to be much removed from his remote predecessors in the news business in twelfth- and thirteenth-century Germany, sixteenth-century France, or seventeenth-century England. We notice first that Purdie's letter is addressed to a man of importance, a man who presumably will use the information, indirectly at least, to help him make decisions of public consequence. Purdie is acting as a "servant" in a real as well as stylized sense. In the previous two centuries, this had been the job of the French *nouvelliste;* in England, the role of hired correspondents of the country nobility in keeping their employers informed of the news of London and Westminster had only recently been assumed by the "public prints,"[10] and even then as supplement rather than replacement. In his role as reporter of intelligence, Purdie does not distinguish between his private function as a businessman and his public function as a supplier of information to an influential legislator. He uses the very words that he will use in the coming issue of the *Gazette.* The "news," which is indistinguishable from "intelligence," has already become embalmed in the actual language that will carry it from newspaper to newspaper, from colony to colony, and, in this instance, from printer and private correspondent (there is no difference) to public figure. Like the correspondents of the English secretaries of state during the Restoration, Purdie was playing a double role that it did not occur to him to question or to separate. Purdie's status as postmaster, government printer, and private publisher was not such a giant step removed as we often assume from that of the Restoration secretaries of state, who for reasons of state not only supervised the collection of intelligence but also monopolized the publication of news.[11]

The modern reader of Purdie's newsletter is next struck by its style, reminiscent not of what is read in the morning newspaper but of what is heard on radio or television. The style is terse, telegraphic. It assumes a knowledge of the context and provides only what the reader needs to know to keep abreast. Little explanation is necessary, and only in the case of the court-martial item, in which case it is gratuitous, does the author find the need to comment. Purdie's newsletter continues:

> Baltimore, July 21. Count D'Estrange's Fleet, two of the largest excepted, safe arrived within Sandy Hook, where they lie at Anchor. 4000 Troops landed from this Fleet at Black Point in Shrewsbury, New Jersey, to cooperate with the American Army.—All the American Sloops of War are ordered to join the French Admiral, who had himself invited them to come and help him to destroy and capture the Enemy's Ships; those which the Americans take to be their whole Property.

The elements of style for reporting intelligence in this way had not changed in a hundred years. Between 1634 and 1695, the Earl of Huntingdon received regular newsletters from a number of paid correspondents. Among them was Henry Muddiman, who like Alexander Purdie a century later produced a newspaper, or "newsbook," as the Civil War and Restoration predecessors of the *London Gazette* were called. The letters to Huntingdon varied somewhat in style and format, depending upon the correspondent. They also became increasingly standardized over time. By 1691, Huntingdon was reading something like this:

> The Close of laste weeke one Canning was committed to Newgate for Printing and Publishing dangerous Papers reflecting upon the Government, at the same time a Private Printing Press was seized, which was constantly employed by ill affected Persons to Print Scurrilous Bookes.
>
> The Earle of Suffolk was the other day married to the Lady Maynard.
>
> Yesterday the House of Lords heard a cause between the Earle of Monmouth and Mr. Danvers about an Estate which the latter claimes, . . . their Lordships adjourned the further debate thereof till tomorrow.
>
> This afternoon the Morocco Ambassadour was present at the Acting of a Play called the Emperor of the Moon.
>
> The Earle of Torrington has been admitted to the Honour of kissing his Majesties hand.[12]

And so on. Each compact item is packed with current intelligence on political, religious, military, diplomatic, judicial, or mercantile matters, or at least with court gossip of interest to the country nobility. There is no need to elaborate upon the simple facts; it is presumed that the reader has all the background needed to make sense of them.

By 1693, some of the letters to Huntingdon were disclosing an even greater consciousness of format and style. Flourishes of penmanship served as a kind of heading for the whole piece and to introduce each new item. In one such letter, the words "My Lord London November 16 1693" are spread in a bold and fancy hand across the top of the page. Then the news begins:

> By letters from Rome of the 31 past Wee are advised that the Pope seems very zealous to procure a Peace between the house of Austria & ffrance. . . .
>
> Turin [with a flourish of penmanship] the 2nd instant on the 26th Our Army decamped & marched. . . .
>
> Vienna [with a flourish] the 5th The Grandvisier is decamped from Belgrade & has sent his Army into winter quarters. . . .[13]

There are seven more items, each treated stylistically and calligraphically in the same way. This one series of newsletters, simply one of many examples in a genre that was still developing even as the newspaper began, demonstrates an evolving consciousness of style in the communication of intelligence. The emphasis was upon simplicity, brevity, a businesslike dignity of tone befitting an address to an employer or important personage, an ignoring of what a modern newsman would call "background," and the development of a predictable system by which the reader could easily separate one item of information from the next.

We need now to notice two remaining attributes of the Purdie-to-Jefferson and the Huntingdon newsletters: the order of events reported and the use of the dateline. At first glance the order may appear random, since our impulse is to look for groupings according to subject or other such relationship or to try to discern some assumed hierarchy of importance. We can find neither of these, but we do find, even though it is not apparent at once in every detail, the most obvious order of all: chronology. The news writers of both Huntingdon's and Jefferson's centuries thought of intelligence as history, as did the compilers of the printed newspapers. The format was narrative, or at least linear, with little or no discrimination among events as to their importance and little heed to whether the report showed any signs of connectedness among its parts. But the various pieces of recent history—even Purdie's personal business with Jefferson, which was inserted in the letter amongst the larger events in its proper chronological place—were presented in the order of their occurrence. The *London Gazette*, the first "newspaper" by our definition, followed this logic even when reporting so momentous an event as the death of William III. The March 9, 1702, number of the *Gazette* began with a relatively minor action of the House of Commons on March 7, followed by an account of the King's death on March 8, followed by the official proclamation of Queen

Anne by various public bodies, and concluded with several proclamations by the new sovereign. News, according to this logic, is history, and the record of the official history of the government of England is properly reported in the order in which it happened.[14]

The tradition of transmitting intelligence in handwriting and in print incorporated yet another seventeenth-century invention, that of periodicity. Milton Mueller has suggested provocatively that the serial publication of news at regular intervals during the English and Continental upheavals of the early seventeenth century acted, somewhat like the town clock of medieval Europe, as a common time standard for a dispersed readership. A fixed publication cycle, such as that adopted for the seventeenth-century news publications, "coordinates literate comunication among people who are not in direct contact with each other, extending a common sense of immediacy over greater distances and larger populations."[15] The practice of reporting at regular intervals began with private correspondents engaged to report official and diplomatic news. This same periodicity was picked up as a matter of course by the publishers of the English newsbooks and their Continental equivalents, called "corantos."[16]

The influence of the newsletter tradition is obvious in practically all of the experimental London newspapers that appeared soon after the lapse of the licensing act in 1694, but in certain of these papers it is reflected more strongly than in most. The publishers of *The Post Man, and the Historical Account* and of the *Flying Post*, among others, conceived of their papers as devices to facilitate correspondence from London into the country. That is the significance of both titles. Each paper provided blank space for the correspondent to add his own news. Here is how Richard Baldwin, publisher of the *Post Man*, explained his plan:

> This paper having found a General acceptance, the Publisher has thought fit to add a postscript on the 3d side of a whole Sheet, which shall be done upon good Paper and shall contain, all the most Remarkable occurrences. If any Gentleman or News Writer shall think fit to make use of them, they may have them at a very reasonable rate at the Publishers . . . ; there will be a space left, for business or what other news they shall think proper to incert. . . .[17]

The *Flying Post* took pains to notice that its special postscript for country correspondents was "done on good Writing Paper, with Blanks so ordered, that any one may write of their Private Affairs into the Country."[18] Ichabod Dawks, publisher of *Dawks's News-Letter*, went a step further (or backward) by trying to imitate the appearance of a manuscript newsletter, providing at the top of the page the large salutation "Sr" (Sir), evidently cut in wood to resemble handwriting, followed by "London" in similar characters and the date. Obviously, no recipient of one of Dawks's papers was fooled into thinking that it was addressed to him alone, but Dawks apparently thought the tradition worth preserving, at least in form. The text is entirely in script type and runs all the way across the page rather than in columns as in the other newspapers of that time and since. Like the sockets for buggy whips that were preserved for tradition's sake in some of the early horseless carriages of our own century, Dawks's whimsy lacked both imitators and longevity.[19]

The power of the newsletter tradition as it was practiced in England is also noticeable in the practice around the turn of the eighteenth century of printing polemic pamphlets in the form of letters written to "a friend (or gentleman) in the country," and in fact, one short-lived periodical of the 1690s, *The Gentleman's Journal*, used *By Way of Letter to a Gentleman in the Country* as a subtitle.[20] Finally, the first newspaper in America to last beyond one number was entitled the *Boston News-Letter*. Its birth in 1704 coincided with the period of experimentation in the London press, and John Campbell, its publisher, had recently been in the habit of sending out occasional handwritten summaries of the news to some of the leading men of New England by virtue of his access as postmaster of Boston both to information and to the mails.[21]

Propaganda and "Gazettes"

But the newspapers of the eighteenth century were not simply "intelligencers." They were vehicles of propaganda, literature, and commercial advertising as well. They were meant not only to inform but also to persuade, entertain, and sell. None of these other functions is a part of the newsletter tradition. In fact, as we have seen already, there was to some extent a parallel evolution of both newsletter and newspaper; the manuscript newsletter tradition continued to develop even after the introduction of the printed newspaper. Moreover, for half a century before some English newspapers actually tried to fill the place of the newsletter, the nation's periodical press had been given over mainly to propaganda. This implies something very different about the intended audience and the communicator's perceived relationship with that audience than is implied by the notion of intelligence. In the one case the intent is to inform, in the other to persuade or manipulate. Far from being the servant of his reader or in league with him, the propagandist tries to bring a largely anonymous and therefore impersonal audience into sympathy with his own view or compliance with his purposes.[22] The difference could hardly be more profound. Yet newspapers of the eighteenth century—and of today—did, and do, both.

The use of the press as a manipulator of public opinion had long been taken for granted in England. The Tudor and early Stuart monarchs controlled the printing press, including its use as a primitive dispenser of news, for their own political purposes. They did so, for the most part, with the cooperation of the printers. Then, with the outbreak of the Civil War in 1642, we find the full-fledged use of the press for propaganda. And it was in the publication of news in the form of periodical "newsbooks" that both sides most effectively revealed their skill and their zeal as propagandists. The royalist *Mercurius Aulicus*, edited at Oxford by the witty John Birkenhead, exchanged clever ripostes, carefully selected and slanted news, and direct attacks with various parliamentary papers in London, most conspicously *Mercurius Britanicus*, whose able assistant editor Marchmont Nedham proved a worthy opponent for Birkenhead.[23]

After the Restoration, a new printing act restored the pre–Civil War controls on the number of printers who could practice in the realm and reinstituted prior licensing. The enforcer of the act after August 1663 was Sir Roger L'Estrange, who also, by virtue of his position, had a monopoly on publishing news. For over two years, until the system changed with the introduction of the official *Oxford* (later *London*) *Gazette*, he used his two newsbooks not only to present a royalist's-eye-view of the news but also to spell out his uncompromising view of the use and misuse of public information. We may take this statement, with which the first number of his *Intelligencer* began, to be the official position of the Restoration government:

> First, as to the point of Printed Intelligence, I do declare myself . . . that supposing the Press in Order; the People in their right Wits, and NEWES, or no Newes, to be the Question; a Public Mercury should never have My vote; because I think it makes the Multitude too Familiar with the Actions, and Counsels of their Superiours; too Pragmaticall and Censorious, and gives them, not only an Itch, but a kind of Colourable Right, and License, to be Meddling with the Government.[24]

L'Estrange's attack on free information, by the way, preceded by only eight years a famous expression of similar views by another Restoration royalist, Governor William Berkeley of Virginia. "But, I thank God, there are no free schools nor printing," reported Berkeley to the Lords Commissioners of Foreign Plantations, "and I hope we shall not have these hundred years; for learning has brought disobedience, and heresy, and sects into the world, and printing has divulged them, and libels against the best government. God keep us from both!"[25] Precisely because of all the mischief that had been caused by disobedence, heresy, sects, and the press, L'Estrange now argued, it is necessary to recognize that the times demand extraordinary measures. One such measure would be a judiciously prepared organ of public information. "There is not anything," he declared, "which at This Instant more Imports his Majestie's Service, and the Publick, then [*sic*] to Redeem the Vulgar from their former Mistakes, and Delusions, and to preserve them from the like for the time to come: to both which purposes, the prudent Menage of the Gazett may contribute in a very high Degree." He promised to use his paper to work on the minds and affections of the common people "by convenient Hints, and touches," and "to detect, and disappoint the Malice, of those scandalous and false Reports which are daily Contrived, and Bruited against the Government."[26]

L'Estrange's newsbooks contained far more foreign news than domestic, and such domestic news as he reported was designed either to promote affection and loyalty to King and Church or to set an example for prospective offenders. Parliament's prohibition on printing reports of its own affairs applied to all printers and publishers, whether or not they enjoyed a royal monopoly, so the newsbooks contained no news of Parliament. Nearly all the news from England concerned the comings and goings of the royal family, the grand occasions of church and state such as the consecration of bishops, and the trials and punishments of criminals and traitors. It was with particular glee that L'Estrange fastened upon the arrest, trial, condemnation, and execution of John Twyn in February 1664 for having printed *A Treatise of the Execution of Justice*, which justified revolution and regicide. L'Estrange, who as surveyor of the press had searched Twyn's home himself and seized the incriminating proofs of the book (the author of which Twyn never disclosed), devoted one and a third of the eight pages of his February 22, 1664 *Intelligencer* and one full page of his February 25 *Newes* to this affair and to several related cases.[27] Two months later, L'Estrange roundly defended his selection and slanting of the news and disclosed his essential purpose, as if it were not already plain, in publishing his newsbooks:

> . . . I reckon it an Essential Part of my Duty, to endeavor to make any Party Ridiculous, that labours to make the government odious to the People, and that I do further resolve, to follow the same course still, till either Authority stop my hand, or those People should mend their Manners.[28]

With the replacement in 1665 of L'Estrange's two newsbooks by an established organ of government, the *Gazette*, the propaganda function of the English press changed from the partisan railings of L'Estrange to a dignified presentation of official news and announcements that could be called "propaganda" only in the sense that it functioned to forward the interests and business of the realm. But both the tone and purpose of the official announcement, as introduced by the *Gazette*, and the vociferous partisan warfare of a Roger L'Estrange and his predecessors became a part of the practice of eighteenth-century journalism.

Although the term "gazette," which originated in Venice in the middle of the sixteenth century, did not always mean a bulletin of official announcements, that became its principal definition as soon as Joseph Williamson and Henry Muddiman began publishing the *Gazette* on behalf of the government on November 16, 1665.[29] The influence of the *Gazette* on English and American newspapers during the next century was enormous. By the end of the colonial period, there was scarcely a colony without its "Gazette," which surely implied in every case that the printer considered his journal committed to the public business, perhaps even quasi-official, even though it was not, like the *London Gazette*, a government enterprise. But since many such printers were postmasters with the franking privilege for exchanging the news and may have held the government printing contract as well, they were, in fact, public servants who discharged part of their responsibility to the public by printing the news—albeit for private profit.

One such postmaster (though not a printer) was John Campbell, who published the first successful newspaper in America. His *Boston News-Letter*, like the *London Gazette*, carried the phrase "Published by Authority" for its first sixteen years, and then his successor began a competing newspaper, the *Boston Gazette*, also "Published by Authority." While the government of Massachusetts Bay never acknowledged either the *News-Letter* or the *Gazette* as its own publication in any official way, Campbell thought of himself and his newspaper as enjoying some sort of special relationship with the government.

While Campbell's *News-Letter* and Brooker's *Gazette* played the role of gazettes in early eighteenth-century Boston, the third newspaper in town, James Franklin's *New-England Courant*, waged outright propaganda. Unlike that of L'Estrange, this was propaganda directed *against* authority, and therefore Franklin and his two competitors fought one another in print. The *Courant* carried no official proclamations or governor's addresses of the sort that appeared in both the *News-Letter* and the *Gazette*. What it did carry was plenty of sharp-tongued satire that would remind the reader of L'Estrange if it were more heavy-handed and not so clever. Franklin and his club of "couranteers" satirized not only the prevailing government and religion but also the competition.

One could perhaps argue that Franklin's *Courant*, like its predecessors in London at the turn of the century—Daniel Defoe's famous *Review* along with publications with less illustrious but more colorful titles such as *The Politick Spy*, *The English Lucien*, and *The Jesting Astrologer; Or, the Merry Observator*—contributed more to the art of satire than to the art of propaganda. But it was a satire designed, like most satire, to persuade as well as to entertain. We can think of it, therefore, as propaganda as easily as we can think of some small part of it as literature. And gazetteers and propagandists alike contributed to the making of the eighteenth-century newspaper.

Printing and the Printing Trade

The great contribution of the *London Gazette* to newspaper history as a whole was really its form rather than its function: its leap to what we recognize even today as the newspaper format.

Though the *Courant* of Amsterdam had been printed in columns on both sides of a half-sheet as early as 1618 and, in fact, had been imitated briefly in London in 1621,[30] successive English news publications prior to 1665 were invariably in the form of booklets and pamphlets. The practices of English printers and booksellers had become well ingrained over the past two centuries. It was only natural that the customary format of the book would be retained when the printing press was enlisted in the unfamiliar role of publishing current news.

The few news publications that appeared before the Civil War used the familiar codex—octavo format with title page, blank verso, text beginning on page three, and lines of type running across the entire page. During the war years, the press of events required more production and more speed. Publishers of newsbooks, therefore, gradually came to compress the title and the beginning of the text onto the first page and to use page two, but that was the only mechanical concession to this new use of printing. Some of the earliest newsbooks of the war period anticipate what we think at first we recognize as the idea of a headline, skipping ahead to a development that the newspapers of the eighteenth century missed. For example, the second number of *The Diurnall Occurrances in Parliament* (January 24, 1642) carries this summary of its news on the title page:

> The Diurnall Occurrances in Parliament from the 17. of Jan. to the 24 Contayning the Scotch Commissioners desires to the King, and the Order of the house of commons thereupon, and many other particular passages concerning Ireland. much bloud was shed, but the Scots got the day, and obtained the Victory. Also many other remarkable Occurrances, truly and exactly set doune.[31]

In somewhat more orderly and sophisticated form, *The Faithful Scout*, another parliamentary newsbook, listed on page one of the May 25, 1655, number a capsulized version of the important news under the title.[32]

These were not, however, headlines. They were titles. This was simply the adaptation to the newsbook format of the lengthy title pages that one finds in almost any book of that day. If considered whole, the title varied from issue to issue. Not even the full import of what we understand as a serial publication had yet occurred to these publishers, and certainly no advanced notions as to how to present timely information about recent events as opposed to the less perishable commodities with which they were accustomed to dealing as makers and sellers of books.

The leap to a newspaper format came with the *Gazette*. The official court paper was printed on both sides of a half-sheet of paper slightly longer but more than an inch narrower than our standard business letter. A compact title, not a rambling one like those of the Civil War and Interregnum that had taken up much of the first page, was placed neatly in large type at the top of the page, and each page was divided into two columns.

P. M. Handover, author of a short but definitive study of the *Gazette*, has come up with a convincing explanation for the sudden change. Leonard Lichfield, printer of the *Gazette* when it began at Oxford, was a printer of Bibles. Bible printing, a highly specialized and carefully restricted branch of book printing in seventeenth-century England, demands the use of small type packed onto a page as economically as possible.

The London Gazette.

Published by Authority.

From **Monday** July 31. to **Thursday** August 3. 1704.

Windsor, July 29.

THE following Address from the Clergy of the Diocese of *York*, was presented this day to Her Majesty by *John Sharp* Esq; being introduced by the most Honourable the Lord Treasurer.

To the QUEEN's *Most Excellent Majesty.*

The humble Address of the Clergy of the Diocese of *York*.

May it please Your most Excellent Majesty,

WE Your Majesty's most Dutiful and Loyal Subjects, the Clergy of the Diocese of *York*, being deeply affected with Your Majesty's surprizing Goodness, in settling Your whole Ecclesiastical Revenue to be a perpetual Fund for the augmenting small Benefices throughout England; do humbly beg Leave at this Season, when we are met together in our several Districts, to repeat and renew in our own Persons those Solemn Thanks for this Royal Benefaction to the Church, which have been already offered to Your Majesty by our Representatives in Convocation.

Indeed we are glad of all Occasions to express our great Satisfaction and Joy in having Your Majesty to Reign over us, whose Principles must always keep You entirely to the Interests and Religion of the Church of England, and who has given us so convincing a Proof of Your Care of both by this late Act of Grace to Your poor Clergy.

We heartily pray God long to preserve Your Majesty, and so to direct and influence all Your Counsels, that You may ever pursue those Glorious Principles and Inclinations which God hath inspired You withal; and that it may never be in the Power of Your Majesty's or the Church's Enemies to obstruct or frustrate the happy Effects of them.

Which Address Her Majesty received very Graciously.

Dantzick, July 23. N. S. Our Advices from *Warsaw* say, That Preparations were making there for the Coronation of their new King *Stanislaus*. The King of *Sweden* has complimented him on his Election, and has, tho' not without great Difficulty, prevailed with the Cardinal Primate, the Crown-

General, and several more of the Confederates who opposed it, to acknowledge him; and has promised him a powerful Assistance. Some Letters add, That 3 Commissioners are appointed on the part of *Sweden* with the Character of Ambassadors Extraordinary, viz. Lieutenant-General Count *Horn*, the *Swedish* Envoy *Wradisleven*, and the Vice President *Palmberg*, to treat of an Alliance with *Poland*. In the mean time the King of *Poland* had for the third time issued his Summons to the Nobility to mount on Horseback for the Defence of his Person and Government against the *Swedes*, and those who are in their Interest; and, according to the last Accounts from *Sendomir*, was preparing to depart from thence, in order to join the Succours that are marching from *Muscovy* to his Assistance.

Paris, July 28. N. S. The Marquis d'*Elbeuf* arrived from *Piedmont* the 26th Instant at night at *Versailles*, who, it is said, brings Advice of the Surrender of *Verceil*, and that the Duke of *Vendosme* intended to dismantle that Place, and to attack *Ivrea*. Our Letters from *Germany* say, the Marshal *de Villeroy* had been to view the Imperial Lines at *Bihel*, in hopes to have been able to force them, now that most of the Forces which were there are marched with Prince *Eugene* to observe the Marshal *de Tallard*; but that he found them so well guarded, that he did not think fit to attempt them.

Kinsale, July 23. On the 21st Instant came in here the *Owner's Adventure, Michael Staples* Master, of 240 Tuns, 10 Guns and 20 Men; the *Samuel, Richard Holland* Master, of 230 Tuns; and the *Lyon and Lamb, Joseph Green* Master, of 150 Tuns; all three belonging to *London*, and homeward-bound with Sugar and other Goods from *Barbadoes*; The first of these Ships was attacked off of this Harbour by a *French* Privateer of Twelve or Fourteen Guns, who boarded her twice; but the Master and his Men made so good a Defence, that they killed as many of their Enemy as entered on board the Ship; and, with the Assistance of one of the other Merchant Ships, obliged the Privateer to retire. The *Owner's Adventure* had in this Action two Men killed, and one or two slightly

Number 4041 of the *London Gazette*, which after nearly 39 years of biweekly publication still looked almost exactly the same as it did when publication began in Oxford in 1665. Note that this number begins with an official announcement from Queen Anne's Court. Such announcements, when they appeared in this journal and those that imitated it, always preceded the news. This is one of the numbers of the *Gazette* that would have influenced John Campbell, the Boston postmaster, early in the life of his *Boston News-Letter*. (*Courtesy, American Antiquarian Society*)

Because of the very small type used for this purpose, the pages of Bibles were usually set in columns. Lines of small type spread entirely across the page would have been hard on compositor and reader alike, and potentially disastrous at the critical point when the compositor must remove the several lines he has set from his composing stick and, squeezing them tightly together with the thumbs, index fingers, and middle fingers of both hands, transfer them gingerly to the galley tray.

Both Lichfield and Thomas Newcomb, printer of the London edition of the *Gazette*, were part of the small, privileged group of printers in England that had access to the restricted business of Bible printing. Both were experienced with this format and owned the appropriate type.[33] If Hand-over is right, it was the application of an almost esoteric branch of the printing industry to the problem of news publication that contributed to the breakthrough in format and presentation that the *Gazette* represents. With the outpouring of news publications of all kinds thirty years later when the licensing act expired, it was only an eccentric few, such as Ichabod Dawkes, who reverted to an older format. In every physical respect, the *Gazette* had become standard. It was this that the others copied. Joseph Williamson, its founder; Henry Muddiman, its editor; and Leonard Lichfield, its first printer, had to this extent invented the English newspaper.

The organization of the English printing trade also influenced the earliest newspapers. Since its incorporation in 1557, the Company of Stationers had regulated access to the craft in London and overseen every aspect of its practice and its relationship to publishers and booksellers, who dominated the company. For most of that time, printing had been forbidden outside of London except at the two university towns of Oxford and Cambridge, and there it was under the supervision of the Crown. Government licensing of books had been the rule.[34] Naturally, such a tightly controlled craft produced conservative members, cautious lest they trespass against some company or Crown regulation and lose their livelihood or worse. Moreover, the division of labor in the making of books was a rigid one. Authors were not printers, and printers were not bookbinders or booksellers; in the print shops themselves (called chapels), there was a division even between compositors and pressmen. The daily and weekly regimen and methods of work were decreed by tradition and by a closed system of apprenticeship. Toward the end of the seventeenth century, the printers had the advantage of manuals, or instruction books, which improved the quality of printing but also further encouraged standardization and adherence to established practices.[35]

When it came to printing the news, therefore, there was little reason that it should have occurred to anyone that the standard divisions of labor and the standard practices of publishing should not apply. As a consequence, newspaper publishing during its developing stages in London stuck largely to the conventions of the book trade. Typically, there would be a publisher who conceived and underwrote the publication. Quite often he would be a bookseller. He might do all or some of his own writing, in which case he would call himself the "author" of the paper, or he might hire an editor to collect and assemble the materials and perhaps do some of the writing. The printing would be done in the office of whatever printer he had contracted to do the job and by men steeped in the methods, traditions, and protective devices of the Company of Stationers and the habits of bookmaking. This arrangement suited especially the newspapers and journals with a literary tone and, in fact, must have helped such papers flourish.

The first American papers were published under similar circumstances. The abortive *Publick Occurrences* was published by a London bookseller temporarily resident in Boston. John Campbell published the *Boston News-Letter* and as "undertaker," as he called himself, collected and arranged the materials that went into it. He hired Bartholomew Green to print it. All but one of the first six newspapers in Boston were supervised either by the postmaster or by amateur writers, either alone or in "clubs." By mid-century, however, the American practice had become what in the 1720s was the exception: the printer, by and large, did it all. But the American printer was free from the encumbrances of either a strong bookmaking tradition or a guild. He came to serve as editor, business manager, writer, and advertising salesman as well as compositor and pressman. In the process, he risked his own capital. He became much more than a tradesman, free in a way that his London counterpart was not free to work out a new occupation centered on the making of newspapers. In these ways the craft of printing and the organization of the trade contributed to the origin and evolution of the newspaper—and to some degree impeded that evolution.

The genealogy of the newspaper can teach us a lesson in the history of technology. The private publishers who began to put out the first English newspapers after the official *London Gazette* drew upon a cluster of existing technologies, examples, traditions, and habits. They combined them in such a way as to meet new opportunities and new demands. They drew upon the newsletter tradition; the propagandistic journalism of the Civil War, Interregnum, and Restoration; and the methods of book printing and the organization of the printing trade. The newspaper press flourished at this juncture, having been furnished an eminently workable model of organization and format by the *Gazette* and freed to experiment by the lapse of the licensing act in 1694. It now hurried to meet an appetite for news that was whetted by political change and foreign wars and to accommodate the demand for organs of advertising and communication by the growing commercial community and for a medium of expression by the literati, both serious and hack, who were carrying the culture of England from the Restoration to the Augustan age. New technology was responsible for none of this development. It was only the application of old technologies, techniques, and ideas to new situations.

There were many inventive approaches to editing and designing newspapers between 1695 and 1720, some of which will make their appearance in the next chapter. In general, however, there was not a long life in store for those that departed most radically from the physical layout of the *Gazette* or for those that tried for the greatest variation from what was becoming the standard combination of primitive news reporting, transcripts of public documents, occasional letters and essays, shipping notices, and advertisements. By a process of experimentation, trial, and elimination, there gradually occurred a rough standardization of the product. And while in London there remained some room for specialization, the "provincial" newspapers of both England and America came invariably to combine the roles of intelligencer, gazette, advertiser, and propagandist, and, in some cases, to add the function of literary journal. Theirs was a mixed ancestry, and they showed it.

Chapter 2

The Metropolis

The Setting

The distance from St. Paul's to Whitehall was about a mile as a waterfowl would fly between the two points across the curve of the Thames. It was perhaps a mile and a quarter by way of Fleet Street and the Strand. About these two strangely different centers, London was spreading in the 1690s like a great ellipse.

The court of King William and Queen Mary at St. James's Palace, home of the revised monarchy now balanced by a powerful Parliament of lords and rich gentlemen sitting nearby in ancient Westminster Palace, formed the hub of political power. Here also was centered the command of armies and navies, the conduct of diplomacy, classical learning and the fine arts, the adornment of leisure, and the tasteful display of the sort of wealth that was derived from inherited lands. Here in Westminster, the fashionable part of the metropolis as well as the political capital of the nation and the empire, had risen over the past century the stately houses of nobles along the Strand and around newly laid-out squares. Here also were "pleasure gardens" and incipient nurseries of upper-class immorality, such as Covent Garden and the Restoration theater. To its medieval function as seat of royal authority, Westminster was swiftly adding the more modern role of stylish suburb. This was the West End.[1]

To the east, downstream, stood the ancient walled "City"—London proper—which was at once the older and the younger of the two centers of

32

the metropolis. The walls and fragments of the famous "tower" recalled the Roman occupation of Britain, abandoned thirteen centuries before. London's equally famous City companies, or guilds, despite the erosion of the system since medieval times, remained the key to both the economic and the political life of the City. They thus provided a living link with the Middle Ages.

London, however, had in the quite recent past undergone two mighty purges, the plague of the summer and autumn of 1665 and the Great Fire of September 1666. The first had killed about 70,000 in the metropolis, the vast majority in the City. Charles II and the royal entourage had set up temporary court in Oxford, Parliament had sat in the same place, and nearly all the rich and noble had deserted the town for the countryside.[2] Carried by the flea whose host was the black rat, the bubonic plague was primarily a disease of the crowded poor.[3] The Great Fire had raged for five days, devouring 13,200 houses, eighty-seven parish churches, six chapels, most of the company halls, the Royal Exchange, the Guildhall, twenty wharves, and London's principal landmark, St. Paul's Cathedral. Something over 373 acres, more than three-quarters of the area within the old city walls, had been leveled. The loss was reckoned imperfectly in the millions of pounds.[4]

On the ruins of the old City had risen the new London of Sir Christopher Wren. Orderly rows of connected brick dwellings replaced the prefire medieval buildings of lath and plaster. Fifty-one new parish churches, abandoning the Gothic lines of their predecessors, displayed the neoclassic proportions and embellishments of the English Renaissance. There were new company halls in the new style, set off with courtyards and gardens, and there was a new Guildhall and a new Royal Exchange. Humped and brooding over the rest towered Wren's new St. Paul's Cathedral, the great domed landmark of London from that time to this.[5]

The business of the City, as an American president would say of his country some two and a quarter centuries later, was business. In 1747, the author of The London Tradesman catalogued 363 different trades and crafts, from anchor smith to woollen draper, most of them practiced within one of the City's ninety incorporated companies, or guilds. The numbers could not have been far different half a century previous, since only two companies, the watermen and the fan-makers, had been incorporated since 1700.[6] Here was the center of manufacturing, the throbbing heart of this "nation of shopkeepers," and one of the preeminent seaports of the world. Though London was supplemented by other English shipping centers, such as Bristol, Liverpool, and Newcastle, she was never even remotely challenged during the century to come as the focus of trade for the entire empire.

At the peak of the commercial pyramid stood the great trading companies. The East India Company had been incorporated in 1600, Hudson's Bay in 1670, the Royal African in 1673. Yet to come, in 1711, would be the

South Sea Company. These enormous corporations, chartered to monopolize trade in their respective areas of interest and often wielding political and military as well as commercial power, were based in London and owned mainly by London stockholders. Their activities, and those of more modest owners of shipping, had led recently to the birth of the new industry of marine insurance, also based in the City.[7]

The creation of private wealth from sources such as these coincided in the 1690s with a dramatic increase in the public debt, brought about by King William's war against Louis XIV of France. The War of the League of Augsburg (1689–97) was the first in a series of conflicts in the long Anglo-French struggle for empire and naval supremacy that extended in a sense even through the War for American Independence nearly a century later and the Napoleonic Wars a generation after that. The prosecution of large-scale warfare demanded large-scale borrowing. The lenders, of course, were the newly wealthy merchants and stockholders of the City; the new financial relationship between government and business thus resulted in yet another new industry, modern banking. The Bank of England joined the other powerful institutions of the City in 1694.[8]

The social hierarchy of the City was based not on land or on inherited titles, as it was at the western focus of the metropolis, but on money— money from overseas trade, from selling goods at wholesale or retail, from practicing professions such as law or medicine, or from manufacturing. The decline of the liveried companies had by no means spelled the end of the time-honored system of apprenticeship by which boys learned one of the traditional handicrafts such as cabinet-making, brick or stone masonry, tinkering, printing, or refining gold, and then graduated to the status of free journeyman. Through success and careful saving as a wage-earning journeyman, one could hope to become a master mason or printer and thus join that class of minor capitalists who hired journeymen and raised up apprentices of their own. And in a very practical sense, economic power was linked with political power, because a successful tradesman whose craft or business made him a member of one of the twelve specially privileged incorporated companies could aspire to be an alderman and eventually Lord Mayor.

Recently in some of the trades, notably watchmaking, shoemaking, and silk-weaving, the introduction of specialized tools and a crude division of work had made possible the "putting-out" system of labor by which relatively unskilled women and children in their homes fulfilled various steps in the production of these important London manufactured goods. Nor was even the supervision of manufacturing and conduct of trade exclusively a male activity. A tradesman's widow might succeed to the proprietorship of the business upon her husband's death, as happened also in eighteenth-century America. Of the twenty-three London printing houses recorded for the era by a modern scholar, five were run by printers' widows.[9]

Undergirding all this feverish activity, amongst which the various English classes were discovering that new phenomenon of social mobility—and nowhere was English society more mobile than in London—was a great multitude of the "meaner sort." The streets teemed with peddlars, chapmen, basket women hired to carry goods from one place to another, servants, unemployed laborers and sailors, beggars, pickpockets, and prostitutes.[10]

Together, Westminster and London formed the two disparate centers of a rapidly expanding metropolis that included the Borough of Southwark on the opposite side of London Bridge and the various parishes that comprised the City "Without the Walls."[11] Taken as a whole, this was home for perhaps 575,000 people by the end of the seventeenth century, having in the past fifty years surpassed Paris as the largest city in Europe.[12] What was true according to the first official census report of 1801 had been true for more than a century: this was "the Metropolis of England, at once the Seat of Government and the greatest Emporium in the known world."[13]

The Conduct of Business

It was the milieu of the City—the Royal Exchange, the coffee houses, the docks, the crowded and filthy streets, the guild halls, and the shops—that spawned the London newspaper. Just as the *Gazette* was the organ of Westminster, most of the unofficial journals that followed the lapse of the licensing act in the spring of 1695 were voices of, or at least from, the City. The rebuilding after the fire had been accompanied by the appearance of several printed advertising sheets presumably aimed at helping the restoration of business. Sir Roger L'Estrange, the government's Surveyor of the Press, apparently sanctioned one or two of the earliest ones and joined in sponsoring a weekly advertising paper lasting from 1675 to 1681 called the *City Mercury*. It listed a small subscription fee but most of its 8000 weekly copies were distributed free by London's 121 parish clerks. At the same time, a few unlicensed and therefore illegal sheets appeared on the scene, unmolested either by L'Estrange or by his successor as official monopolizer of the news, Joseph Williamson, publisher of the *London Gazette*.[14] In 1692, two more had appeared, John Houghton's *Collection for Improvement of Husbandry and Trade*, which contained business news and information as well as advertising, and an unofficial revival of the old *City Mercury*.[15] A brief look at the newest *Mercury* will teach us some things about the conduct of London business at the end of the seventeenth century, especially the emerging role of the press.

Its full title reveals much by itself: *The City Mercury; Published (GRATIS) Every Monday for the Promoting of TRADE*. Its publisher, a bookseller named Thomas Howkins, distributed a thousand copies a week without charge *"to all* Booksellers-shops, *and the Principall* Coffee-Houses *and* Inns *in* London *and* Westminster."[16] By July 1692, four months after the paper began, Howkins was sending his *Mercury* to the main provincial towns of England, encouraging advertising from all over the realm, and proposing to have his printer run off still more weekly copies.[17] Howkins must have died sometime between July 1692 and June 1694, for by then the *Mercury* was being put out by one Sarah Howkins, presumably the founder's widow.

The paper's format and contents were the same under both managements. It was printed on both sides of a half sheet, or folio of paper that was seven by either thirteen or fourteen inches, close to the size of the *London Gazette* from which the format was obviously copied. Each page was divided into two columns, and the title, like that of the *Gazette*, appeared in large bold type at the top of the front page, surmounted by the centered arms of the City of London. The *Mercury*'s entire content was advertising, placed in return for "very Reasonable Rates." The top of the left-hand column on page one, the space that the *Gazette* often gave over to a royal proclamation or official palace announcement, was devoted in the three surviving numbers of the *Mercury* (July 4, 1692, and June 11 and December 10, 1694) either to an announcement from the publisher, which was a sort of advertisement for the paper itself, or to an unclassified advertisement to which, probably for an extra payment, the publisher gave special prominence. The rest of the *Mercury* consisted of what we should call today "classified" advertisements, organized by type and, in the case of the larger categories, actually labeled with headings: "Books Newly Published," "Houses to be Let," "Physicians Advertisements," and so on.

In the announcement of July 4, 1692, by which Howkins sought to draw the attention of provincial readers to the potential benefits of advertising in the *Mercury*, the publisher enumerated the kinds of merchandise and services that might be publicized in this way: ". . . the Titles of *Books*, Advertisements of *Auctions*, or *Publick Sales*, things *Lost* or *Stole*, *Houses* to be Let or Sold, *Doctors Bills*, Persons Removing from one Place to another, Either *Trad[e]s-Men*, *Shopkeepers*, *Stage Coaches*, *Wagoners* or *Carryers*, with the Days of their Coming In and Going Out, and to what *Inns* they Come; with anything Else of this Nature. . . ."

By far most of the advertisements in this paper and in the more general ones that succeeded it fell into one of two categories: newly published books or medical cures of various kinds. The book lists always came first, immediately after the opening announcement or unclassified advertisement. Naturally, the Howkinses used the "Books Newly Published" section to announce their own wares, but only five of the thirty-three titles advertised in the three surviving numbers were offered for sale by themselves. The *Mercury* is not best understood, therefore, as a house organ; its publishers treated their journal as a profit-making enterprise on its own account, not simply as a device to promote the other aspects of their business. For "Physicians Advertisements," the same three numbers contain offers to cure, among other things, gout, stomach ache, "Freckles,

Pimples, Worms, and Morphew in the Face," "tooth-ach," and "Convulsion Fits, and the Falling Sickness."

Despite the small sample of *Mercuries* that is available to us—only three out of at least 142 numbers published[18]—we can be confident in our generalizations about the relative predominance of booksellers' and physicians' advertising, because the same pattern is evident in the swarm of newspapers that appeared after the repeal of the licensing act. Not only is this the clear impression conveyed by a cursory look through the files of the 1690s and 1700s, but it is an impression confirmed by R. B. Walker's more systematic comparison of the advertising content of two of the earliest of these papers, the *Post Boy* and the *Flying Post*, with that of the *London Gazette*. Of the *Post Boy*'s 360 advertisements in the first quarter of 1700, 200 were for books and 24 for medicine—a total of 224, or 62 percent of all the advertising in those 39 numbers. During the same three-month period, the *Flying Post* printed 375 advertisements, of which 178 were for books and 57 for medicine—a total of 235, or 63 percent.[19] This observation allows us to catch a glimpse of the way in which print was starting to change the way Londoners did business.

The change at first was by way of supplementing rather than altering established business practices. The center of trade was the Royal Exchange, an elegant arcade-like building near St. Paul's. Here merchants, brokers, factors, and traders came each day to conduct business in the particular "walk" of the Exchange that was appropriate to one's own market or trade. Beginning in the late 1690s, certain specialized businesses, starting with the stock brokers, deserted the Exchange for nearby coffee houses, and some eventually centered in exchanges of their own, such as the Corn Exchange, completed in 1750. The Royal Exchange, however, supplemented by the activity in the coffee houses and by specialized exchanges, remained the principal place of daily business for the merchants and large-scale traders of a London that was still largely without business offices.[20] On the retail level, the shop had been an important and conspicuous feature of London economic life since the middle of the seventeenth century.[21] As in the case of the Royal Exchange and its satellites, business in London's hundreds of shops was carried on face to face.

The earliest printed advertisements, such as those in the *City Mercury*, were not aimed mainly at doing for a merchant or a tradesman what he could do by personal contact and word of mouth. We find no food or drink advertised, for example; nor do we find clothing or clothstuffs or much by way of ordinary shopkeepers' goods and services or reference to the great mercantile enterprises. Part of what we do find are notices relating to real estate, employment, transportation, and similar matters obviously connected with a growing and changing economy for which the existing facilities and methods provided no way to bring buyer and seller together in a systematic way. The *London Post* of January 1 and 3, 1701, carried an especially revealing solicitors' announcement describing a firm in Chancery Lane that brokered jobs, real estate, and loans and represented clients to government departments as well as in the courts. The other part of what we find does consist of traditional goods and services but is limited to the two special commodities already noticed—books and medicine. There is, I believe, a separate explanation for each.

Book notices, by far the most numerous of advertisements in the early years of newspapers, were also perhaps the most obvious use of the first advertising columns. The publishers of many of the turn-of-the-century newspapers were booksellers themselves, and the newspapers were sold in bookstalls and appeared conspicuously in taverns and coffee houses, where, along with the more ephemeral news sheets and broadsides, auction notices, prices-current lists, and the new essay journals, they were passed from hand to hand, discussed, and often read aloud.[22] In short, the makers and vendors of newspapers had a stake in the sale of books, while the consumers of newspapers, demonstrably thirsty for newsy conversation and the printed word, were a perfect target audience. As the satirical *English Lucien* pointed out in 1698 with only partly justified ridicule, "Many People here [in London] are still tainted with the *Athenian* Itch, and the *News-mongers* continue Scratching them, by Publishing (three days in the Week) a Parcel of *Flying* and *Lying Intelligences*, partly patcht up out of old *Gazettes*, and the rest, generally, very Silly and False; notwithstanding which, some Persons swallow it down as greedily as they do their Coffee."[23] Published book notices admirably served the needs of potential customers since they were thus saved the trouble of going from one bookstall to the next and browsing amongst the latest pamphlets, as Samuel Pepys did in London and Samuel Sewall did in Boston, to learn about the most recent productions of the press.[24] To at least one London observer at the turn of the century, those productions presented a confusing scene indeed. "THE multiplicity of Pamphlets that now crowd the Press," wrote a contributor to the *Weekly Miscellany*, "from such various Subjects under consideration, silences my Pretensions of making Reflections and Observations of whatever happens. For I think it now, a Task sufficient to know the Titles of what is dayly publish'd, whilst I find the *Hawkers* confounded with their medly of Wares, crying out aloud their *Plots* and *Projects* in one hand, whilst *Poetry*, having no Body to speak for it, and not being able to speak for it self, lies carelessly neglected in the other hand."[25] The practice of advertising presented at least a potential alternative, presumably more systematic and doubtless more attractive to bookishly inclined consumers, to these older street methods of marketing. Booksellers and printers obviously thought as much, because book announcements continued to appear in even greater numbers throughout the eighteenth century.

The prominence of medical advertising has another explanation. The practice of medicine in this period, such as it was, was a pretty freewheeling affair. It was still primitive, often unsuccessful, and sometimes undertaken without even the rudimentary forms of authorization that this slowly evolving profession provided for itself. Physicians, surgeons, apothecaries, midwives, unlicensed practitioners, and quacks[26] all suffered in some degree from a reputation of incompetence and chicanery to which the satirical columns of the *English Lucien* again provide us one among many possible clues: "A hue and Cry after the *House*-Doctor, if any person can give notice what part of the world he hath taken upon him to depopulate for this Winter season, let him give timely notice at our office, that so all such people as are sick and weary of their lives may repair to him upon occasion, and that all those who have neither estates nor employment in this Town *may go and take possession of that country, after the destruction of said Inhabitants.*"[27]

Instead of relying upon building up a regular practice through reputation and earned confidence, therefore, some practitioners and mixers of potions took advantage of this new opportunity to announce their discoveries or specialties to a largely anonymous public. All the medical advertisements mentioned specific diseases or ailments and implied that the cure being announced was the result of an exclusive and often recent finding of the advertiser—the latest contribution, as it were, to the gradually unfolding and highly competitive field of medicine.

The relative anonymity of doing business through newspaper advertising rather than by means of the face-to-face contacts by which most London business was transacted in these years well suited the needs of the doctors' prospective clients. This was true especially in the decade or two following the lapse of the licensing act, during which the successors of the *City Mercury* carried substantial advertising offering to cure one variety of illness in particular—venereal disease. By perusing, let us say, the *Post Boy* in 1701 or the *Weekly Journal* in 1717, the unfortunate sufferer from "a Clap or running of the Reins" could be directed to the "Antivenereal Antidote" sold with printed directions by "Mr. Needham, Surgeon," at his house in High Holbourn, meticulously described down to "the blue Balcony Rails with a Golden Head thereon," or to Dr. Wright, who offered his "Diuretick or Cleansing Tincture" for the treatment of a long list of ghastly venereal symptoms at ten shillings per bottle, also with directions. Dr. Wright's house in Wine Office-Court, Fleet Street, was distinguished by *two* golden heads and two square lamps, while an unnamed physician of forty years' experience offered to cure "the French Disease and Clap" at his home "at the Blue-ball in Whale-bone-Court."[28] By such advertising, which as the years went on became ever more graphically clinical in its description of symptoms, patients could be spared the embarrassment of seeking such specialized treatment through personal inquiry. As one physician noted in a long advertisement in 1717, this was by definition a secret disease: ". . . nor will the Medicine cause the least *Suspicion* in the most intimate *Friend* or *Bed Fellow*, it Operating with the utmost *Ease* and *Secrecy*; and since 'tis improper to let One Patient be the Informer of *Another*, for as the Disease is, so the Diseas'd must be *Secret*, there can be no other way for those Dissident People to be satisfy'd, but by Tryal. . . ."[29]

This particular variety of medical advertising began to flourish only in the very late 1690s, after the newly legal newspaper press of those years had taken over the commercial function of extra-legal but politically harmless and therefore tolerated sheets such as the *City Mercury*. But the columns of the *Mercury* make it clear that the practitioners had found the printed advertising medium nicely adapted to their purposes right from the beginning of its availability.

The London business community that Thomas and Sarah Howkins designed the *Mercury* to serve was becoming increasingly sensitive to new developments in communication. The national postal service, first made official in 1629, had died during the Civil War but had been restored under the Commonwealth and improved after the Restoration. The post took mail to and from London, usually on horseback and with considerable efficiency and frequency, but not until 1680 had there been a systematic means of circulating correspondence and printed materials within London. That had come with the Penny Post, originally two competing private postal services operating out of coffee houses but taken over by the government when the courts ruled in 1682 that this was an infringement on the legal postal monopoly of the Duke of York.[30] Under government sponsorship, the Penny Post continued for a while to use certain coffee houses as pickup points for the mail and, in recognition of its prime purpose as an adjunct to the London mercantile community, located its main office very close to the Royal Exchange.[31] Private enterprise, nevertheless, often intruded upon and bettered the official mail service, albeit illegally. When the Post Office abandoned the use of coffee houses, it could not abolish the elaborate systems that their proprietors had devised for collecting mail bound overseas and distributing it to the appropriate shipmasters. The coffee-house mailbag thus remained a conspicuous feature of the London communications system throughout most of the eighteenth century. At the same time, the ubiquitous and extremely versatile coffee house (there were 551 of them in London according to one report of 1739) and the rising newspaper developed an intricate partnership that included the designation in advertisements of this or that coffee house as the place to leave a letter, collect the reward for a lost or stolen item, respond to an inquiry, or complete an assignation.[32] Newspaper advertising thus discloses a connection between print and the coffee houses that is even more intricate and diverse than the more well-known diffusion of the coffee-house culture by the essay journalists of the period.[33]

Improved communications, involving the gradual rise of the printed word as a supplement to the oral culture of the seventeenth century, obviously were one key to an increasingly complex business economy. In this development the early newspapers played a part. But when we move beyond the *City Mercury*, we find that the emerging new world of communications had applications well outside the immediate concerns of trade and commerce that dominated the life of the City. E. A. Wrigley has suggested that London was "a potent engine working towards change in England in the century 1650–1750."[34] Economic, demographic, and sociological changes centered in the metropolis were among the agents of "modernizing" English society as a whole, especially since at least one English adult in six in this period had experienced life in London directly.[35]

Moreover, the late seventeenth and early eighteenth centuries were a time of dramatic political reorientation within England and diplomatic change abroad. In a rapidly changing communications culture, the taste for news of such affairs could not long be confined to the ministers of Whitehall and the country parliamentary class which was the traditional recipient of handwritten newsletters. Finally, social and political change was working with the development of urban tastes to produce the beginnings of a literary flowering. The essay journals of the turn of the century rose along with the newspaper, enlarging the public discussion of politics, manners, morals, and the arts through yet another use of the expanding world of print. This form of "journalism" inevitably both reflected and influenced—and overlapped—the less polished and more ephemeral news sheets that primarily concern us here. These journals, too, quickly found an audience throughout an England that to some extent was beginning to shed some of its local and regional particularism in favor of a more unified national culture focused on an unquestioned metropolitan capital.

The Practice of Journalism

The independent unlicensed newspaper emerged from the business milieu of the City, but its genesis was not solely commercial. Politics was also involved. George Ridpath, whose name is most closely associated with the first newspaper after the expiration of the licensing act, was a Whig and Presbyterian who intended his *Flying Post* to advance his party's cause as well as to make money.[36] Benjamin Harris, whose short-lived *Intelligence, Domestic and Foreign* appeared on May 14, 1695, only three days after the first number of the *Flying Post* (and not quite five years after he had tried to start a newspaper in Boston), was even more explicitly a political controversialist on the Whig side. Abel Roper, on the other hand, founded the *Post Boy*, which first appeared on May 17, 1695, purposely as a political rival to Ridpath's *Flying Post*. Roper seems to have been a Tory and high churchman by conviction, though his enemies accused him of writing for whichever party paid him best.[37] It is possible to detect the political leanings of the two rivals, the *Flying Post* and the *Post Boy*, from not much more than a cursory reading.

Politicians both in and out of the ministry made good sponsors for the writers of the new unofficial newspapers during the faction-ridden reigns of William III and Queen Anne. Eventually, in 1712, the Tory leadership favored by Anne dealt with the problem of printed opposition with the blunt instrument of repression—this time in the form of a stamp tax, which achieved its immediate end by putting several newspapers out of business. It did not, however, achieve the long-term Tory goal of controlling printed criticism of the government altogether.[38]

But not even the potent combination of commercial opportunity and partisan politics accounts completely either for the explosion of print in 1695 or for the form and content of the many new journals. To the business and political context of the age we must add a localized London tradition of a certain kind of literature—or, to be less charitable about it, hack writing.

Writing for pay was, to be sure, a kind of business, one that meshed well with the long-established trades of printing and bookselling and with London's emerging culture of the coffee house. By most lights of the day, however, it was not entirely respectable. Hired pens had first been used in seventeenth-century England to write propaganda for both sides during the Civil War. It was then that the term "Grub Street" had become current, applying the name of an actual short street in the City (now Milton Street near Moorgate) to a school of political pamphleteers who found even more work for themselves after the Restoration, branching out from politics into whatever kind of quick productions sponsors or publishers were willing to pay for. By the 1690s, and especially after the lapse of the licensing act, it had actually become possible to make a precarious living in this way.[39]

It is not as easy as one might suppose to locate the exact line that separates the "Grub Street hack," such as the riotous Tom Brown, from his more serious, well-remunerated, and well-remembered contemporaries, such as Jonathan Swift, Daniel Defoe, Joseph Addison, and Richard Steele. Brown is one of the few of his particular ilk whose name emerges from the near anonymity in which most of them lived and wrote, but all of the canonized writers just mentioned wrote political and other pieces for pay, contributed to or edited journals, and got into political or legal hot water or both. All or most of them wrote perishable prose for newspapers as well as works that have endured. As a prolific contributor to that new genre, Swift must have meant to include himself when he equated the periodical press of his generation with "Grub Street," and Defoe matched some of the rougher aspects of the typical "Grub Street" writer's life at least on the occasion in 1702 when he stood in the pillory and then spent two years in prison.[40] On the other hand, a newspaper's "author" without a lasting claim to literary fame, one who might seem to fit the "Grub Street" mold, could win a superior local reputation among his contemporaries. Jean de Fonvive, a French Protestant émigré, edited the almost universally trusted and admired *Post Man* and received the real accolade of an offer to serve at the unprecedented annual salary of four hundred pounds—a hundred pounds more than Steele got for the job—in the highly respectable position of "Gazetteer," or editor of the official *London*

Gazette. Even more to the point, perhaps, he could afford to turn it down.[41] But then there were Tom Brown, a notorious drunkard and brawler; Ridpath of the *Flying Post,* who ran off to foreign parts without waiting to be convicted for libeling Queen Anne; and John Tutchin of the *Observator,* who on a technicality escaped sentencing for libel in 1704 but three years later was found beaten to death.[42]

The way a newspaper got started during the decade or so following 1694 and the precise way it was carried on are both less clear than the somewhat standardized picture that emerges after 1712. The first newspaper sponsors were individual entrepreneurs. Most, apparently, were booksellers, such as Abel Roper, who hired a "newswriter" identified only as E. Thomas to edit his *Post Boy.*[43] But a publisher might also be a printer, such as Ichabod Dawks,[44] or even a professional writer, like the essay-journalists or George Ridpath. After a couple of decades of experimentation with the new medium, the individual newspaper entrepreneur came to be overshadowed by a new phenomenon in the news business, combinations of booksellers who pooled their resources to form what in effect were newspaper publishing companies.[45]

Physically, the new newspapers were much like their prototype, the *London Gazette.* The *Flying Post,* the *Post Boy,* and most of their rivals appeared on seven- by twelve-inch folio leaves, printed in two columns on both sides of the leaf. (Dawks's eccentric *News-Letter,* with its script-like type stretching across the full page, was an exception.) The title was centered in large type at the top of page one, while the second page—or last page if there were more than two—was rounded off with a colophon. Most continued the convention begun by the *Gazette* of emphasizing foreign news, placed at the beginning of the paper unless there was a special reason for it to be usurped by something else. Domestic news in most papers consisted of little more than a sequence of snippets beginning near the end of the back page. Advertisements were few at this stage, accounting for a small proportion both of space and of the publishers' income,[46] despite the great potential of the London advertising market demonstrated by sheets such as the *City Mercury.*

The first private newspapers came out three times a week, their publication days of Tuesday, Thursday, and Saturday timed to coincide with London's thrice-weekly post days. Both the publication schedule and the titles of the early thrice-weeklies—*Flying Post, Post Boy, Post Man, St. James's Post, St. James's Evening Post,* and even Dawks's *News-Letter*—point unmistakably to their publishers' intention that their journals, aimed for a national distribution, should be identified in their subscribers' eyes both with the speed and comprehensiveness associated with the national postal service and with the venerable newsletter tradition of communicating intelligence from the metropolis to the country. The *Post Man, Post Boy,* and *Flying Post* also eventually placed their titles between a pair of woodcut "ears" (to use a modern term), one of which invariably depicted a mounted postman blowing his horn, thus visually conveying the same connection.

By getting out their papers in time to be taken to their "country" destinations by the departing post riders, however, the first thrice-weekly publishers were not able to include any news that arrived on that post day. Abel Roper's *Post Boy* led the way in meeting—or perhaps creating—the demand for better timeliness. The paper announced in 1701 that on each publication day it would offer for sale at three City locations, including Roper's bookshop, *"a Written Postscript, containing all the domestick Occurrences, with the Translations of the Foreign News that arrives after the Printing of the said* Post-Boy." The *Post Boy* had in fact been following this practice at least occasionally since 1697.[47] The *Post Man* and the *Flying Post* both responded in 1703. The *Post Man*, having provided from close to its beginning an extra page of news and space to write in for those of its London readers who wanted to pay the extra price, now put on sale at a coffee house what was in effect a handwritten evening edition containing *"all the Remarkable Occurrences of the Day, and the chief Heads of the Foreign Mails that came in after the Printing of the* Post-Man."[48] A month later, the *Flying Post* took the next logical step by offering to deliver a *printed* "postscript" to its London subscribers each publication day, containing news that had arrived in the foreign mails after the morning edition and combining with it the familiar blank page for personal use.[49] A 6 p.m. delivery would enable an alert and fast-scribbling correspondent to get his embellished copy of the *Flying Post*'s "Postscript" into the mail to a country recipient before the post rider's departure in the evening.[50]

It was then only a matter of time before a few thrice-weekly publishers would aim deliberately at the in-town market with an evening post-day paper featuring the news that had arrived only hours before publication. That must have been the idea behind the *Evening Post*, which started up in 1711, and *St. James's Evening Post*, which the combination of booksellers that published *St. James's Post* began in 1715 as a supplement to their first paper, begun earlier the same year. Both these evening papers took pains to supply blank space on what the "St. James" group called "fine Writing Paper," suggesting that the evening market included London's corps of correspondents "into the country."[51] The evening papers, at first a minority, began a trend that by the early 1730s was standard among papers with a post-day publication schedule, attesting to the growing recognition of timeliness as the supreme value in the marketing of news.[52]

The thrice-weekly press, which along with the official twice-a-week *Gazette* dominated the London newspaper scene for the first two or three decades after 1695, was aimed at a national readership. This it appears to have achieved, with broad geographic distribution and a circulation apparently as large as three to four thousand in the case of both *Post Boy* and *Post Man* throughout the first decade of the new century and a much smaller but rising circulation for the *Flying Post*.[53] There were other papers directed more specifically at the London market, published weekly and daily. Because this market was large, dense, and varied, there was room for a degree of specialization that is not apparent among the more-or-less standardized combinations of content that one finds in the London-based tri-weekly "national" press. Some of these papers were devoted to general foreign and domestic news, much in the manner of the tri-weeklies and most of the developing provincial press of the period. Others aimed exclusively at translating, reporting, and sometimes interpreting the news of Europe for the benefit of their London readers. Still others sought primarily to entertain or edify their urban audience by means ranging from "polite" essays on contemporary manners and morals to crude and often vulgar satires on the newspaper genre itself.

The first daily newspaper, the *Daily Courant*, appeared in broadside form—on only one side of a half-sheet of paper—on March 11, 1702. Despite its sparser content (*"half the Compass,"* its publisher put it, *"to save the Publick at least half the Impertinence, of ordinary News-Papers"*), *the Courant* marks an advance in newspaper practice even beyond its innovation in frequency. Designed simply to keep its London readers abreast of the news of the world as reported in the foreign press, the *Courant* stands out among its contemporaries to a modern eye for its cleanness of appearance, its readability, and its orderliness of presentation. Its two unruled columns of highly legible type are well spaced and contain a sequence of European news items, each group of which is headed by the source from which the items in that group were translated: "From the Harlem Courant, Dated March 18. N.S.," "From the Amsterdam Courant, Dated Mar. 18," and "From the Paris Gazette, Dated Mar. 18.1702," to use the three examples in the *Courant*'s first number.[54] The *Courant* at first printed no advertisements, but that soon changed, as did the one-page format. Shortly after it began, the paper was taken over by Samuel Buckley, who later worked in the office of the secretaries of state for much of his career and became Gazetteer for life in 1717. Buckley, eventually using his access to the official news reports of the secretaries of state as well as translations of the foreign press, printed the *Courant* on both sides of the sheet and incorporated paid advertising.[55]

The *Courant*'s move toward rationalizing the presentation of foreign news followed a much more elaborate but short-lived attempt at systematic presentation and interpretation in a remarkable weekly journal that had appeared the previous year. The *New State of Europe* evidently took both its title and concept from a cluster of monthly news magazines, one of which, the *State of Europe*, first published at The Hague, had originated thirteen years before with the Glorious Revolution.[56] Though the *New State* gave the appearance of a newspaper rather than an essay journal or magazine, it was much more carefully composed and laid out than most of its contemporaries and filled four pages instead of the standard two—a full sheet folded to produce two folio leaves, each the usual seven by thirteen inches. The first two of the *New State*'s four pages was filled with a succession of news items organized under appropriate headings by their country of origin. In several cases, the segment of news from a given country was followed by a few inches of comment: the Portuguese news by "*Reflexions on PORTUGAL*," the Spanish news by "Reflexions on *SPAIN*," and so on. The third and fourth pages were devoted to the *New State*'s two other departments, "The Geographical Part of the New State of Europe" and "A Character of the Works of the Learned." The first consisted each week of a substantial essay on some fairly little-known place in Europe that had lately figured in the news—the "country" of Tyrol in the case of the paper's first number. The second, a very early predecessor of the modern newspaper's book-review section, consisted of synopses of recent books, divided into foreign and London imprints.[57]

Either the *New State of Europe* or the dynastic revolution in Europe to which it was primarily a response, and which after the accession of Queen Anne would result in England's becoming a principal combatant in the War of the Spanish Succession, stimulated other attempts to educate English readers about the context as well as the facts of the news. During the two months following the appearance of *New State* on May 23, 1701, the *London Gazette* advertised two new monthly publications along the same plan in addition to an English reprint of the most recent volume of the original *State of Europe*, still being published at The Hague.[58] It may well be that the *New State of Europe* and its related literature played some role, at least, in inspiring Daniel Defoe's *Review*, which he began in 1704 while serving out the end of his two-year term in Newgate. The successive full titles of his journal from 1704 to 1713 suggest a similar intent and method.[59]

The *New State* changed printers, and possibly proprietors, at least twice during its eight-month life. Gradually the format and quality of the too-ambitious experiment diminished. By July 8 had come the first of many numbers with only two instead of four pages. Most of the typographical innovations with which the paper had begun in May gradually disappeared during July and August, and the content of the geographical and literary sections became greatly attenuated. Sometime during the fall, there was a switch to a thrice-weekly publishing schedule. By December, under at least its third printer, only the title remained to distinguish *New State* from any of its competitors. In format, content, and typography, it was now like all the rest, and with the number of January 22 the surviving file ends.[60]

The rather different but equally serious attempts of the *Daily Courant* and the *New State of Europe* to inform a London readership about contemporary foreign affairs in a systematic and reliable way contrast strikingly with what might be considered the "Grub Street" end of the newspaper spectrum in the earliest decades. The most obvious representatives of journalism's underside in these years are the satirical weeklies, the *English Lucien*, which appeared in 1698, and the *Jesting Astrologer*, which came along in 1701. Neither of these, nor those like them, lasted long, but their scurrilous tone and bawdy wit not only provide a vivid glimpse into the less respectable corners of London life but were occasionally imitated with only slight moderation by the general tri-weekly press.

Both of these "Grub Street" productions satirized the follies of metropolitan life while they parodied the newspaper genre itself, a temptation too strong to resist for two publishers of 1705, one of whom briefly put out the *Diverting-Post* and the other the even shorter-lived *Whipping Post*. The format of both *Lucien* and *Astrologer* imitated exactly that of their chief serious contemporaries, except that the *Astrologer*'s lines ran across the entire page instead of in columns. The parody extended even to the *Lucien*'s colophon, which changed after the first three numbers to "*LONDON*: Printed, and Sold by the General Assembly of *Hawkers*, 1698." London's affliction with the "Athenian Itch" and the sometimes unscrupulous attempts by news publishers and the coffee-house crowd to satisfy the craving for the latest news and gossip were favorite topics for both. The *Lucien* contrasted a London with a Persian coffee house, where "Quarrel[ing] very much about State-affairs" reportedly had been cured by the appointment of a "*Moullah* to be there every day betimes to entertain the *Coffee-quaffers* with a Point of Law, History, or Poetry." If some authority would only effect the same change in the coffee houses of London, the satirical piece went on, "it would be far more deverting than reading a parcel of dull sham NewsPapers."[61]

Occasionally the *Lucien*'s attack on newspapers crossed the line that to modern sensibilities separates the clever from the downright vulgar, raising the question of how far up the scale of gentility this and similar expressions of the grosser side of post-Restoration culture would have been found admissible:

> *Stocks-Market*, Feb. 4. A Gentleman being taken with a violent motion in his body, was hastily going to the public *Squerting-Office* to ease Nature, but groping in his Pockets for a *Fundament-Wiper*, could find nothing proper for that purpose, when at the same instant, a Woman came bawling by, *The Flying Post*, *The Post-Man* and *The Post-Boy*, he call'd her to him, and ask'd for one of her *NewsPapers: Which Sir*, said she? *Either of them*, reply'd the Gentleman, *will serve my turn*; upon which she deliver'd the *Post-Boy*, he ask'd the Price of it; she answered *a Penny*; the Gentleman tears it in the middle, and return'd her one half again, with a *Half Penny*, saying, *this part will do my business well enough*; The Woman, perceiving herself trick'd, gave him as many Curses as a *Fish-Woman* bestows upon a *Car-Man* that oversets her Basket; and so left him.[62]

The same question arises in connection with the *Jesting Astrologer*'s jocular treatment a few years later of the twin social problems of prostitution and venereal disease. Neither, though both were discussed openly in print on all sides, was usually treated as a joke. For the *Jesting Astrologer*, however, these troublesome issues combined nicely with the greed and pomposity of the medical profession to provide ideal grist for its satirical mill:

> . . . Professing thus both Physick and Astrology, as I was, the other Day, sitting in my Study, . . . a Female Patient, Mask'd, wrapt up in Velvethood and Scarf, came and thump'd at my Door, with as much Authority, as a poor Cuckold at Midnight, knocking for a Midwife . . . who in plain Words, told me, she was Clap'd, and ask'd me for what Mony I'd undertake to Cure her; I told her, five Pounds; Confound you, says she, for an old groping fumbler, I have been a Trader in this town, almost this twenty Years, and never gave above a Guinea in my Life. Indeed, Madam, said I, I cannot undertake the cure for so inconsiderable a sum. Well, says she, I'll defer Physicking a little, and Kiss on a Fortnight or three Weeks longer, for the Benefit of your Profession; and if you wont undertake me then for the Mony I have offer'd, you are the most ungrateful old Tuzzy-muzzy-mender, that ever handled Surringe; and away she trip'd, without another Word. . . .[63]

Like the *English Lucien*, the *Jesting Astrologer* reserved some of its choicest barbs for its fellow newspapers and for the frequenters of coffee houses. And like the more serious essayists of the age, its writers worried in print about the more fundamental values that underlay contemporary public and private morality. Among the "astrologer's" predictions for 1701 were these:

> THE Beards of Coffee-house Politicians, will Wag mightily, during this Session of P[arliament]; and every flying Gull, and foolish Imposition, inserted in the News Papers, will go down as glib, with the Sipers of Ninny-broth [coffee], as a *White-Fryers* Falsity, Publish'd by sham Authority, does oftentimes with the too credulous Multitude.
>
> Great talk of strange Plots will addle the Noddles of the Publick. . . .
>
> It will be hard for a poor Man to be thought a good Man, or a rich Man an ill Man, in this Age; whilst Men shall be esteem'd Honest for their Wealth, much rather than their Vertues. . . .

The same passage attacks dishonest church wardens and improvident husbands and laments that, despite the work of the "Reforming Society," the reformation of manners "crawles backwards like a Crab."[64] Beneath all the *Jesting Astrologer*'s ribaldry, therefore, lay the ostensibly serious purpose, perhaps only partly hypocritical, of drawing critical attention to the moral follies of the age.

That there were limits to the transgressions of decency that would be tolerated by at least a portion of the newspaper readership of the early eighteenth century is evident from an explicit concern over obscenity that made its way into *St. James's Evening Post* in 1718. A publishers' announcement acknowledged that several letters had complained of frequent "obscene Advertisements," asserted that such material had been taken in without the knowledge of the publisher, and promised to avoid "any such Occasion of Offence" in the future. The voicing of such concern, however, though it informs us that limits did exist, does not help us very much in understanding what the limits were. Had the complaints been directed at the ubiquitous and ever more clinical ads for venereal cures, or perhaps for certain book titles recently advertised in *St. James's Evening Post*? The recent announcement of *Eunuchism Display'd*, for example, had listed that book's rather graphic chapter headings; another had advertised a five-volume treatise on a similar topic, *The Causes of Impotency and Divorce*, and yet another *The Diseases of Women with Child*.[65] When compared with the scurrilous examples of "Grub Street" writing, the mere advertising of books such as these hardly seems grounds for provoking a row over obscenity.

Just a few days before the concern was voiced in *St. James's Evening Post*, however, another paper had printed an obviously satirical and potentially libelous advertisement depicting an unnamed but probably identifiable china shop near Charing Cross as only a front for a house of procurement where, for the benefit of her female customers, the proprietress provided, among other erotic paraphernalia, "Men of all Sorts and Sizes, ready to serve their carnal Desires."[66] It is possible that the same advertisement had appeared in *St. James's Evening Post*, though it is not apparent from the surviving file. If so, this sham announcement, with its details, comes as close as any London newspaper during the quarter-century after the end of licensing to transgressing the limits of decency according to the standards of most modern communities. Whether this or something rather different is what the readers and publishers of *St. James's Evening Post* understood in 1718 as "obscene," I am still uncertain. It is obvious only that the bounds of acceptable taste in newspapers, though apparently broad, were not limitless. They seem, in fact, to have been drawn more narrowly at this stage of the Augustan period than during the Puritan era seventy years before.[67]

One might, of course, speculate that those bounds would be different depending upon whether one was a habitual reader of papers such as the *London Gazette* and the *Daily Courant* and the serious essay journals or a devotee of the "Grub Street" end of the periodical spectrum. Was the literate population, in other words, already dividing itself, even at this early stage, as it does with great self-consciousness in contemporary Britain, between the readers of "quality" newspapers on the one hand and consumers of the "downmarket" popular press on the other? Probably not. The deliberate coarseness of some of the material in the newspaper parodies was mixed with some good examples of genuine wit that it would have taken a reader of some sensitivity and familiarity with the rest of the printed culture to appreciate. Chances are that most literate and public-minded Londoners knew the whole range of what the press had to offer, not just a part of it, even though each of the various political and social sectors of that readership must certainly have had its preferred journals and may have shared their publishers' scorn for the competition.[68] The coffeemen, we know, subscribed to everything,[69] and what was read and discussed and argued over in the coffee houses was no doubt what was also discussed in the shops, in the Exchange, in the taverns, and in the most posh gentlemen's clubs. Addison, Steele, and later Samuel Johnson were familiar with all these settings and did not write as if they had one segment of their audience more in mind than another—though we must remember that there were very large segments of London's, and Britain's, population that were not part of any reading audience at all. William Hogarth marketed his visual portrayals of the ugliest and most brutal scenes his great reportorial skills could communicate to all who could pay the price of a print, and these portrayals often ended up as framed adornments of the most fashionable rooms. "The gross and the elegant," to use a phrase of L.C.B. Seaman,[70] co-existed in eighteenth-century English culture, not only within many of the same social circles but often in the same individual mind. And, needless to add, in many of the same newspapers.

A Closer Look

Along with the obvious disadvantages of the filing scheme used by the British Library's Burney Collection, by which some of its many thousands of newspapers were collected in volumes with greater attention to chronology than to title, there is one great advantage. By leafing through a volume of intermixed titles in which numbers are arranged in chronological order, the modern reader gains a particularly dramatic sense of how a segment of the press as a whole was responding over a period of months to the world of events and communications that presumably all newspapers shared. What such a reader finds, instead of a unified vision of that world, is one that is utterly fragmented. Except on the rarest of occasions, such as the death of a sovereign, different newspapers in the same week or even of the same date might well, so far as one can tell, be describing different Europes, different Englands, different Londons.

One such volume[71] contains interspersed numbers of the first three thrice-weeklies, the *Post Man*, the *Post Boy*, and the *Flying Post*, for the year 1698. Despite their similar sources—foreign newspapers translated by their own staffs, their own correspondents in a few European and English cities, and London gossip—these three otherwise very similar newspapers, published on the same three days each week and containing the same two identically sized pages to fill on each publication day, gave their readers with rare exceptions entirely different pictures of each day's events. To read the three papers on a given day was like getting letters from three different friends, each of whom for reasons partly but not entirely related to politics traveled in somewhat different circles, had different sources of information, and had different interests. Obviously, there was no cooperation among the three, no mutual copying despite the common accusations of plagiarism directed at newspapers as a whole, and little copying even from common sources such as the *Gazette*. More to the point for one who seeks to understand the long way that the news business had yet to travel from these beginnings, there was nothing like consensus on what our own day understands as "news judgment." As Addison's *Spectator* observed, although the papers of the period "receive the same advices from abroad, and very often in the same words . . . their way of cooking it is so different, that there is no citizen, who has an eye to the public good, that can leave the coffee-house with peace of mind, before he has given every one of them a reading."[72]

In certain respects, however, the three publishers displayed remarkable unanimity. The papers were similar in size, layout, typography, general method of collecting and presenting news, adherence to the newsletter tradition in the order and standard phraseology of news items, and contents. For all of them, and for all of their contemporaries with a few eccentric exceptions, "news" meant primarily the affairs of state, with particular emphasis on what was reported from abroad. The news tastes of the time, however, also extended to natural and human curiosities and to occasional small triumphs and tragedies of ordinary people. In printing such reports, the newsmen agreed on yet another convention—the *impersonality* of the news. Except when reporting the activities of royalty and other great personages, who created news because of who they were no matter what they did, these newspapers and their contemporaries reported human events while preserving the perfect anonymity of the actors and tragedies without naming the victims. The following examples of this convention of news reporting were picked at random from another volume in the Burney Collection,[73] this one covering the second half of 1701 and adding the *London Post* and the *English Post* to the three original thrice-weeklies.

The first is from the *Post Boy* for September 20, 1701, which reported: "Yesterday a Man stood in the Pillory at Charing Cross, for putting off Counterfeit-Money." One might ask the purpose of the item. Is it to make us feel either sympathy or repugnance for the victim? We know neither his name nor anything of his family, occupation, or background, save that he has been convicted of counterfeiting. Is it to satisfy any curiosity that a reader might have built up over the case? The paper had apparently not mentioned it before, though the story may have made its rounds by word of mouth. Is it to provide the *Post Boy*'s "country" readership with insights into an ugly but very public slice of London life? The stark report lacks details, description, and color. If there was a conscious rationale for printing this one-dimensional story, it may have involved the idea of a printed supplement to the deterrent that the theater of punishment was intended to supply in the first place—a printed warning that counterfeiters risk punishment. The identity of the offender, we can assume, was no more important to the many hundreds of readers who now shared this public experience than to the other hundreds who had been first-hand witnesses at Charing Cross.

A similar example appears in the *Flying Post* for October 11: "This week the two High way Men were seized that robbed the two Stage-Coaches last week on Hounslo-Heath." Here the writer seems to take for granted some prior knowledge of the crime, even though none of the five previous numbers of the *Flying Post* (or any of the other four papers in the volume) had carried an account of it. The function of the newspaper in this instance seems to be to provide the conclusion, at least for the moment, to a story that had been circulating by traditional means, word of mouth. At the same time, it used the comforting authority of print to announce to what may have been a concerned population that two dangerous criminals were now out of circulation. Again, however, the defendants remain unnamed and unexplained; the item has had a public purpose, but in no sense a personal one.

Finally, there is this from the *Flying Post* of October 9: "Yesterday a Labourer belonging to St. Paul's was interred in St. Faith's Church, having been accidentally killed the Day before by the fall of a Stone, which broke his legg short off, so that he died immediately." Does the story evoke sympathy? Yes, but for whom? Horror? Yes, though we are spared the details. But in the absence of personal information of any kind, is either of these human reactions the aim of the writer? No doubt many readers recognized the victim and were glad to receive the information about the place of his burial. For those who knew no more than was contained in this report, however, it served only as a kind of public statistic, perhaps reported with no very clear purpose in mind at all.

This impersonal convention in reporting, with the puzzles over motive that it sometimes raises, perservered without great refinement well into the century and was extended into the provinces on both sides of the Atlantic. Its contemplation, along with reflections upon the meaning of other dimensions of news publication, belongs to a later section of this book. It is enough for the moment to note that the newspapers appear not only to have been serving here as a kind of bridge between the oral culture and the more formal and authoritative culture of print but also to have been moving in an inchoate way toward the enlargement of the public sphere.

It would be to misrepresent the content of the earliest London newspapers, however, to place too great an emphasis upon the small events and the nameless people who strayed into print according to a publisher's whim. It is true that before the Stamp Act of 1712, as an immediate consequence of which the twenty or so newspapers then appearing in London were reduced to about twelve,[74] one could find a small supply of the more-or-less scurrilous and usually short-lived journals that played up the local and the trivial. To an overwhelming extent, however, the serious newspapers of whatever frequency and intended audience, both before and after the Stamp Act, stressed the affairs of state, reported in surprisingly large measure from abroad. After the Stamp Act, it was mainly these that survived, despite the many illegal and ultimately unsuccessful attempts to undercut the market with unstamped competitors.[75] In their emphasis upon affairs of state, and especially upon foreign intelligence, of course, they followed the lead of the official *London Gazette*.

We shall see the same phenomenon repeated even more dramatically when we consider the first successful attempt at a newspaper in America. Since the American publisher's emphasis was essentially a matter of copying English precedent, we need to address as best we can the reasons for the London publishers'—and presumably their readers'—preferences.

It could be argued that in an era still not free from the continual threat if not the fact of governmental interference with the press, even though neither licensing nor actual censorship had been in effect for some time, foreign news was a "safer" political commodity than too intense a scrutiny of domestic affairs. Government possessed the power not only to punish indiscretion but to reward useful newspaper allies, whether by outright subsidy or by the more indirect means of purchasing copies of a newspaper for use in its own intelligence or propaganda efforts. Copies of *St. James's Evening Post*, for example, were among those distributed in 1725 by the secretaries of state.[76]

Governmental interference, or the anticipation thereof, does not by itself, however, explain the newspapers' preoccupation with foreign affairs. If a publisher wished to avoid offense, plenty of bland alternatives to foreign news were available. Obviously, the publishers sought to meet what they perceived as a public demand for such news. The demand was grounded in part on the centrality of foreign policy to English politics in the period after the Restoration. Perhaps it was also related to the habit, begun with the receipt of the earliest English-language news publications from Amsterdam early in the seventeenth century and reinforced and perpetuated by the main emphasis of the *Gazette*, of regarding the very idea of "news" primarily as foreign intelligence. Certainly, it was easy for a publisher to come by, possibly easier than the most interesting kind of political information from his own country. British diplomats and army officers, the foreign contacts of the vast London mercantile community, traveling gentlemen and scholars, Continental religious sympathizers with English dissenting groups, and newspapers from all the European capitals, not to mention the intelligence service of the secretaries of state, were among the many sources of information, impressions, and opinion about the events and personages of Europe that flowed into London in the eighteenth century and readily found their way into the columns of its newspapers.[77]

The serious thrice-weekly press made up most of London's newspapers in the first part of the eighteenth century. The daily press shared with the thrice-weeklies an emphasis on general news, but their frequency, smaller length, and almost entirely urban audience made these papers a distinct genre. The twice-weekly *London Gazette* was also mainly a general (and very serious) news organ, but its government sponsorship gave it a character of its own, especially in its function as the bearer of official announce-ments. The weekly newspapers and journals provided great variety, since each tended to have a distinct method, message, and audience.

Variety and specialization such as this was possible in the thriving market for print that was London and the national audience beyond that to which the products of London presses were distributed. It was not, how-ever, possible in provincial England, which was spawning newspapers of its own, or in the overseas provinces of the empire. In both these settings, the publishers of "news" papers discovered sooner or later that to be a real success, their products needed to be more than that alone.

Chapter 3

The Provinces

London's Hinterland

A simplified road map of Britain in 1700 would make it clear that London was "metropolis" in more than overwhelming size alone. Like the hub of an eccentric wheel or the off-center core of an incomplete spider's web, it sent off spokes, as it does today, to every part of the kingdom. Counting clockwise from east northeast around to north, the six main spokes were post roads connecting London with Harwich on the North Sea, with Dover on the Channel, with the West Country towns of Exeter, Plymouth, and Falmouth by way of Salisbury, with the principal Atlantic port of Bristol, with Chester and the Welsh port of Holyhead on the Irish Sea, and with Edinburgh by way of the four-hundred-mile Great North Road.[1] The Harwich and Dover roads provided part of a land–sea link between London and the European continent, while through Holyhead the London-based political and commercial leaders of England kept in touch with their dependency of Ireland. The Cornish and Bristol roads had a part in London's Atlantic commerce, though the bulk of England's overseas shipping still sailed directly out of the Thames.

Just as all the main roads fanned out from London, so did the principal sea lanes of the empire. English ships sailed in the higher latitudes of the North Atlantic from early spring to late autumn, providing London's link with the American ports of Portsmouth, Boston, Newport, New York, and Philadelphia. The southerly route by way of the Azores or the Canaries to the Caribbean sugar islands, Charleston, and the ports of the Chesapeake was usable most of the year.

Despite its great metropolis, England was a rural nation. Three-quarters or more of its five million people were country dwellers. The trading center for the farm or hamlet in which most of them lived was one of five or six hundred market towns located not more than six miles away. To such a center, the farmers and villagers brought their animals and produce on the weekly market day, exchanged news and gossip of neighbors and country matters, and carried away whatever supplies they had bought or traded for. In such centers, where the town population ranged from about 400 to 1800 people, most economic activity was just about that fundamental, consisting mainly of the exchange of country goods among farmers. Even little trading towns like these, however, usually held a few local craftsmen who could exchange their products for the goods that were brought in on market day or find ways of sending them farther afield, and even the small agricultural hinterland of such a place might occasionally produce a surplus. Thus it was a rare market town, however small, that did not at least occasionally find its simple economic life enriched by some remote participation in a broader trading network. This, of course, meant an ultimate, though tenuous, connection with London.

A few of the market towns, not more than fifty, could boast a more complex pattern of trade, populations ranging from two to five thousand, a wider trading hinterland than that of most towns, and sometimes an organized industrial base, such as the home manufacture and distribution of worsted cloth under the sponsorship of a local company of wool merchants. In a notch still higher than these in the urban hierarchy, scattered throughout the country were the major regional centers, industrial clusters, important seaports, and national social or cultural centers such as certain cathedral cities and the university towns of Oxford and Cambridge, all of which supplemented London as secondary centers of urban life. Of about thirty such towns with populations over 5000, a handful stood out as the largest and most important cities of the realm outside of London. Each of these large provincial cities, ranging in size from Norwich with nearly 30,000 people to York with just over 10,000, combined a strategic location with special industrial, commercial, or social functions and, in most cases, a direct road link with London.[2]

The "big seven," if we may so designate the places at the top of this secondary rank in the urban hierarchy, were Norfolk's county and diocesan center of Norwich, the great Atlantic seaport of Bristol, the northeastern coal-exporting port of Newcastle, the West Country regional center and Channel port of Exeter, the North Sea fishing port of Yarmouth, the Essex clothmaking town of Colchester, and the ancient northern regional capital and cathedral city of York. Ultimately, it was primarily through these well-distributed regional centers that materials and people flowed to the metropolis. It was these same major centers that formed most of the main links in the intricate distribution network that, in turn, carried goods, information, and ideas from London out into the English hinterland.

Not even the largest of these provincial cities remotely approached the metropolitan center of the nation in size, complexity, influence, or prestige. Norwich, the largest, was only about one-twentieth the size of London. Setting aside for the moment all considerations of political, commercial, and intellectual centrality, consider that in 1700 about one Englishman in nine actually lived in London. Only about one in 45 lived in one of the seven largest provincial cities.[3] It was, however, in towns such as these, probably beginning with Norwich in 1701 and Bristol in 1702, that the English provincial newspaper was born.

Before either the *Norwich Post* or the *Bristol Post Boy* were the *News-Letter* of Dublin and the *Edinburgh Gazette*. The newspapers of the Celtic fringe, like the readers for whom they were intended, looked to London as their chief source of information and imitation. In 1700, only Wales among the non-English countries of the British Isles was fully integrated with England politically, as it had been since 1536. Though the Welsh language could still be heard and read throughout its 8000 square miles of mountains, hills, plains, and valleys, only English-speaking Welshmen could hold administrative office in the principality. The central political authority for the 400,000 people of Wales, fewer than the population of London, was the King and Parliament at Westminster.[4]

Scotland, junior partner in a political relationship with England that had included a joint sovereign since 1603 and would culminate in a union of parliaments in 1707, was also an outpost of London. The Reformation had introduced to Scotland the English Bible and prayer books, and largely by these vehicles the language of England had superseded Lowland Scots, a vernacular English dialect, and the Gaelic of the Highlands as the common coin of literature, commerce, and politics as well as religion.[5]

Edinburgh, while possessing unusual symbolic and administrative importance as the ancient national capital for Scotland's million inhabitants and the site of a renowned university, was now taking its place as another regional center, somewhat larger than Norwich, in London's hinterland.[6] The newspaper-publishing history of the royal borough, reaching back to the Civil War era, was somewhat parallel to that of London. From the 1640s to the 1660s, some Edinburgh printers occasionally turned out reprints of London Interregnum and Restoration newspapers or, in a few cases, published their own titles, using the London prints as their main source. An *Edinburgh Gazette* appeared briefly in 1680, but it was in 1699 that a new *Edinburgh Gazette*, published twice weekly by James Donaldson, instituted a new era of continuous newspaper publishing in Scotland.[7]

Ireland, where newspapers had a more precocious development than in Scotland, was a conquered English province. Inflamed by the eight-year-old memory of the Irish massacre of Protestant planters in Ulster, Oliver Cromwell had undertaken a quick and vicious campaign in 1649 to bring all of Ireland under parliamentary rule. He had then installed English Protestant landlords to take control over most of the land. The conquest had been confirmed in 1690 with William's victory at the river Boyne over the French-supported attempt by the deposed James II to lead an Irish rebellion against the revolutionary settlement of 1689. By 1700, the two and a half million largely landless Irish[8] were dependent politically and economically on England and subordinate in their own country to a Protestant ruling class whose political and cultural center was Dublin. As its standard for social, intellectual, and religious life, Protestant Dublin looked to London.

As in Edinburgh, a few Dublin printers had done a little news publishing during the Civil War and immediately after the Restoration. Dublin's era of continuous newspaper printing, however, began as early as 1685 with the institution of Robert Thornton's *News-Letter*. This little sheet and its many successors in the 1690s and the first half of the eighteenth century, all published only in the capital city and aimed almost exclusively at a Protestant readership, depended overwhelmingly for content and example upon the newspapers of London.[9]

Each English colony in America, like each outlying town and county in the British Isles, was a separate part of the fringe of a world whose core was London.[10] Coastwise commerce, to be sure, provided a limited economic bond among most of the twelve mainland colonies (Georgia would not fill out the complement of thirteen until 1733), as did the "down and back" trade between the fish and timber ports of New England and the sugar ports of the West Indies. The necessity of at least a rudimentary common defense against French-led Indians engaged in the American phase of the War of the League of Augsburg enforced a small degree of cooperation among colonial governments, but such cooperation was achieved with grudging difficulty, and the necessity was mostly confined to New England. The colonial postal service was still in its most primitive stage of development, and roads were notoriously poor. Religious diversity from region to region ruled out ecclesiastical cooperation as a basis for intercolonial unity. The string of colonial colleges that in a few decades would provide a common intellectual base for the American professional and merchant classes was confined in 1700 to two unlike and widely separated institutions in two very different colonies, Harvard in Massachusetts and the infant William and Mary in Virginia. Since the collapse of the short-lived Dominion of New England in 1689, the only political connection among colonies was the one they shared by reason of a common relationship with Whitehall. And for each little incipient colonial metropolis, as for each provincial city of Britain, the point of reference and standard of comparison was the single great metropolis of London.

News for the Provinces

When the independent presses of London started the great deluge of printed news in the second half of the 1690s, much of it was designed for nationwide distribution. The *Flying Post*, the *Post Boy*, the *Post Man* and their kin all came out on a schedule aimed at the departing post every Tuesday, Thursday, and Saturday. Their titles and iconography linked them unmistakably with the newsletter tradition. Circulation figures of 3000 to 4000 apiece for the *Post Boy* and *Post Man*, the most successful of the early papers, demonstrate a receptive country readership for the London newspapers.[11]

For such receptiveness there was good reason. The European war was of vital concern not only in London but anywhere that English investments were at stake or English lives and property were potentially in danger. This included all the major seaports and manufacturing centers. Restoration culture in the form of theaters, music festivals, literary societies, and membership in national associations such as the Royal Society was spreading to provincial cities, accompanied by a widening interest, among the growing minority who were sufficiently literate, in reading.[12]

All of these new realities of provincial life at the turn of the century combined with an awareness of the newspapers, the essay journals, the clubs, and the coffee-house culture which were flourishing at the metropolitan heart of the empire but which a burgher of Norwich or Bristol could share only in part and only with difficulty. The proliferation of London newspapers had made available an extraordinary diet of printed news compared with any time prior to 1695. To keep abreast of what was being discussed in the capital, a literate rural Englishman or one dwelling in one of the regional towns needed to subscribe to all of them. This was an expensive and time-consuming option, available only to the well-to-do, to whom neither literacy nor the burgeoning interest in public affairs was confined. After the lapse of the licensing act, some London-trained journeymen responded to the new opportunities—and the newly competitive printing environment of the City—by heading for the larger provincial centers to open shop on their own. There, in addition to meeting the job printing needs of local business communities and beginning to supply local booksellers with provincial editions of books and pamphlets, some of them saw their chance, as G. A. Cranfield has put it, "to provide in one cheap newspaper the most important items contained in the various London newspapers of the previous week or so."[13]

Lacking confirmation of the possibility that *Sam Farley's Exeter Post-Man* may have beaten him to it, historians usually award to Francis Burges of Norwich, the largest town in England outside of London, the prize for putting out the first English provincial newspaper.[14] The ancient cloth-making city of Norwich, more prosperous and more dependent upon woolen manufacture in 1700 than ever before, had the disadvantage of being off the beaten track. Located some one hundred miles away to the northeast of London in the bulge of East Anglia, its main link with the metropolis was over a northern spur from Colchester off the London–Harwich post road. Its postal needs were thus served by a privately contracted "bye post" from Colchester rather than the Post Office itself. While not having the advantage of as regular or as rapid communications with London as some of its sister cities, Norwich stood in particular need of such connections because of the special nature of its cloth trade. For several decades, the stylish lightweight, brightly colored fabrics that were the hallmark of "Norwich stuffs" had depended mainly on the London market rather than on foreign trade. Norwich weavers sought constantly to update their knowledge of contemporary London tastes and fashions and to supply their clothstuffs to the urban market quickly before the fashion faded.[15]

More than 90 percent of Norwich's population lived within the city's medieval walls, which surrounded the largest enclosed urban space in Britain. Unlike most walled cities, however, the enclosure included fields and pastures as well as the usual closely settled streets. At the center, not far from the cathedral precincts and close to the intersection of several converging Norfolk roads, lay a large open marketplace, still in use, which served as the city's principal retailing center for fish, meat, and produce during thrice-weekly market days. Norwich functioned as a regional distribution center as well as market town for its own immediate hinterland. Thus, the agricultural surpluses of all of Norfolk, including livestock on the hoof, arrived in Norwich by road to be bid upon by agents or dealers from London, who then arranged for subsequent shipment to the markets of the metropolis. Likewise, goods from London destined for distribution throughout the county arrived first at Norwich, either by wagon or through the nearby seaport of Yarmouth, on consignment to the city's wholesale merchants. However, neither woolen worsteds, the city's fundamental commodity, nor raw wool, the main ingredient, were usually bought and sold on the local market.[16]

The sizable population and compactness of Norwich, its position as the regional market center, its relatively high literacy, and its constant export of a vital commodity to London made this provincial city a conspicuous one in London business circles and an obvious destination for a journeyman printer of London looking for a likely place to work his trade after the expiration of the licensing act. Burges set up his print shop in Norwich in 1701 and, as far as we know, put out the first number of his *Norwich Post*, probably the first English (but not the first British) newspaper to come off a press outside of London since the *Oxford Gazette*, early in September the same year. Unfortunately, we have no surviving samples of the *Post* as it was published during Burges's lifetime, which lasted only until 1706.[17] His widow, "E. Burges," however, continued the paper after his death, at least until July 1712, the month before the Stamp Act put some newspapers out of business and forced most others to change their format. The eight extant weekly numbers between May 3, 1707, and July 5, 1712, give us a good glimpse of the *Post* during Mrs. Burges's proprietorship, when it probably was not far different from its earlier version.

The *Norwich Post* came out, or at least was dated, on Saturday: "Saturday, April the 26th to Saturday, May the 3d, 1707," to use No. 287, the first one available, as an example. Saturday was the chief of the city's three weekly market days, but, more to the point, it was a post day as well. Part of each week's paper was devoted to a few items copied from a London newspaper that had left the metropolis in the departing Thursday post and was now just arrived in Norwich, usually under the heading: "*This Days Post brought the following Advices.*" The *Post*, along with its rivals, the *Norwich Post-Man* and the *Norwich Gazette*, both begun in 1706, must have been on the streets and in the marketplace sometime Saturday afternoon.[18]

All of the surviving *Posts* are printed on sheets folded to produce two leaves each between 6 and $7\frac{1}{2}$ inches wide and varying in length between $10\frac{1}{4}$ and $11\frac{3}{4}$ inches. Each of the four pages is divided into two columns. The title in Gothic letters is flanked by a woodcut on each side—on the left, a crude rendition of the city arms with its castle and heraldic lion, and on the right, the indispensable mounted horn-blowing postman that links the paper's contents with the swift carriage of mail over the post roads. Unfortunately for the effectiveness of the imagery, the horse in 1707 appears to be in more of a canter than a gallop—though by the next May, both the horse and the city arms, having swapped sides, had been considerably improved, the horse now apparently moving with greater purpose. Under the title is the line, "To be Publish'd Weekly: Containing an Account of the most Remarkable Transactions, both Foreign and Domestick."

The order of contents, with one exception, is much the same as had become standard in London: news from Europe, news from England, local news, and advertisements—the first category, European news, getting by far the largest allotment of space, unless overshadowed by the text of an official announcement or, as happened in the first number available to us, the Queen's speech to Parliament. The exception to the standard London order is the space reserved, just prior to the small bits of news from Norwich, for a few items arrived in "This Days Post." It was this space, usually a part of the first column of page three, that was hastily filled by a compositor before a short press run in the hour that one Norwich newspaper said in 1707 was necessary between the arrival of the post and the distribution of the paper. The two outside pages, the first filled with news from London newspapers and newsletters that had arrived earlier in the week and the fourth with local and regional advertisements, obviously had gone through the press well ahead of time. It remained only to run off the other side of the sheet after the small space kept open for the most current news had been filled. Some provincial printers elaborated on this idea further, organizing the entire news content of their newspapers according to the arrival of the post deliveries, in most cases three, since the last weekly number. This allowed for systematic type-setting throughout the week as the successive posts came in.[19]

The *Post*'s advertisements between 1707 and 1712 filled the fourth page of the paper and usually a small part of page three as well. Compared with that of most other provincial newspapers of the time, British and American alike, this was a very large allocation of space for advertising, especially since the *Post* had local competition in this period. In most newspapers outside of London, advertisements were sparse in the beginning, coming to occupy as much as one to two pages by the 1740s. The *Newcastle Courant*'s average of 5.7 advertisements per number in the years 1711 and 1712—about half a column—is much more typical of provincial newspapers, and many carried far fewer than that during the first half of the century.[20] The earliest surviving copy of the *Bristol Post-Boy*, for example, that of August 12, 1704, carries only one two-inch advertisement, and the first number of John Campbell's *Boston News-Letter* the previous April would have carried none at all had the publisher not inserted one on his own behalf.

The somewhat complicated nature of the local economy of this isolated city and its role as trading center for a large region probably explain the relative abundance of advertising in the Norwich newspaper. Though most of the advertisements are from within the city walls, others, including a few announcements offering real estate for sale, are from elsewhere in Norfolk. Thus the surviving numbers of the *Post* inform us that certain segments of local trade at this stage were relying rather heavily on the printed word.

There is no such evidence, on the other hand, that the newspaper played much role in public affairs. Statistical lists of baptisms and burials, sometimes supplemented by the prices of grain, were the only consistent features of local news. When the occasion demanded, the *Post* did run the results of mayoral and parliamentary elections, and once in a while readers could find a report of a fire or an accident either in Norwich or in one of the nearby towns, or an announcement such as "This week a Man was brought to the Castle from Fettenham, upon Suspicion of Stealing two Horses."[21]

By far the bulk of the news in the *Post* was of the sort that the local oral grapevine could not supply. At least half of every number, usually all of the first two pages and up to half of page three, consisted of foreign and domestic news copied out of the London newspapers, especially reports from the various battlefronts of the War of the Spanish Succession. This was the sort of information, after all, that the country newspapers were designed to provide.

What was true of the demand for news in Norwich was also true for Bristol, the second provincial city to produce a newspaper. Located at the head of Bristol Channel and provided with a superb harbor (as well as a thirty-foot tide), Bristol lay 115 miles almost due west of London by road. While its population in 1700 was only about two-thirds that of Norwich (20,000 compared with Norwich's 30,000),[22] it served a hinterland that was even broader and much more diverse. The river Avon furnished a waterway for imported goods all the way into Warwickshire and Gloucestershire, which in turn sent grain and cheese back to Bristol for export and local consumption. A similar trade flourished by land between the city and a broad territory surrounding Bristol Channel, including the counties of Somerset, Wiltshire, Monmouthshire, Worcestershire, Hereford, and much of southern Wales. The population of Bristol's market region in 1701 has been estimated at about 948,000, or about 16 percent of the population of England and Wales. And this does not count Ireland, to which Bristol sent both English manufactures and imported colonial goods in exchange for Irish woolen cloth and yarn, linens, tallow, and hides.[23]

Moreover, the second seaport of England, "a place very early addicted to trade,"[24] was on the verge of its "golden age." Already a major shipping center for trade with Africa, the West Indies, and the American mainland, Bristol was about to enter half a century of spectacular growth in population, in Wren-inspired public buildings, and in the Atlantic trade. Human cargo as well as English cloth and glass and iron ware, Spanish wool and Iberian wines, Baltic timber and naval stores, and colonial sugar, rum, and tobacco filled the holds of Bristol ships. Before 1700 the shippers of the city, responding to the Caribbean and Chesapeake planters' desperate quest for affordable labor, had already carried 10,000 indentured servants from Britain to the New World; in the next fifty years, England having taken over the African slave trade from the Dutch, scores of vessels sent out by Bristol merchants would be sailing the infamous Middle Passage instead.[25]

The city's elaborate economic structure included manufacturing as well as the flourishing import-export business upon which most of its great fortunes were founded. In addition to the usual urban trades, most of which were organized into companies that regulated apprenticeships and admitted freemen like the liveried companies of London, Bristol had long had a flourishing cloth-making industry. In addition, it was home to certain specialized industries related directly to maritime commerce. Shipbuilding, the most obvious of these, with its dozens of particular trades, was supplemented by an important barrel and hogshed industry and by the makers of the famous Bristol glass, who furnished the bottles for the reshipment of the Spanish and Portuguese wines that had been imported in bulk.[26] At the peak of the economic pyramid of Bristol stood a simplified version of the great trading companies of London, the single Society of Merchant-Venturers incorporated in the sixteenth century by Edward VI.[27]

The "corporation," or government of the city, with its twelve aldermen, thirty common councilors (including two sheriffs), and Lord Mayor, was

much like that of the City of London. Though there was less explicit
linkage between the organized trades and the municipal corporation than
was the case in London, the actual working of the system was no different.
It resulted in the perennial selection to office "of the better and more
discreet citizens," to use the words of an eighteenth-century chronicler.[28]
Like the London corporation, Bristol's met in a guildhall, or "Council
House," soon to be rebuilt according to the new tastes in 1705.

One of the corporation's powers was to admit to freemanship, or the
status of burgess, men who had not acquired that status by birth, marriage, or apprenticeship. Burgesses could not only practice a trade in the
city but vote in the elections for Bristol's two members of Parliament and
be eligible for selection by the aldermen to fill vacancies in the common
council.[29] In April 1695, only a month after Parliament refused to renew
the licensing act, the corporation bestowed such status upon William
Bonny, a printer from London.[30]

The evidence for Bonny's first *Bristol Post-Boy*'s having come out in
November 1702 is of exactly the same kind as that for fixing the establishment of the *Norwich Post* in September 1701—the serial number and date on
the first extant issue. Only John Campbell's rather vague and possibly ill-
informed statement in the *Boston News-Letter*, and the longer stretch of
undocumented years involved, have inhibited historians from applying the
same evidence and method to *Sam Farley's Exeter Post-Man* and concluding
that Farley beat both Burges and Bonny by starting the Exeter paper in
1700.

Whether the *Bristol Post-Boy* was the second or the third provincial
newspaper (and therefore the first or the second in the West Country), it
served a very different community than the one served by the *Norwich Post*.
But despite the wide separation in geography and character between Norwich and Bristol, their two newspapers were much the same. Both obeyed
the canons of content and format established by the *London Gazette* and
continued by most London newspapers of the 1690s, and both largely
ignored the events of their respective cities.

The earliest of four extant numbers of the *Bristol Post-Boy* is that of
August 12, 1704, Number 91. Unlike the four-page *Norwich Post*, all four of
these numbers have but two pages, one on each side of a leaf 11½ by 7¼
inches, about the same size as that of the *Norwich Post* in 1708 and 1709.
The title, centered in bold roman type at the top of the page, is followed by
the legend, "Giving an Account of the most Material NEWS both Foreign
and Domestick." Publication day was Saturday, but apparently on at least
one occasion Bonny put out an extra, because Number 287 is dated from
Wednesday, September 7 to Saturday, September 10, 1709, instead of the
stretch from Saturday to Saturday that the paper normally purported to
cover. Both pages, in the conventional style of the day, are divided into
two columns. Nearly all of the content of this and the other three surviving
numbers, one each from 1708, 1709, and 1710, is war news. All four num-

bers are completely devoid of local material except for the thirteen Bristol advertisements scattered among them.

Bonny's *Post-Boy* lasted until 1712, the year the Stamp Act served its intended purpose by putting a number of newspapers out of business. The second generation of Bristol newspapers began with the founding of *Sam Farley's Bristol Post Man* and the *Bristol Weekly Mercury* in 1715. Because they were printed within the thirteen-year period in which an unintended loophole in the act encouraged the publication of newspapers in "pamphlet" form, all the surviving numbers of both papers take on the appearance of a small magazine, complete with an elaborate title page. As in the case of the *Post-Boy*, Bristol news is entirely absent.

By 1715, however, both *Farley's Bristol Post Man* and the *Weekly Mercury* were taking advantage of Bristol's direct trade with Europe and America by occasionally bypassing London sources for foreign news. This was an option not available to Norwich printers, and perhaps had not occurred to Bonny during the early years of the *Post-Boy*. Henry Greep announced that the "Fresh Advices" in his *Mercury* were from "Holland, France, Spain, &c. . . . Far Exceeding all other News Papers." It appears from the *Mercury* of December 1, 1716, in fact, that he might even have had his own correspondent in Paris. Greep preceded an extensive run of European news with the announcement that much of it had arrived in the mail from France the previous Monday and on Saturday, the day of publication. The most recent news from Paris was dated November 28, only three days before it appeared in Bristol print. Greep attributed the rest of his news from Europe to two of the nationally circulated London newspapers, *St. James's Evening Post* and the *Evening Post*, and to one of the few regular newsletters that London authors were still sending into the country and which remained a popular source for some provincial printers into the 1730s. The same number of the *Mercury* also contains a brief item of colonial news—a visit to Boston by a New Hampshire delegation to greet Samuel Shute, recently arrived in America to serve as governor of both Massachusetts and New Hampshire—from the *Boston News-Letter* of October 15, just over six weeks earlier. [31]

Bristol's Sam Farley, son of the founder of the *Exeter Post-Boy*, made the London connection with his *Post Man* as explicit as possible by announcing in the standing matter on his title page that the paper would come out two hours after the arrival of the London post every Saturday morning, the news "carefully Abstracted from the Gazette, Post-Man, Post-Boy, and Evening Post, with Domer's and other Written Letters; free from all Party Cause, or Personal Reflections." Clearly, however, Farley supplemented his London sources with items received in the mail from France, Holland, and Flanders. On January 28, 1716, among the news that had arrived in "two mails from France and one from Flanders," the *Post Man* carried three short items with New York datelines. Each of the three, it turns out from checking the *Boston News-Letter* file for 1715, originated in a separate number of that American newspaper, the only one then published in the colonies.[32]

These bits of evidence that the Bristol publishers departed at least occasionally from the normal provincial newspaper practice of copying directly from London are immensely provocative. Among other things they demonstrate an eastward flow of American printed news for which it is difficult to find much evidence in the London press of this period. Interesting though these departures certainly are, however, they are small exceptions to the general rule that the country newspapers of England copied the newspapers of London.

Norwich and Bristol were soon joined as newspaper publishing towns by Exeter, Shrewsbury, Worcester, Stamford, Newcastle, Nottingham, and Liverpool—all located, as R. M. Wiles has pointed out, a considerable distance from London.[33] At the end of July 1712, a dozen English newspapers were being published weekly outside of London, supplementing and largely dependent upon the twenty or so weekly, thrice-weekly, and daily productions of the metropolitan press. The Stamp Act of August 1 caused the death of seven of the provincial papers along with about eight London titles, but the loopholes discovered by the publishers of *Sam Farley's Bristol Post Man* and the *Bristol Weekly Mercury* led fairly swiftly to a recovery of numbers. By the time of the much strengthened act of 1725, which slowed down the increase in new titles dramatically for the rest of the century, the number of provincial newspapers had risen again to 24.[34]

Sold over the counter on market days, hawked on the streets of some of the larger cities such as Norwich, delivered to in-town subscribers by printers' boys, and distributed throughout the hinterland of each publishing town by a system of traveling "newsmen" and resident agents,[35] the provincial newspaper became the prime vehicle for spreading the print culture of the metropolis, second-hand, to the ordinary country reader.

Boston

Three thousand nautical miles across the Atlantic from Bristol, west southwest by west, on the edge of a continent that the English had only begun to explore during their century of settlement, another provincial town was experiencing the transforming power of print. As the capital of Massachusetts Bay province, chief town of New England, and still the most populous seaport of British America, Boston combined some of the characteristics of several of the regional centers of Great Britain. At about 7000, its population was roughly a quarter the size of Norwich's and about a third that of Bristol's, though there were few other English provincial towns that were its match. Like Norwich, it was market town for a broad hinterland, consisting of much of New England. Like Bristol, it was an Atlantic port, the busiest in North America. It built ships and traded with other mainland American ports, the West Indies, and Britain. Like Plymouth and Yarmouth, it sent out fishing fleets and exported processed fish. Like Edinburgh, it was a political capital and a center of both religion and higher learning. Like all of them, its source of authority, its prime example, its only real point of reference was London, the place at the end of its main highway.

Except that in this case, the main highway was the sea.

Everything about Boston's most obvious physical features pointed to its orientation to the Atlantic: its peninsular, almost insular setting on Shawmut Neck, long before the Back Bay was filled with soil from the peaks of the Trimountain to make room for urban growth and connect the city more substantially with the mainland; the navigation tower atop Beacon Hill; wharves and shipyards rounding the bulge of the North End, lining Town Cove, and reaching around much of the south side of the peninsula almost to Boston Neck itself; the waterfront taverns to accommodate travelers and sailors; and the short-lived "Barricado," a fortified dock-like structure closing off the inmost cove of Boston Harbor to protect its wharves from enemy fire ships that never came. This unused and inconvenient barrier, built between 1673 and 1681, was superceded as the harbor's most conspicuous landmark between 1710 and 1715 by a remarkable 1600-foot wharf, lined with shops and warehouses (like London Bridge) and extending the town's main thoroughfare of King Street well out into the harbor to serve even the deepest-draft ships. Far from a barricade, Long Wharf functioned as an inviting avenue from the sea squarely into the center of Boston, since at the head of King Street stood the wooden medieval Town House with its official meeting rooms and library above and an open market place "for Merchants, Mr of Shipps and Strangers as well as the towne . . . to meete in" underneath—a provincial equivalent of the Guild Hall and Royal Exchange combined.[36]

If the environs of the Town House and marketplace at the intersection of King Street and Cornhill were Boston's "City"—an analogy heightened by the location directly across Cornhill Square of the meetinghouse of First Church—the town also had its "Westminster." During the fourteen-month residence in Boston of the Earl of Bellomont, royal governor in 1699–1700, he urged the province to build an official residence "in the best part of the Town, where Sir Edmund Andros lived."[37] The "best part of town" to which Bellomont referred was perhaps a quarter-mile walk from the Town House along Cornhill and Marlborough Street (both of which have now been blended into the modern Washington Street), a route that led the townsman of 1700 into what was then called the "South End." By far the most conspicuous structure there was an elegant three-story brick house with a cupola very much in the Restoration style of Sir Christopher Wren, built twenty years earlier by a wealthy merchant named Peter Sargeant. By 1716, far too late for the popular Bellomont to benefit, this handsome building would come into public hands as the official gubernatorial residence. The "Province House," in the seventeenth century a distinctive exception to the crowded medieval look of most Boston streets of that era (like the streets of London before the Great Fire) remained a prominent Boston landmark until it burned in 1864.[38]

In the last few years of the seventeenth century, the daily talk of the Town House and other mercantile gathering places, such as the better taverns and the only two London-style coffeehouses in North America,[39] would have been almost as likely to center upon provincial and imperial politics as upon trade. The Restoration had prompted Whitehall's rediscovery of America and a reorganization of the empire, with some special attention to Massachusetts. Charles II had revoked the original charter in 1684, bringing the colony for the first time in its history directly under royal control. James II had established the Dominion of New England the following year. News of the Glorious Revolution had brought about a local revolt, abetting a mutinous militia garrison just returned from duty at the frontier outpost at Pemaquid, against the imperious Sir Edmund Andros; fifteen of the province's leading citizens had met at the Town House in April 1689 to draw up a proclamation urging Andros to surrender the government to a caretaker committee pending instructions from the new sovereigns. The proclamation was read to an approving crowd outside in the marketplace, then printed by Samuel Green, Jr., Boston's only printer. Conscious of the strength of his opposition, Andros had given up without a struggle. Increase Mather, meanwhile, had sailed to England intending to plead with James II for an amelioration of Andros's harsh regime. He had found himself dealing instead with William and Mary, a more sympathetic audience, and a changed agenda. The result had been the Province charter of 1691. Mather and Sir William Phips, whom the joint sovereigns had named first governor under the new charter, had returned to Boston in triumph.[40]

With the new monarchs had come war with France, and with war had come a new function for Boston. It had now become a naval base and staging area for military expeditions against Canada, a function it would retain for much of the century to come.[41] And with royal governors had come English office-holders and bureaucrats. "Thus," wrote Samuel Sewall sadly in 1701 after the swearing of William Atwood, newly arrived Admiralty Court judge, "a considerable part of Executive Authority is now gon[e] out of the hands of New England men."[42]

The rapid transformation of Boston from a largely self-contained colonial outpost to England's most vital provincial link in a now flourishing overseas empire naturally enlarged and partly changed the role of the printing press. As this happened, the press in turn played its own part in the transformation of Boston.

Printing had come to the Puritan colony in 1638 with the establishment of Stephen Day's press in Cambridge under the sponsorship of Harvard College. In 1649, Day had turned over the press to Samuel Green, who would go on to become founder of an exceptionally long, far-flung, and distinguished printing dynasty. By 1674, there were two printers at work in the colony on three presses, but the General Court had used its licensing power to keep them all in Cambridge. Marmaduke Johnson got permission to move his shop to Boston in 1674, but died before he printed anything there. It was John Foster, Harvard graduate, Dorchester schoolmaster, and friend of Increase Mather (just appointed licenser of the press), who in 1675 bought Johnson's equipment and began the first printing in Boston. The first two items off his press were sermons by Mather.[43] By 1700, there were three printers in Boston—John Allen, Bartholomew Green, and Timothy Green. Of these, only Allen was neither a son nor a grandson of Samuel Green, although he was a partner of the patriarch's son Bartholomew.

During the first half-century of printing in Massachusetts, the bulk of the output by far consisted of pieces commissioned to serve the formal ends of state, church, or college. These had included some of the most famous—because earliest—productions of the American press, such as "The Freeman's Oath," *The Whole Booke of Psalms*, and John Eliot's Indian Bible. Much more numerous were ephemeral publications such as broadside notices, gubernatorial proclamations, legislative resolutions, a few private advertisements and announcements, and the annual lists of Harvard graduates with the *Quaestiones* to which the graduates were to give Latin responses during the commencement exercises. More substantial productions included almanacs, catechisms, various editions of the Massachusetts laws and orders of the General Court, and many printed sermons, though not as many as in the century to come. As early as 1667, the Cambridge presses of Samuel Green and Marmaduke Johnson were beginning to respond to what was apparently a readers' interest in worldly events in Europe. Each printer put out a separate edition of Thomas Vincent's *God's Terrible Voice in the City of London*, describing the plague and the fire, and in 1669 the two collaborated on an edition of an account of that year's eruption of Mount Aetna. In 1673 Johnson printed a semi-humorous collection of maxims called *Old Mr. Dod's Sayings*, and in 1668, quite daringly, even a mildly erotic piece of fiction, popular in England, entitled *The Isle of Pines*, for which he was fined by the authorities.[44] These few departures from the standard governmental and sectarian uses of the press, while significant because they demonstrate both a broadening of reading tastes and an early inclination, perhaps, toward a metropolitanization of culture of the sort that was still far in the future, were exceptional. Of all these publishing ventures, the one that came the closest to an instance of actual "news" reporting was the colonial reprint of the Mount Aetna piece, since the event itself had been in the comparatively recent past. But the New England press even then was producing nothing remotely like the *London Gazette* or any of its predecessors.

It was Samuel Green's eldest son, Samuel Jr., who broke out of the mold, perhaps unconsciously. This Green printed in Boston from the death of John Foster in 1681 until he himself died at forty-two in 1690. Until late 1684, he was actually an employee of Samuel Sewall, whom the General Court had licensed at Foster's death to supervise the sole Boston press. In mid-April 1685, just after Sewall had resigned the license leaving Green in charge, there came off the press a broadsheet of an entirely new kind—a reprint of the *London Gazette* of the previous February 9 that reported the death of Charles II and what was for Bostonians the portentous news of the accession of James II.[45]

This reprinting of the *Gazette*, whether Green and his customers recognized it as such or not, was a new departure for this or almost any other English provincial press. For the first time, a printer had used his press to inform his readers about a recent event; a provincial printer had become an "intelligencer." It is significant that this first use of the Boston press for this purpose concerned an event of imperial importance in London. From that time on, the productions of the Boston press included occasional broadside reports of world events—an English naval victory over the French in 1692, an earthquake in Naples in 1694, an entire *London Gazette* of 1700 containing news of the new King of Spain and the coronation of a new Pope. In 1698, Bartholomew Green and John Allen even reprinted an article from the *Monthly Mercury* entitled "The Turkish Fast." Broadsides occasionally reported domestic intelligence as well, such as "A Relation of Captain Bull, Concerning the Mohawks at Fort-Albany," which Samuel Green, Jr., printed in 1689.[46]

In the spring of that same momentous year, the rebellion against Andros stimulated a flurry of productions from Green's press in the form of both pamphlets and broadsides. The central document of the lot was of course the address to Andros already mentioned. But late in the year, perhaps November or December, there came another breakthrough in the rapidly developing printing history of the town. Combining two letters from Increase Mather in England with an excerpt from a London publication imperfectly identified as "the publick News-Letter" (probably the *Gazette*), Green produced a newspaper-like broadside entitled *The Present State of the New-English Affairs*.

This was a one-time publication, undated and without serial number. But in its appearance and format it duplicated the *London Gazette*, with its centered title at the top of the page, its two-column presentation, and even a line in small gothic under the title reading "This is Published to prevent False Reports"—in place of the *Gazette*'s date. All three items, the first from a letter from Mather to Governor Simon Bradstreet dated September 3, the second a newspaper extract dated July 6, and the third a part of a letter from Mather to his son Cotton dated September 2, concerned the progress of Mather's attempt to get a new Massachusetts charter approved by Parliament and Mather's appearance before the King. Whether *New-English Affairs* was printed with official sanction by Green on his own account or commissioned by another, such as the governor or perhaps

Cotton Mather, the record does not disclose. What had happened here, however, was the adaptation of the concept and form of the *Gazette* to the presentation under a local title of a collection of related European intelligence, all with a specific bearing upon local interests—and upon the personal reputation, it might be added, of Increase Mather. This in itself constituted an immense leap in the sophistication with which a provincial printing press was applied to the dissemination of current information. In addition, the decision to use the press for such a purpose, whether made by the government, a Mather, or by the printer himself, discloses the most interesting assumption that to intrude the authority of print into the oral culture—to impose in this limited way a printed substitute for word of mouth—was an obvious way to "prevent False Reports."[47]

Compared with the imaginative leap that had produced this important news broadside, the idea of issuing such a publication serially was only a short step. Less than a year after the appearance of *New-English Affairs*, by which time young Samuel Green had died in the smallpox epidemic of 1690, Bostonians had in their hands the three-page sheet that has been long and widely celebrated as the first American newspaper. *Publick Occurrences Both Forreign and Domestick*, issued on September 25, 1690, differed from *New-English Affairs* in the one vital respect that its publisher intended "Numb. 1," as it was labeled, to be the first in a series. The paper was to be *"furnished once a moneth (or if any Glut of* Occurrences *happen,* oftener)." It also differed from its broadside predecessor and its newspaper successors in its emphasis upon American rather than European news and in its publisher's strikingly cavalier disregard of the province government's claim of authority over the press. Both these differences contributed to the paper's swift demise; "Numb. 1" never had a sequel.

The publisher of this abortive newspaper was Benjamin Harris, a refugee from Jacobean London. His time in Boston coincided almost exactly with the final revival of the licensing act, 1685–94, which occurred after a temporary lapse in the act between 1679 and 1685. The timing could hardly have been accidental. For violating the revived act, in fact, he had been pilloried and imprisoned just before coming to Boston in 1686. Prior to that, as an associate of Titus Oates, the vehement anti-Catholic publicist, and opponent of the accession of James, he had been prosecuted under common-law seditious libel proceedings during the earlier hiatus in the act. In Boston he set up shop as a publisher, opened the London Coffee House, and engaged the printers of the town to print books and an almanac. His peak year as publisher and bookseller came in 1690, and in the following year his Boston fortunes improved even more when he established a printing partnership with John Allen, another refugee from London. Despite his rapidly growing prosperity in this provincial town, he returned in 1695 to a freer London than the one he had left nearly a decade before, and published newspapers—this time legally.[48]

Harris's main printer in 1690 was Richard Pierce, a relative by marriage of the Mathers, the Cottons, and several other prominent Boston families, who as it turned out would not live out the decade.[49] Pierce's most notable production by far in that or any other year, certainly for long-term importance, was the first edition of *The New England Primer*, commissioned and possibly compiled by Harris. *Publick Occurrences*, however, which Pierce also printed for Harris, has found an even more conspicuous place, whether deserved or not, in most history books.

To a modern reader's eye, *Publick Occurrences* is a much more engaging publication than most of the provincial newspapers, English or American, that appeared in the two or three decades after 1700. It is, in the first place, printed legibly and neatly, a tribute perhaps more to Pierce's craftsmanship than Harris's editorial supervision. The writing is also original and lively by comparison with anything that appeared subsequently in America before the appearance of the *New-England Courant* in 1721, and the topics are drawn overwhelmingly from local surroundings—a thanksgiving observance by Christian Indians, the state of the harvest, a suicide, "*Fevers* and *Agues* . . . in some parts of the Country," the abatement of the Boston smallpox epidemic, the second disastrous Boston fire within a few weeks, and extensive news of the American theater in King William's War then in progress. Toward the end of the paper, not at the beginning as standard practice would later dictate, appeared "intelligence," mostly in the form of war news, from the West Indies, France, and Ireland. *Publick Occurrences*, like *New-English Affairs* which preceded it, had a different underlying purpose than its eighteenth-century successors, which during at least the first several decades of their history were designed primarily to involve their American readership in the affairs of Europe as seen through English—and specifically London—eyes. Harris intended primarily to save Bostonians during an exceptionally critical time from rumors and "False Reports" of the events and affairs, especially the martial affairs, of their own province.

It was primarily Harris's wartime news and comment that aroused the ire of the magistrates. The publisher intruded himself into matters of diplomacy with his criticism on the inside pages of the Iroquois Indians, ostensibly allies of the English against the French. First suggesting in the course of a long description of a two-pronged English expedition against Canada that the Mohawks were reluctant to join in as promised, he went on to express gratitude that Canada might in fact be taken "without the assistance of those miserable Salvages, in whom we have too much confided." A conquest by Christians alone, the argument went, would prevent the occasion for sacrificial offerings to "the Devil," and "God alone will have all the Glory." Harris added, "'Tis possible, we have not so exactly related the Circumstances of this business, but this Account, is as near exactness, as any that could be had, in the midst of many various reports about it."[50]

Quite aside from Harris's lack of official sanction to print his newspaper, this insult to an ally in the midst of delicate negotiations in an anxious wartime climate was too much for the revolutionary and essentially ad hoc government of Governor Bradstreet and his council to tolerate. They may also have been offended by Harris's published report that part of the reason for domestic unrest in France stemmed from the dauphin's resentment that Louis XIV *"used to lie with the Sons Wife."* The order for suppression came four days after the newspaper's appearance. After noting that the paper had been printed *"Without the least Privity or Countenance of Authority"* and that it "contained Reflections of a very high nature: As also sundry doubtful and uncertain Reports," the governor and council declared "their high Resentment and Disallowance of said Pamphlet." They not only ordered *Publick Occurrences* "Suppressed and called in" but took the next step to forbid the further printing of anything without license.[51]

That was the end, for the time being, of newspaper publishing in Boston. The able and too high-spirited Harris returned to London and Pierce died, both in 1695. Boston printers, however, continued to produce broadsides, presumably with governmental sanction, that occasionally reported public events by printing excerpts from the London newspapers. In addition, the postmaster of Boston, a Scottish bookseller named Duncan Campbell, began exchanging news of Europe and the colonies with correspondents elsewhere in America. Thus the familiar device of the handwritten newsletter took its place in the American communications chain in the 1690s.

Clearly a growing, thriving, war-anxious Boston was thirsty for news. As to how the news could be collected and dispersed, all the necessary examples had been set, and most of the necessary lessons had been learned. It remained only for a successful pioneer to do the job. The pioneer turned out to be Duncan Campbell's son John, who when his father died in 1702 succeeded him in the post office. In 1704, John Campbell began the extraordinarily long-lived *Boston News-Letter*, America's first successful newspaper.

Part II

AMERICA: NARRATIVE

Chapter 4

John Campbell, Pioneer American Newspaperman, 1704–1719

The Man and His Enterprise

Among the tradesmen of post-revolutionary Boston in the early days of the new charter was Duncan Campbell, a bookseller recently come from Glasgow. In 1693 he became Boston postmaster. A fellow Scots émigré, Governor Andrew Hamilton of New Jersey, headed the newly reorganized colonial postal system, which may have helped. As postmaster for the largest and most important seaport in British America, Campbell could make his office a center for more than the routine taking in and dispatching of other people's mail. He had both the franking privilege and frequent contact with the masters of incoming ships who came to Boston with news in the form of hearsay reports and the London prints.

Around 1700, Campbell began sending occasional handwritten newsletters to Governor Fitz John Winthrop of Connecticut. In so doing, he was continuing quite a venerable tradition of such correspondence between Boston and Hartford. A small collection of newsletters in the Massachusetts Historical Society contains similar reports from Boston to John Winthrop, Jr., the younger Winthrop's father and predecessor, even in 1666. There is also evidence here of similar correspondence from London, New York, and Philadelphia to Boston later in the seventeenth century.[1]

In 1702, Duncan Campbell died. His son John (1653–1728), about whose first forty-nine years we know next to nothing, now succeeded him in the Boston postmastership.[2] John Campbell now took his place in an existing system of news distribution among the colonies. He sent weekly letters to Winthrop and perhaps other New England notables as well. Though there is no direct evidence to that effect, we can assume that he exchanged such letters, as Duncan Campbell apparently did before him, with some of his fellow colonial postmasters.[3]

Like their predecessors, John Campbell's newsletters were written by hand, adhering closely in all respects to the newsletter tradition. What Winthrop learned from the Boston postmaster had overwhelmingly to do with European and Atlantic affairs: various premature reports of the union of England and Scotland; naval actions and privateering activity in the Caribbean; a dynastic marriage; the Portuguese entry into the War of the Spanish Succession; sketchy bits of war news from Europe; and extensive shipping news. Campbell salted this heavy fare of overseas intelligence with occasional reports of Indian skirmishes on the New England frontier, small doses of political news from Massachusetts and New York, and, on June 1, 1703, a description of the recent elaborate ceremonial surrounding the annual Massachusetts election day. With the rare exception of local events that he had observed at first hand, Campbell's news had come to him by way of oral reports from mariners in arriving ships or, more usually, by British "public prints" carried in the same vessels. Campbell also occasionally mentions "letters," providing the only real evidence that he may have exchanged newsletters with correspondents in other colonial capitals.[4]

The usual explanation for the appearance on April 24, 1704, of the *Boston News-Letter* is that Campbell moved naturally from handwriting to print in order, as Arthur Schlesinger phrased it, "to improve and commercialize this service."[5] The explanation makes sense as far as it goes and is reinforced by the unusual title Campbell gave his paper, which suggests continuity with the prevailing practice.[6] Surely the idea of improving his system of correspondence in this way is part of what he had in mind.

But the example of the English newspaper press, with which Campbell was well familiar by 1704, must also have been a powerful influence on the postmaster's decision to begin publishing a newspaper. He copied the *News-Letter*'s format exactly from that of the *London Gazette*, and much of its content from the *Gazette* and its unofficial London counterparts.

Moreover, the very concept of a printed newspaper and its audience moved Campbell beyond mere continuity with his former practice of exchanging newsletters into a rather different world of communications. Commentators have remarked, correctly, upon the tiny circulation of the *News-Letter* in its earliest years,[7] but that fact does not lessen the contrast between exchanging newsletters and publishing a newspaper. The 250 copies that Campbell's printer turned out at first were aimed at a readership that was partly anonymous and located principally in or around the publisher's own city. One of Campbell's aims in moving to a printed *News-Letter*, without doubt, was to "improve and commercialize" his intercolonial traffic in news. But whatever hopes Campbell may have had for the commercial success of his undertaking had to rest on its reception by his fellow Bostonians, not his correspondents in other places. And although, as we shall see, he consciously addressed his paper to a particular segment of the local audience, there is a difference between carrying on a personal (even though not necessarily private) correspondence and broadcasting information through multiple copies to anyone who will buy it. Campbell's role as simple intelligencer became expanded instantly to the role of one who creates, produces, and markets a product. At the same time, he made himself an early and crucial agent in the transformation, by depersonalization and enlargement, of the public sphere.[8] By imitation, Campbell very quickly reenacted on American soil the transformation that the harnessing of the printing press to the purpose had brought through a long period of evolution to the handling of news in Europe.

An Index to Provincial Culture

Modern readers may find it a paradox that the quickly suppressed *Publick Occurrences* of 1690 came closer to meeting our contemporary standards of journalism than John Campbell's *Boston News-Letter* of 1704. The writing in Harris's paper was livelier and the printing neater. More telling, Harris's paper was full of local news that he had collected on his own; Campbell's was devoted overwhelmingly to European news copied from the London prints.

It was not just that Harris was an experienced journalist and controversialist from Restoration London and Campbell a provincial postmaster, nor that Campbell took more care to avoid offense. Both these factors obviously helped make the difference, but it is more significant that the two publishers had separate purposes in mind. Harris had intended to keep a local audience informed of confusing and fast-breaking events in its own community "to prevent false reports." Campbell aimed with his *News-Letter* at linking provincial Americans with the metropolitan center of their pan-Atlantic English world. For the next thirty-five years, it would be Campbell's aim, and not Harris's, with one or two vivid exceptions, that would dominate American newspaper publishing. And although the trans-Atlantic emphasis in American newspapers came to be challenged after 1739 by other concerns, it was not abandoned entirely for a quarter-century after that.

Any reader whose expectations are conditioned by modern newspaper practice, and that includes most historians, is bound to be disappointed at the first encounter with the *News-Letter* or one of its early contemporaries if the search is for direct and abundant light upon the locality of publication. One reaction to this disappointment has often been the assumption that the resort to foreign news was a matter of using "filler" for space that would have been used in more interesting and locally relevant ways if the publishers had only been more creative, resourceful, or daring—more, that is, like those of our own day. Even so astute a student of early American printing as the late Stephen Botein, not to mention a number of earlier and lesser commentators, regarded the European emphasis in American newspapers before 1765 as an innocuous alternative to locally relevant political controversy.[9]

For Campbell, however, this overwhelming diet of European news was a deliberate and positive choice, not a negative one. The evidence is overwhelming. For one thing, the obvious purpose of his and his father's handwritten newsletters, which had no need for filler, was the sharing of intelligence from abroad. For another, there were Campbell's elaborate, sometimes desperate attempts, to be discussed in due course, to systematize the European news and bring it up to date. Without question, the news of the world across the Atlantic was for Campbell a deliberate priority, not filler.

It is easy to see how by printing this sort of information the *News-Letter* provided a service that was not otherwise available. For very few of Campbell's readers was there any other regular link to the world at large at all. Provincial officials, merchants, the more conspicuous divines, and perhaps some of the more recent émigrés from Britain were in positions to correspond with superiors, counterparts, or relatives across the sea. But not even that correspondence, important as it was for the elite groups involved, could provide a comprehensive and systematic record of the quite dramatic contemporary history of the Europe of Louis XIV or even the England of Queen Anne and the Duke of Marlborough. And for the general run of Bostonians, there was no such source at all.

The more interesting question, however, is why, at this time, American readers might have been curious about such matters. Colonials of the seventeenth century seem to have done without this sort of information quite nicely, though the times in Europe, especially in England, had been no less exciting. Printed intelligence was of course far more sparse in England before 1694 than subsequently, but it was not altogether lacking either before or after the Restoration. There is no evidence that much of it ever made its way to America, and the extensive personal correspondence among members of Old and New English Puritan families that David Cressy describes seems to have dealt largely with private rather than public affairs.[10] Harris's *Publick Occurrences*, along with the Mathers' proto-newspaper *Present State* and the various associated broadsides, all came out at a particular moment of crisis in Massachusetts when colonial minds remained fixed, with yet greater intensity, on local conditions, the same category of affairs with which they had been mainly occupied since the time of settlement.

If we look to a relaxation of local tensions to explain an apparent new willingness on the part of Campbell's readers to involve their minds with the affairs of the world, the explanation fails. The political crisis had passed, it is true, but New England, like the mother country, was at war. Unlike the vast majority of their English counterparts, many hundreds of New Englanders in 1704 were immediately at risk of losing their homes, their families, or their lives at the hands of the French and the Indians. Yet Campbell's newspaper, while copying out in profusion the English accounts of the European theater of the war, paid only slight and sporadic attention to the American side.

Here among other things is evidence that the print culture as exemplified by Campbell's *News-Letter* was still a long way from supplanting the oral culture. What was easily and habitually transmitted by word of mouth, the assumption seems to have been, it was not necessary to replicate in print. But we are still not left with a wholly satisfactory explanation for what was apparently an acute interest in intelligence from across the sea.

What does seem to work in accounting for the shift in emphasis that occurred between *Publick Occurrences* and the *Boston News-Letter* is the notion of communication as ritual.[11] Over the past generation the people of the British American colonies—and this was perhaps nowhere quite as true as it was in Massachusetts—had come to learn that their lives and welfare were in fact connected with the course of transatlantic events. With the new charter, a new sequence of royal governors, and new importance as an imperial outpost, all of which had accompanied a waning of the insularity of seventeenth-century New England Puritan culture, Bostonians were awakening to a new sense of their own Englishness. Therefore, a newspaper such as Campbell's, with its deliberate stress on the news of Europe as seen through the eyes of London, served as an expression and further shaper of an emerging provincial identity that was markedly different from the more isolated colonial identity that had been expressed by *Publick Occurrences* fourteen years before. The *News-Letter* affirmed this awakening Englishness of its small circle of readers as it took some first steps toward embodying the values and solidity of the community whose printed voice it became.

Campbell, we may be sure, had no idea he was a pioneer of culture in this sense as well as a pioneer in American journalism. But this communal, identity-shaping, ritual role of his newspaper, to be furthered and refined by his successors in the decades to follow, mattered more to the eventual place of newspapers in provincial society than the actual information the *News-Letter* transmitted to its readers.

Intent and Audience

Campbell thought of his publishing enterprise as an extension of his duties as postmaster. Like other colonial postmasters and certain other officials, he owed his livelihood not to a salary, but to whatever profits he could extract from an enterprise of the Crown.[12] One of the ways he tried to do that was to use his office to publish and distribute a newspaper. But it was not just as a supplement to his income that Campbell saw the *News-Letter*. It was, as he phrased it in a publisher's announcement in 1705, "a Publick Good," from which he hoped to receive sufficient "encouragement" both from subscribers and from government to meet its expense.[13] Although the Massachusetts House of Representatives never cooperated in this "Publick Good" nearly as much as Campbell believed appropriate, in his eyes the *News-Letter* was a way of expanding the postmaster's official role as a disseminator of public information.

Campbell aimed his paper not at anything resembling a mass audience, but at the leading men of Boston and those in the province with real or imagined interests in common with them. In the *News-Letter*'s early years the publisher—or "Undertaker," as he usually called himself—often mentioned the "Gentlemen, Merchants and others" who contributed to its support.[14]

A small part of his readership, Campbell acknowledged, might have private access to much of the news with which he filled his paper, but the public interest demanded its broader distribution partly, in the tradition of Benjamin Harris, to avoid the spreading of false rumors during dangerous times. After he had published his paper for a year, Campbell took pains to spell out his own view of the public value of the enterprise. He explained in the *News-Letter* of April 9, 1705, that "This Public Printed News-Letter was undertaken to be Published for a Publick Good, to give a true Account of all Foreign and domestick Occurrences, and to prevent a great many false reports of the same. . . ."

Three weeks later, he elaborated: the first year's file of the *News-Letter*, he reminded his readers, contained "all of the Foreign Occurrences of Europe, from the 1st of November, 1703, to the middle of December, 1704." He then explained the importance of that accomplishment:

> And if any will consult the Publick Prints of England in that time, considering that they Print 2 or 3 times in a week, & that we did Print here but once in a week; they will find no one piece of material News that is in them, omitted in ours: As also in our Prints you have the publick occurrences from the West-Indies and other parts: and likewise those from our Neighbouring Provinces, besides those of this and the Province of New-Hampshire. All which Intelligence, tho' some few Gentlemen and Merchants might have all or some part thereof, yet for the most part the people in general, in this and the Neighbouring Provinces, have it not, and what they have, variously, and often falsely reported: and a great many Providences now Recorded, that would otherwise be lost. . . .[15]

Campbell does refer in this announcement to "the people in general." He also alludes, at the end of the excerpt quoted here, to a religious assumption undergirding the reporting of the news that had not previously figured in Campbell's own explanations of what he was doing. The recording of "illustrious providences" as marks of divine approval, promise, warning, or disfavor had been central to Puritan homiletics since New England had begun, and had indeed formed a significant part of the output of New England printing presses.[16] Here, almost as an afterthought, Campbell offers this pious motive as another aspect of his paper's "Publick Good."

By and large, however, the content of the *News-Letter* was designed to meet the needs and interests of the political, economic, and social leadership. Nearly all of it was organized around the comings and goings of ships. At least during the fifteen years, 1704–19, that it had the field to itself, the *News-Letter* gave Boston its main glimpse of the outside world, and Campbell served as the eyes, ears, and voice of the town's maritime interest. He served also as the voice of the royal government of the province, and reflected the opinions of the mainstream clerical leadership as well. To whatever extent, therefore, the *News-Letter* was intended for ordinary Bostonians and other New Englanders, Campbell and his principal patrons would have conceived of its role as an instrument of social control.

The leading men to whom the *News-Letter* was mainly addressed must have found its contents of some practical use in the conduct of their affairs. To acknowledge that likelihood does no violence to the notion that the *News-Letter* is best appreciated as a ritual expression of community identity, nor does it deny its other possible social or religious functions. Certainly Campbell believed in the utilitarian value of his enterprise, and obviously hoped his patrons agreed.

There were indeed substantial pressures to keep abreast of news of the Atlantic world, however long it was before that news actually appeared in *News-Letter* print. The economy of the town turned on the sea. News of naval actions and piracy, ice-clogged or storm-damaged ports, domestic upheavals in any of the sugar or wine islands, market conditions in London, the movement of ships anywhere in the trading network, and all of the more far-reaching developments in politics, diplomacy, and war might conceivably affect a merchant's decisions and would have a bearing upon whether risks already taken would result in profit or loss. The royal office-holding establishment of the province also looked to the sea, its only link with the source of its authority in Westminster. Official correspondence conveyed instructions and acts of government, but a wise and effective governor, especially one responsible for the safety of his province in time of war, needed all the most timely information, official or unofficial, that could make its way to him and his fellow office-holders from the outside world. The postmaster was perhaps the closest equivalent on the provincial level to the Restoration secretaries of state who had collected and distributed foreign intelligence for the King, a function eventually taken over by the editor of the *Gazette*.[17] The sequence of events in Massachusetts, and the usefulness of Campbell to the Crown's representatives in Boston first as postmaster and correspondent and then as publisher of printed news, was a rough provincial parallel to the development of official information services in England a few decades earlier.

The Technicalities

The time would come in provincial America when all newspaper publishers would be printers, and when many printers would be postmasters as well. Campbell, however, was not a printer, nor were any of those who would succeed him in the Boston postmastership and continue to publish newspapers. Like Benjamin Harris before him, therefore, Campbell had to hire a printer for his newspaper. His choice was Bartholomew Green, the current leading representative of New England's foremost printing family. Green would eventually take over the *News-Letter* himself, but not until 1722.

Like all printing jobs of the period, the mechanical task of putting out America's first newspaper began with the selection of a sheet of paper of appropriate size. There were several standard sizes from which to choose, determined by the dimensions of the mold with which the paper-maker had scooped the mixture of rag pulp from his vat.[18] Contemporaries gave each size a name: "pot," "crown," "foolscap," and so on. The sheet upon which Bartholomew Green began to print the *Boston News-Letter* was of the size called "pot."[19] By measurement, the sheet was about 12 by 15 inches in 1704; by 1708 it was somewhat larger. The *News-Letter* was printed in half-sheet, or "folio" form, as had become almost universal for London newspapers by now and would become standard in America. If a folio newspaper were to have four pages, two pages would be printed on each side of the sheet and the sheet folded in the middle to produce two folio "leaves," each with a page on both "recto" and "verso." If, like most numbers of the *News-Letter* during Campbell's time, it were to have only two pages, it would use only half the sheet. By using the "work-and-tumble" method,[20] the pressman could print both pages on one side of the sheet, then flip the sheet and print the same two pages on the other side. The result, if the forms were positioned properly in the chase and the paper turned the right way, would be two recto-verso pairs on each sheet. The sheets could then be torn in half along a straightedge after going through the press. The size of the *News-Letter*'s leaf began in 1704 at about 12 by 7¼ inches, barely larger than the dimensions of the *London Gazette*, but changed slightly several times thereafter.

The terms "sheet," "folio," "leaf," "page," and the rest were of course all associated with the making of books. That is entirely natural; neither in England nor in Campbell's and Green's America was the production of a newspaper, pamphlet, or broadside understood as being very far removed from the printer's traditional primary activity of book manufacturing. It was merely an extension and simplification of a very old and rather complex craft; the essential materials, methods, and terminology remained the same for newspapers as for books, and would remain so for a century or more to come.

In format as in Campbell's understanding of what he was doing, the model for the *News-Letter* was the *London Gazette*. Like the *Gazette*, the *News-Letter* was laid out in two columns. The treatment of the nameplate and other matter at the top of page one was identical in the two papers, right down to the line in small gothic letters announcing "Published by Authority." Both papers treated even the date of publication in exactly the same way: "From Monday April 17. to Monday April 24. 1704." This method of presenting the date (though not necessarily the precise typography used by both the *Gazette* and the *News-Letter*) had become fairly common in England and would be adopted almost universally in America. The paper was presumed to be issued on the latter of the two dates, at the end of the span of time that it covered.

Contemporaries, however, seldom referred to an issue of a newspaper by date as we do today; they referred to it by its serial number. Accordingly, an arabic number was placed in the upper right-hand corner of the first page of both papers, preceded in the case of the *Gazette* by "Numb." in small gothic and in the case of the *News-Letter* by "Number" in small roman type. The only other variation from the *Gazette*'s appearance was in Campbell's insertion of a centered "N. E." (later changed to "New England") in small gothic letters immediately above the title. At the bottom of the last page of each number of the *News-Letter*, in keeping with another standard English newspaper practice, appeared a colophon very much like the imprint at the bottom of a book's title page.[21] For its first four numbers, the *News-Letter*'s read: "*Boston*, Printed by *B. Green*. Sold by *Nicholas Boone*, at his Shop near the Old Meeting-House." Beginning with the fifth number on May 22, the wording changed: "*Boston*: Printed by *B. Green*. Sold at the Post-Office. 1704."[22] Eventually, after more experimentation, the colophon consistently carried Campbell's name as well as the printer's.

The *News-Letter* followed the *Gazette* in arrangement of content as well as in format. Whatever the actual habits of perusal may have been, all newspapers of the period were laid out to facilitate only one order of reading: from the upper left corner of page one straight through to the bottom of the righthand column of the last page. The normal order of content was this: important official documents such as proclamations, if any, which in the case of the *News-Letter* appeared at first only rarely, foreign news (the bulk of the *News-Letter*'s content by far), news from Campbell's correspondents in other American ports, Boston news, occasional official notices, and advertisements. For the first year, Campbell ran his small amounts of local news above the even smaller squibs of news from his American correspondents, but apparently realized in 1705 that the logic of both chronology and geography by which he arranged his paper demanded that the Boston news should come at the end, which is where it stayed throughout the rest of his ownership.

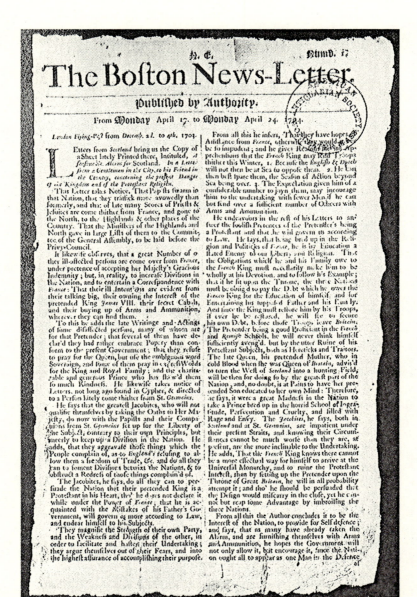

The first number of the *Boston News-Letter*, begun by John Campbell on April 24, 1704. Compare the details of this paper's format with those of the *London Gazette* (p.28), which Campbell followed with great precision. The small gothic "N.E." above the title stands for "New England." This number, like most of its successors over the next few years, consisted, as did the *London Gazette*, of just two pages, the front and back of a "folio," or half-sheet of paper. (*Courtesy, American Antiquarian Society*)

The *News-Letter* appeared weekly on Mondays from its first number on April 24, 1704, to very early in Green's proprietorship in 1723, when he moved it to Thursdays in order to make it available to "People of the Country" who came into town for lecture day.[23] The *News-Letter* and most of the subsequent papers in Boston apparently were printed and delivered in the morning of publication day; when Green announced his change, he specifically noted that the *News-Letter* would come out "every Thursday Morning" rather than "on Mondays," and when Thomas Fleet replaced the *Weekly Rehearsal* with the *Boston Evening-Post* in 1735, his announcement that he would publish on Monday evenings instead of Monday mornings implied that the new schedule would be a novelty for Boston.[24] We may take it, then, that at least for several decades, Monday morning was the standard publication time for the newspapers of Boston.

The publication schedule for this and most succeeding American newspapers was keyed to the comings and goings of the weekly post. Notices in six numbers of the *News-Letter* in 1704 state that the "western post," which carried mail between Boston and New York (where further connections began with Philadelphia and points south), was set to arrive in Boston every other Saturday and leave the following Tuesday morning.[25] The "eastern post" arrived in Boston from the northeast each Saturday and set out again for New Hampshire and Maine every Monday evening. Beginning in 1719, the western post also adopted a weekly schedule, leaving Boston each Monday.[26] Campbell timed publication so as to use the news in the incoming Saturday mail and to send his newspaper out to points northeast and southwest with the post riders on Monday or Tuesday. Other Boston publishers followed suit, whether or not they were postmaster, because they depended equally upon the postal service for both news and distribution. Similar patterns were adopted in Philadelphia, New York, and successive publishing towns.

In this respect the American publishers differed from their provincial counterparts in England, where the mail arrived in most towns not once a week (or once every other week), but three times a week—carrying the London thrice-weeklies and the few written newsletters that survived well into the eighteenth century. While the English printers of course relied on the mail for incoming news, they did not depend upon the postal service as heavily as American publishers for distribution of their papers. Most English provincial weeklies, therefore, were timed for market day, a weekly institution in all the larger towns, when country people in town for the day could pick up their papers or buy them from street hawkers. Green's shift of the *News-Letter* in 1723 to Boston's Thursday lecture day, the success of which is not documented, was the closest colonial counterpart to the standard provincial procedure in England.[27]

Rarely did the *News-Letter* contain news from the day before publication, and occasionally even news that arrived on a Saturday had to wait a week. On February 23, 1719, a communication from Philadelphia dated

January 21 was accompanied by the reason for its tardiness: "The Western Post came late in on the Lord's Day Night so that we could not give you the above Paragraph in our last." On March 17, 1720, the paper reported the arrival of a traveler from Virginia with a complicated account of a pirate action and other news. His arrival was reported as "Saturday last," meaning Saturday the 8th, not the 15th. It therefore heads the Boston news, which is listed in chronological order. On March 23, 1719, on the other hand, Campbell or his printer managed to squeeze in at the very bottom of the Boston news, "On the Lords Day Night arrived here Capt. Child from Cowes had a long Passage." That obviously meant the night before publication (there was not even time to correct the grammar of this hasty communication), and the paper, or at least pages one and four of that full-sheet number, could not have been run off until the sentence had been set and forced into the chase. Was this unusual, and very minor, insertion done Sunday night or Monday morning, and when were the approximately 300 sheets run off the press? The first job would have taken only a few minutes, the latter about an hour and a quarter if there were only one side left to print, not counting "making ready" before the run and folding the copies afterward.[28] From what we know of Puritan Boston even in the relatively secularized atmosphere of the early eighteenth century, and of Campbell's own strict attitude toward sabbatarian observance, the best guess is early Monday morning, before the paper's distribution to the in-town subscribers. Almost certainly this small exception to the usual routine was just that, imposing only a minor addition to the normal Monday morning task of running one side of the sheet off the press. As the autumn days were shortening in November, 1719, Campbell asked his patrons to get their advertisements to him "as soon as may be after two a Clock in the afternoon on Saturdays, if not sooner that they may be sett with Day light."[29] Again, it appears, the aim was to lock up the paper by the end of the working day on Saturday in readiness for a Monday morning press run.

Collecting and Reporting the News

Campbell was explicit about what we might call the "editorial" side of his operation. At the end of the *News-Letter*'s first year, he published an announcement listing "some of the Charges and trouble that arises" from putting out the paper:

> 1. The Undertaker has several setts of the several Prints from England, & sent him in several Vessels, that being time of War might have one sett if the rest should be taken, which are ordered to come by all Vessels coming to our Continent where the Post is settled almost 500 miles from E. to W. from N. Hampshire to Pennsylvania.
>
> 2. Correspondents settled in several other Ports & Places our Shipping goes to, for sending Intelligence.

3. Waiting on Masters, Merchants and others when Ships & Vessels arrive to have from them what Intelligence they can give.
4. Waiting on His Excellency or Secretary for approbation of what is Collected.
5. Paper & Printing, &c.[30]

Campbell's first duty to his readers as he saw it, therefore, was to supply news from abroad. It was to this effort that he devoted the greatest expense of collection and by far the most space in his paper. As we have already seen, the *News-Letter* was oriented toward the waterfront. Campbell's list of "Charges and trouble" confirms what is already obvious from the paper's content, but it also allows the modern reader a glimpse into the actual process of collecting the news.

The most important stop on Campbell's "beat," to use modern newspaper language, was the waterfront. After July 1713, he could make the stop more expeditiously than during the first several years of his running the *News-Letter*, because it was then that the town's maritime center moved to Long Wharf, just down King Street (modern State Street) from his post office in Cornhill (the northern end of modern Washington Street). Alongside this magnificent structure, extending 1600 feet into Boston harbor from the end of King Street, the deepest-draft ocean-going ships of the era could tie up even at low tide opposite the warehouses that lined its north side.[31] This was now by far the largest wharf in Boston harbor, where Campbell would most frequently have taken delivery of the all-important London "prints" and conducted dock-side interviews with arriving ships' captains. The result of such an interview, reported with the Boston news because that is where the news was gathered, might appear like this in the *News-Letter*:

> *Boston*, on *Tuesday* arrived here *Thomas Ball* from *Montserat* 25 days Passage, by whom we have the following advice, That Capt. *Moules* Commander of a Briganteen private Man of War from *Barbadoes,* has had several Encounters with the *French* Privateers near that Island, in one of which he had kill'd *Lambert* one of their Captains, and several of his men; the next day he shot off both the Legs of another Privateer Captain. The Cartell is settled between *Martinice* and the Leward Islands man for man, but the Governour of *Barbadoes* would not settle it till he had Orders from England. . . .

On rare occasions, Campbell could become a bit more sophisticated, combining two bits of waterfront news into a single report made coherent by a central theme—in the following case a concern about French privateering in New England waters early in Queen Anne's War:

> *Boston*, On Monday last was Launched here, The Province *Galley*, who will be ready to Sail a Cruising in 4 or 5 days. The talk of French Privateers being on our Coast this Week, was occasioned by Capt. *Wilde* of *New-York's* desiring to speak with some Fishing Shallops he met with to be informed by them if the Fleet for *England* was gone, and to get a Pilot for *Piscataqua*, whom the

Shallops took to be a Privateer, and fled from him, and another Vessel that
went hence for *Newfoundland*. . . .[32]

Besides the London newspapers and interviews with mariners, Campbell's sources included correspondents in other American and West Indian
ports. Judging from the paper's content, this was the weakest part of his
operation. Like the Boston news early in the life of the paper, news from
other American towns was concerned almost exclusively with the arrival
and departure of ships, primarily in reports from Rhode Island and New
York. The most frequent exceptions to this perfunctory notice of the rest
of Anglo-America were in the form of local war news and the movements
of the provincial governor. During Campbell's proprietorship of the *News-
Letter*, it was not unusual for several weeks to pass virtually without correspondents' reports from elsewhere in America. There is no clue in the
News-Letter as to the identity of these occasional correspondents, but one
can easily surmise that most of them were Campbell's fellow postmasters.

The following news items from three sister American seaports, appearing in the *News-Letter* for February 1, 1720, are unusual only in that they
reflect a seasonable variation from the usual stark shipping lists in the
news. They illustrate well the personal tone and essentially maritime orientation of Campbell's correspondents:

> Philadelphia, Jan. 18. Our River is fast with Ice, that great Numbers of People
> daily go and come over it, as also Horses and Sleighs frequently on it. Capt.
> Owen from New-York lies at Princehook. Capt. Newcomb in a Schooner
> from Salem, New England, who lost his Mast in bad Weather at Sea, is put in
> to the Horekills, its said he was bound here. Outward bound Drasos for
> Surranam.
>
> New York. Jan. 19. On the 9th, 10th, 11th and 12th Instant great Numbers
> went over Hudson's River upon the Ice, from New York to New Jersey, since
> which the Weather has been very warm like Spring, and all the ice gone. On
> the 16th arrived Jackson in a Sloop from Boston. Cleared Out, Robert Hayes,
> Benjamin for Barbadoes; Capt. Barington in Pink Shepherd, designs to sail for
> London the middle of next week.
>
> Rhode-Island. Jan. 29. No Vessels arrived here since my last, but Israel
> Hardin in a Sloop with Grain from Connecticut. Several Vessels bound out
> for Barbadoes and Leeward-Islands, Philip Harwood for Madera and Capt
> Lawrence for London. Cleared Out, John Draper for Jamaica.

Even those readers whose business did not bring them into frequent
contact with the details of seaborne commerce could not help becoming
acquainted through the newspaper with the maritime geography of the
mainland colonies and the West Indies. Frequent references, as in the item
from Philadelphia, to such points as the Delaware Bay anchorages of
Whorekill Road at Cape James and nearby Princehook Creek, and the
constant litany of the sugar islands and other southern ports, must have
made these names almost as familiar to the circle of Boston newspaper
readers, whatever their occupation, as Salem and Cape Cod.

A much less frequent but often more detailed and entertaining source of news than Campbell's established correspondents were his occasional interviews with visiting travelers. One of his earliest uses of a traveler's story turned out to be for Campbell a source of embarrassment and for the modern reader a splendid lesson in yet another aspect of newspaper practice as Campbell perceived it.

On November 5, 1705, the *News-Letter* devoted almost half of its second page to the incredible adventures and misfortunes of one "Henry Burch, a Quaker." The current stop in this young man's remarkable odyssey was Boston. The main source of Burch's troubles, the story made plain, was a "cruel uncle," Henry Burch of London, "a Doctor of Physick," to whom young Henry had been indentured by his father nine years before. "This whole information," concludes the unusually lengthy article, "was taken from Mr. *Henry Burch's* own mouth." For the first time since his paper had begun, it appeared, Campbell had himself a real human interest story that had originated with an interview in his own newspaper office.

The trouble was that the story was a hoax. Campbell exposed Burch as a liar in the following week's *News-Letter*, but not by way of a correction or apology. Instead, he headed the November 12 article "*A further Continuation of a Remarkable Relation, begun in the Last News Letter.*" Continuing the painfully transparent pretense that he had known the full story all along, Campbell prefaced the second part of the account by reminding his readers "That in some of our *News-Letters*, for want of Room, we have *broke off in the middle of a Matter.*" As to Henry Burch, "According to Good Manners, we have let him tell his Story first." But now, he concluded, "We will take leave . . . to tell ours: For plainly, the most Remarkable part of it, is yet behind."

After some more stalling, Campbell at length disclosed the truth about himself as well as about Burch—that he had been hoodwinked: "But I *tell ye friends* nay pritty *Remarkable*—That a Blade should be so desirous to have such a formal Story Printed about himself, and yet that in less than 2 days time, he should be detected for an horrid CHEAT, and it be palpably found, that probably, *There is not one word of Truth in all the Story.*" Burch, it turns out, had stolen money and clothing from Bostonians who had entertained him before he disappeared. This the victims had made extremely plain to Campbell, who had become, one suspects, something of a laughing-stock. Still worse, there was the matter of the wronged uncle in London, who, if he existed, had been grievously libeled. Obviously, Campbell was aware that the reputation of his paper had suffered seriously. Not only, then, did he offer a reward for the return of the imposter, but tried to vindicate himself to some extent as follows:

> And now, I hope, this has become such an useful Story, that the Gentlemen my Subscribers will not complain either of the *Introduction* to it in our former, or of the *procedure* of it, in our present, *News-Letter*. Our *News-Letter* also will, I hope sufficiently preserve its Reputation, if any Paragraph of it, not setting a

thing in all its *true light*, shall in one weeks time supply all that is defective, and perhaps there are few Readers, but what have themselves now & then told a Story that needed a further *Elucidation*.

Campbell discovered by trial and error, therefore, one of the chief hazards of journalism. He was very conscious of the problems of his enterprise as a business. His annual appeals for support make that manifest, and his recent list of "Charges and trouble" demonstrates that in his brief career as publisher Campbell had taught himself most of the essential steps of the newspaper business as he and his eventual competitors practiced it. The Quaker boy hoax, however, taught him something else: that when a man sells information, his reputation depends upon its being true.

It is to expect too much to add that it ought also have taught him what from a much later perspective is an obvious corollary, namely that a purveyor of news is therefore obliged to take special pains to assure the quality—that is, the truth—of his product. It is obvious from Campbell's statement at the end of his rather weak vindication, in which he suggests that some of his readers may themselves have been caught in a similar embarrassment, that he did not think of himself as in any way set apart from the rest of the community with regard to his ability or responsibility in handling information. Michael Schudson, in discussing the concept of professionalism in the history of journalism, has suggested that a "professional" in any field regards himself as being qualified by special knowledge or special skills, or both, to do a job that the unqualified cannot do.[33] Campbell had no such notion of his own qualifications, nor did any such idea of professionalism in journalism appear for at least a century.

The *News-Letter* and the Government

Not only did Campbell not think of himself as a professional journalist in any modern sense, but he had a very different attitude toward his relationship with official authority than that held by our own contemporaries in the news business. Campbell appended the phrase "Published by Authority" to the nameplate of his journal in emulation of the *London Gazette*, but just what the words meant to him is difficult to say. It meant at least that the newspaper was published with official approval, as in strict fact was required by law.[34] Among the "Charges and trouble" listed by Campbell in his announcement of April 9, 1705, is that of "Waiting on His Excellency or Secretary for approbation of what is Collected."

There is a difference, however, between official approval and official sponsorship. The *London Gazette*, which provided the model for Campbell's *News-Letter*, was much more than sanctioned by the government; it was an official publication. The government of Massachusetts Bay never acknowledged the *News-Letter* as its own publication in any official way, but it is clear that Campbell nevertheless thought of himself and his newspaper as enjoying a special relationship with the government that went well beyond mere "approbation."

Evidently, Governors Joseph Dudley and Samuel Shute cooperated with Campbell as much as he could expect. The small sections of local news disclose plainly that next to the waterfront, the most important stop on Campbell's weekly "beat" was to talk either with the governor or the province secretary. This call was not merely to receive "approbation" for what he proposed to print; it was to collect a substantial part of the local news of the week.

The item heading the Boston news on August 20, 1705, concerns a report of guns firing at Casco Bay on the coast of Maine. It begins, "By an Express to His Excellency from SachoFort . . . we are acquainted. . . ." The ensuing paragraph of Boston news concludes with the planned journey of "His Excellency" to Connecticut to hear a dispute between some Indians and the government of that colony. There seems little doubt that the whole parcel of local news was collected that week during a single visit to the governor. On December 10 the same year, the four inches or so of Boston news consists largely of a list of acts passed by the General Court, the governor's proroguing of the Assembly, his departure to visit New Hampshire, and plans for the Boston merchant fleet bound for the West Indies to sail under naval convoy in the coming week. Almost certainly in these instances and many others, the governor or an assistant was the source, not simply the countenancer of news.

And there were times when "news" expanded into opinion, as when after reporting on October 29, 1705, that John Rogers, a Connecticut drover, had been convicted and jailed for driving cattle through Dedham to Boston on a Sunday, Campbell explained the reason for the report: "It was thought meet at the Desire of several persons to Publish this as a Caveat to others, to let People know, That *Open Profanation of the LORDS-DAY, will not pass unpunished.*"

A little more than seven months later, the *News-Letter* ran its first full-fledged essay of opinion, a piece that modern newspaper readers would label without hesitation an "editorial." The essay, urging legislative encouragement for the importation of white indentured servants in order to reduce the province's reliance on black slaves, occupies more than a third of the unusally hefty thirty inches of Boston news. It offers no moral argument, only an economic one, ostensibly prompted by the publication three months earlier of the annual bill of mortality for Boston, which listed "*44* Negroes dead last year, which being computed . . . at *30 l. per* Head, amounts to the Sum of One Thousand three hundred and Twenty Pounds. . . ." Noting that blacks do not perform military service as white servants do, and asserting that they are "much addicted to Stealing, Lying and Purloining," Campbell rested his appeal to individual owners for a heavier reliance on white servants on two main arguments. First, it is much cheaper to buy a white servant for a limited term of years than to buy a black slave outright, and there is therefore a smaller loss if the servant dies. Second, a farmer who owns a white servant's time can send the man to war if he is required to fit out a soldier from his household, and thus "perhaps save his Son at home," but he cannot send a black.

He also appealed to the greater good of the province on several grounds, the most telling one being that white servants would populate and defend the frontiers as freemen after they had served their time. To encourage men of means in the province to import servants of this desirable kind, he suggested a government subsidy of forty shillings a head.[35]

Campbell may well have written both of these pieces, but there is every indication that the opinions thus expressed appeared in the *News-Letter* not because they were Campbell's but because they reflected an official position that he had been asked to state, as in the case of the Sabbath-breaking story. Legislative action on the question of servants had been a part of Governor Joseph Dudley's agenda since early in his administration in 1702.[36] In June 1707, just a year after the extraordinary published appeal in Campbell's newspaper, the legislature passed the first of two laws bearing on the issue. It skirted the central concern voiced by Campbell, but did authorize town selectmen in the province to require "free negro's and molatto's" to do their share of public road work and the like and to perform military service on the same terms as whites. Then in February 1709, "An Act to Encourage the Importation of White Servants" put in place the very forty-shilling bounty that the article in the *News-Letter* had urged.[37] It appears the executive leadership of the province enlisted the *News-Letter* in what proved eventually to be a successful legislative campaign.

At other times, Campbell published official notices or proclamations in his news columns, much as though he were making available to the governor, Council, and courts a public bulletin board. These were usually printed without comment or context, and are easily distinguished from paid advertisements, which were invariably grouped together at the end of the paper under the heading "Advertisements." It is clear from the wording of such a notice published December 1, 1707, that the Council, at least, viewed the *News-Letter* as an official organ which it was free to use for this purpose. Hostility to Dudley's faltering wartime administration had climaxed with the publication of Cotton Mather's tract, *A Memorial of the Present Deplorable State of New England*, which repeated among other things the popular charge that Dudley had traded with the enemy.[38] In response, the House on two occasions and the Council on one had passed resolutions condemning the reports as "a scandalous and wicked accusation." Campbell, on orders of the Council, printed all three resolutions, preceded by the Council's order to do so. *"Ordered,"* the Council had voted, *"That* [the three 'votes'] *be Published and Printed in the Publick News-Letter."*

During his postmastership, therefore, Campbell operated the *News-Letter* at least some of the time as though it were an official organ of the

executive branch of the province government. And the governor and
Council used it that way whenever it could serve the purposes of state or
politics. This relationship, however, was by and large an unstated one,
probably taken for granted by both parties rather than conceptualized by
anyone. This was, after all, pioneering ground, and Campbell's main
English example was the *Gazette*, despite the alternate examples offered by
London's private press. It was natural for Campbell to approach his task of
publishing from the point of view of royal office-holder, which he was,
rather than from that of independent journalist, an occupation that had yet
to be defined.

But while there flourished a symbiotic relationship between Campbell's
publishing activities and the governor and Council, the publisher enjoyed
no such sustained relationship with the popular Assembly. Repeatedly, in
both print and petitions presented formally to the General Court, Campbell suggested that the *News-Letter* both deserved government support and
needed a subsidy in order to survive. He did receive a legislative grant
during his first three years in the postmastership, and was exempted from
militia duty. Perhaps the increase in the grant from twenty to forty pounds
in the second year, 1704, was related to his starting the *News-Letter* that
year.

In any case, his regular provincial subsidy as postmaster stopped after
October 1706.[39] It could not have been coincidence that on the very next
occasion for his annual printed plea for support, in the *News-Letter* of
March 24, 1707, Campbell included for the first time a gentle suggestion
that governments as well as individuals might come to the aid of his
newspaper.

For the most part, however, government help did not come, at least not
in the amounts Campbell requested. In the period 1715 to 1718, toward the
end of Campbell's postmastership (and the end of Dudley's governorship),
the Assembly was as indifferent even to Campbell's bills for ordinary
official postage as it was to his pleas for help with the newspaper. On at
least four occasions in that period, the House either reimbursed Campbell
for less than he claimed for official postage expenses or refused to pay him
at all. When, no longer postmaster but still publisher of the *News-Letter*, he
submitted a bill in March 1722 for "Printing Advertisements, &c. By
Order of the Governour and Council," the House refused payment of the
five pounds eight shillings "because he could not produce any Order for his
Printing them."[40]

The "Thread of Occurrences"

We have now reconstructed a part of Campbell's weekly newsgathering
routine: visiting the waterfront with the arrival of each ship to receive the
packets of London "prints" along with the mail that it was his duty as
postmaster to take into his custody and interviewing arriving captains and

important passengers; collecting the weekly shipping list, probably from the naval officer of the port; meeting each week personally with the royal governor or the province secretary; occasionally interviewing travelers at his post office; opening the mail from his correspondents in other colonial ports; and receiving occasional visits from Bostonians with news to report, letters to share, or advertisements to place. Sometimes, one presumes, depending upon relative social standing, it was Campbell who did the calling at another's home. We can imagine, for example, his calling at the Roxbury mansion of Joseph Dudley, the former governor, to gather the information for Dudley's obituary and funeral notice, which occupied an unprecedented nine inches of space in the *News-Letter* for April 11, 1720.

Except for the contents of the foreign press and the rare and normally brief reports from his American correspondents, everything Campbell collected in this manner was printed as local news, almost always in a block on the last page of the paper just before the advertisements. The exceptions to this rule were occasions such as the issuance of an important gubernatorial proclamation or the opening of the General Court, when the *News-Letter* generally carried the text of the proclamation or of the governor's address to the Council and Assembly and the formal replies of the two houses on page one, exactly the way the *London Gazette* reported the opening of Parliament. Except on occasions of state such as these, the Boston news rarely occupied more than about one-fourth of the total space in the paper, sometimes much less.

By far the greatest amount of space in the *News-Letter*—typically all of page one and a quarter to a half of page two in a two-page number—was taken up by foreign news, copied straight out of the London newspapers. Campbell's selection and arrangement of this all-important part of his paper disclose some of the most significant truths available about how the pioneer journalist of America conceived of his audience and his job.

To read the *Boston News-Letter* as a true document of its time and place, you have to put aside all twentieth-century notions of what it means to be informed about current events. Our concern as we turn on the evening news or scan the front page in the morning is to keep up-to-date. Campbell's concern, like that of most of the London publishers from whom he copied, was to construct a historical journal of recent events. In a sense only somewhat different from what we mean when we apply the phrase to our most serious contemporary newspapers, the *News-Letter* was meant to be a "paper of record." It almost always fell short of that ideal, primarily because there wasn't nearly enough space for the job. One of Campbell's chief editorial frustrations was his frequent inability to follow through on a projected plan of coverage because he lacked sufficient room in his paper.[41] The idea that it was possible to include in one weekly newspaper every "piece of material News" found in the semi-weekly and tri-weekly press of London, especially in the form of the complete record that Campbell attempted, was of course unrealistic.[42] Falling short of an ideal, however, is not the same thing as failure. Within severe limitations, Campbell approached his goal of presenting to his readers a coherent report that for fifteen years was the only systematic record of the great events of Europe generally available in America.

Campbell was frank about his sources, but after his first three numbers took no special care about attribution. He had access to a much larger variety of London "prints" than his sporadic attributions indicate: on June 10, 1706, the *News-Letter* announced for sale, besides copies of the first two years' *News-Letter*, copies of the *Monthly Mercury*, the *Gazette*, the *Flying Post*, the *Post Boy*, the *Post Man*, the *Observator*, London bills of entry, and London prices current. Campbell's favorite source, however, was almost certainly the *Gazette*.

The *News-Letter*'s normal method of presenting foreign news differed from that of the London press—and the conventions of the newsletter tradition—only in that it was complicated by the multiplicity of sources from which already processed news was copied and the irregularity with which those sources arrived in Boston. A fundamentally chronological presentation had been standard English newswriting practice for at least a century. Campbell's problem was to adapt the chronological ideal to the *News-Letter*'s role as the single organ through which the reports collected and printed by half a dozen or more London newspapers were communicated to British America.

His plan was to construct what he called a "thread of occurrences," beginning, as it happened, in November 1703 (only three months later than the last European news reported in Campbell's last surviving letter to Winthrop) and continuing from number to number, theoretically without a break. Sometimes upon the arrival of a fresh supply of newspapers, he would interrupt the continuing "thread" by printing what he judged to be the most important of this most recent news before returning to the chronology from which he had broken away. When such a break in the "thread" occurred, there was usually an accompanying announcement.[43]

Because Campbell copied his news from several sources, usually in fairly large segments, his attempt to sustain a single "thread" was sometimes further spoiled by chronological overlap as he moved from a segment consisting of many small items, let us say, from the *Gazette* to a similar segment taken from the *Flying Post*. There might even be an occasional repetition of an item, either within the same number or, more likely, in a subsequent one. By 1713, Campbell had found a way to deal with redundancy without damaging what for him was an even greater concern, the integrity of the record. That was by making frequent use of an entry such as "*Amsterdam, July 13*. See our Numb. 444."

Though Campbell seldom did any kind of editing or rewriting, he did make this one concession to concision. More interesting than the concession, however, is his refusal to do what must have seemed equally obvious:

eliminate the second reference to the item from Amsterdam altogether. But that would have broken the chain of events that had been reported as a unit by a correspondent of one of the London newspapers, and therefore damaged the integrity of the record. It was as if the London press was not simply a source, but a kind of canon. For Campbell to have conceived of it in this way is not quite as ridiculous as it appears on its face if we think again in terms of ritual. If the forging of a bond of identity with the metropolis is what mattered, then the language and the constructs of the London newspapers were actually more important than the events they reported. One essential purpose of these reports, therefore, would have been spoiled by editing or paraphrasing.

Some notion of both Campbell's method and its ultimate impracticality can be gained from his attempt to provide a complete documentary record of the end of the War of the Spanish Succession. On August 31, 1713, he announced his intention to publish the "Articles of Peace," signed the previous April. The serial publication of the Treaty of Utrecht began as promised on September 7 and continued on September 14, both times occupying more than half the paper. That took care of the main body of the treaty, but there were still the "renunciations" by which Philip V, the now-recognized Spanish King, guaranteed that the Crowns of Spain and France would remain separate, one of the chief war aims of Britain. The renunciations came next, stretching over seven weeks of *News-Letters* and ending finally near the top of the second page on November 2. The paper, however, had skipped an installment on October 19,"By reason," explained Campbell, "of the following Intelligence from London," which turned out to be the official account of the ending of Queen Anne's fourth Parliament on July 16, including the speech of the Queen transcribed in full. Working through November, the *News-Letter* carried the complete texts of the British and French sovereigns' grant of treaty-making powers to their respective ambassadors extraordinary and the Queen's proclamation for a public thanksgiving before admitting, finally, that the game was up. Campbell would continue to add to the documentary record of the peace, but some pieces of it would have to be left out. As usual, the blame rested not with him, but elsewhere. With his customary petulance, he announced to his readers on November 11, 1713, that he would have given them the rest of the record had he received "any Tollerable encouragement."

Hardly had the *News-Letter* settled back into its normal chronology of European news when Campbell had to deal with another great event, the death of Queen Anne. Again, this was a matter of adjusting the regular order of things to the intrusion, not so much of the event itself as to a profusion of official, largely ceremonial documents that demanded priority in the record over mere correspondents' reports of scattered events. It was through these documents, of course, that Campbell's provincial readers could participate, down to the minutest detail, in the awesome imperial ritual of a royal succession. Campbell tried to minimize the disruptive effects of the intrusion as much as he could, but of course received a setback in his ongoing struggle to keep the running record both intact and as current, or almost as current, as the minimum six-week Atlantic sailing time allowed. Partly as a consequence of his attempt to juggle the competing demands of immediacy and chronology, Campbell's readers got the news of Anne's death and the accession of a new sovereign piecemeal—and in a singularly undramatic way.

The Queen's death occurred in the morning of Sunday, August 1, 1714, and was duly reported in the next *London Gazette* on August 3. Obviously, all of London if not most of the realm knew of that event and the subsequent proclamation of George I well before the publication of the official printed account, if only because the proclamation, issued by the Privy Council according to immemorial custom, had been ceremoniously read aloud at all the ancient designated places in London and Westminster long before Sunday was over.[44] Here is one of those innumerable cases in which the printed news medium supplemented the traditional oral culture by adding relative permanence and a broader geographic distribution, but did not replace it as a means of telling the news first.

The same was true in Boston. Word of the event, in the form of "Letters and Prints" not including any copies of the *Gazette*, arrived in Boston in two ships on Wednesday, September 15, six weeks and three days after the Queen's death. On Friday, still three days away from the *News-Letter*'s next scheduled appearance, another ship arrived from Britain with copies of the August 3 *Gazette*. Not until Monday, September 20, was the *News-Letter* able to announce the news to its readers, practically all of whom by now had almost certainly heard it the old-fashioned way: by word of mouth. Campbell's treatment of the announcement silently acknowledged that fact—and reveals his determination to forge ahead with his "thread" at almost all costs. The first page and more than half of the second of that Monday's two-page paper picks up the chronology from where he had left it the previous week, beginning, ironically, with a report of the death of a fairly obscure German princess in June and ending with an item from London dated August 3 (three days *after* the Queen's death) reporting rumored activity at the French court. The thirty-three separate items in this large batch of foreign news include one dealing with Queen Anne—her appearance before Parliament on July 9. Then follow brief shipping reports from Philadelphia, New York, Rhode Island, and New Hampshire, and, finally, well down the right-hand column of the second page, the Boston news:

> *Boston*, On the 15th Currant, in Letters and Prints brought by Two Vessels arriving Here, one from Great Britain, and the other from Cork in Ireland, we received the Sorrowful News of the Death of Our Late Most Gracious Sovereign Lady Queen ANNE of Blessed Memory, And of the Accession of the Most High and Mighty Prince GEORGE. . . . Which News was confirmed

by the London Gazette from the 31st of July to the 3d of August past, brought in a Ship from Great Britain arriving the 17th Currant. . . .

There follow a few more squibs of Boston shipping news. These include the customary paragraph headed "Entred Inwards," which contains the names and commanders of the two ships already alluded to, and also include two more brief references to the transition in Britain.[45]

If, therefore, Campbell's readers had had to depend upon their newspaper for a full and timely report of one of the most significant events of an eventful decade, their introduction to this news would have been fragmentary and almost casual. But that was not the case, because over the past five days the word had spread. Campbell fully intended to provide the complete record that he had by now read in the *Gazette* and that he knew would be elaborated upon in subsequent papers yet to arrive. For now, it was enough to note the arrival of the news. Since the demands on space would be great in the weeks to come, it would be better at this stage to clear the decks of "thread" than to launch immediately into preserving the official record of the death of the Queen. The community knew the essential facts. There was no compelling pressure, as he saw it, to do more until next week.

When next Monday did come, the September 27 *News-Letter*, temporarily relieved of the burden of the "thread," was devoted almost entirely to the single subject of Anne's death. Anyone reading it through the spectacles of today's assumptions about newswriting—that the point is to use as few words as possible—would be appalled, given the *News-Letter*'s limitations, by Campbell's lavish expenditure of space, in which he managed to say quite little. But that would be to misunderstand the main end of a journal such as the *News-Letter*, which was neither efficiency nor immediacy, but the systematic construction of a printed record. Moreover, it should take but a moment's reflection by modern readers over a certain age to comprehend the ritual importance of such a record. It is necessary only to recall the minutely detailed reportage of the ceremonial public events occasioned by the death of John F. Kennedy that commanded the communal attention of a nation of television viewers in November 1963. In essential purpose, function, and effect, only the medium was different.

Campbell dedicated nearly all of the September 27 number to a separate "thread," dealing only with the shift in sovereignty. The entire first page and first two or three inches of page two contained these official documents from the *Gazette*, in order: a formal notice dated August 1 recording the death of the Queen, the immediate convening of the Privy Council to order the proclamation of her successor, and the public reading of the proclamation at five named places in Westminster and London; the text of the proclamation followed by the names of all 134 dignitaries who had signed it; the names of 26 Privy Councilors and other lords who by prior legislation would administer the government until the new German King arrived in Britain; and the full text of the order detailing all eighteen changes to be entered in the Book of Common Prayer (scarcely owned in New England) as a result of the change in sovereigns. There followed a fragment of Campbell's general "thread," beginning with an appointment by Queen Anne on July 30 and concluding with a long memorial by the Dutch Assembly on the occasion of the change of affairs in Britain. Next came an unusually long fifteen inches of American news in which the normal shipping reports were supplemented by accounts of ceremonial responses in Portsmouth, Salem, and Boston to the death of the Queen and the accession of King George. The *News-Letters* of October 4 and 11 went back to pick up the chain of events prior to the Queen's death.

The eight numbers from October 18 through December 6 reported in detail the official and ceremonial matters attending the accession of George, but the ten after that, through February 14, 1715, went back again to pick up the sequence of mostly ordinary events prior to August 1. These included, finally, on February 14, a long obituary of Queen Anne dated August 1. Having now caught up, the *News-Letter* began most of its numbers for the next few months with news of the first events of George's reign. The coronation, which occurred on October 20, 1714, was reported on May 23, 1715. The next week, on May 30, Campbell ran an announcement of the now-familiar kind:

> [Having for these Nine Weeks past given you the most Remarkable Occurrences of the Court of Great-Britain, we must retire back to give you the Less Observable of the said Court, with the most Remarkable of Europe: had the Undertaker any suitable encouragement . . . , he would have Printed a Sheet a Week, which would . . . have forwarded the same Nine Weeks that is now behind. . . .]

The End of the Monopoly

Campbell's running struggle to keep up with the increasing flow of European news in the desperately inadequate columns of the *News-Letter* became more hopeless as the years went on. By the summer of 1718, he was behind in Continental news not nine weeks but thirteen months! His subscribers were complaining, or so at least we can surmise from a printed explanation of his attempted remedy the following summer. He was trying, he said, to "make . . . the News Newer and more acceptable."[46] In January he had begun to put out a four-page *News-Letter* every other week, alternating with a two-page one. In virtually every four-page number that year, the "extra" space was devoted to foreign news.

The experiment continued throughout 1719; the British news got a little newer but not much. There was noticeable improvement both in the amount and in the currency of news from the European continent. On

August 10, Campbell offered a reminder of the change in progress along with the predictable whining about his sacrifices:

> And in regard the Undertaker had not suitable encouragement, even to Print half a Sheet Weekly, seeing he cannot vend 300 at an Impression, tho' some ignorantly conclude he Sells upward of a thousand: far less is he able to Print a Sheet every other Week, without an Addition of 4, 6 or 8 Shillings a Year. . . .
>
> And considering the great Charge he is at for several setts of Publick Prints, by sundry Vessels from London, with the Price of Press, Paper, Labour, carrying out the News Papers, and his own trouble, in collecting and composing, &c. . . . Such therefore as have not already paid for the half Year past . . . are hereby desired to send or pay the same unto John Campbell. . . .

Campbell thus ended his years of monopoly on the same note with which he had begun. But we must not denigrate Campbell's accomplishment. Despite his editorial and financial frustrations, he did teach himself during those fifteen years to publish, not without success, an American newspaper.

Chapter 5

Competition, 1719-1732

December 1719

Newspaper publishing in America, monopolized for fifteen years by the postmaster of Boston, entered a new phase at the end of 1719. John Campbell acquired a head-on competitor in the person of his successor in the Boston postmastership, and a young printer of Philadelphia began a newspaper that for most of the decade to come would have to itself the news and advertising market from New York to the Chesapeake. By contrast with the long monopoly of the *Boston News-Letter* in British America, the provincial cities of England were sprouting newspapers for a vastly larger readership at a rapid rate. By the end of 1715, there were 23 country newspapers in 11 English towns outside of London; over the next decade, when exactly four newspapers would be founded in the mainland colonies and one in Jamaica, another 25 would appear in provincial England.[1]

While the introduction of Boston's second newspaper was accompanied by deliberately competitive rhetoric and strategies on both sides, Philadelphia's Andrew Bradford simply aimed at making his *American Weekly Mercury* as useful as possible to a readership that stretched over a remarkably broad geographic area. The day would come when he would be dividing that far-flung market on friendly terms with the New York branch of his own family, and still later be facing outright and not so friendly competition in Philadelphia itself. The first of those events, however, was still more than six years and the second nearly a decade in the future.

The competition in Boston produced an uneven match between a superseded and very nearly superannuated postmaster and his younger and more imaginative successor who had the additional advantage of being fresh from London. While Campbell continued to publish his *News-Letter* in the unaccustomed capacity as political outsider, the new postmaster William Brooker now proceeded to use his office to publish a rival newspaper "by authority." He called it the *Boston Gazette*.

Campbell's tenure in the post office came to an end in 1718, when he was sixty-five. His published assertion that he stepped down voluntarily is unconvincing. Complaints about Campbell had made their way over the head of his American supervisor, Deputy Postmaster General John Hamilton, to the postmaster general in London. Communications from London to Hamilton suggested Campbell's removal, but before Hamilton decided to act, the postmaster general himself, on June 27, 1718, appointed a successor to Campbell in the person of Philip Musgrave. At some point during the next eleven weeks, Hamilton, unaware of the action in London, removed Campbell and named Brooker to the job.[2] Brooker served until the spring of 1720, when Musgrave arrived from England to assume the office to which the highest authority in the British postal service had appointed him two years before.[3]

Brooker's *Boston Gazette* appeared on December 21, 1719, after the new postmaster had been in office fifteen months. Brooker chose as his printer James Franklin, now not quite twenty-three, who just two years earlier had set up his printing shop in Queen (now Court) Street, a short walk around the corner from the post office.[4] Franklin was then the only printer in Boston who was not a member of the Green clan. To many Bostonians who had been on the scene much longer than the new postmaster, this young upstart must have seemed an unlikely choice for printer of the only newspaper in town that claimed to be "published by authority." On the other hand, Franklin was also the only printer in Boston with London training and experience, which may well have been a factor in Brooker's choice. Franklin held on to his printing contract only as long as Brooker remained in his temporary appointment as postmaster. When Musgrave arrived late the next summer to take permanent charge, he quickly provided the postmaster's newspaper with a more credible link to the Boston establishment by replacing Franklin with Samuel Kneeland, nephew and former apprentice of Bartholomew Green, the long-time printer and future publisher of the *News-Letter*.

If Massachusetts had its Greens, a smaller and less cantankerous American equivalent to the extensive clan of Farleys that dominated provincial news publishing in southwestern England in the first half of the century,[5] the middle colonies had their Bradfords. William Bradford, formerly of Philadelphia and now of New York, had not yet established quite the dynasty that had proceeded from the shop and loins of the original Samuel Green, but his was at least a dynasty in the making. In New York he had trained and taken into partnership his son Andrew, who was now in his sixth year as the sole printer in his native Philadelphia, where he served as official printer both to the province government and to the Society of Friends.[6]

The elder Bradford, raised up to the printing trade by Andrew Sowle, the chief Quaker printer of London, had married his master's daughter and joined his master's sect. Arriving in Pennsylvania with his printing press and paraphernalia in 1685, Bradford had gone into business but got entangled in a series of legal troubles with both the government and the Quakers. In 1693, enticed by an offer of the public printing contract there, he took his equipment, wife, and seven-year-old Andrew to New York, where he abandoned the Friends for the Church of England and settled in for a long career of printing and public service.[7]

Since arriving in Philadelphia under his father's sponsorship in 1712, Andrew Bradford had established a thriving printing business and miscellaneous retail shop, as was common among printers. Unlike the two Boston publishers, he was not the postmaster of his town, though he would acquire that appointment in 1728 and serve in it until he lost it to Benjamin Franklin in 1737. There is no question that the appointment became an asset to his newspaper.[8]

As far as anyone knows, only coincidence explains the separate decisions that brought the second and third American newspapers into being at the same time. That Brooker's *Gazette* appeared one day before Bradford's *Mercury* is due simply to the different postal schedules of Boston and Philadelphia.[9]

Bradford must have been aware of at least some of the developments in Boston, though not necessarily of Brooker's plan to start a new newspaper, because he had laid elaborate plans for distribution all along the seaboard before his first number appeared. He listed at least two postmasters, including the postmaster of Rhode Island, among his ten subscription agents from Williamsburg to Newport. Bradford, it seems, hoped to attract both subscribers and advertising everywhere outside the immediate range of the *Boston News-Letter* and, if he knew of its existence, its new competitor.

The Shape of the Competition

In purpose, content, and general appearance, Brooker's *Boston Gazette* had much in common with the *Boston News-Letter*. It was identical in size, two-column layout, placement of the title, and treatment of the publication date. Like the *News-Letter*, the *Gazette* inserted the phrase "New-England" and the serial number of the issue at the top of page one, and a centered "THE" in the next line, just above the title. During Brooker's short tenure, the colophon at the end of the paper did not mention the publisher's name, but only the printer's.

What must have struck the Boston readership more than similarities in format between the two papers were the differences. The most immediately visible one was the creation of what was by Boston standards an exceptionally dramatic nameplate. Brooker flanked all three lines of the title, including its "*NEW-ENGLAND*" preface, with two woodcuts an inch and three-eighths square. The picture on the left—today such embellishments are called "ears"—was of a full rigged ship under sail. On the right galloped a mounted postman sounding his horn. The pair of devices, though an obvious enough choice for a publisher wishing to link his newspaper graphically with the post office, was not original. The *Post Man and the Historical Account* had used identical illustrations with the same placement since its founding in London in 1696, and by 1715, both the *Post Boy* and the *Flying-Post*, two other London newspapers whose names were intended to suggest an association with postal communications (by implication, of course, the most rapid available), had begun using identically placed woodcuts with similar, though more allegorical, iconography.

The resulting difference in appearance between the *Gazette*, with its rather interesting design combining print and pictorial elements at the top of the page, and the *News-Letter*, with its prosaic line of print stretching across a narrow band at the top of an otherwise gray page, was heightened by the occasional use of still another device that broke the visual monotony of brevier or nonpareil set in unrelieved columns.[10] Brooker's italicized publisher's announcements, of which there were several during his period of ownership, were spread across the entire width of the first page beginning just under the date. The division of the remaining matter into columns began only after the announcement ended, often quite close to the bottom of the page. The effect was obviously much more dramatic than Campbell's method of almost burying his announcements in a single column near the end of his paper, and added to the visual interest of the first page. Like the woodcut ears, this treatment undoubtedly was adapted from one or more of the London papers of the past decade or two. Richard Steele, for example, had opened his famous essay journal the *Tatler* with an explanatory address to the reader treated typographically in exactly the same way,[11] and the same model could be found in the first number, May 23, 1701, of the *New State of Europe*. Finally, the *Gazette* used substantially larger and more varied type than the *News-Letter* to present the proclamations and other official documents with which both papers often began. On the whole, partly by combining with some of these small departures in composition a more judicious use of white space, the *Gazette* consistently presented to its readers a neater, livelier format than that of its competitor. Visually, the *Gazette* resembled to some degree several of the independent London newspapers such as the *Post Man*, the *Post Boy*, the *Flying Post*, and *St. James's Post*, while the *News-Letter* continued to stick closely to its own earlier—and duller—model, the *London Gazette*.

Brooker began publication, as Campbell had in 1704, with two pages. By this time, however, the *News-Letter* was struggling to carry the burden of the "thread" by publishing more four-page numbers and, in 1720, four "post scripts," or supplements. Brooker soon found himself pursuing the trend toward bigger papers. The first known full-sheet number of the *Gazette* was the twelfth, March 7, 1720, and there were at least twenty more through the end of 1720. Several of the full-sheet numbers, however, unlike any of the *News-Letter*'s, were printed on only three pages. Brooker also published at least one supplement early in 1720. Boston readers and their correspondents were now getting a much heavier diet of printed news than had been the case fifteen years before. In the year 1705 the *News-Letter* published 110 pages of news; in 1720, the *News-Letter* and *Gazette* together turned out a minimum of 290 pages, two and two-thirds times as many.[12]

Brooker introduced the first number of his *Gazette* with a statement of intent that could not help but draw an ill-tempered reaction from Campbell. He announced that the new paper came at the request of *"several of the Merchants and others of this Town,"* but especially of *"those People that live remote from hence, who have been prevented from having the News Paper sent them by the Post, ever since Mr.* Campbell *was removed from being Post-Master."* Point one: subscribers who "live remote from hence" need a newspaper published by the postmaster, who can send it free through the mail. Point two: Campbell had been fired.

Point three was actually another dig at Campbell's *News-Letter* though not phrased that way. It raised the question of whether Campbell had been serving his primary readership adequately. *"To make this paper the more Acceptable to the Trading part of this Town, and other Parts of America,"* Brooker went on, *"Every other week will be published an Account of the Prices of all Merchandize, how they govern at this Place, in the Nature of a Price Currant."* An obvious idea, it would seem, especially since lists of London prices were among the regular publications that Campbell had been receiving in his packets of prints for years. But it had not occurred to Campbell to adapt this long-standing London practice to the immediate needs of the Boston mercantile community. As it turned out, Brooker would soon abandon this innovation under pressure from local merchants who did not want to share this valuable information with distant readers.[13] While circumstances therefore found him wrong about what was acceptable to his chief Boston patrons, he was not wrong about Campbell's relative lack of initiative. Campbell's way, by and large, was to copy what was already in print or sent to him by letter; the *News-Letter* was fundamentally a compilation of "news" already processed, a systematic arrangement of an existing record, not primarily an instrument for the *creation* of the record. Brooker seems to have recognized that limitation in his rival's approach, and he recognized one thing more, point four: that Campbell too often printed *old* news. *"The greatest Care will be taken,"* the new publisher promised, *"that this Paper shall always contain the latest News that can be met with from the public prints."*

Point five brought his case for support back to another of the special advantages of being a postmaster in the newspaper business: *"And as for the other Occurrences of the adjacent provinces, the several Post-Masters communicate all Matters of that kind to this Office every Post: And it is hoped the Method that will be observed in carrying on this Paper, will be such as to render it agreeable. Those therefore that are willing to promote it, are desired to signify their Intentions at the Post Office accordingly."*

Campbell let the next week's publication day go by without comment, but the January 4 number of the *News-Letter* was the first of a new year, by Campbell's usage, and it was time for the annual appeal for support; the recent appearance of a rival newspaper could hardly escape notice. Campbell's plea began historically, a reminder to his readers that the *News-Letter* had been serving them faithfully for "near upon Sixteen Years." But now there has occurred an intrusion on the scene: "And it [the *News-Letter*] was the only Intelligence, on the Continent of America, till the two last Monday's of December past, there came forth here a Paper, Intituled, The Boston Gazette. . . ." Campbell then took issue with the contention of "the Nameless Author" that he had been removed from office. "He is necessitated to Affirm," Campbell wrote of himself, "He voluntarily resign'd it, because he would not take up with less Annual Allowance than Brooker, who succeeded him, that was superceded by Mr. Musgrove [*sic*] from England." Then there was the matter of Brooker's contention that out-of-town subscribers had been unable to receive the *News-Letter* since Campbell left the post office. This was untrue, pronounced the former postmaster. His explanation lacked clarity but not conviction. Anyone who chose, he said, could have the *News-Letter* sent by post (by paying postage, it turns out later), and many subscribers recently had been having the paper "carryed them by private hands on the Post Road, which they still may, and these three Months past by agreement with Mr. Musgrove, they had it by Post." The final clause, cryptic though it is, suggests that Campbell had gone over Brooker's head to Musgrave, once his appointment to the postmastership had become known but before he stepped into the office, and regained postal privileges for the *News-Letter* that Brooker had revoked. Those privileges did not extend, however, to the free postage to which the *News-Letter* had been entitled over the past fifteen years. This becomes obvious at the end of the publisher's long announcement, at which point he offers "such as have a Mind to pleasure their Friends with it per Post" the option of having the paper printed on a whole sheet, "one half with the News, the other half good Paper to Write their Letter on." The advantage would be that a correspondent could pay only "single Postage, for both the News and their Letter every Post." This, said Campbell, "will fully Obviate that insinuation of People's being prevented from having it that live remote from hence."[14]

Brooker, naturally, could not ignore such a challenge. His signed response filled most of the first page of the next Monday's *Gazette*.[15] Most of it aimed at setting the record straight, as Brooker saw it, about the postmastership. He set forth in some detail the sequence of events, including the appointment of Musgrave in London and his own subsequent appointment by Hamilton. He also undertook to clear himself of Campbell's charge that he had misrepresented the availability of the *News-Letter* in places remote from Boston.

By far the bulk of Brooker's long retort was just that—one side of a public quarrel consisting mostly of a disagreement over facts, a debate carried on by the crude method of assertion and denial. The first few sentences and the very last, however, gave Boston's readers a sample of the journalistic tone of the future, betraying at the same time the assumption that provincial newspapers were derived from those of the metropolis— that, in fact, their validity and excellence depended upon the fidelity of the provincial publisher to his metropolitan model.

Brooker's discourse, pointedly datelined at the "POST OFFICE," begins, *"THE good Manners and Caution that has been observed in writing this Paper, 'twas hoped would have prevented any occasion for Controversies of this kind; But finding a very particular Advertisement published by Mr.* Campbell *in his* Boston News-Letter *of the 4th Currant, lays me under an absolute Necessity of giving the following Answer thereunto."* There is an effort here not simply at accuracy, completeness, and timeliness, nor only to serve the practical needs of the community—all of which were values espoused repeatedly by Campbell in his ragged, barely articulate fashion—but at gentility. Brooker's language throughout this statement and in others like it is, if not elegant, at least coherent and correct. Campbell's written English was not like that—one reason, perhaps, though not the main one, for his great preference for copying over doing his own writing. "Will Whetstone," one of the *New-England Courant*'s ebullient contributors in 1722, would be unnecessarily cruel but not far from the unfortunate truth in his description of Campbell's "Stile" as "blundering and vile," marked by a "confus'd and incoherent Manner of Speech."[16] Beyond Brooker's more graceful language was the phrase "good Manners and Caution." The *Gazette* was a very long way from the *Tatler* and the *Spectator*, to be sure, but it is significant that it occurred to Brooker even to mention urbane qualities such as these in reference to the operation of a provincial news sheet. The day was not far off when Boston publishers and "authors" would be trying much more deliberately to incorporate their own version of London's polite letters into their newspapers.

Brooker followed by chastising his rival for his apparent ignorance of newspaper conventions in the metropolis: *"Mr. Campbell begins in saying,* The Nameless Author—*Intimating as if the not mentioning the Authors Name was fault: But if he will look over the Papers wrote in* England *such as the* London Gazette, Post-Man, *and other Papers of Reputation) he will find their Authors so."* One could hardly ask for a more forthright statement of the assumption, shared not only by Brooker and Campbell but also by most of the Americans who would put out newspapers during the next few decades, that it ought to be the aim of a good provincial publisher to do in Boston as it was done in London.

The spat between Campbell and Brooker continued for another round and a half of exchanges, then died out. Campbell's parting shot in the February 1 *News-Letter* was a feeble one: "All the Reply he [Campbell] thinks fit to trouble the Publick with . . . is that he has lived and traded here many Years, and is known."

Here ended the first newspaper controversy in America. If the readers of the two papers were bored by it, they had a right to be. The question of whether Campbell had resigned or been dismissed from the post office two years earlier was hardly a public issue worth much discussion. There would, however, be matters of far greater consequence debated in the press a short time in the future, and Brooker and Campbell had set a precedent of personalized controversial journalism that seemed at this early stage of newspaper rivalry an inevitable concomitant of competition.

Under Brooker's brief direction, the *Gazette* lived up quite faithfully to the promises with which its life had begun. The frequent lists of Boston prices current and relatively recent European news—three months behind, on average, as opposed to the *News-Letter*'s six—set the new arrival off from its veteran competitor, as did its fresher, neater appearance. Readers could also find in the new journal most of the *News-Letter*'s standard features such as the Boston shipping lists, maritime news from other colonies, and a small amount of advertising. Official news of the province in the form of proclamations and public announcements appeared with equal prominence and timeliness in both papers. On the whole, the *Gazette* offered an attractive alternative to the *News-Letter* indeed.

However, Brooker and Franklin achieved the *Gazette*'s greater visual appeal at some cost in substance. The eye is drawn to regularity without monotony, to variety without confusion. When it looks at the printed page it is attracted to neatly arranged contrasting areas of black and white more than it is attracted to a large field of unrelieved gray. This was the visual difference between the *Gazette* and the *News-Letter*, but the fact is that the crowded, virtually marginless columns of an average *News-Letter* contained more reading material than an equal number of nicely spaced columns, punctuated with an interesting variety of type sizes, in an average *Gazette*.

On March 14, 1720, the thirteenth number of the *Gazette* and number 830 of the *News-Letter* began with the same item, a transcript of Governor Shute's 500-word proclamation for a general fast on the coming March 31. If both printed versions of the text were lying side by side, no reader would hesitate to pick up the *Gazette*. The arrangement on the page, the spacing, the use of a horizontal rule at the end of the item, even the size of the print both in the heading (larger than the *News-Letter*'s) and in the body of the proclamation (smaller than the *News-Letter*'s) all announce the special official nature of the document, inviting the eye first to the bold letters spelling out the governor's name, then down through graduated sizes of

An early number of the *Boston Gazette*, showing how John Campbell's successor William Brooker and his printer James Franklin took advantage of their recent London experience to produce an attractive alternative to Campbell's *Boston News-Letter*. This issue of March 14, 1719/20 (the eighteenth-century owner of the file used pen and ink to change the Old Style date on the paper to 1720) used an especially dramatic combination of fonts, in contrast with that day's *News-Letter*, to present a gubernatorial proclamation. (*Courtesy, American Antiquarian Society*)

type to the preamble and finally the body of the proclamation, all with the visual assurance that the piece is of a finite length and that what one is invited to begin can thus be easily finished. The *News-Letter* version, by gloomy contrast, is almost forbidding in its density, the document scarcely separated visually from the news from Europe that follows it. But the *Gazette*, already having used a third more space than its competitor for its nameplate, now squanders almost another two inches of the left-hand column for big letters and attractive white space before beginning the preamble of the proclamation. Instead of the eleven words to a line that the *News-Letter* squeezes on average into its crowded columns, the *Gazette* manages only nine. While the *News-Letter* has polished off the proclamation in 9½ inches, leaving another two inches at the bottom of the first column and 11½ inches in the second for news on the same page, the *Gazette* uses almost 12 inches for the proclamation, leaving only three more inches of usable space on page one. There was a price for relative readability and attractiveness.

There was also a price for timeliness. Campbell lagged several months behind Brooker in his presentation of most of his European news, but it was not for lack of the same sources on the same schedule. During much of the time Campbell and Brooker were in competition, in fact, both publishers were working from shipments of English newspapers that had come in late December of 1719, since the supply could not be refreshed by transatlantic arrivals during the winter.[17] But while Brooker was choosing the most recent—or interesting—papers from the December cargoes, Campbell remained the victim of his "thread," unwilling to sacrifice continuity of record for contemporaneity. The *News-Letter* was thus a more complete and more systematic "paper of record" than the *Gazette,* while the *Gazette* may have seemed to its readers somewhat livelier.

It was also more enterprising. As early as March 7, 1720, the *Gazette* sported an exceptional number of advertisements by Boston standards, a total of 14, occupying 15½ inches of space. The *Gazette* did not repeat this performance during 1720, and did so only rarely for the rest of the decade. Its competitor under Campbell, however, never came close. Generally both newspapers ran at most seven advertisements and often far fewer, filling between two and eight inches of space at the end of the last page.

But it was in another way that Brooker got the drop on his older rival more spectacularly, just two weeks after the apparent advertising coup. Since early in the year, Campbell had been publishing a two-page "Postscript" to Monday's *News-Letter* every other Thursday. Since this was the dry news season, his purpose could hardly have been to score "beats" on his competitor with news that might arrive between Mondays. It was to keep up with his continuing project of printing a systematic record of European affairs. The idea was the same as his plan the year before of putting out full-sheet numbers in alternate weeks in the hope of staying somewhat up-to-date. The extra space at this time of year also allowed him to incorporate material of a kind for which there had never before been a place in the *News-Letter*. The regular number for February 22, for example, led with an article describing how the Russians made tar, and the "Postscript" for Thursday, March 17, filled most of page one with "Rules for Raising and Making Hemp," ending with a parenthetical reminder of a provincial law encouraging hemp-making. Perhaps these articles were Campbell's way of demonstrating his commitment to his maritime and mercantile audience, a counterpart to Brooker's prices current. Certainly, taken together with the *Gazette*'s page-two article on Louisiana, excerpted on March 14 from September's *Political State*, they served to introduce to Boston and America the idea that newspapers were for more than news. But more than anything, Campbell's "Postscript to the Boston News-Letter," as each of the special numbers was called, enabled him to move forward a bit more rapidly with his thread of news.

About the beginning of March, however, the sea lanes were becoming active once again, and ships from Britain starting to arrive in some of the more southerly American ports, though not yet in Boston. Campbell published a "Postscript" on March 17, probably planning his next one for the thirty-first, two weeks away. On Monday the twenty-first, both Boston publishers delayed as long as they could the printing of their regular editions, hoping for the arrival of the biweekly "western post," now two days late. Finally, both *News-Letter* and *Gazette* were committed to the press, run off, and distributed. The post rider galloped into town along Boston Neck at noon, too late to meet the printing schedules of either the present postmaster or the former one, carrying the mail from Philadelphia and New York and points along the way. The mail included copies of the *American Weekly Mercury* for Tuesday, March 8, which carried the *London Gazette*'s account of King George's speech before Parliament on November 23, 1719, reporting optimistically upon the progress of the Anglo-Spanish war then winding down. It is doubtful that it ever would have occurred to Campbell on his own to take extraordinary measures to rush this admittedly interesting but less than critical news—or hardly any other news—into print. Brooker, however, took just such measures. Perhaps because this was the first direct news of English public affairs to make its way to the colonies this season, but also likely casting a nervous eye at Campbell's new habit of printing periodic "Postscripts," Brooker came out the very next day, a Tuesday, with his first "Supplement" to the *Gazette*, more than half of which was given over to the King's speech of November 23. Brooker headed the account with an announcement of the arrival of the news, "*which for the Satisfaction of the People of this town, and the adjacent Places, we take the Occasion of publishing in this Manner, sooner than delaying it till Monday next; at the same time assuring 'em, that News of Moment will be communicated in this Nature, so soon as it shall come to the Knowledge of this Office.*"

Brooker had just added a new rule to the rapidly evolving game of newspaper competition in Boston, drawing not only upon his familiarity with the bustling news scene in London, with its twice-weekly, thrice-weekly, and daily press, but also upon his superior understanding of the developing public thirst for the most *recent* news, however trivial or removed from context. He had now beaten his rival in a contest that Campbell had never bargained for and scarcely understood, serving notice in the process that he was prepared to do it again and again. The purpose of extra editions had now been redefined; the idea was not to provide more space for old news, but to respond at once to the urgency of the new—not on a predetermined schedule, but whenever the occasion arose.

Faced with the fact that he had been scooped, what was Campbell to do now? To print the royal speech in the next regular *News-Letter* would give his readers what they had read in the *Gazette* nearly a week before. His next "Postscript" was not scheduled until the Thursday after that. One option might have been simply to refrain from playing the newspaper game according to Brooker's new rules, sticking to his own method and schedule without concern for the competition. But Campbell, despite the dignity of his years and his long experience in the business, was not sufficiently secure in his own counsel for that. Instead, he responded to Brooker's pressure while trying to make it appear otherwise, failing to hide his embarrassment at having to adopt Brooker's rules at the point at which he had already lost the game.

Campbell published his next "Postscript," not on Thursday the thirty-first when it was scheduled, nor even on the next available Thursday, the twenty-fourth, but on the very next day, a Wednesday. The Postscript led, of course, with the same text of the King's speech that Bradford and now Brooker had published before. Hidden among the advertisements at the end of the paper was this lame explanation for the unusual printing schedule: "Thursday the last Day of . . . March being the Day appointed . . . for the Publick Fast, and the Day for the other Weeks POSTSCRIPT, the Publisher of this Intelligence, thought fit to Print it this Week, and the rather because of the KINGS Most Gracious SPEECH to both Houses of Parliament coming to his Hand by the Post, which came late in on Monday last." The March 23 "Postscript to the Boston News-Letter" is the last one on record.[18]

A Paper for All America

For the publisher of the *American Weekly Mercury*, there was for the moment no need to enter the competitive game. Andrew Bradford had the field to himself, not only in Philadelphia but along the whole middle coast of English America from New York to Virginia.

Only speculation can account for the exact motives behind the naming of our earliest newspapers, Bradford's included. Anna Janney DeArmond, who produced a detailed and perceptive study of Bradford and his newspaper nearly half a century ago, included a brief discussion of the printer's choice of title. The passage points out, correctly, that the name of the messenger of the gods was not only a popular title for English newspapers of the seventeenth and eighteenth centuries, but was a generic term often applied to hawkers of pamphlets and news sheets and even as an equivalent to the term "newspaper" itself. DeArmond also noted the recent success of the *British Mercury*, an English commercial journal, suggesting that Bradford may have chosen the title as a "good omen."[19]

Fine, but why the *American*, rather than the "Philadelphia" or "Pennsylvania" Mercury? Neither of the two Boston publishers had seen fit to identify his newspaper with an entire continent, and it would soon become the custom for nearly every publisher in the colonies to incorporate the name of his particular locality or province in his newspaper's title. Before dismissing the question as being without significance, or answerable by a printer's simple whim, we ought to consider the geographic scope of Bradford's publishing vision, and the extent to which he actually achieved something like continental patronage. His, in short, was not a paper for Philadelphia or Pennsylvania alone. Within the obvious limitations of its time, the *American Weekly Mercury* was true to its title in becoming, far more than its Boston counterparts, an "American" rather than a regional newspaper.

Like the two Boston publishers, Bradford aimed his paper at the mercantile community, stating explicitly in the third month of publication that his "design" was to "Promote Trade."[20] The first twelve *Mercuries* were all two-page numbers, printed on the front and back of a half-sheet of "pot" paper, a sheet slightly shorter and wider than the "printing foolscap" of the two Boston papers. This format remained the rule, with an occasional four-page exception, from the paper's birth in 1719 until 1728, when four-page papers began to dominate.[21] Like the two Boston papers and virtually all those in England, the *Mercury*'s pages were divided into two columns, unruled for the first seven numbers and ruled thereafter. The nameplate, at first a simple combination of large roman and gothic letters in two lines, acquired new sophistication beginning with the thirty-third number on May 17, 1720. From then until 1740, when it gained still further elaboration by the addition of a woodcut view of the Philadelphia waterfront, the paper's title, set in three lines, was bordered on either side by square "ears," one showing a mounted horn-sounding post rider and the other a rather crudely drawn Mercury. The appearance of the page became much like that of the *Boston Gazette;* the iconography, of course, was a variation of the standard images that adorned many British newspapers.

Bradford's way of appealing to his mercantile audience was much like that of the two Boston publishers. The principal supplements to the main diet of European news were simple lists: the Philadelphia, New York, Boston, and occasionally Rhode Island shipping lists and prices current for Philadelphia and New York. Weekly presentation of these two fundamen-

The AMERICAN
Weekly Mercury,
TUESDAY *December* 29, 1719.

LONDON, Auguſt 30, 1719. By Letters from *Spain*, we have the following Advices.

ON the 11th inſtant 750 French, among them two Companies of Granadiers, commanded by the Chevalier de Givry, Major General, and M. la Motte, Brigadier, were imbarked at Port-Paſſage, on ſeveral Tranſports, under the Convoy of Captain Johnſon, commanding the Britiſh Men of War, which have their Stations on this Coaſt; and Collonel Stanhope, his Britannick Majeſty's Envoy, went on Board, to be preſent in an Enterprize deſigned on San Antonio. They ſet ſail that afternoon, and the next Evening arrived before San Antonio. The Harbour being narrow at the Entrance, and having Breaſtworks caſt up from thence along the Sides to the Town, with near 50 Pieces of Cannon placed upon them, it was thought adviſable not to attempt going into it, but rather to endeavour to land upon the Back of it, in a ſandy Bay; to the Weſtward of the Harbour. Upon getting thither, it was ſeen the Enemy had raiſed two Batteries, behind which they had about 600 Men drawn up to oppoſe the landing of Troops. The Cannon of the Britiſh Ships fired upon them for ſome Time, as the Batteries did alſo upon the Ships, to which they did no other Damage than the tearing two or three of the Sails. That Place being at the Bottom of the Bay of Biſcay, where the Sea conſtantly runs high, there were very great Swells, which made the Waves break with violence upon the Shore: However, at Six a Clock it was determined to put the Troops into the Boats, and try if it was poſſible to land them there, but when they were got near the Shore it was judged extreamly hazardous, if not impracticable; they therefore put off again, and went about a Mile further to the Weſt, into another leſſer Bay, where the Sea appeared to be ſomewhat ſmoother. The Enemy not expecting them in that Place, the Forces immediately landed without Oppoſition or Loſs except four or five Seamen drowned, and three Boats overſet; all the Officers and Soldiers getting ſafe aſhore. It being then almoſt dark, they immediately made themſelves Maſters of the Top of a Hill, which is cover'd with thick Wood, and lies between the two Bays, where they remained all that Night; and at Break of Day upon the 13th they marched down, in Number 750 French, and about 200 Engliſh Seamen, to the firſt mentioned Bay, where

they ſaw no Enemy appear, the Batteries being abandoned, which they immediately took Poſſeſſion of. Whilſt they were there, the Magiſtrates of the Town came to make their Submiſſion, telling them they would meet with no ſort of Oppoſition, for that the Militia and ſome Companies of Invalids, which had appeared the Night before, were all diſperſed, and had left even the Forts upon the Harbour without one Man to defend them: From thence the Forces marched through the Town ſtreight to the Harbour, where were in two Forts and upon the Mole 47 Pieces of Cannon, all loaded, which were deſtroyed by burſting a great part, and nailing the reſt. Then the Forces went to the Ship Yards, where lay on the Stocks three Men of War, one of 70 Guns, the other two of 60 Guns each; the firſt was decked, and wanted very little to be launched, the other two were not altogether ſo forward, tho' they were quite built up but not decked. Theſe three Ships were entirely burnt to the very Ground by the Engliſh Seamen; they alſo burnt a vaſt Quantity of the fineſt Planks newly brought from Holland, ſufficient for what could be imploy'd in the Building of five or ſix Men of War. There were alſo a great many Barrels of Pitch and Tar, which with ſome other Naval Stores were burnt, in order to ſet on Fire a great Quantity of fine Timber that was provided for the Building of more Ships. Having thus effectualy executed what was propoſed by this Expedition, the Forces imbarked again the ſame Evening, and arrived here at the Camp laſt Night, with no other Loſs than what is above-mentioned. Collonel Stanhope finding it neceſſary to encourage and animate Troops which had not been uſed to Enterprizes by Sea, was the firſt that leaped into the Water when the Boats approached the Shore. Captain Johnſon and the other Commanders of the Britiſh Men of War, were very zealous and active on this Occaſion. In the River of San Antonio were found two Dutch Ships lately come thither, one loaded with Powder, which had been ſent to Pampelona, and the other had brought Naval Stores; Men were ſent on board them, but found nothing, every thing having been landed ſome Days before.

All our Advices from the Baltick agreed for a while that the Ruſſians have quitted Sweden upon the Approach of the Britiſh Squadron, and are retired, the Gallies in particular, with ſome Precipitation; and that their whole Fleet

The first American newspaper outside of Boston, Andrew Bradford's *American Weekly Mercury*. This is the second number, dated December 29, 1719. Note the detailed narrative, copied from one of the London newspapers, of an episode in the war between Spain and the Quadruple Alliance, even though this brief struggle, in which England and France were allied, did not involve the American colonies. Bradford shared the assumption of his contemporary publishers in Boston that American readers were interested chiefly in the affairs of Europe, news of which was not easily available in any way other than these newspapers. (*Courtesy, American Antiquarian Society*) tal kinds of business data, he presumed, would facilitate the trading that underlay the Philadelphia economy. When Bradford announced his "design" early in the life of the *Mercury*, he expressed the hope that it would be "Incouraged by the Merchants of this City, by Acquainting Us with the true price Current of the Several Goods imported in it, which we presume may be Serviceable to All concern'd in Commerce. Especially to them, that have any of those Goods to Sell, who will find a quicker Sale, by our Informing those persons that want them where they may be Supplied." He added to his request for price information, "We likewise Desire those Gentlemen that receive any Authentick Account of News from *Europe*, or other places, which may be proper for this paper, that they will please to favour Us with a Copy."[22]

While Bradford's statement of "design" seems to have been addressed explicitly to an audience of Philadelphia businessmen, the paper actually reached very much farther—and not simply by accident. The publisher obviously laid his plans for broad distribution with care, working primarily with his father in New York but with contacts elsewhere as well. He worked out a three-tiered subscription rate depending on distance from Philadelphia: ten shillings a year for subscribers in his own province, fifteen shillings for New Jersey, New York, and Maryland, and twenty shillings for Virginia, Rhode Island, and Boston. Subscriptions could be entered with either of the two Bradfords or with other named persons in Annapolis, Maryland; Williamsburg and Hampton, Virginia; Newcastle, Delaware; Salem, Perth Amboy, and Burlington, New Jersey; and Newport, Rhode Island.[23]

We have no subscription lists to judge how well this plan for virtually continental distribution worked,[24] but almost from the beginning, the *Mercury*'s advertising took on a geographic breadth that by Boston standards was breathtaking. The paper was only a week old when a planter from Green Springs, Virginia, advertised a runaway slave. Advertisements as a whole were few over the next few months, but those that did appear included announcements of fleeing servants from Virginia, Maryland, New Jersey, and various parts of Pennsylvania. One such advertisement asked for the return of the runaway either to Andrew Bradford or to William Bradford in New York.[25] In subsequent years, advertising was placed from Long Island, New York's Westchester County, Rhode Island, and even Milton, Massachusetts, to the north and from James River and Yorktown, Virginia, to the south, with a rich array of localities throughout New Jersey and Pennsylvania between.[26] Correspondence and news items provide additional evidence of broad distribution. On May 31, 1722, Bradford reported receiving a letter from Long Island requesting that the *Mercury* print "a particular Account" of a mineral spring west of Philadelphia. The next June 7 the paper printed an account of serious lightning damage in Cecil County, Maryland, received from "one of our Subscribers." From mid-1720 until the elder Bradford started his own *New-York Gazette* at the end of 1725, the *Mercury*'s colophon offered to sell the paper and take in advertising at William Bradford's New York office as well as at the publisher's own shop in Philadelphia. Obviously, William was also providing his son with material such as the New York shipping and price lists, so that in a sense the *Mercury* had a branch office for several years in New York.

The dominant content of the *Mercury* by far was European news copied from the London prints, usually unattributed. Bradford printed Governor William Keith's address to the Pennsylvania Assembly on the first page of his fourth number on January 5, 1720, but not for another seven months did he depart again from his normal practice of filling that page and most of the rest of the paper with news from Europe. The second departure from standard practice came on August 18, 1720, in Bradford's thirty-fifth number, when he led the paper with a proclamation by Governor Keith. The next occasion was the following October 20, when he printed both Governor Keith's speech to the opening of the province assembly and the comparable performance by New York's new governor, William Burnet.

The first ten numbers of the *Mercury* contained no American news at all aside from the governor's proclamation and the shipping and price lists. Beginning with the March 1 number, which carried two brief items concerning shipping from Boston, the *Mercury* carried occasional excerpts from the two Boston newspapers or accounts sent by correspondents elsewhere in America. News from Philadelphia itself, after the model of the *Boston News-Letter*, remained scarce until the coming of other American newspapers encouraged more frequent and systematic mutual copying.

In the dull season when the ships from Britain were not sailing, Bradford showed imagination and enterprise at least equal to William Brooker's. And he was far less restrained than either Brooker or Campbell in expressing an opinion. In the winter of 1721, he made especially effective use of a piece of "old" news from a London paper that had been on hand for some time.

He warned his readers on January 17, 1721, that since no vessel had arrived in the past week, "Our Readers must not expect Impossibilities, or that we can entertain them with fresher Advices from England, Spain, France, &c. than those already published by us in our preceeding Papers." For current news, he announced, he would substitute a series of "modest Reflections" on the conduct of the various European powers. He began that day with a lengthy and judgmental commentary on Spanish diplomacy. Whether the piece was composed in his office or copied from London it is difficult to say, but it is reminiscent of the essays found a decade or two earlier in the various *State of Europe* publications.

No more such "Reflections" appeared for a time, but three weeks later, on February 7, Bradford planted the seed for something better. One of two items datelined London, October 29, reported the embarkation of a large shipload of "malefactors" destined for "transportation to America." Bradford obviously knew at the time he selected the item what he would do next. In the next number, October 14, appeared a lengthy article that began: "Those Malefactors mentioned in our last as sent from Newgate and Marshalsea to be transported into the Plantations, are now arrived in Maryland, to the Number of about 180." The long discussion that followed combined a vehement attack on the policy of transporting criminals to America with a warning to the *Mercury*'s readers to be wary of the unsavory characters they might encounter as a result of the recent shipment. This essay could have been written only in America; its timing establishes that, even disregarding its obvious point of view. Appearing as it did under a Philadelphia dateline, it must have been the work either of Bradford or of one of his close associates. It is worth adding that the "editorial," which is what it would be called today, addresses a continental rather than a strictly provincial concern. Bradford was speaking to all America.

One is tempted, perhaps, to attach greater significance to this interesting statement than is actually there. For an American publisher, at the extraordinarily early date of 1721, to attack British policy while embracing a continental vision of the American colonies does provoke thoughts of the revolutionary future and raises, however briefly, the question of possible antecedents to resistance, rebellion, and intercolonial unity. It is true that this was the first American newspaper statement critical of British colonial policy. It was also a rare statement for the first half of the century, if not unique in that respect, preceding by thirty years Benjamin Franklin's famous suggestion that the colonies pay for British convicts with American rattlesnakes.[27] Far from anticipating separation, however, Bradford's piece articulates a provincial self-awareness, at which John Campbell's copying of the London newspapers only hints, that was expressed in perceived links between the home government and culture and the interests and identity of British Americans.

The *Mercury*'s monopoly in all that rather vast area that Bradford claimed as his own ended with the establishment of his father's *New-York Gazette* late in 1725; it ended in Philadelphia in December 1728. It was at that latter point, or shortly afterward, that Bradford would begin to face the dynamics of competition that were already in place in Boston. Unfortunately for him, it was precisely this turbulent Boston scene that was nurturing the skilled competitor with whom Bradford would have to contend. Before examining the special training ground of Benjamin Franklin, however, we must return briefly to John Campbell's first competitor, the *Boston Gazette*.

The *Boston Gazette* Under Three Postmasters, 1720–1732

The details of the transfer of the *Gazette*'s ownership from William Brooker to Philip Musgrave, and the printing from James Franklin to Samuel

Kneeland, are obscured by a small gap in the newspaper record and by the ambiguity of the record that remains. Certainly both changes were associated with Musgrave's succession to the postmastership sometime during the spring or summer of 1720.[28]

At least by September 26, more likely by the third or fourth week of August, Philip Musgrave was publishing the *Gazette* in his capacity as postmaster, using Samuel Kneeland as his printer. The connection continued until Musgrave's death almost five years later on May 18, 1725.[29] During his ownership and that of Thomas Lewis and Henry Marshall in the seven years after that, the appearance and general character of the *Gazette* departed little from the norms established during the brief and creative tenure of its founder, William Brooker. The *Gazette* continued to present a far neater appearance typographically than that of the *News-Letter*; it stuck overwhelmingly to news rather than literary material; it tended to emphasize currency and interest in the news over continuity; and it never hesitated to print letters criticizing a rival, whether the *News-Letter* or the obstreperous newcomer on the scene after August 1721, the *New-England Courant*.

Musgrave's *Gazette* was aimed at the same primarily mercantile audience that Brooker had had in mind and Campbell was still trying to cultivate. Shipping lists, not only for Boston but also for Rhode Island, New York, and Philadelphia, continued to be a conspicuous regular feature of the paper, and the news communicated to Musgrave and his successors by fellow postmasters or copied from the *American Weekly Mercury* usually was of a distinctly commercial character, sometimes in the form of price lists. On January 30, 1721, Musgrave inserted between the Boston news and the advertisements an italicized announcement from the government of Ireland announcing a new lighthouse on the western Irish coast. This was a service to mariners analogous to Campbell's much earlier copy of Queen Anne's proclamation of the new Union Jack after the union with Scotland, complete with a woodcut copied from the *London Gazette* illustrating the revised merchant ensign.[30]

The first two and a half years of Musgrave's five-year ownership of the *Gazette* coincided with the protracted end of the aging Campbell's long reign at the *News-Letter*. During this period, the *Gazette* tended to devote somewhat more of its space to Boston news than the *News-Letter*, though its main emphasis was still on copied reports from abroad.

Whatever the explanation for the *Gazette*'s slightly larger budget of local news than the *News-Letter*'s—probably nothing more than Campbell's habit and Musgrave's inclination—it apparently has nothing to do with any particular advantages of access that Musgrave may have enjoyed by virtue of his official position. There is no evidence that Campbell's relationship with the province authorities, whether executive or legislative, changed very much after he left the postmastership or that Musgrave ever achieved important "beats" over the *News-Letter* as a result of official privilege.

At the beginning of the 1722 session of the General Court, the House of Representatives as usual elected its own speaker and clerk and, subject to the governor's approval, the twenty-eight members of that year's royal Council. Both publishers received the election results from the province secretary and printed them in their newspapers. The list of councilors, however, included only the twenty-six names approved by Governor Shute, with whom the House was carrying on a heated struggle for power, rather than all twenty-eight elected by the House. Musgrave further offended the tender sensitivities of the House by referring to the electors of the speaker and clerk as the "General Court," by which one might understand (despite the wording of the Charter of 1691) the entire bicameral legislature rather than the House alone.

The House summoned Musgrave and Campbell in turn to answer in person for their errors, and directed both to print its future transactions only from copies legally attested by either the province secretary or clerk of the House. Musgrave got some extra attention, either in tacit recognition of the quasi-official status of the *Gazette* or because it was thought necessary to set the new publisher on a straight course from the beginning. "Mr. Speaker by Direction of the House Admonished him therefor, and Ordered him to Amend those Mistakes in the next Gazette. . . ." Campbell apparently escaped admonishment, but his treatment was no gentler than Musgrave's. Later on the same day in which the House dealt with the two publishers' "errors," it "Read and Dismist" an account of five pounds six shillings from Campbell for government advertising in the *News-Letter*.[31]

This episode merely confirms the general sense the newspapers convey that both Campbell and Musgrave were on better terms with the government of Samuel Shute than with the popular assembly. This was by no means a new position for Campbell, but there must have been political implications in being identified with one or the other in the 1720s that would not have been as obvious or as inconvenient for Boston's sole newspaper publisher a decade or two earlier as they were for the two "establishment" publishers in this rancorous decade. Not only had the popular, or "country," party of Elisha Cooke achieved dominance of the House and reached new heights of contentiousness with a governor stubbornly protective of the royal prerogative, but the obvious identification of the *Courant* with the popular party forced both the *News-Letter* and the *Gazette* to entertain partisan writings on the other side. And to complicate things still further, the *Courant* carried on a series of personal attacks against Musgrave, even accusing him, early in 1721, of dishonesty and malfeasance in his postmastership.[32]

Thus Musgrave's paper, whether he wanted it that way or not, became recognized along with Campbell's by the dominant party in the legislature as a vehicle for its opponents. No doubt this was more significant for him, a newcomer on the scene with a reputation and a fortune still to gain and with pretensions toward being the "official" voice of the province, than for Campbell, a nearly superannuated fixture whom the legislative leaders had dismissed long since as a nuisance.[33]

Musgrave's tenure in both post office and newspaper, however, was cut short by his death on May 18, 1725.[34] By that time, Campbell, whose failing health is dramatically disclosed in the shocking change in his handwriting between 1721 and 1723,[35] had turned the *News-Letter* over to Bartholomew Green. The *Courant* was in decline and nearing its end: the end of the smallpox scare had taken from the *Courant* its favorite issue, and the furtive flight to Philadelphia of the teen-aged Benjamin Franklin had robbed it of its best writer. As for the *Gazette*, its familiar character remained in place under two new publishers; generalizations as to size, format, arrangement of content, amount and nature of advertising, and overall tone and purpose during Musgrave's time would be nearly as valid for the first nine months of 1732 as for 1725.

There were some minor changes, to be sure. Thomas Lewis, who took over the *Gazette* soon after Musgrave's death, dropped "Published by Authority" from the nameplate in September 1725, but Henry Marshall restored it three years later.[36] In 1727, Marshall switched printers from Kneeland, who now began the *New-England Weekly Journal*, to Bartholomew Green, Jr., whose father now both printed and published the *News-Letter*, but the change in printers between these first cousins produced no noticeable change in the appearance of the paper. Beginning in 1728, however, perhaps under the stimulus of the distinctly literary *Weekly Journal*, Marshall supplemented the news with more verse, letters, and essays. This trend continued much more dramatically after John Boydell succeeded to the post office and the *Gazette* and changed its format late in 1732.

American newspapers did indeed pass through a "literary" phase in the 1730s that had its effects more or less everywhere newspapers were published and contributed to the evolution of a standard product. It is a further measure of Boston's particular eccentricity as a publishing center, however, that only there do we find, for a time, a small cluster of specialized journals that can best be described as "literary newspapers." The full flowering of this genre came in an atmosphere of enthusiasm for the genteel literary and artistic models of Augustan England, a new and liberating experience for the best-educated young heirs of New England Puritanism. Its seeds were sown, however, in the superheated atmosphere of political—and medical—controversy. It is to that tumultuous and transforming chapter in the history of American print and culture that we next turn.

Chapter 6

The Couranteers, 1721–1726

The Birth of the *New-England Courant*

In midsummer, 1721, Boston still had only two newspapers, the *News-Letter*, gasping toward the end of John Campbell's eighteen-year regime, and the quite new *Gazette*, now early in the term of Postmaster Philip Musgrave. The *Gazette* was somewhat livelier and better looking than the more systematic but less varied *News-Letter*, but there was little to distinguish the two publishers politically. Both were respectful of Governor Samuel Shute and his administration, both carried on the same mildly contentious relationship with the Assembly, dominated by the popular, or what has been variously called the "country" or "old charter" party,[1] and neither had ever engaged in any hostilities with the clerical and intellectual leadership of the province. Both publishers addressed their newspapers primarily to the economic and political elite. Both treated the lower orders of town and country with anonymity and occasional contempt.

There is a certain pleasant irony, therefore, in the recognition that the first American newspaper to deal largely in the "polite" letters of Augustan England was also the first to identify itself to any degree with some of the segments of society that the *News-Letter* and *Gazette* mostly ignored. It used a device whose origins and essential nature were learned and genteel to attack learning and gentility, and to espouse causes identified mainly with the common sort of people.

The founding of the *New-England Courant*, its role in the great controversy over smallpox inoculation, and its successful defiance of official attempts at suppression make up one of the best known and possibly most significant episodes in early American journalism, the more so because it includes the novitiate of Benjamin Franklin.[2] While it is impossible to ignore the familiar cast of characters and the main events, the emphasis here will be on the nature of the *Courant* as a new genre of newspaper and of its sponsoring "club" as a new kind of publisher.[3] Both genre and publisher flourished briefly in Boston, but never elsewhere in the American colonies.

In one respect, the *Courant* did anticipate the standard: like Andrew Bradford's *American Weekly Mercury* but unlike either of its Boston competitors, the *Courant*'s nominal publisher was its printer. James Franklin, however, did not do it alone. He was but one of a club of "Couranteers" who provided the meat of the paper's irreverent and usually witty content. Though there are no surviving records to prove it, there is some reason to suppose some of Franklin's fellow writers shared with him the financial risk of the undertaking as well. The publisher of the *Courant*, then, was probably not Franklin alone but the Couranteers as a group.

The *Courant* owed its birth to the congruence of two circumstances, set against a broader background of political and social conflict early in an especially rancorous decade. Franklin had printed the *Gazette* from its founding by William Brooker in 1719, but when Philip Musgrave took it over in the summer of 1720 he replaced Franklin with another printer, Samuel Kneeland of the important printing family of Greens. This little drama, the reasons for which are entirely lost but which undoubtedly contributed to putting the young Franklin into a combative frame of mind, preceded by only a few months a new epidemic of the fearful smallpox and the local introduction in 1721 of a controversial new method of dealing with it. This was a cumbersome and risky procedure, still decidedly in its experimental stage, involving the implantation of infected tissue into a surgical incision in the uncertain hope that the resulting preventive case of smallpox would be mild enough to avoid death or disfigurement.

It was Cotton Mather, having read about inoculation in the Royal Society's *Philosophical Transactions*, who on June 6, 1721, suggested to the physicians of Boston that they use it to fight the further spread of smallpox.[4] In the *Gazette* of July 17, Dr. Zabdiel Boylston announced in a lengthy paid advertisement that he had successfully inoculated one of his children and two of his slaves, and that he intended to continue "Artificially giving the Small-Pocks," recommended as the method was by "gentlemen of Figure & Learning," despite an "abundance of Clamour and Ralary" against him for trying it. The chief source of the "clamour" turned out to be William Douglass, a Scottish-born doctor of medicine from Edinburgh and therefore the only physician in Boston with a university medical degree. Ironically, it had been he who had lent Mather the *Philosophical Transactions* that had set off the storm in the first place. There can be no doubt that Douglass, soon to become one of the chief Couranteers, was the author of the long criticism of the local application of the experiment, signed "W. Phi-lanthropos," that John Campbell published in the *News-Letter* on July 24, a week after Boylston's advertisement in the *Gazette.* The controversy that had been swirling angrily around Boston's oral culture for several weeks now became formalized by print.

The Boston selectmen invoked what turned out to be a very temporary ban on inoculation[5] while six Congregational ministers of the town, in-cluding both Mathers, signed a letter to John Campbell—although it was printed in the *Gazette*—taking the publisher to task for allowing the *News-Letter* to be used for "Philanthropos"'s attack on Boylston.[6] As the lines were becoming thus drawn in what may have been the angriest debate in eighteenth-century Boston before the Stamp Act, the *New-England Courant* burst upon the scene, transforming the issue by making it its own, indeed by making itself (as many newspapers have done since) part of the issue.

The inoculation controversy alone, however, is not enough to explain the founding of the *Courant*, any more than a new outbreak of smallpox accounts for the vehemence of the fight over inoculation. Both occurred against a broader background of conflict.

Most obviously, it was a conflict between political factions. T. H. Breen's revival a generation ago of the contemporary terms "Court" and "Country" helped clarify the fundamental political division in Massa-chusetts, as does Richard Bushman's much more recent and politically specific explication of the conflict in terms of the New Charter and Old Charter parties, the latter dominated in the province Assembly by the Boston Caucus of Elisha Cooke. Both explanations also point to the cul-tural divisions that underlay the political conflict.

In the decade before the smallpox crisis, the most divisive issue in Massachusetts had been money—specifically, the question of how best to deal with the province's endemic shortage of specie. The problem became especially severe in the years following the Peace of Utrecht when the conduct of business and commerce depended almost entirely on now-deflated wartime bills of credit. The same issue remained central to Massa-chusetts politics until after mid-century. Predictably, the larger mercantile interests and those such as ministers and government officials who lived on fixed salaries opposed the most permissive and inflationary paper money schemes, while their opponents sought the incorporation of a private bank that would issue bills of credit secured by its members' real estate. Hutchinson characterized supporters of the land-bank scheme in general as "persons in difficult or involved circumstances in trade, or such as was possessed of real estates, but had little or no ready money at command, or men of no substance at all."[7]

Over this and other issues, the two parties contended in the various arenas available for partisan debate in provincial Massachusetts. The Country usually carried the day in the Assembly, where Elisha Cooke, Jr., led the popular forces year after year, but their Court opponents could claim governor, Council, most of the pulpits, the college, and a part of the press—including, in a very general and not overly articulate way, Boston's two newspapers, the *News-Letter* and the *Gazette*.

The background of conflict had a cultural and stylistic as well as a political dimension. Breen includes this dimension within the Court-Country scheme, identifying "the movement toward a cultural Angliciza-tion" specifically with the Court.[8] In general, the identification works, but there were anomalies.

Take, for example, the Congregational clergy. Though for very specific reasons the Mathers opposed Governor Joseph Dudley (1702–14) and his egregious assaults on Puritan traditions in politics and religion,[9] they and most of their clerical colleagues aligned themselves with Governor Samuel Shute (1716–27) and Lieutenant Governor William Dummer, who was in charge of the province in Shute's absence during the last five years of his term, and against Elisha Cooke and his followers. Such predilections are easily explained from personal and political standpoints; as salaried men they opposed the bank and easy currency, and as victims of the general waning of deference in their society, they participated through sermons and pamphlets in the efforts of magistrates and the "better sort" to restore a sense of social hierarchy. But the ecclesiastical system to which they owed their identity and their livelihood had more to fear from Court than from Country, if by "Court" we are to understand in part an attachment by some royal officials to the Church of England or at least a sympathy to the encroachments of Anglicanism in New England.[10]

On the other hand, the Old Charter Assembly listened to the arguments of Timothy Cutler and Samuel Myles, rectors of Christ Church and King's Chapel respectively, rather than to the leading ministers of the province when it was called upon in 1725 to approve a seventeenth-century style synod that Cotton Mather hoped would redefine and reinvigorate the place of the standing churches in Massachusetts. Governor and Council, unlike the Assembly, approved the synod, only to have their position denounced by the Lords Justices in England.[11] Similarly, the voices of New England Anglicanism found a much more available and sympathetic sounding board in the *Courant* than in either the *News-Letter* or the *Gazette*, oriented though the two older newspapers were toward the Court side in politics.

When we turn from religion to literary matters, the case of the *Courant* confronts the Court-Country scheme with yet another anomaly. Breen is certainly right to label the *Courant*, as he does, the "Voice of the Coun-try."[12] Not only in its uniformly whiggish political essays and in its some-times incautious jibes at the province's officialdom, but even in its satirical treatment of higher education and the pretenses of the learned, the *Courant* follows the Country pattern culturally as well as politically. But if we consider the whole meaning of "anglicization," it was the *Courant* and not its rivals that was advancing this supposedly Court-related phenomenon most completely. The point is not only that the *Courant* was quoting the letters of "Cato" from the *London Journal*, as Breen and others have correctly pointed out, but that its publishers decided to introduce to an American audience a journal devoted primarily to this and other forms of controversial and "polite" literature at all. Both the concept and the form, needless to say, were copied directly from some of the most popular and most polished British periodicals of the day.

As a chapter in the history of journalism, therefore, the *Courant* has a rather different significance than it does in Massachusetts politics. Far from acting as a force against cultural anglicization, James Franklin and his sophisticated associates continued on a new level of imagination and intensity the trend in newspaper publishing already begun by William Brooker and Philip Musgrave, whose *Gazette* was offering a stylish contrast to John Campbell's dull and utterly provincial *Boston News-Letter*.

The cultural role of the *Courant* thus understood hardly comes as a surprise once we consider the background of those chiefly responsible for it. James Franklin had been trained in a London print shop and helped Brooker, himself an English émigré, establish the format of the *Gazette*. The most conspicuous Couranteer next to Franklin was William Douglass, the university-trained physician from Scotland. Two other contributors, George Steward and John Gibbons, apparently also enjoyed the title of "Doctor." The author of the introductory essay in the *Courant*'s first number of August 7, 1721, and of an intemperate attack two weeks later on a *Courant* opponent, was John Checkley, a Boston-born but Oxford-educated collector and seller of rare books, paintings, and manuscripts and dealer in pharmaceuticals. Checkley had traveled widely in Europe and was perhaps the most outspoken Anglican in the province. Because of his expressed sympathy with the nonjuring bishops, he was even suspected for a time of Jacobitism. Another contributor, the Reverend Henry Harris, was assistant rector of King's Chapel, where Checkley was a conspicuous communicant. Thomas Fleet, who had moved his printing business from London to Boston a decade earlier, now joined his fellow printer Franklin as a contributor to the *Courant*, anticipating his future role as printer of the *Weekly Rehearsal* and publisher of the *Boston Evening-Post*. Though the immediate cause of Fleet's emigration to the colonies had evidently been his outspoken hostility to the High Church party at the peak of its ascendancy during the reign of Queen Anne, he did not hesitate as a printer in Boston to print the controversial doctrinal works of Checkley, which argued some of the same views that Fleet had opposed in his homeland.

This part of the *Courant*'s stable of contributors, therefore, is characterized by British origins or experience, a distinguished education and broad foreign travel in the case at least of Douglass and Checkley, a cultivated taste for the arts in the case at least of Checkley, and an attachment by several to the Church of England. All of this cannot help but suggest an impulse toward "anglicization," whatever one's specific understanding of the term might be. One might also expect to find here a more than ordinary familiarity with contemporary literary fashions, a well-developed sense of the current terms of political and religious controversy, a knowledge of science, and an interest in the arts—in short, an attachment to all that their century meant by "polite."

But the Couranteers did not consist entirely or even predominantly of British émigrés and High Church Anglicans. There was also ample representation of Boston's provincial and middle-class majority, having in common with the Douglasses and Checkleys only their exclusion from the main centers of power and influence in the province, a gift for satire or something like it, and a compulsion to write. The printer and presumed chief Couranteer himself, though his London apprenticeship is obviously significant, was the tradesman son of a Boston tradesman who had piously raised his large family within the congregation of Old South Church. Two other Couranteers, Fleet and the younger Franklin, shared James Franklin's trade. The author of seven articles in the *Courant* during its first year, later identified by Benjamin Franklin only as "Capt. Taylor," was most likely Christopher Taylor, a mariner. His career had recently climaxed with command of a ship out of Boston, but he was his family's profligate black sheep, the father of an illegitimate son by his maid, a repeated litigant in the courts, and likely holder of property interests in New England forest lands. This last would have been his link with the anti-government policies of Elisha Cooke's party. The most prolific early Couranteer of all, whom Franklin called "Mr. Gardner," was probably Nathaniel Gardner, who along with Matthew Adams, another contributor, was a Boston leather dresser. Gardner, who wrote 32 of the 93 articles identified by Franklin, was, like Adams, a faithful and active Congregationalist despite some of his anti-clerical writings. He was also a perennial servant of the town, being elected or appointed to some municipal office in every year but six from 1717 to his death in 1770.[13] This side of the stable balanced the urbanity of the other with deep roots in the workaday town culture of New England, which in the *Courant* found its public voice for the first time.

The list of Couranteers so far has not included more than passing reference to Benjamin Franklin. It may seem suspiciously pat to say that the sixteen-year-old apprentice's "Silence Dogood" letters neatly combined the voices of both sides of the *Courant*'s stable. In truth, however, they did—though perhaps no more thoroughly than the much more numerous but far less studied and therefore less appreciated writings of his master and elder brother James.

The *Courant*'s first number of August 7, 1721, took its logical place in the sequence of exchanges that had begun with Boylston's announcement in the *Gazette* of July 17. Douglass's "Philanthropos" letter had followed by a week in the *News-Letter*, and that in turn had been followed on the next publication day, July 31, by the six ministers' attack on Campbell and

"Philanthropos" in the *Gazette*. If the exchange had followed the pattern thus begun, Douglass would have used the August 7 *News-Letter* to continue his narrative of the introduction of inoculation to Boston, taking the occasion to respond to the July 31 letter from the clergy. The Mathers and their associates, however, had now closed off that possibility by chastising Campbell, whose defiance of their disapproval would have been out of the question. But Douglass was not to be denied his next shot—right on schedule. The ministers had not counted on Franklin and the Couranteers.

The *Courant* adopted the same publication day, Monday, that its two competitors used, presumably for the same reason: the weekly postal schedule. Though the first number announced that it would appear only "once a Fortnight," the paper in fact came out every Monday from August 7, 1721, to June 19, 1725, and every Saturday from June 26, 1725, at least to June 25, 1726—the last number anyone has yet found—and probably for more than six months beyond that.[14] Its general appearance in 1721 was not far different from that of either the *News-Letter* or the *Gazette* except that it was printed on a slightly smaller sheet; Thomas called it "crown," as opposed to the *Gazette*'s "printing foolscap."[15] Franklin, like his rivals, used a half-sheet format for his newspaper, resulting in a folio page about 12 by 7 inches. The great majority of the *Courant*'s numbers throughout its life were of two pages, one on each side of a half-sheet leaf. A four-page number appeared only rarely. The text was laid out in two unruled columns under an ordinary-looking nameplate that had more in common with the plain letters of the *News-Letter* than the well-illustrated title of the *Gazette*. Beneath the dateline of the first number, however, appeared an italicized hint that the new journal would not be all seriousness. "*Homo non unius Negotti*; Or, *Jack of all Trades*," the motto read. Though its nameplate contained no embellishment like that of the *Gazette*, the *Courant* did, starting with its fifth number on September 4, use a factotum, or large decorative initial letter, to begin the leading article each week. The same elaborate woodcut, showing a ship above the letter and a mounted postman and Mercury below it, was used throughout the life of the *Courant*. The colophon identified Franklin as the printer and announced that advertisements would be "taken in" at his printing house in Queen-Street, an offer that had little effect: the *Courant* never could boast much advertising, and for the first several weeks virtually none at all except that placed by Franklin himself. Beginning with the second number, however, "advertisements" was expanded to "advertisements and letters," an invitation that did prompt substantial response as the paper flourished after several months of operation.

Douglass's column and a third on inoculation, which he entitled "A Continuation of the History of Inoculation in *Boston*, by a Society of the Practitioners in Physick," had to wait until the new paper had been properly introduced. It therefore began at the top of the right-hand column of page one, being preceded in the left column by the introductory essay written, if we are to trust Benjamin Franklin's memory, by John Checkley.

Like the Latin motto at the top of the page, the essay was an entirely new way to begin an American newspaper. The author, taking on somewhat crudely the persona of the journal itself, introduces himself—and thus the paper—to its readers. This device would be refined in the more skillful hands of subsequent contributors to the *Courant*, but Checkley's effort was sufficient to set the tone. Like the English journalists he was imitating, Checkley tried to create a fictitious character to serve as the journal's presumed "author," with whom its readers, entering into the game, would interact. The specific device with which the essay begins is lifted directly from the first *Spectator*.

"I have observed," Joseph Addison had written in 1711, "that a reader seldom peruses a book with pleasure, till he knows whether the writer of it be a black or a fair man, of a mild or choleric disposition, married or a bachelor, with other particulars of the like nature, that conduce very much to the right understanding of an author." He had then gone on, as he put it, "to open the work with my own history."[16] Checkley's version, unlike its model, expresses impatience: *"It's a hard Case, that a Man can't appear in Print now a Days, unless he'll undergo the Mortification of Answering to ten thousand senseless and Impertinent Questions like these, Pray Sir, from whence came you? And what Age may you be of, may I be so bold? Was you bred at Colledge Sir? And can you (like some of them) square the Circle and cypher as far as the Black Art?"* But, like Addison, he goes on, though in much smaller compass, to *"give my gentle Readers some Account of my Person and my rare Endowments."*

In fact, however, the only question he addresses is one of those that Addison had explicitly avoided, that of his character's age. He says he is *"some odd Years and a few Days under twice Twenty and three,"* which, given Checkley's actual age of about forty-one, was close enough to the truth. What he and his associates obviously were sensitive about, however, was the age of James Franklin, then only in his mid-twenties. Without question, the views of the Couranteers would be open to challenge and contempt on the grounds of the youth of the only person whose name was publicly associated with their journal. Correctly anticipating just such a challenge, Checkley has his character say, *"I hope no One will hereafter object against my soaring now and then with the grave Wits of the Age, since I have dropt my callow feathers, and am pretty well fledg'd; but if they should tell me that I am not yet fit nor worthy to keep company with such* Illustrious Sages, *for my Beard do'sn't reach down to my Girdle, I shall make them no other Answer than this,* Barba non facit Philosophum." The self-description then ends as abruptly as it began with a promise, never fulfilled, that his readers will find him more thoroughly "dissected" in the next number.

It is just here, however, that Checkley's character utters the often quoted rhyme that links the introduction with the piece by Douglass that follows. He says he will often be found *"in the good Company of a certain Set of Men,"* meaning the Matherite clergy,

> Who like faithful Shepherds take care of their *Flocks*,
> By teaching and practising what's Orthodox,
> Pray hard against *Sickness*, yet preach up the POX!

The only similarity, then, between Checkley and Addison is the formula with which both the *Courant* and the *Spectator* begin, a partial description of the narrator in response to the assumed curiosity of the reader. But "Mr. Spectator" is a detached observer of the passing scene, a "looker-on," as he describes himself, who "never espoused any party with violence." His social role, like that of Richard Steele's *Tatler*, is that of overseer, or gentle "censor" of the manners and morals of the day.[17] Checkley's provincial character, completely unlike his metropolitan model, is a partisan, and hardly a gentle one.

At the bottom of the left column, right after Checkley's essay and its concluding rhyme, comes a publisher's notice, either added by Checkley as a part of his initial contribution or inserted as a separate item by Franklin. Having already taunted Boston's leading clergy, the *Courant* now proceeds to pick a fight with its competition. "This Paper will be published once a Fortnight," the notice reads,"and out of meer Kindness to my *Brother-Writers*, I intend now and then to be (like them) *very very dull*; for I have a strong Fancy, that unless I am sometimes flat and low, this Paper will not be very grateful to them."

Douglass's renewed attack on inoculation fills the entire right column of page one and runs about four inches onto the back page. Its central argument, which will become one of the persistent themes of the *Courant*'s approach to this topic, is that the town's leading ministers have urged support of their stand on inoculation on the basis of their authority alone. Not the least hazard of defending inoculation "on the Merits of their Characters, and for no other reason," is that to the clergy's own reputation. The best way for the ministers to retain their "sacred" character is for them "not to give the least Occasion to have it called in question." The clergy thus is warned, contrary to the most venerable of New England traditions but in harmony with the sentiments of a growing number of previously inarticulate ordinary people of Boston, not to meddle further in secular affairs. It was as plain to Douglass as it was to Cotton Mather that the issue of clerical authority was in large measure what the inoculation controversy was all about.

By what was probably an accident of timing, the *Courant* had yet one more opportunity to publicize the Country's cause in its first number. As it happened, the election of Boston's delegates to the Assembly had occurred during the previous week, and so a conspicuous piece of news on page two was the choice of Elisha Cooke and four other representatives on the popular side "by a great Majority," as the *Courant* put it, of the town meeting. The rest of the news on that page, except for a one-inch item from Westfield reporting by roundabout means a disastrous fire in Quebec, is under a Boston dateline, though one of the Boston items quotes at length a letter from a French physician (undoubtedly received by Douglass) concerning the plague then rampant in Europe. The Boston shipping list, the last entry in the paper, accounts for about a third of the news.

Thus was launched the *New-England Courant*, which during its brief life transformed the practice of Boston journalism in many ways, not all of them for the better. For while it introduced real controversial writing, thereby giving sustained expression to a significant body of opinion hitherto confined to the impermanence and relative powerlessness of the unaided and unrecorded human voice, it too often descended to the level of fatuous argument, inside jokes, and plain gossip, some of it puerile and vulgar. All of this, however, like adolescence, was a necessary stage for the development of a mature periodical press in the American colonies. For all its silly faults, the *Courant* taught American publishers that they could incorporate the features of a British literary journal into their newspapers, fought and won a courageous battle for press freedom, printed some truly readable and memorable prose, and for a short time performed the salutary office of entertaining what was probably still a too-solemn Boston. For an impertinent and precocious brat that never survived its own adolescence, that is no mean record.

The Short and Merry Life of the *Courant*, 1721–1726

The newspaper war that the *Courant* began with its attacks on inoculation and its jibes at the "very, very dull" competition could not of course remain a one-sided conflict. Not only did Campbell and Musgrave enter the fray, however reluctantly, but the young minister of Roxbury, Thomas Walter, took the assignment of delivering the clerical response to Checkley's opening gun.

Walter, a nephew of Cotton Mather who had once been a member of Checkley's circle of wits but had more recently undertaken to give the orthodox answer in print to a published attack by Checkley on predestination, chose as his format a mock newspaper broadside called *The Little-Compton Scourge; Or, The Anti-Courant*. Franklin cheerfully printed the broadside and even advertised it for sale that day in the August 14 *Courant*. The essayist contented himself with a minute dissection of Checkley's opening discourse in which he made it plain by references to an "apothecary's shop" that he knew the author's identity and threw a series of dull barbs at "Couranto"'s wit by ripostes of his own which if anything were more pathetic than the original.[18]

The one-time *Little-Compton Scourge* did have a significant effect on the *Courant*'s future, not because of its own rather weak content but because of the reply it generated from Checkley in the third number of the *Courant*. This consisted of the coarsest kind of personal attack, accusing Walter of brawling, unchastity, and drunkenness. Its overall design was to encourage the notion that the *Scourge* could easily be dismissed as a product of its libertine author's alcoholic stupor. A somewhat milder response to the *Scourge* by a different author in the same number of the *Courant* advanced the same theory. By the use of his victim's initials and occupation ("clerk"), and the nickname "Tom" in a bit of closing verse, Checkley left his local readers in no doubt as to identity.[19]

That was Checkley's last appearance in the *Courant* by Benjamin Franklin's recollection, and it was an appearance for which the printer felt called upon to offer a sort of apology. The bounds of admissible printed discourse in Boston had been tested and very readily discovered, at least when it came to dealing with the clergy. "Several Gentlemen in town believing that this Paper (by what was inserted in No. 3) was published with a Design to bring the Persons of the Clergy into Contempt," read a statement in the *Courant*'s fifth number, "the Publisher thinks himself oblig'd to give Notice, that he has chang'd his Author; and promises, that nothing for the future shall be inserted, anyways reflecting on the Clergy or Government, and nothing but what is innocently diverting." The notice adds that the *Courant* will welcome "any short Piece" on either side of the inoculation question if it contains no "malicious Reflections." This time the *Courant* and its printer avoided legal trouble, but Franklin would not long remain immune from official action against him.

Once we modern readers make our way through the *Courant*'s early exchanges with Campbell, Musgrave, and Walter and reach the point where we can take for granted the voluminous essays on inoculation that dominated the paper for the first ten months of its life, we can begin to reach some generalizations about the *Courant* as a newspaper rather than as an episode in the political life of eighteenth-century Boston.

The *Courant* differed dramatically from its competitors in that it almost never began with the news. In the important left-hand column of page one, where Checkley's introductory essay led the first number of the paper, there usually appeared either a sprightly article from one of the London literary journals or, still more frequently, a piece of prose or verse composed by Franklin or another member of the club. These were often disguised as letters to the printer or "author," but we know from Benjamin Franklin's annotations that for at least the first forty-five numbers, "letters" of this kind were all either inside productions or from correspondents known to the publisher.[20] The "leading article," to use a term introduced in British newspaper circles early in the nineteenth century, generally occupied approximately the entire left-hand column, sometimes falling slightly short, more often extending a few inches into the right column. Here the authors discussed a wide range of subjects from politics and religion to personal problems and contemporary manners. When the featured essay was not about inoculation, it might deal with marriage, human foibles such as pride or flattery, political theory, the shortcomings of Musgrave as postmaster, the burning contemporary issues of episcopal as against presbyterian ordination and "regular" singing in church, the true date of Christmas, or speculations on the end of the world. Starting in April 1722, when Benjamin Franklin began his anonymous submissions to his brother, the Silence Dogood letters often appeared in the place of honor.[21] On January 21, 1723, the day the *Courant* began appearing over Benjamin's name because of an order of the General Court against James, the persona and format of the paper became more systematized by the creation of a fictional "club" headed by one "Dr. Janus." From then on, the leading article more often than not was disguised as a letter to Janus, frequently with a reply. Both the Dogood letters and the Janus column that in effect succeeded them carried the strong marks of the younger Franklin's now well-known admiration of the *Spectator*.[22]

The rest of the *Courant*'s content, again unlike that of its competitors, followed no particular pattern as to placement except that its relatively sparse advertising always came at the end, usually preceded immediately by the shipping list from the Boston custom house. Most numbers carried news from both home and abroad, following the conventional order in placing reports from remote places before those closer to home, and the Boston news usually, though not always, last. News from Britain as well as from other places in Europe appeared under the heading "Foreign Affairs," an indication of a distinctly American self-consciousness that was not so evident in either the *News-Letter* or the *Gazette*.

We should stop for a moment to consider the *Courant*'s self-conscious Americanism, which may seem at first glance to be incompatible with the growing "anglicization" of the American press that I am also suggesting. However, the crudest and most thoroughly "provincial" way for an American publisher to imitate the English model was simply to copy content, as both the *News-Letter* and the *Gazette* had been doing. Thus the Boston newspapers to date—Bradford's *American Weekly Mercury* had been a little freer with original material—had, by reporting the same news that had appeared in the metropolitan press but for the benefit of a far different audience, performed a different function with respect to its own community than the newspapers of London. Franklin and his associates, by contrast, strove to produce a paper that served much the same function for Boston that the livelier English journals were serving for London by adapting contemporary English forms of writing to their local situation. This was at once a more sophisticated and a more accurate form of imitation.

The news content of the *Courant* was subordinated both in placement and in its allotted space to material of other kinds. Its placement was unpredictable; sometimes it would begin on page one immediately after the leading article, but just as often a letter, piece of verse, whimsical article, or bogus announcement or advertisement would take precedence.

There was no attempt like Campbell's to present the news systematically; Franklin simply picked from the London prints whatever seemed timely, interesting, or amusing, and developed ties with like-minded correspondents who sent him engaging reports from around New England.

In the *Courant* for December 25, 1721, a letter from Saybrook, Connecticut, includes a paragraph of news about a case of arson and an accidental death but begins with the writer's introduction of himself and his announcement that he will begin a correspondence because "The political and humorous Letters of your Correspondents, with which you entertain us in these Parts, [have] sufficiently recommended your paper to us." Franklin may not have had to do much active solicitation of newsletters; it appears rather that many towns in the region had small but receptive audiences for the *Courant*'s form of journalism, including in each case a local wag or aspiring writer who was only too eager to see his own prose in such a notorious and clever journal without being asked or paid. The volunteer could be confident of a welcome for his contributions, provided they passed muster, because of Franklin's standing invitation for letters.

The correspondent from New London had a good eye and ear for the sort of situation and language that made for an especially acceptable *Courant* news item. He may have been inspired by the piece that Franklin picked out of one of the London newspapers for the number of November 27, 1721:

> *London, Aug. 19*. On Monday Night last a little Fellow that turns the Wheel at a Razor-Grinders in Butcher-Row, eat up at one time a Leg of Mutton, weighing about eight Pounds, and afterwards, to make up his Meal, he eat about half a Pound of Candles.
>
> Some days before, the same little Cormorant eat two Dozen of Cucumers, Rine and all, for his Breakfast, to the great Mortification of the Gentleman-Taylors in that Neighbourhood.
>
> We hear he hath likewise undertaken to eat a roasted Cat or two, with a Dozen of fry'd Mice set round to garnish the Dish, and other proper Sauce.

The provinces, as the *Courant* reported two weeks later, could do the London razor-grinder one better when it came to bizarre behavior. Franklin had been quoting from a letter from New London giving an uncomplimentary account of the life of a Baptist minister named John Rogers, whose death the letter reported. Then came an abrupt change of subject:

> The same Letter adds, That a certain Man at Stonington (who has a Wife and several Children) lately castrated himself, which has occasion'd abundance of Waggish Talk among the looser Sort of the Female Tribe, who are so incensed against him, that some of them talk hotly of throwing Stones at him, if he lives to come abroad again. He is very much swell'd, but seems rejoyc'd at what he has done.[23]

Throughout 1722, the year the smallpox epidemic came to an end and the inoculation issue gradually ceased to dominate the *Courant*, there evolved a more highly developed pattern of correspondence. More and more of the paper's content took the form of droll letters, responses, and counter-responses. Though these were more often than not the production of Franklin's regulars, appearing over fictitious names such as Ann Careful, Anthony de Potsherd, Fanny Mournful, Will Coatless, Ben Treackle, and James Franklin's own favorite pseudonymn Timothy Turnstone, some were from anonymous outsiders. Benjamin Franklin was unable to identify, for example, the contributor who in the April 9, 1722, number described in detail the behavior of a "Female Debauchess" of the town who was often called to her window at night by a sequence of different admirers, each of whom she would loudly scold for an hour before finally letting him in. The purpose of the communication, in keeping with Franklin's announcement the previous January 29 that one purpose of the *Courant* was to "expose the Vices and Follies of Persons of all Ranks and Degrees, under feign'd Names," was to let the lady know "that her Actions are watched more narrowly than she may imagine" so that she will "give less Occasion for their being expos'd for the future."

This was also the ostensible purpose of a still more titillating letter on March 5, 1722. Benjamin Franklin attributed it to Captain Taylor, whose own reputation, it will be remembered, was somewhat sullied. It was this sort of gleeful exposure of organized debauchery (combined in this case with a sly suggestion of clerical negligence), though not the heavy-handed apology for doing it, that as much as anything linked the *Courant* with some of its London contemporaries:

> We have lately read some of your Papers, whereby we perceive that one great Intention of them is to detect Vice and Prophaneness; which is certainly very commendable, especially at such a time as this is, when Wickedness prevails among us, more than has ever been known: And that lewd and disorderly Persons may take Warning and reform (if they purpose to escape a *Grand-Jury Presentment*) is the Reason of our sending you this to publish in your next *Courant*. We have therefore thought it necessary to acquaint the town, that there is an House not an Hundred Doors from the *old South Church*, said to be kept by a very remarkable *British* Woman, who in the Summer Season sometimes makes her publick Appearance in a handsome Jacket, edg'd with a fashionable Gold Lace, wearing a monstrous hoop'd Petticoat and a black Hat with a Gold Edging. This *little Prude of Pleasure* would do well to advertise her Nocturnal Gallants (such as Lawyers, Sea-Officers, Journeyman Gentlemen, Merchants Apprentices, and the like) that they do not dance naked any more with young girls; and to give a very particular Admonition to Two or Three of the chief and most brazen fac'd of them, not to act over their loose Behaviour with herself, at her Window, on the Lord's Day in the time of Divine Service, in the Hearing if not in the Sight of the Minister.

Many of the *Courant*'s "letters" were designed specifically to provoke a clever response from the "Author" or one of his pseudonymous friends—a device that Benjamin Franklin did not forget during his *Pennsylvania Ga-*

zette days. Normally the reply came right after the original, as when Franklin responded to Ben Treackle's request for advice on a matter of love and to Will Coatless's feigned criticism of the *Courant*'s habit of describing particular persons "and point[ing] at them as it were with the Finger."[24] Both Ben and Will were in fact Nathaniel Gardner, one of the *Courant*'s most prolific and versatile writers.

Though the letter, often combined with editorial response, soon emerged as the Couranteers' favorite structural device for conveying their opinions, wit, and satire, they could call other forms into service as well. For example, the satirical advertisement (this was on page one):

ADVERTISEMENT

A very good second-hand Post-Master's Sword, never drawn but once; also a Case of Pistols, never discharg'd, to be sold by Vendue or Outcry about Three Months hence.[25]

Or the tongue-in-cheek announcement:

ADVERTISEMENT

Whereas several Persons sitting together in a Pew, in a Church at the south Part of Boston, for some Time past by their irregular singing, have considerably distirb'd that Part of Divine Service. This is to advertise them, that for the future they keep time with the rest of the Congregation, that so that Part of Worship may be the more decently perform'd.

JOHN HARMONY.[26]

Or the resolution of an imaginary assembly, or the ballad, or the bogus news item. But the favorite device by far was the letter.

The *Courant* passed through several distinct stages in its brief life. From its birth in August 1721 to about the middle of March 1722, when the smallpox scare abated, the paper was preoccupied by the inoculation issue. The first of the Dogood papers appeared on April 2, 1722, prompting the thought that young Benjamin saw his opportunity with the loss of the *Courant*'s first great cause and deliberately picked that moment to slip his first letter under the print shop door. The Silence Dogood letters lasted until December 3, 1722, overlapping during the second half of the year with James Franklin's protracted troubles with the province authorities. These troubles climaxed with his month-long imprisonment from early June to early July and culminated in an order of the General Court on January 16, 1723, prohibiting him from publishing the paper without the supervision of the province secretary. During this second and liveliest period of its life, April 1722 to January 1723, the *Courant*'s most conspicuous features were the *Spectator*-inspired productions of Mrs. Dogood and extensive discussions of provincial political controversies in the light of Whig theory.

The third brief period began on February 11, 1723, when the *Courant* announced that because of the order of the General Court, its publisher would henceforth be Benjamin Franklin, not James. This change marked the introduction of the Janus column, which now succeeded the Dogood letters as the paper's main literary vehicle, a somewhat more varied range of subjects, and a slightly—but only slightly—more cautious tone in its political criticism. It lasted through the end of September 1723, when Benjamin Franklin, tired of his brother's beatings and jealousy and armed with a disingenuous discharge of his apprenticeship with which the Franklins had planned to fool the authorities if Benjamin's proprietorship of the *Courant* were called into question, ran away.[27] Janus failed to appear in the *Courant* for three weeks following Benjamin's departure. When he was restored, it was plain that the spark, though not yet gone, had begun to dim.

The fourth period from October 1723 to June 1726, therefore, during which the paper continued to appear over Benjamin Franklin's name, was the time of the *Courant*'s gradual decline. The content remained varied and there were still occasional instances of very good writing. But original material became increasingly rare, the local news increasingly routine. The imagination and spirit so evident during the *Courant*'s first two years simply withered away.

The *Courant* began its life, according to Checkley's intemperate reply to Thomas Walter in the third number of the paper, with the "chief Design" of opposing inoculation. For that task, especially since it involved the attraction of using the anonymous medium of print as a weapon against the political and clerical establishment of the day, it was easy to attract an enthusiastic and even brilliant coterie of allies who had never before enjoyed an outlet for their wit and satire. It is easy to suppose, though the supposition contradicts Benjamin Franklin's fifty-year recollection of the matter, that James Franklin was in fact persuaded to start the newspaper by one or more of those allies. One thinks especially of the physician William Douglass, who at little risk to himself thereby gained the organ he needed to carry on what had become almost a personal fight against Boylston and the Mathers.

But even the early *Courant* was not an anti-inoculation organ exclusively. In the hands of James Franklin and his little club of contributors, it became a satire, not only on government and religion but also on newspapers themselves. With its fictitious letters and advertisements, its sometimes droll selection of the news, its mock-serious attention to trivial subjects, and its overall tone of literary buffoonery, the *Courant* in its early stages mocked the very genre that John Campbell, William Brooker, and Philip Musgrave had struggled so earnestly to establish for the benefit, so they believed, of Boston. Unlike, however, the *English Lucien*, which had been London's satirical and bawdy response to the first flurry of private newspapers in the 1690s, or the *Jesting Astrologer*, of a few years later (a possible source of some of Benjamin Franklin's later work), the *Courant* tempered its spoof with material that was intended to be taken seriously.[28]

As the paper matured and flourished through its post-smallpox stages in

1722 and 1723, it gave more and more evidence of striving to be an authentic local newspaper. This does not mean that it gave up on buffoonery, or that it began to devote a larger share of its space to news. But at the same time that it was diversifying its content and responding to legislative assaults with letters and essays on constitutional liberties during the second half of 1722, its small budget of news was directed more and more toward the affairs of town and province. The Dogood letters and their sequel, the Janus column, treated issues of general human, religious, and political interest, but the topic of the day often had specific application to some contemporary local concern. In the *Courant*, therefore, much more than in the *News-Letter* or *Gazette*, the Boston readership began to learn that a local newspaper was for reporting and discussing matters near at hand. The *Courant*'s adoption of the role of reporter and commentator on its own time and place constituted, however paradoxically, a far more faithful adherence to the best English journalistic models than the mere large-scale copying of British newspapers that still made up the main content of its two rivals.

It is, in fact, the diminishment of original and local material in the *Courant*'s waning years that marks its decline as a distinctive journal. Through 1724, the paper devoted much of its space to various aspects of the running quarrel between Congregationalists and the newly assertive apologists for Anglicanism in New England. This provided fodder for a good bit of provocative and publishable material, but aside from that and a protracted exchange on the relative advantages of city girls and country girls, the *Courant* was starting to give evidence that its creative energies had been exhausted. It is particularly shocking that thirteen straight numbers, from October 9, 1725, to January 1, 1726, were filled with the life of the recently executed English criminal Jonathan Wild. Sensational though that highly publicized life certainly was, and as interesting as it may have been to New England readers, Franklin's cast of writers in the prime of their original energy would never have thought of squandering so much of the *Courant*'s space over an entire quarter of a year to a narrative copied from England.

The last number of the *Courant* anyone has yet found, that of June 25, 1726, offers sad testimony that the end of the road had indeed been reached. There was no Janus column (there had been only seven since the first of the year), no letters, no Boston news except a single item on a drowning and several inches of shipping lists, and as usual only a tiny handful of advertisements. The paper led with a long extract from the proceedings of the Irish Parliament—this in the same journal that in 1722 had uproariously and repeatedly flailed Musgrave for giving so much space to similar proceedings from Carolina[29]—and filled the rest of its space with the texts of a petition and opposing advertisements from the *Daily Courant* over regulating elections in the City of London.

Either then or soon afterward, the Couranteers, out of energy, enthusiasm, imagination, and probably money, gave it up. James Franklin moved his printing business to Newport and founded the *Rhode-Island Gazette;* Benjamin by then was already about to end the London phase of his early career; William Douglass continued a conspicuous figure in Boston medicine and did some important historical and descriptive writing; and John Checkley continued his controversial career, eventually reaching his long-sought goal of entering Anglican orders.[30] Most of the other Couranteers vanished from the record.

The *Courant's* demise was as quiet and decisive as its brief appearance was brilliant. The creativity of its producers could not be long sustained, but they had shown the way to a new kind of journalism. The literary fashions of contemporary England had been blended with the more utilitarian functions of a newspaper and harnessed to the social and political concerns of a particular provincial community. Others would soon follow where the *Courant* had led.[31]

Chapter 7

"A Fine Taste for Good Sense and Polite Learning": The Literary Newspaper, 1727–1735

"Politeness" Comes to Boston

The *New-England Courant*, boisterous and short-lived, gave to the printed discourse of the 1720s a temper and a method that was new to British America. Besides taking on an audacious political role and transforming the public sphere in the process, it introduced its audience to a locally produced periodical literature.

At the end of the decade the literary newspaper came of age, joining the very "establishment" against which the *Courant* had spent its brief career in opposition. The new representatives of this genre, the *New-England Weekly Journal* and the *Weekly Rehearsal*, came far closer than the *Courant* to replicating in general nature and tenor, though never in quality, the much-admired work of earlier English journalists. This was, however, only a brief stage in the movement toward the relatively standardized newspaper model that would emerge by about 1740.

The new cultural forces at work in the Boston of the 1730s are glimpsed in the efforts of a visiting bookseller from London to sell his wares by flattery. Like John Dunton, who had come to sell English books to the colonials back in 1688, Richard Fry set up shop for a time in the New England capital with a stock of books and stationery items. Moving in with fellow English émigré Thomas Fleet, who from his shop in Cornhill would soon be printing Jeremiah Gridley's *Weekly Rehearsal*, Fry began supplementing his other activities by underwriting American editions of contemporary English prose and poetry and offering them for sale at Fleet's print shop.

"For the pleasing entertainment of the Polite part of Mankind," Fry announced in two Boston newspapers in the spring of 1732, "I have Printed the most Beautiful Poems of Mr. Stephen Duck, the famous Wiltshire-Poet: It is a full demonstration to me that the People of New-England, having a fine taste for Good Sense & Polite Learning, having already Sold 1200 of these Poems."[1] The following month Fry applied the same sales strategy to a far more ambitious undertaking, a subscription edition of *The Spectator*. Fry's announcement of the *Spectator* project appealed directly to the cultivated American reader's pride in his—and her—own learning and public spirit:

> It will be needless to acquaint the Learned & polite part, that nothing more demonstrates the fine Genius of a Country, than to have the curious Art of printing brought to perfection. . . . I dont doubt but every Gentleman that is a true Lover of his Country will Subscribe, and I justly flatter ny self I shall have a number of Lady's Subscribers, the Authors of these Books have always been justly esteemed among them.[2]

Fry's proposed American edition of *The Spectator* never materialized, though Thomas Cox, another London bookseller who came to Boston, imported an edition of *London Magazine* for his American customers later in 1732, and by 1734 was offering English volumes of both *The Spectator* and *The Tatler*.[3]

The Augustan attachment to the adjective "polite" did not signify primarily an interest in good manners, except by extension. The main use of the word in the eighteenth century, by which time it had moved beyond its earlier literal meaning of polished or smooth in the physical sense, was in connection with artistic or intellectual pursuits, especially literature. The "polite" literature of the period, says the *Oxford English Dictionary*, was "polished, refined, elegant; correct, scholarly, exhibiting a refined taste." By the early eighteenth century, the adjective had also become applied to certain fields of study. "Polite learning," as understood by Addison, had the same meaning as "liberal education"—learning, that is, appropriate to gentlemen. In the words of a French contemporary, translated for an English audience, this meant primarily "Morality, Politicks, and the Knowledge of good Literature."[4] Politeness, in short, was an ideal explicitly at odds with the "plain style" of writing, preaching, and illustrating professed and practiced by several generations of New England Puritans.

Fry may have misjudged the number of American buyers who could pay the very handsome price of three pounds in these cash-short times, but his flattery of American urban tastes was grounded in firm evidence. Under John Leverett, its first non-clerical president, Harvard College had moved between 1708 and 1724 toward a concern for producing cultivated scholars, physicians, and merchants as well as Congregational ministers. In 1721 its students began producing the first American college periodical, *The Telltale*, and a club of pious but urbane undergraduates met thrice weekly to "read members' poems, and indulge in learned conversation, pipes, tobacco, and beer."[5] In 1723 Benjamin Colman, pastor of the Brattle Street Church, gathered in 1699 on eighteenth- rather than seventeenth-century principles, aimed at a symbolic burial of much of the intellectual baggage of the old century in his sermon on the death of Increase Mather, *The Prophet's Death Lamented and Improved.*[6] John Smibert brought professional painting from London to Boston in 1729, and the next year, to the delight of his new fellow townsmen, held America's first art exhibition. Mather Byles's poetic tribute in the *Gazette*, "To Mr. Smibert, on the Sight of His Pictures," introduced art criticism to Boston. Before the artist's arrival, wrote the twenty-three-year-old Byles, "Solid, and grave, and plain the Country stood,/ Inelegant, and rigorously good."

That had now changed ("The tuneful Nine begin to touch the Lyre")[7] and was continuing to change. By the 1740s, four American publishers would be testing the provincial market with magazines in imitation of the English model. None of them lasted long, but the most essential functions of the magazine were already being served by the newspaper. In fact the most persuasive evidence of all that Bostonians, at least, were acquiring a "taste for good sense and polite learning" was the flourishing in the 1720s and 1730s of a specialized kind of newspaper, the kind represented by the *New-England Courant*, the *New-England Weekly Journal*, and the *Weekly Rehearsal*.

The distinguishing features of this genre were not confined to Boston. William Parks's first incarnation of the *Maryland Gazette* began its life in 1728 and 1729 by devoting a huge proportion of space to essays on such topics as reading for women, philosophical doubting, poetry and painting, the dangers to religion, and the European balance of power.[8] When Thomas Whitmarsh started the *South-Carolina Gazette* in January 1732, he treated his readers in verse to a *Spectator*-like disclosure, signed "Philo-Carolinensis," of his own character and predilections.[9] But it was only in Boston, with its oversupply of printers, a tradition of newspaper competition already in place, and at least the rudiments of an actual literary community, that produced journals sufficiently specialized to be considered a truly distinct genre.

Beginning the *New-England Weekly Journal*, 1727–1741

In 1720, Philip Musgrave took over the post office and the *Boston Gazette*, promptly fired James Franklin as printer, and replaced him with Samuel Kneeland. Just a year later, James Franklin started his own newspaper, the *New-England Courant*. In 1727, probably by an agreement within the

Green family and an arrangement with the new postmaster Henry Marshall, Bartholomew Green, Jr., took over the printing of the *Gazette* from Kneeland, who soon started his own newspaper, the *New-England Weekly Journal*.[10]

It was fitting that Franklin's young contemporary and former rival, Samuel Kneeland, should now succeed him as publisher of Boston's only literary journal, just as he had succeeded him seven years earlier as printer of the *Gazette*. At thirty, he was still among the youngest master printers in Boston. He had served his apprenticeship under his uncle, the elder Bartholomew Green, but he had been in business on his own since 1718.

Kneeland's main clientele came from precisely those segments of provincial society from which Franklin and his friends had been most alienated. Early in the smallpox epidemic Kneeland had printed a pro-inoculation broadside by Increase Mather. He had already printed or published most of the thirty-five works of Cotton Mather that he would print over Mather's lifetime, and since 1722 he had shared with his former master the lucrative contract as official printer to the House of Representatives. He had printed an edition of the *Bay Psalm Book*, and with his younger partner Timothy Green II, would soon add to his orthodox credentials by being entrusted with three further editions of the psalm book, an edition of the Westminster Confession, two editions of the Shorter Catechism, and many works of the pro-revival side of the Great Awakening. These would include some sermons and journals of George Whitefield, the younger Thomas Prince's *Christian History*, and fifteen of the most important works of Jonathan Edwards. All this, of course, was—or would later be—in addition to his record as printer of the *Boston Gazette* under Philip Musgrave and Thomas Lewis.[11]

Kneeland was the nominal publisher of the *Weekly Journal*, but was not nearly as close to it as James Franklin had been to the *Courant*. Four months after the paper started, in fact, Kneeland took young Timothy Green as his partner and began to devote most of his own energies to a bookshop in nearby King Street, leaving Green in charge of the Queen Street printing office where the *Journal* was produced.[12] The editorial functions of the newspaper were mostly in the hands of an informal club of writers. The *Journal's* literati, however, were a far cry from the now-defunct Couranteers. No one could possibly have conceived of labeling them, as Campbell had labeled Franklin's group, a "Hell-Fire Club."[13]

Isaiah Thomas, whose authority in such matters one must at least begin by presuming, names three men as the main editorial influences on the *Journal*: Mather Byles, Samuel Danforth, and Thomas Prince. All three were linked with the very causes, factions, and social circles that the *Courant* had attacked and satirized. Two other men, both named Adams, have since been identified as the authors, with Byles, of the "Proteus Echo" pieces that were the dominant feature of the *Journal* during its first year.

Byles was a Mather in much more than his baptismal name. His father, a respectable but not very prosperous saddle maker in Boston's North End, had died when the child was less than a year old. His mother, the second daughter of Increase Mather, was left alone in charge not only of her own infant but of several step-children as well. Increase Mather had taken a particular interest in this talented grandson, whom he decided should be educated for the ministry, and it had fallen to Cotton Mather to carry out his father's wishes in this respect. The relationship between Byles and his uncle and near neighbor was close to that between son and father. Byles was only twenty in 1727, having finished Harvard two years before, and thus was not yet ready for ordination. Instead of filling the years between college and pulpit in the usual role of schoolmaster, he wrote voluminous verse, corresponded with the great English hymnist Isaac Watts and (less successfully) with his grand poetic hero Alexander Pope, and helped start up the *Weekly Journal*, of which he was probably the prime instigator.[14]

"Judge Danforth," as he was called by Isaiah Thomas and all his copiers,[15] was Samuel Danforth, the thirty-year-old schoolmaster of Cambridge and future representative, province councilor, and chief justice of the Middlesex County court of common pleas. A member of a conspicuous ministerial family, Danforth may have become friendly with Byles during the younger man's undergraduate days by virtue of the Cambridge schoolmaster's close association with Harvard. Byles could also have taken an interest in the help that Danforth was giving Thomas Prince in compiling the materials that would later be used in *The Chronological History of New-England*, and certainly was linked to him by the bond of the *Courant*'s disfavor, since in 1721 Danforth had submitted to Boylston's inoculation.[16]

Byles and Danforth, reported Thomas, were the "principal editors" of the *Weekly Journal* and "often corrected the press"—normally a responsibility of the printer. He added that Thomas Prince "was supposed to have taken an active part in the publication of this paper, and for a time to have assisted in correcting the press."[17]

Prince's association with the *Weekly Journal* would have been natural. Kneeland was a member of Old South Church, where Prince began his lifelong pastorate in 1718. Prince was probably the most scholarly and literary person in Boston next to Cotton Mather, and certainly one of the most anglicized. He was already busy accumulating his huge library and perhaps starting to write his two-volume providential history of New England. He had been well introduced to London's most fashionable literary modes during eight years of travel in England, from which he had returned in 1717 splendidly bewigged and boasting that many a cultivated native-born Englishman had mistaken him from his accent for one of their own.[18] His scholarly association with Danforth, his friendship with Byles, and his parish connection with Kneeland were enough to make him an obvious partner in the enterprise. Moreover, his factional allegiance was clear. In 1721 he had been one of the six signatories of the clerical letter in the *Gazette* that had helped to define the sides in the inoculation controversy. In 1727 he was still identified so closely in theology, sentiment, and style with his counterpart at North Church that Perry Miller did not hesitate to count him among the "Matherians."[19]

The likelihood that Prince was in fact one of the *Journal's* three original editors gains force when one surveys the paper's opening statement on March 20, 1727. Obviously some "Matherian" historian had a hand in it. After promising that the *Journal* would record *"with fidelity and Method . . . a Collection of the most Remarkable Occurrences of* Europe . . . ,*"* the unsigned prospectus turned its attention to domestic affairs. Correspondents, identified as *"the most knowing and ingenious Gentlemen in the several noted Towns in this and the Neighbour-Provinces"* (meaning, one supposes, some of New England's most conspicuous Congregational ministers), were well in the process of being recruited. Their task was to *"Collect and send what may be Remarkable in their Town or Towns adjacent worthy of the Publick View; whether of Remarkable Judgments, or Singular Mercies, more private or publick; Preservations & Deliverances by Sea or Land."* These would be published *"together with some other pieces of History of our own, &c. that may be profitable & entertaining both to the Christian and Historian."*[20]

Remarkable judgments, singular mercies, and preservations and deliverances, of course, were the stuff of providential history, in which New England intellectuals specialized and of which Prince's *Chronological History of New-England*, published in 1736 and 1755, would be the best full-blown example after *Magnalia Christi Americana.* Could Prince perhaps have seen the *Journal's* system of correspondence as part of his own collection effort? In any case, the *New-England Weekly Journal*, the second newspaper in America to incorporate the features of a literary journal, was the first such publication in the English-speaking world with an express intent to collect providential history. Fortunately for the paper's plan, its correspondents and writers had the best possible material for such a purpose before the year was out—the New England earthquake of October 29, 1727.

The *Weekly Journal*, however, blended its Puritanism with "politeness." Besides anticipating the publication of remarkable judgments and singular mercies, the *Journal's* maiden number promised entertainment more in line with the Augustan values of contemporary England. This part of the prospectus announced that "a Select number of Gentlemen, who have had the happiness of a liberal Education, and some of them considerably improv'd by their Travels into distant Countries; are now concerting some regular schemes for the entertainment of the ingenious Reader, and the Encouragement of Wit & Politeness; and may in a very short time, open upon the Public in a variety of pleasing and profitable Speculations."[21]

In one such "Speculation" several months later, one of the *Journal's* gentlemen essayists addressed explicitly the compatibility between Christianity and a polished and pleasing human character. "There is no Notion more false," he began, "than that which some have taken up, that Religion is inconsistent with a Gentleman." Taking aim at a lingering roughness among a remaining few of the more serious professors of New England religion, the *Journal* urged Christians not to scare off unbelievers with "a dull sordid Temper" or by being "scrupulous about the most innocent and indifferent things," but to attract the lukewarm and the doubtful to the faith by cultivating the social graces. "All the World," wrote the essayist, "is charmed with a Gentleman who at the same time that he is religious, is also complaisant and obliging. . . ." He contrasted the present state of manners with an earlier situation, much as Mather Byles, in three years' time, would contrast the cultural eras in New England before and after the coming of Smibert. "This Age is too polite," he wrote, "to bear the same Ill-manners and Roughness as the former. Then a Man was thought the more Religious for being a Clown, and very honest because he used no Ceremony but downright plain dealing. But now the world cannot endure the Absurdity to see a Man behave himself as if he were under the Reign of Queen *Elizabeth*. Refusal to conform to "the innocent customs of the times in which we live" demonstrates "a high Degree of Pride and affectation" and "a Meanness of Soul, which it is impossible should take place in a Man of generous and enlarged Sentiments."[22]

The author of this particular piece evidently was John Adams, Byles's slightly older fellow poet who was just then beginning a brief and unsuccessful pastorate in Newport.[23] The essay's theme, however, the relationship between gentility and Christianity, was a central concern of the writers of the *Journal*, especially young Mather Byles. Indeed, the theme of his Master's essay, submitted to Harvard in 1728, was that "polite literature is an ornament to a theologian."[24] Just as the third Earl of Shaftesbury, according to one recent interpretation, was joining to "politeness" the classical ideal of civic virtue, Mather Byles and his associates were joining "politeness" to Puritan piety.[25]

About the same time, early in the life of the paper, Byles opened his long correspondence with Isaac Watts by sending him copies of the *Journal* containing some of his poems and essays. Watts's first reply that is still on record was dated November 7, 1728, and sounded a note that persisted until the end of their exchange in 1742. "May your Soul grow like his [Cotton Mather's] in every Grace and Zeal for the honor of Christ in Love to souls & in pious conversation & Devout temper," wrote the great man to his devotee, and added: "May your politer writings as much edify the age wherein you live & do equall honor to the religion of Jesus!" A few months later, Watts reinforced his message, apparently concerned that the nephew of Cotton Mather might be letting poetry replace rather than serve religion: "May New England flourish in polite Learning but let her not decay in Strict religion lest her chief Glory vanish! . . . Poesy & polite writing which seem to be your darling Studys may Contribute much to encourage the passions on the side of Vertue & Piety."[26]

The time would come when an ordained and possibly more pious Mather Byles would explicitly abandon "poesy" for the serious work of the pulpit. For the moment, however, it was the *New-England Weekly Journal*, with its attempt to merge New England piety with "politeness," that was commanding his chief attention.

The *Journal's* "Proteus Echo," an American Spectator

During the *Journal's* first twelve months, the chief vehicle for the literary speculations of Byles and his fellow writers was a weekly essay over the name of "Proteus Echo." Like the *Courant's* Janus, Proteus Echo almost always led the paper, but his "lucubrations," as he called them in imitation of his English models, were usually longer. Janus and Silence Dogood had been features of the *Courant*, but they had not dominated it. Proteus Echo was more like Mr. Spectator or the *Tatler's* Isaac Bickerstaff in that for twelve months he served as the voice of his paper; all other content was subsidiary. A Proteus Echo piece commonly occupied all of page one of the *Journal* and often more; when the *Journal* had four pages, Proteus Echo usually took two of them. The essays, generally between 1000 and 2000 words, were about the same length as the *Spectator's* whereas the comparable features of the *Courant*, because of the necessary economies of space, had usually been much shorter.

On April 10, 1727, the *Weekly Journal's* fourth Monday,[27] Bostonians were suffered to read yet another Addisonian introduction to a series of essays, the third such imitation the town had seen in six years. Proteus Echo, however, was far more faithful to his model than either John Checkley or Benjamin Franklin's Silence Dogood had been, especially in the first few lines. Mr. Spectator had begun, "I have observed, that a reader seldom peruses a book with pleasure, till he knows whether the writer of it. . . ." Proteus, acknowledging his debt at the outset without naming his source, used some of the same words: "An ingenious Author has observed, that a Reader seldom peruses a Book with Pleasure, 'till he has a tolerable Notion of the Physiognomy of the Author, the Year of his Birth, & his Manner of living, with several other Particulars of the like Nature, very necessary to the right understanding of his works." The significance of the pseudonym becomes apparent during the course of the opening essay when the writer describes his childhood ability to "imitate any thing that I saw or heard." With his protean ability to assume any appearance or character, he now intends "frequently to write in Quality of the Imitator." Later he refers to "an ingenious Author [obviously the Spectator] whom I am now imitating."

The second essay in the series, on April 17, continues the almost literal emulation of his model by describing, just as Richard Steele had done after

Addison's opening number sixteen years before, the various members of the fictional "Society" in which the author kept frequent company.[28] Subsequent entries, usually in the form of exchanges of letters between Proteus and correspondents with names such as Will Pedant and Jack Sneer, repeatedly make comparisons between *The Spectator*, *The Tatler*, and *The Guardian* and Boston's "Imitator."[29]

The subjects of Proteus Echo's essays resembled those of the British writers who served as his model: the manners and morals of the day, human virtues and errors, and speculations about religion, philosophy, and the natural world. If only because just fifty-two of the essays ever saw print, however, the variety was not nearly as rich.

Nor was the wit quite as elegant. The "Jack Sneer" letter that occupies the bulk of the twenty-eighth Proteus Echo column purports to describe the members and practices of a "Laughing Club" at the American Cambridge, more reminiscent, perhaps, of the *Spectator*'s Oxford-based "Ugly Club" than of any of the handful of other antecedents that the letter actually names. But as in an earlier Proteus essay in which by way of criticism a shoemaker, for example, hopes that each page of the *Journal* may be its "last," the chief humorous device here is a series of heavy-handed puns: "It requires Art to manage this *ticklish* Affair with a proper Dexterity: for which reason, that I might proceed with some Method, I should inform you First of all, whence our Society took Its Origin; or, in other words, by what lucky Chance we became *shaken* together." The club's president, "Mr. *Gorgon Grin*, . . . has been frequently heard to compare himself to the Planet *Jupiter*, and our Club he calls the circum-*jovial* Satellites."[30]

Though the Proteus Echo writers strove for a light touch and occasionally achieved a humorous turn of phrase, there was nothing here remotely like the sprightly young comic genius of Benjamin Franklin that had produced some truly hilarious passages in a few of the *Courant*'s better Dogood letters. These writers also lacked Franklin's capacity, or inclination, to domesticate the essay form. Instead of adapting the techniques of *Spectator* to an American setting, Proteus Echo more usually paraphrased his English model without much alteration of theme or substance. The tenth essay, for example, discusses "Dick Grub-street," the personification of the London hack writer, in terms of "Songs, Lampoons, with Pieces of Bawdry and Ribaldry," and of political essays "in the Form of News-Papers, Gazettes, Mercuries, Flying-Posts, Examiners, Observators, &c., which have, by a benumming kind of magick, lull'd the Publick asleep, and made the whole Nation a sort of reading Drones." Even more inappropriate for a Boston audience, if possible, is the essay's association of its subject with the theater, still outlawed in the Puritan capital and which only a tiny fraction of the *Journal*'s audience at best could ever have experienced. "His Plays," wrote John Adams in this particular piece, "have very frequently been clapt upon the Stage, and as often, to his great mortification, hissed off."[31] When sixteen-year-old Benjamin Franklin had undertaken a similar topic just five years earlier, it had been in the form of Mrs. Dogood's incomparable "Receipt to Make a New England Funeral Elegy."[32]

Proteus Echo did show some originality in two respects. One was in harnessing the essay form to the religious norms of the time and place. The other was in the occasional topicality of his essays. Unlike the Addisonian model, the writings of Proteus Echo often reflected specific local current events. Not exactly *comments* on the news, these occasional topical essays, usually reflections upon some grand theme such as death or eternity, were nevertheless *prompted* by the news; if not "editorials" in the modern sense, they were nevertheless brief topical sermons in print, reflecting both the training of the *Journal's* principal contributors and the paper's general tone of polite Puritanism.

Byles's reflections on death in the seventeenth Proteus Echo essay, for example, were prompted by the mysterious and widely discussed suffocation of two young men who had been lowered into a well on July 19, 1727. A running scientific speculation on the cause of the tragedy, copied in New York, occupied much *Journal* print for three weeks following the original report. The Proteus Echo entry, on the other hand, reflected on the religious and philosophical lessons to be learned from contemplating this and other instances of sudden death. Though the essay is much concerned with divine providence, it differs from the traditional New England sermon in its occasional classical and historical allusions and in the complete absence of specific citations of Scripture. Though it is not lacking in orthodoxy, its language is elegant rather than plain, its deity benevolent rather than stern, the future a promise rather than a threat:

> I know of but one Way to arm my self against the Terrors of Dying, and that is, by securing the Friendship and Protection of the Being who maintains my Breath. . . . not Doubting but He will support me in the last Agonies of Nature, and give me to see Everlasting Glory dawn behind the Evening of my Present Life.

Despite allusions in the piece to the Boston event that inspired it, the author takes pains to maintain the fiction that Proteus Echo is an *English* rather than an American author. Referring to another instance of unexpected death from an apparently innocent cause, that of a young English noblewoman who had bled to death from the prick of a needle, the essayist writes, "I have often beheld her Statue in *Westminster Abbey*, in which is emblematically intimated the Manner of her dying." Byles, who never in his life got within three thousand miles of Westminster Abbey, then goes on to describe the statue and its setting in detail.[33]

Another such essay and accompanying poem, this time by Matthew Adams, the uncle of John, was provoked by unusually violent lightning storms. Adams's reflections on instances of phenomenal lightning damage culminate in contemplations in prose and verse on the Last Judgment, when the earth, "being fired perhaps by the Tail of some blazing Comet," will be burned up according to Biblical prophecy.[34] The death of George I likewise prompted responses from Proteus, largely in the form of Byles's and Matthew Adams's poetry,[35] but no event of the *Weekly Journal*'s brief era produced more sustained attention than the earthquake of October 29, 1727.

Both the *News-Letter* and the *Gazette* reported it in due course as a significant item of Boston news, the *News-Letter* six days after the event and the *Gazette* a full week later than it might have because the earthquake had occurred late Sunday evening and Henry Marshall's printer, Bartholomew Green, Jr., did not stop to insert this news before running off the paper Monday morning.[36] The *Journal*, by contrast, managed to include a fairly substantial report, complete with spiritually edifying comment, in its Boston news on October 30:

> Last Night and this Morning we have in this Place felt several Shocks of an Earthquake, but that which was the first (as is suppos'd) was the most surprizing and awful, which was about three quarters of an hour after Ten a Clock, the Noise was like hard Thunder, which lasted for the space of about two Minutes, when the Earth trembled and shook to a very great degree, the Houses rock'd as if they would have fallen down, and many of the Inhabitants being amaz'd ran out into the Streets, and there seem'd to unite the Cry, *Lord our Flesh trembleth for fear of thee, and we are afraid of thy Judgments.* But to make just and religious Improvement of this unexpected and unusual Event of Providence among us in these Parts, we shall doubtless be instructed by the Philosopher and the Divine.[37]

Proteus Echo's reflections on the event, penned by John Adams, came the very next Monday, in the same November 6 number that contained Mather Byles's poem *The God of Tempest* (later to be reprinted in broadside on the occasion of an earthquake in 1755),[38] an appeal to *"The Rev Ministers, and especially the Correspondents with the Publisher of this Paper"* to contribute from around the region to a *"compleat . . . History"* of the earthquake, and an advertisement for Kneeland's forthcoming pamphlet on the subject.[39] Adams's topic was fear, and his method of composition an instructive lesson in the construction of a topical essay of the period.

Though the occasion for the essay was the earthquake, Adams did not use that event as his "lead" or "handle" for the rest of the piece, as a modern writer almost certainly would if handed a similar assignment. Instead, he began, Spectator-like, by setting forth his topic, which according to the genre was usually some human quality, habit, foible, or emotion: "There is not any one Passion of the Mind which more distracts it, and throws it into greater Confusion than Fear."

The opening paragraph develops the idea of fear in general terms, ending with the maxim that "our Fear always rises in Proportion to the Worth and Excellence of what it is probable we shall part with." The second paragraph develops the implications of the maxim with which the first one ended, observing in due course that the most valuable and excellent thing that anyone has is his soul. A transitional sentence then contains the first explicit reference to the earthquake: "We may all then be able to judge into what uncommon Agitations of Mind the late unusual Convulsions of the Earth flung the Profligate and the Wicked." The third paragraph discusses that gloomy proposition at some length.

With the fourth paragraph, the train of thought that has been developed up to now undergoes a slight change in direction so as to include the effect of the earthquake on all minds, not just those of the manifestly guilty. It begins, "There is nothing so capable of surprizing and damping a humane Creature as *Earthquakes*." The fifth paragraph builds on the fourth by devoting itself wholly to the notion that from an earthquake there is no escape. "When the earth rumbles under us, and begins to wave and quiver, where shall we run for Refuge and Safety?" the topic sentence demands. The answer, of course, is nowhere. Adams's rhetoric suggests the method of the 139th Psalm: "If we ascend the Tops of Hills, the Earthquake is there. . . . If we imagine to fly to the Waters, Flames may belch out of the Sea . . . , or our Foundation may fail us before we can get thither." The paragraph concludes by implying a link between one theory of the cause of earthquakes and the doctrine of hell, so that the notion of helplessness achieves a cosmic level: "If it [the earthquake] be caused by Fires, which burn under us, and run in Rivers of Flame, which threaten to blaze out in the most dreaded Eruptions; it must fearfully suprize us to think how the outward Convex Earth which is our present Foundation, is only an Arch, which as it were hangs over a fiery Sea; and that if it should once cave in, we should fall into a Boiling and Sulphurious Lake."

The sixth paragraph is a brief one, further developing this theory of the earth's fiery interior that is held by "the best Modern Philosophers." This time the vision leads by implication to the Last Judgment, "when this large and spacious Arch which is stretch'd over the Hollow that is under it, shall descend down with a mighty Noise, and the waves of Fire breaking out, shall boil over."

The seventh paragraph of the essay, the last, concerns the antidote to fear, the Christian faith, by which alone "we can bear up amidst the Crush of a World trembling to a Dissolution." The earthquake will have proved a blessing if "the Vicious Part of my Countrymen would improve this unexpected Turn of Providence to their Benefit, and admire and pursue the Path of that Innocence which alone can compose the Soul in the general Shipwreck and Dissolution of Nature."

Though this tightly crafted essay contains not a single specific reference to Scripture and flows not from a text but from a *Spectator*-like proposition of the author's own devising, it follows in abbreviated form both the structure and function of a Puritan sermon. Adams's maxim at the end of the first paragraph occupies the place of the sermon's doctrine. The doctrine is then broken down to be discussed bit by bit until at last it is time for a summary ("What Heart at the Consideration of this, is not ready to melt away with Fear!") and then the "improvement," the application of the doctrine to the practical business of life.

Although the occasional use of a sermon-like format in response to particular current events is what sets off the Proteus Echo essays both from their English models and from the *Courant*'s literary pieces, it was not consistently used. The fifty-two writings of Proteus Echo in prose and verse are in fact quite varied in both form and subject. The last of the "lucubrations," contained Byles's veiled revelation of the three authors of the column, appeared in the *Weekly Journal* of April 1, 1728—just ten days before John Adams was ordained over a church in Newport, which may explain why this phase of the *Journal*'s literary history came to an end at this time.[40] The final entry was somewhat rambling, referring to the series now ending as "little Essays at the Advancement of Morality and Politeness among us," apologizing for small errors in construction and typography, rebuking the column's critics, and thanking its patrons. It ended with one of Byles's poems, "To a Young Lady," extolling the many charms of the "Belinda" who had left a silver pen with the printer as a gift for the author. Whether Byles's identity was known to his "fair Benefactress" is not clear, but the poem, of course, was written with the gift pen.

On that flirtatious note, worlds removed from trembling acknowledgments of the God of earthquakes, the versatile Proteus Echo made his exit.[41] Byles, however, continued to use the columns of the *Journal* for his own and others' poetry, and the paper maintained the effort to provide its reader with essays of "entertainment" or "improvement," usually in the same first-page location that had housed Proteus Echo. A publisher's announcement introducing an anecdote about the invention of the stocking loom, which headed the paper the week after Proteus's departure, made the *Journal*'s intention clear: "There are Measures concerting for rendring this Paper yet more universally esteemed, and useful, in which 'tis hop'd the Publick will be gratifi'd and by which those Gentlemen who desire to be improv'd in History, Philosophy, Poetry, &c. will be greatly advantaged. We will take the liberty at this time to insert the following Passage of History."[42]

Even without the help of Proteus Echo, whose essays apparently failed to inspire sufficient encouragement to support the bookseller Daniel Henchman's plan for a printed collection,[43] the *Journal* maintained its essential personality for a short while. The chief hand at the helm for a few years after 1728 was probably still that of young Mather Byles.

The *Weekly Journal* Transformed

The *Journal*, however, was becoming steadily less important in Byles's personal scheme of priorities as the new decade began and he approached his own middle twenties. He had stood at Cotton Mather's death bed in February 1728 to receive his uncle's last blessing.[44] That year he took his Harvard M.A. in course, the normal step prior to ordination. After failing twice to secure a pastoral appointment, he was ordained at the end of 1732 over the newly gathered Hollis Street Church, and in February 1734 was married in the Province House by Thomas Prince to Anna Noyes Gale, Governor Belcher's niece.[45]

There is a gradual but discernible change in the *Weekly Journal* over the few years after 1728 when Byles's attention was being directed increasingly elsewhere. At the beginning of 1729, the paper reinstituted a fairly regular essay, apparently by more than one author.[46] This series did not last, and even the poetry that had been so conspicuous a feature of the *Journal* during its earlier life was soon fading from its columns. By September 1731, Byles's Havard classmate Jeremiah Gridley must have thought the *Journal*'s literary content sufficiently thin and infrequent to risk filling the gap himself with his *Weekly Rehearsal*.

The gradual change in the *Journal* was real enough, but there is no parallel here with the last stage of the ebbing life of the *New-England Courant*. The *Journal*'s transformation was in no sense a decline. The paper continued to be a vigorous and attractive contributor to Boston's varied diet of print until Kneeland and Green merged it with the *Boston Gazette* in 1741. It significantly increased its editorial space by a change in format in 1733 without raising its annual subscription price of 16 shillings, and continued to carry a healthy budget of advertising throughout its life.

Through the thirties, however, the *Journal* came to look more like a printer's than a writer's paper. Original creative material came to be largely replaced by essays from English publications, transcripts of gubernatorial proclamations and legislative records, letters from readers on controversial topics such as the currency issue and the Whitefield revivals, and occasional polite essays submitted in the form of letters. The *Journal* also became much more likely now than in its first years to print European news in substantial quantity—sometimes, especially if a ship had just arrived, at the beginning of page one. Some numbers, on the other hand, contained no foreign news at all. In short, the *Journal*, after dropping its most distinctive literary feature, became an organ of much greater variety, though less originality, than it had been in the beginning. It moved away from the model of the *Courant* with which it had begun in 1727 and toward that of the *Gazette*.

The change is not surprising. It is clear both from internal evidence in the *Journal* and from what we know of the transitions in the life of Mather Byles around 1730 that Byles's role in the publication was diminished beginning soon after the Proteus Echo stage, which was the only period for which he accumulated his own annotated file of the paper.[47] It may eventually have ended altogether. No doubt Danforth and Prince maintained whatever editorial interest and print-shop tinkering they had carried on before, as perhaps did Byles himself, but this would certainly have been on the level of a hobby, very much peripheral to the main business of their lives. Without the continued active participation of a fully dedicated Byles or someone like him to meet the weekly publication commitment, no casual club of literati could maintain the responsibility of getting the paper out on time. There is no evidence that the brace of Adamses who had contributed Proteus Echo pieces retained any later connection with the *Journal* at all.

Therefore, whatever real responsibility for publication that Byles and his group had shared with Samuel Kneeland and Timothy Green shifted sometime around 1730 to the printers alone, primarily to Green, the junior partner. As that happened, the *Weekly Journal* began to shed some of the eccentricities of a predominantly literary newspaper and acquire what were coming to be the standardized characteristics of the better of the general provincial newspaper of the era. Green may well have continued to get occasional help and advice from one or more of the Byles-Danforth-Prince combination, but much of the content of the *Weekly Journal* in the 1730s clearly originated outside that little circle.

That content was lively, however, and often relevant to the presumed interests of Bostonians who might originally have subscribed to the paper because of its emphasis on polite learning and the improvement of morals. Between December 1732 and December 1733, for example, *Journal* readers would have found in the leading position a long essay and accompanying poem from the *London Magazine* on the invention of printing, a two-page collection of edifying biographies and dying words of the fourteen felons hanged on one unusually grand execution day in London, a political essay from the *Free Briton*, verses from the *South-Carolina Gazette* in praise of James Oglethorpe and his Georgia project, a short essay from London's *Universal Spectator* entitled "Prudent Lenity of Parents," a technically precise thirty-one-line poem in iambic pentameter by an anonymous New England mother on the death of her young child, and a gloomy letter from a local reader reflecting on the discouraging current state of the Earth. This last, the obvious contribution of a clergyman, sounded a bit like some of the religious pieces of old Proteus Echo: The "reasonable" response to the signs of decay that surround us is to "lay a good Foundation for the time to come, and to obtain a saving Interest" in God.[48]

By comparison with its competitors, the *Weekly Journal* could be extremely flexible in its use of space. While one number might be filled almost entirely with European news, another might devote nearly all of the paper to excerpts from the records of the Massachusetts Assembly, of which Kneeland and Green were the official printers.[49] Still others would contain a combination of relatively long articles or letters on some topic of current concern and a variety of hard news items from home and abroad.

If any of the three writers usually associated with the *Journal*'s founding continued to enjoy a significant influence over the paper throughout the

decade, it was the hand of Kneeland's pastor, Thomas Prince, that seems
most enduring. The single topic that consumed the most *Journal* type
during 1733 was the important legal controversy over whether ministerial
lands in Rhode Island's Narragansett country belonged by law to an Anglican or a Congregational minister. Surely it was Prince who used the
Journal on behalf of the cause, since the bulk of the long exposition of the
case that ran over four numbers of the paper in October consisted of
the texts of documents we know were in Prince's possession. The *Journal*
did print one Anglican rebuttal to the opening summary of the case, which
had concluded with an appeal for contributions to finance the Congregational side of the dispute, but by far the most space went to Prince's
lengthy and detailed reply to the rebuttal.[50]

While the *Journal* gave as much attention as its rivals to the currency
crisis between 1735 and 1740, and to the developing war with Spain and
France at the end of the decade, it far outdid the others in its pursuit of the
third hot topic of the day, religious revivalism. Even before George
Whitefield began his second American tour in 1739, the *Journal* rarely lost
an opportunity to copy reports of his English successes from the London
prints. Toward the end of 1739 and throughout 1740, during Whitefield's
journey through the northern colonies, the *Journal's* columns were rich
with letters and articles favoring the spiritual awakening and Whitefield's
revival of Calvinist doctrines.[51] Of all the ministers in Boston, none was
more committed to the Great Awakening than Thomas Prince; Mather
Byles, as far as we can tell, stood pretty much aloof from the controversies
it inspired.[52]

At the end of 1740—and not far from the end of the *Journal's* life—the
paper ran in the lead position, ahead even of a long letter opposing a land
bank, an anonymous bit of current providential history. Like a similar
piece late in 1733, and like the more pious of the old Proteus Echo essays,
this one drew a pointed religious message from the signs of the times. In
this case, the signs combined the recent fatal epidemic of "throat distemper" (diphtheria), to which the *Journal* had been paying occasional
attention since 1736, with more mundane acts of providence such as flood-
ing in the Connecticut Valley, coastal storms, and a damaging spell of wet
weather during the past summer and autumn. More specifically here than
in most of the earlier writings, these were signs of divine judgment, demanding revival and reform. The supporting texts were neither classical
allusions nor *Spectator*-like maxims, but quotations from the Bible. The
writer ended his brief diatribe to the once-chosen but now fallen people of
New England with the prophet Malachi's warning to the unfaithful priests
who had corrupted the covenant of Levi: "*If ye will not hear, and will not lay
it to Heart to give Glory to my Name, saith the Lord of Hosts, I will even send a
Curse upon you and curse your Blessings; yea, I have cursed them already, because ye
do not lay it to Heart.*"[53]

The polite Puritanism of Proteus Echo and the early *Weekly Journal* was now translated into a jeremiad, fully enlisted in the Great Awakening. The author's identity is not disclosed, but the themes are those of a Prince in these years, not a Byles.

From 1736 to the autumn of 1741, Kneeland and Green had the job of printing John Boydell's *Boston Gazette* as well as their own *Weekly Journal*. During these years, the printers doubtless welcomed all the help with the *Weekly Journal* that Prince and others could provide. The wonder is that the two papers managed to maintain their distinct characters even after Boydell's death in 1739 transferred the *Gazette*'s ownership to the inactive hands of his widow, Hannah.[54] This uncomfortable arrangement came to an end on October 20, 1741, when on the occasion of Hannah Boydell's death, the *Gazette* and *Journal* merged into one newspaper under the ownership of Kneeland and Green. The *Boston Gazette; or, Weekly Journal* retained the general appearance and numbering sequence of the *Gazette* and the Tuesday publication day of the *Journal*.[55] It became more newsy and less literary than either had been in the 1730s. The end of the *Weekly Journal* as a separate title also marked the end of a distinctly literary form of journalism in provincial America.

The Brief Flowering of the *Weekly Rehearsal*, 1731–1735

For a short time, another literary newspaper flourished alongside the *Weekly Journal*. Its experience drives home the lesson already contained in the brief histories of the *Courant* and the *Journal*: it was able to maintain its original character only as long as an amateur and part-time founder could sustain the enthusiasm and commitment necessary to keep the founding vision alive. The trend in newspaper publishing in Boston, in keeping with what had always been normal practice elsewhere in the provinces on both sides of the Atlantic, was toward printer-owned newspapers, and toward a rough standardization of the product. The town's three literary papers, like its postmasters' papers, turn out to have constituted a stage, influential as well as brief, in that evolution.

In September 1731, not long after the *Weekly Journal* had lost some of its original flavor, yet another aspiring young man of letters decided to enter the crowded arena of Boston newspaper publishing. To the *News-Letter*, *Gazette*, and *Weekly Journal* was now added the *Weekly Rehearsal*, edited and largely written by Jeremiah Gridley, usually called Jeremy. Like Mather Byles, Gridley had taken his first degree at Harvard in 1725, though he was five years Byles's senior, and like him had not yet settled into a permanent vocation. The M.A. awarded to him in 1727, a year before Byles earned one, had moved him not into the ministry but into secondary education; he served from then until 1734 as "usher," or assistant to Nathaniel Williams, master of Boston's South Grammar School. Eventually, after an abortive beginning at reading divinity and some travel in

England, Gridley would make his mark in Boston as a lawyer, and a very good one. He would rise, indeed, to the top of his profession as attorney general of the province. But in 1731, as with Byles only a few years earlier, Gridley's most compelling fascination was with the literary awakening of which the *Weekly Journal* had been a promising, but was now a faltering, expression.[56]

Gridley chose as his printer John Draper, who at twenty-nine was exactly Gridley's age and was then near the beginning of a long and exceptionally prolific printing career. He had learned the trade from his father-in-law, the senior Bartholomew Green, from whom Draper would shortly inherit both the family shop and the *Boston News-Letter*.[57] Just before that important transition at the end of 1732, Gridley would switch the printing and possibly part ownership of the *Rehearsal* to Thomas Fleet.

There is no surviving direct evidence that Gridley was in fact the *Rehearsal*'s founding publisher. We must take Isaiah Thomas's word for it.[58] Thomas, however, was a part of the Boston printing community while Gridley and his two printers were still alive, which by itself strength to his assertion. Our confidence is further strengthened by the unsigned publisher's announcement in the *Rehearsal*'s first number asking that letters and advertisements be sent to him at the South Grammer School, which is where Gridley was employed.

Gridley and Draper tried to set the *Rehearsal* off from its rivals visually by a vertical floral design that separated the two columns on each page, and by an italicized Latin quotation of several lines that often followed the title and the date line. These embellishments along with a varied assortment of decorative initial letters no doubt were intended to draw attention to the new journal's artistic character, but the most striking departure from conventional practice was in the title itself. The *Weekly Rehearsal* was the first provincial newspaper, British or American, not to include its place of publication (even "New England" or "American") in its title. Surely Gridley, like the undergraduate editors of Harvard's *Telltale* in his own college generation, chose his paper's name with the metropolitan literary journals in mind.

The publisher's unsigned address to his readers occupied all of the first page of the maiden number of September 27. For once, an aspiring Boston literary journalist managed such a statement without direct imitation of the *Spectator*. Here was no fictional personage like Janus or Proteus Echo, no elaborate construct detailing the writer's character and the identity of imaginary friends, and no strained attempts to follow some canonical genre. Gridley wrote in the first person without identifying himself, explicitly avoiding his motives in starting up his journal but setting forth in what a modern reader would judge to be far too many words the kind of paper he hoped the *Rehearsal* would be.

The subject matter of its essays would be without limit as long as they were "useful or entertaining," and there would be no editorial policy except to be governed by the rules of restraint that were embodied in the contemporary ideal of politeness. "The Nature of this Design," to use Gridley's words, "is confin'd then to no particular Argument, and in fact will be circumscrib'd by nothing, but Discretion, Duty and good Manners." But since it is beyond the capacity of almost anyone "in this knowing and polite Age" to entertain with complete originality, the *Rehearsal*, as its name implies, will "in the general Course . . . be derivative." The main source, it becomes clear, will be the classics: "The ancient are yet living, and many of these later Ages will forever live with them. They are too pure to displease, too numerous to fail us. And is it not impossible for an industrious Hand to give them a different Course?"

Gridley's opening essay invites contributions from his readers, but also promises that to consider the paper "only in the Essay-kind" is but half true. "For it is intended, to be a Narrative of whatever shall occur in Commerce in the Civil or Learned World as far as it deserves our Attention, and comes within Notice. It will be the Endeavour of the Publisher to procure the best Intelligence, and to digest it in the most suitable Method." In other words, it is to be half an essay journal and half a newspaper, though the news will apparently be selected and "digested" in such a way as to meet the diverse interests of his subscribers.[59] As it happened, the *Rehearsal* proved more true to the second part of Gridley's prospectus than to the first.

The intended format for a standard two-page number would devote the entire first page to a literary essay and the second to a selection of news and the *Rehearsal*'s quarter- to half-column of advertisements. Insofar as the length and nature of the page-one article allowed, it was often set in somewhat larger type than that used for the second page and composed with a decorative initial letter and sufficient white space to be relatively attractive. The second page, intended for material more prosaic and business-like, usually reflected that difference in its denser and less studied appearance.

The format, however, which remained fairly consistent through the *Rehearsal*'s first year, sometimes conveyed a false distinction between the actual contents of the two pages. There were indeed occasional essays, some perhaps by Gridley, some communicated by readers, and some copied from elsewhere. There was, for example, a nice piece on "conversation" on October 4, 1731, and another beginning the following week, communicated by "W.X.," discussing the "two Things that can reasonably employ the Cares of a wise Man," namely "the *Study of Virtue*" and "the *management of Life*." These more than nearly any succeeding page-one articles seem to meet Gridley's implied intention to adapt the enduring wisdom of the ancient writers to the "polite" world of the eighteenth century. But the *Rehearsal*'s primary strength turned out to be its selection of news, much of which was rich in what journalists of our own day call "human interest." This was true in many cases even of the distinctly non-

classical articles that were given the special typographical treatment reserved for page one. The leading article often, though not invariably,
emerged not as an essay of persuasion or reflection but as an extended news
report.

The most spectacular such instance in the *Rhearsal*'s first year was a
series of five page-one installments detailing the sensational seduction in
Toulon of an allegedly innocent young French woman by her Jesuit con-
fessor, Father Jean-Baptiste Girard, followed by an even more sensational
abortion and attempted cover-up. The series, complete with an element of
suspense from week to week, was well calculated to appeal to Puritan
prurience and to New England's still-throbbing terror of Rome, France,
and the Society of Jesus. Months after the concluding episode, the *Rehearsal* ran an update, also on page one, in the form of the young woman's
statement, printed by the French royal printer and evidently translated by
someone, in which she protested her innocence in the affair even though
her French judges apparently had convicted her of libeling Father Girard
and condemned her to death.[60] It was not, obviously, by accident that the
series was preceded by a two-installment account by a "Mahometan
Moore" of the Spanish Inquisition.[61]

But it was not just in the leading article that Gridley showed his talent at
selecting readable news with a special appeal to his Boston audience. He
devoted nearly a column, or not far from half of the second page of October 11, 1731, to the reported efforts of a Greek patriarch to subvert the
Eastern Church by returning it to the jurisdiction of Rome. On November
1, long excerpts from the previous July's *Political State* reported a rare
English view of the spring election in Massachusetts and the abortive first
attempt at a seditious libel trial of Richard Franklin, publisher of London's
popular anti-government paper, *The Craftsman*.[62] The next week, a long
article from an unnamed London paper detailed the circumstances of the
death of a boy who worked in a billiard room and the trial and partial
acquittal of the gentleman player who struck him with his cue. The jury
found the death accidental and convicted the attacker only of manslaugh-
ter, greatly to the applause of the sympathetic reporter who compiled the
account. The question at issue was whether the blow could have been
expected to cause death. Neither witnesses nor reporter ever suggested
that the boy ought not to have been hit at all.[63] The June 5, 1732, number
carried an extensive report from Vienna on vampires, "a sort of Prodigy
lately discovered in Hungary."

Jeremy Gridley's greatest influence on the *Rehearsal*, all the evidence
suggests, came during its first year, between September 1731 and August
1732, when Gridley switched printers from John Draper to Thomas Fleet.
There are ample clues that from the time Fleet began printing the *Rehearsal*
on August 21 to his actual purchase of the paper from Gridley the following March, the printer had a stronger hand in its production while
the founder's influence, or interest, was waning. Very likely, in fact,

judging by an announcement by the "Publishers" on August 28, Fleet assumed part ownership of the paper with the transfer of the printing contract.

The period of Gridley's most intense involvement came just after the time that the *Weekly Journal* had lost some of its original character as a literary journal. Proteus Echo had been dead more than three years, and the *Journal's* brief essay series that succeeded him had been abandoned. Gridley obviously was hoping to fill the gap with his neo-classical essays on the front page of the *Rehearsal.* He got off to a strong start, and in fact managed a short run of interesting speculative writings, some of which prompted responses from readers, between January and June 1732, but even less than Byles and his colleagues, or James Franklin and his colleagues before them, could he sustain a weekly schedule of creative writing. One biographer says Gridley was now beginning to devote his attention to the law, but a more recent version of his career has him staying at South Grammar School until 1734 and reading law some time after that, with a brief interest in the ministry and then a European voyage in the meantime.[64] Whatever else was going on in Gridley's life, the *Rehearsal* was becoming less a part of it. His brief fling with the *Rehearsal* venture, however, by no means cured him of his infatuation with periodical letters. In 1743 Gridley was hired to edit the first really successful magazine in America, *The American Magazine and Historical Chronical*, a Boston imitation of *London Magazine*, which lasted under Gridley's editorship until the end of 1746.[65]

One brief series of essays in the *Rehearsal* early in 1732 hints that part of Gridley's agenda may have been to provide a voice in opposition to the religious views often expressed in the *Weekly Journal*. A four-part philosophical discourse beginning January 31 presents a rationalistic view of the universe, debunking spirits and witches and deploring the "strange Propensity in Humane Nature to Prodigy, and whatever else causes Surprize and Astonishment, and to admire what they do not understand; we have immediate Recourse to Miracle, which solves all our Doubts, and gratifies our Pride, by accounting for our Ignorance."[66] Here is an explicit attack, it appears, upon New England providentialism, including the post-Newtonian version best articulated in Boston by Thomas Prince.

"Whensoever therefore we hear of, or see any surprizing Appearance or Events in Nature, which we cannot trace and connect to their immediate Causes," the first installment concludes, perhaps recalling the earthquake of 1727, "we are not to call in supernatural Powers, and Interest Heaven or Hell in the Solution to save our Credit. . . . We are not to measure the Works of God by our scanty Capacities."

Throughout the series, Gridley accepts the truth of Biblical revelation as well as the Newtonian universe and Lockean empiricism. In the next to last installment, he calls upon all three to support his attack upon a belief in witchcraft. As for demons,

Where are we commanded to believe that the Devil plays hide and seek here on Earth; that he is permitted to run up and down and divert himself, by seducing ignorant Men and Women; killing Pigs, or making them miscarry, entering into Cats, and making Noises, and playing Monkey Tricks in Church Yards and empty Houses, or any where else here on Earth but in empty Heads?

We know that he was cast headlong from heaven, is chain'd fast in the Regions of the Damned, and kept by the Power of the Almighty from doing Mischief to his Creatures; and to say the contrary, seems to me the highest Blasphemy against Heaven it self. . . .

I shall conclude by observing, that the Heathen Poets first invented these Stories, and the Heathen Priests stole them from them. . . .[67]

In this series and in a long letter from "P.N." urging a rational approach to religion, printed on July 17, the *Rehearsal* clearly was establishing itself as the local voice of "reason" as well as another voice of "politeness." Though no specific names were ever called on either side, this was a voice clearly in opposition to that of the spiritual and literal progeny of the Mathers that made itself heard in the *Weekly Journal*. Who, indeed, if not New England's most conspicuous and prolific interpreters of illustrious providences and prosecutors of witches were Gridley's "Heathen Priests"?

Gridley's outspoken rationalism, which in its mode of expression amounts also to a moderate revival of the anti-establishment message that had last appeared in the *Courant*, suggests that Gridley was deliberately seeking out a kindred mind when he engaged Thomas Fleet to print the *Rehearsal* and perhaps become a partner with him in August 1732. A friend of the Franklins and perhaps the most conspicuous printer left in Boston who was not a member of the Green clan, Fleet had been a contributor to the *Courant* and now must have relished the chance for a head-on rivalry with the Byles-Prince-Kneeland group that was associated with the *Weekly Journal*. Under Fleet's ownership, which began in March 1733, the *Rehearsal* and the *Boston Evening-Post*, which succeeded it, were among Boston's most consistent and articulate opponents of "enthusiasm" and the Great Awakening.

The Literary Journals: Metamorphosis and Legacy

By the spring of 1733, three of Boston's four newspapers—the *News-Letter*, the *Weekly Journal*, and the *Rehearsal*—were owned by their printers. The fourth, the *Gazette*, was still under the ownership and active guidance of Postmaster John Boydell. A fifth newspaper, Ellis Huske's *Weekly Post-Boy*, would soon join the ranks on the occasion of Huske's appointment in 1734 to what proved to be a twenty-year tenure as essentially an absentee postmaster. After 1741, when Kneeland and Green took over the *Gazette* upon Hannah Boydell's death and merged it with the *Weekly Journal*, the

Post-Boy held until 1755 the anachronistic position of Boston's only non-printer-owned newspaper.

As for the two papers that had begun as literary journals, the *Weekly Journal* and the *Rehearsal*, their respective journeys away from their original character were contemporaneous and parallel. While there is evidence that Thomas Prince and perhaps others kept making occasional contributions to Kneeland's and Green's *Weekly Journal* for the rest of the decade, both the *Journal* and Fleet's *Weekly Rehearsal* were putting far less emphasis upon original creative material after 1732 than either had done during their enthusiastic infancies. For the home-grown writings of Byles, the Adamses, and Gridley, the publishers of both papers substituted essays and similar material copied from the literary journals of London, but nearly as often used the leading space on page one for foreign news or public documents. Both continued to welcome letters from readers. These were occasionally of a literary cast, but more often dealt with some topical issue of local concern. The *Weekly Rehearsal* published no less than five long letters on the Massachusetts currency issue over a seven-week period in the spring of 1734. All began on page one.[68]

Fleet became especially creative in his handling of local news on the back or inside pages of the *Rehearsal*. The following bit of war news, compiled by the printer in his own words from reports available locally and printed with the news of Boston, is a far cry indeed from John Campbell's mechanical copying two and three decades earlier:

> There is a flying Report in Town, said to be brought from *Lisbon*, by a Ship which arrived here the last Week in 33 Days, *viz.* That the Germans have beat the French upon the Rhine, and raised the Siege of *Philipsburg*; and, that the French Ships before Dantzick have been destroyed by the Russian Fleet. Tho' we cannot vouch for the Truth of this important News, yet we find an Article in the *New York* Gazette of the 12th Instant, which seems to Countenance some Part of the Report, which is as follows:
>
> *Stelpe.* (an ancient Town and Castle in Germany) *May* 30. An Account is just come of a very furious Engagement between the *French* and the *Russians* in the Road of *Dantzick*, but no Particulars of it, so must wait for Confirmation.[69]

On August 18, 1735, Fleet changed the title of his paper from *Weekly Rehearsal*, a literary conceit devised by Gridley, to the *Boston Evening-Post*. The new name, besides reflecting Fleet's move to Monday evening publication, the first in Boston, conveyed the more business-like character that the paper had presented since Fleet had assumed control. Like the *Weekly Journal*, with whose positions it often differed but with which it never openly quarreled, the newly named *Evening-Post* had by now acquired all the marks of an energetic and enterprising printer's newspaper, aimed at a diverse audience bound together if at all by a common interest in public affairs, not a common taste in literature. The days of polite letters had by no means ended in Boston, nor would they end when Kneeland and Green let the *Gazette* subsume the *Weekly Journal* in 1741. But the audience was not sufficient to sustain even one journal devoted mainly to literature, and certainly not two. Nor could the town boast a literary community of sufficient size, dedication, leisure, or talent to keep up a consistent flow of native productions.

A similar and almost contemporaneous pattern can be seen among the much more numerous newspapers of provincial England—a case of parallel evolution rather than of any influence of one case upon the other. Beginning only a few years earlier than the *New-England Courant*, sections of what G. A. Cranfield calls "light-hearted correspondence and humorous advice" began to appear in some provincial papers. From the 1720s through much of the century, the provincial press tended to separate itself into three broad categories: straight "news" papers, those with heavy literary content such as the *Northampton Mercury* and the *Leeds Mercury*, and political papers. The literary journals, exactly like those of Boston, suffered after promising beginnings from a flagging of local contributions, forcing a heavier reliance on essays copied from London and other shifts in character.[70]

While some form of differentiation among papers continued to prevail in provincial England, where the readership was very much larger and many towns supported competing newspapers, the specialized literary papers of Boston were a temporary phenomenon. What a Boston audience could sustain, however, and what Boston printers could provide was a remarkably large selection of comprehensive newspapers composed of news, letters, public documents, advertising, and literature. But after 1732 the literature mainly copied rather than imitated the London originals, usually with explicit attribution. At this stage in the development of provincial culture, it was probably just as well.

Yet the *Courant*, the *Weekly Journal*, and the *Rehearsal* contributed an important dimension to the gradually maturing provincial newspaper in America. They helped readers develop a taste for speculative and imaginative writing, whether copied from abroad or attempted at home. Essays, letters, poems, and even occasional romances now took their expected place at least some of the time in the place of honor of most American newspapers. Specialization and eccentricity gave way to standardization, just as writers' papers gave way to printers' papers. But in the process, the literary journals of the twenties and thirties had left an enduring mark.

Chapter 8

Three Cities:
A Richer Tapestry,
1728–1740

The Explosion of the 1730s

The brief but fruitful lives of the *New-England Weekly Journal* and the *Weekly Rehearsal*, experiments in a distinct genre I have called the "literary newspaper," were not the only contributions to a decade of rapid development in American newspaper publishing. Between 1728 and 1739 the number of newspapers more than doubled, from five to twelve. If we count the two West Indian newspapers that appeared in the same decade, the number nearly tripled. And even this is to disregard the *Maryland Gazette* and the first *Rhode-Island Gazette*, which were founded in this eventful publishing era but did not survive the decade.

Nor do numbers tell the whole story. This was the time when Benjamin Franklin, having built upon his Boston apprenticeship by further printing and writing in Philadelphia and London, now entered direct competition with Andrew Bradford by starting the *Pennsylvania Gazette* on its illustrious career. It was also the time when fierce political factionalism in New York produced both a protracted paper war between rival newspapers and the most celebrated legal action against a publisher in the colonial period if not in all American history. Alongside the literary newspapers of Boston, the printer Bartholomew Green and an all-around man of affairs named John Boydell were carrying their more general newspapers, the *Boston News-Letter* and the *Boston Gazette*, to new levels of variety and maturity. This was most dramatically the case with Boydell, whose aim in life was to be a successful politician but who instead left as his principal legacy an especially creative and transforming editorship of the *Boston Gazette*.

The Achievement of John Boydell

John Boydell began his adult life as a political place nan, and sought to fashion a career by using his "interest" to climb the ladder of patronage. For an uncomfortable decade following the abrupt return to London in 1722 of his principal patron Governor Samuel Shute, he attended to the Boston affairs of his several contacts in his native England and strove vainly to secure a firm place for himself in the appointive colonial establishment.[1]

He acquired the *Boston Gazette* with his provisional appointment to the Boston postmastership upon the death of Henry Marshall in October 1732. This was a job that suited him much better than that of naval officer for the Massachusetts Customs District, which he had held since 1729, because of mutual distrust between him and Governor Jonathan Belcher, upon whom the naval office depended. To be permanent postmaster, however, his appointment needed confirmation by the postmaster general in London. Boydell, his correspondence reveals, was confident that his English interests would eventually prevail, which made all the more devastating the news in 1734 that London's choice for the permanent postmastership would be Ellis Huske of Portsmouth, a New Hampshire political ally of Belcher's.

Even though no official correspondence had yet made its way from London to Alexander Spotswood, the deputy postmaster general for America, Boydell promptly submitted his resignation to him on July 10, 1734, having gotten Huske to agree that this time ownership of the *Gazette* would not be transferred with the postmastership.[2] Spotswood, grateful to Boydell because the resignation had removed the deputy postmaster general from a tight spot, continued the former postmaster's franking privilege for both his letters and the *Gazette*.[3] The agreement prevailed even after Huske started a newspaper of his own, the *Boston Weekly Post-Boy*, not long after he assumed the postmastership in October 1734.

Boydell, his political career now ended, continued to publish the *Gazette* until his death on December 11, 1739, after which the printing firm of Kneeland & Green produced the paper on behalf of Boydell's widow Hannah, who lived another two years. When Hannah Boydell died in October 1741, ownership of the *Gazette* succeeded to the printers, who then combined it with their *New-England Weekly Journal*.

Very soon after Boydell's management began in the autumn of 1732, the *Gazette* took on an entirely new look and a fundamental change in character. Keeping on as printer Bartholomew Green, Jr., whom Marshall had hired in 1727, Boydell moved the *Gazette* as far beyond Brooker's early version of 1719 in aesthetic appeal and sophistication of content as Brooker had moved provincial newspaper publishing in America beyond John Campbell's *News-Letter*. The *Gazette* now became consistently a four-page paper, printed on a smaller sheet than the size used since 1719. The folded sheet resulted in a handy folio of two 8- by 10-inch leaves. Boydell also reduced the size of the *Gazette*'s nameplate, using a neater type, though the phrase *"NEW-ENGLAND"* and the appropriate serial number remained in place above the title and *"Published by Authority"* below it. The two wood-cut "ears" retained the same iconography—the ship and postrider—but were redone, resulting in less crowding at the top of the page. The text on page one now began consistently with an inch-square factotum. All four pages became embellished with a much more lavish use of rules, the advertisements at the end of the paper now taking on a look approximating display advertising. In early 1733, Boydell or Green thought better of that particular innovation and dropped most of the horizontal rules between advertisements, though an occasional one was illustrated with a wood-cut—usually a stock figure of a ship, used with announcements of projected sailings.

It was not only in format that Boydell transformed the *Gazette*. By mid-1733, essays, letters, satirical or polemical pieces on public affairs or on contemporary manners and morals, general interest articles, or even occasional verse would almost always get billing in the *Gazette* over any but the most immediate or otherwise compelling piece of news. Whereas the main competitive stimulus that had faced the *Gazette* in Philip Musgrave's day had been the now-defunct *New-England Courant*, Boydell had to keep his eye on the *New-England Weekly Journal* and the *Weekly Rehearsal*. The challenge from these two papers, though no less real, was far more subtle than the *Courant*'s crude personal attacks, which had demanded a direct response even if it was against a Musgrave's or a Campbell's inclination. The new journals were heirs to the *Courant*'s literary pretensions but not to its legacy of confrontational journalism, and it was up to any rival publisher to decide whether to try to compete in the arena of literature or to stick to the news. Like Marshall before him, Boydell steered a middle course between the two literary newspapers and the *News-Letter*, which under the ownership of Bartholomew Green continued as essentially the same news sheet with which John Campbell had begun.

Marshall had started the trend toward a livelier and more varied content with caution, mainly by obliging readers who submitted light verse on love or fashion, either of their own composition or copied from other sources.[4] Boydell went much further. During his first two years in charge of the *Gazette*, a substantial portion of his paper, often as much as half of a given number, contained such features as a dialogue on the English constitution, an article on raising children, an essay on Christianity and infidelity, poems on love and marriage, a long version of the story of Pocahontas, spoofs on the reluctance of Boston maids in the form of fables about Chinese virgins and an elaborate scheme for a lottery in which various

categories of prospective brides would be the prizes, and lengthy controversial letters on the overbearing public concern of the decade, the shortage of currency.[5]

Advertising took up more space in most numbers of Boydell's *Gazette*
than in its earlier versions, though with no particular consistency for the
first two years. By 1739, the year of Boydell's death, the entire fourth page
of the paper, and sometimes part of the third page as well, was filled with
advertising. The things advertised remained for the most part small items
for sale at retail, with the rare offering of a slave or a servant's time and a few
public notices. By the end of the decade, the use of newspaper advertising
had expanded to include, most conspicuously, the marketing of real estate.

Though Boydell expanded the total space available in the typical *Gazette*
from 41 to 66 column inches,[6] his great emphasis on feature material and
gradual increase in advertising required sacrifice somewhere. What got cut
short was news from Europe, the presumed demand for which had moved
John Campbell to found an American newspaper in 1704, and which even
in 1732 remained an important staple of the *News-Letter*. Not that the
Gazette stopped printing excerpts from the London newspapers altogether,
or even that such material was inevitably excluded from page one. Sometimes the arrival of a ship with especially recent or important news would
occasion a departure from what had now become the rule that the first
page, and often the second page as well, belonged to opinion or entertainment. On the whole, however, in part because European affairs seemed
less pressing to Americans in a time of international peace than they had
seemed before the Peace of Utrecht, foreign news now was less important
in the *Gazette* than in all its years before Boydell, both in proportion of
allotted space and in its placement in the paper. An occasional *Gazette*, in
fact, contained no news from the London press at all, even during the
summer sailing season.

What the new *Gazette* lacked in *news* from the London papers, however,
it more than compensated for in essays and letters either copied directly
from one of the English journals or composed by provincial literati in
imitation of the English model. Thus the ritual function of the provincial
press in providing a communal sharing of British consciousness and identity was hardly compromised by the *Gazette*'s diminishment of European
hard news in favor of softer material such as this. If anything, it was
strengthened.

Another new use of space, however, was an enriched diet of news from
other colonies. Now that Newport, New York, Philadelphia, Annapolis,
Charleston, and Barbados all boasted newspapers for which Boydell could
exchange his *Gazette* post-free, he devoted some of the attention that might
otherwise have been given to news from the London press to items copied
from other places in America. Since all the colonial newspapers copied
from the papers published in other American towns, there quickly developed an intercolonial exchange of news and opinion. Readers in one of the

publishing towns could now expect with some confidence that important developments in the other seaports would appear within a few days in their local newspaper. And because a publisher scanned an out-of-town paper especially for news of the place from which the paper came, there was mutual incentive everywhere for a publisher to pay more attention to reporting the news of his own town than, for example, Campbell had done between 1704 and 1719.

The Boston newspaper reader's world, therefore, had greatly changed in the thirty years since the launching of the *News-Letter*. Then it had been understood that the newspaper reflected only a part of that world, the part not available through daily discourse in the marketplaces, weekly assemblies at lecture and at meeting, regular conversations with assemblymen, councilors, and selectmen, and visits to the tavern. These traditional expressions of the local culture, supplemented by other products of the press such as broadside announcements and ballads, advertising handbills, and a steady stream of recent sermons, could easily serve the internal information needs of a town of perhaps 7000. For a small minority of that population—possibly a quarter of the town's 1500 adult white males—the need was greater.[7] For them, the *News-Letter*, along with private correspondence, had expanded their world to one defined by the sea lanes of the Atlantic and the Caribbean. It was a geographic world of some breadth but an intellectual world of little depth or variety, in part because the times demanded that the concerns of a gentleman of affairs, the presumed reader, be overwhelmingly practical. Wars, diplomacy, imperial politics, shipping, storms, piracy, and more wars—these had been the stuff of the news from 1704 at least to 1721, when the *New-England Courant* began to challenge Boston's journalistic conventions. When official documents from province or town appeared beside these staples in early *News-Letters* and *Gazettes*, it was not so much to inform as to sanctify by print those decisions and pronouncements of which most readers already knew; their publication in a newspaper, like publication by a herald, was a public ritual of confirmation.

The Boston newspaper reader's world of 1734 was no larger geographically than that of 1704, but certain parts of it, especially those comparatively close at hand, could be seen in sharper focus. On the local level, the town's four newspapers still served to supplement and confirm the oral culture rather than substitute for it, just as any small-town newspaper does today. The town had doubled in size between Campbell's postmastership and Boydell's,[8] so there was an inevitable loss of intimacy in the conduct of daily business and official life and a corresponding increased reliance upon printed news and advertisements. The news of Boston in the *Gazette* and its competitors, while far more varied in scope and occupying a larger portion of space than in the early days of the *News-Letter*, was still almost haphazardly selective and obviously far from comprehensive. On the other hand, the newspapers collectively offered a forum for debate and comment on matters of local interest and for the airing and criticism of works by local talent under the influence of one or another muse. Never had the oral culture been able to provide a stimulus to discussion and creativity in the community comparable to this emerging function of print. The public sphere was becoming profoundly transformed.

At the same time that Boston readers were becoming more keenly aware of their own place through the medium of the newspaper, their knowledge of their sister American colonies reached unprecedented heights. Whatever news of his town or province a Philadelphia reader might find in his *Weekly Mercury* or *Pennsylvania Gazette*, for example, would very likely make its way into the columns of at least one of the Boston papers a week or two later. What a reader gained from this, of course, was not a comprehensive contemporary history of any of the other colonies, but a realization that he shared with his neighbors in New York, Pennsylvania, and South Carolina similar interests and problems and the same potential for wealth or ruin, hazards to health and safety, general form of provincial government, and relationship to the authority and culture of Britain that he shared with his fellow townsmen in Boston. Not only did the newspapers create new kinds of bonds within the local community, therefore, but they also stimulated the creation of an American intercolonial community that had been bound heretofore only by coastal trade and a common, though seldom discussed, political relationship with the British Crown.

While the Boston reader took from his newspapers a heightened awareness of his expanding and tightening relationships on his own side of the Atlantic, he also found in them a complementary theme. At the same time his newspapers were inviting him to participate imaginatively in an American community that transcended colonial boundaries, they were also urging upon him a greater involvement in the culture of *England*. The reader's world now included letters, the theater, music, and the arts as well as war and politics. It included a new familiarity with if not always sympathy for the Church of England and other expressions of Protestantism that had once seemed far more alien to the New England Way than they were now beginning to seem. It included controversy over political and religious ideas and questions of public morals and manners. The specific dress in which this newly variegated world was presented to the Boston newspaper reader, when not in verse, was most often that of the polished, sometimes even witty essay, a form borrowed directly from the British essay journal. Twenty years earlier, the form in which Bostonians would have been most likely to encounter commentary on subjects such as these was the Puritan sermon.

None of the other three papers in Boston presented this richer world to its readers in as balanced a way as John Boydell's *Gazette*. The *News-Letter* continued to emphasize news of the traditional sort, stressing European events as it always had. The *Weekly Journal* and *Weekly Rehearsal*, as self-conscious purveyors of literary culture, tended to slight—though not ignore—the more prosaic kind of newspaper content. The *Gazette* fought provincialism on two fronts—on the one hand by drawing its Boston readers into more conscious communion with their colonial neighbors, and on the other by acting as a vehicle for the anglicization of Boston culture.

Philadelphia

What the polished but failed English politician John Boydell contributed to the advancement of newspaper-making in Boston the Boston-trained runaway printer's lad Benjamin Franklin accomplished in Philadelphia. It is difficult for writer and reader alike to consider this period in Franklin's career as if one were dealing simply with one more publisher of newspapers. All the hackneyed scenes of one of our best-loved American legends insist upon crowding in. The phrase "B. Franklin, Printer," however accurate as a tradesman's simple self-description, insists upon being taken at a hundred times face value. Even at twenty-three, when he and a partner took over the *Pennsylvania Gazette* and a very long time before he ascended Olympus, Franklin resists demythologizing; his early road to success seems to us an inseparable part of the canon.

The young Benjamin Franklin, nevertheless, was a simple and nearly penniless printer who had learned to be a better one than he had been in Boston by working for a year and a half in the shops of two superb London printers, Samuel Palmer and John Watts.[9] The year or less that he worked for Samuel Keimer in Philadelphia before that had added nothing to his knowledge or skill in printing, but had introduced him to the business and public life of Philadelphia and the inadequacies, as he saw it, of both its printers.[10] Franklin, of course, had more going for him than what was probably a slightly better-than-average printing background for a young American journeyman. He had little money of his own, and the most promising connection of his early Philadelphia experience, which had given him the false promise both of financial sponsorship and of the security of the government printing contract, failed to pay off. Governor William Keith, Franklin discovered to his dismay, was a notorious maker of promises he never fulfilled and in any case was replaced in office during Franklin's absence in England.[11] On the other hand, Franklin was already learning from this and other experiences how to be resourceful and self-reliant, and he was a talented writer who continued to work at refining that side of his arsenal. Franklin made full use of this combination of advantages in putting himself into the newspaper business.

For almost exactly nine years—December 22, 1719, to December 12, 1728—Andrew Bradford had newspaper publishing to himself in Philadelphia, though Samuel Keimer competed with his printing business beginning in 1723. Bradford's *American Weekly Mercury*, until early 1729, was more like the *Boston Weekly News-Letter* than the *Boston Gazette*. It stuck fairly closely to reporting the news. Most of it was from Europe, usually copied from the London newspapers. With the availability of New England items from the several Boston newspapers, however, and especially the correspondence of official documents and business data from New York by William Bradford, the *Mercury* continued throughout the 1720s to report vital information from several places in America as well. Usually Bradford was able to print a sizable array of advertising from Pennsylvania and surrounding colonies, occasionally as much as an entire page. Practically never until 1729, however, did Bradford print material at all like the satirical essays of the *New-England Courant* or even the derivative literary pieces that appeared from time to time in the *Boston Gazette*. When material other than straight news appeared in the lead position on page one, it was usually a governor's address from one of the American colonies or an official proclamation copied from London.

There were occasional exceptions, appearing during the winter hiatus in shipping and typically taking the form of a political or practical essay, such as the one on hemp culture that led the paper on January 30, 1722. As late as February 28, 1727, Bradford was essentially apologizing for printing quite an interesting letter on mourning from the *London Journal*, one of his favorite sources. He printed the letter, he explained, "having but few remarkable Occurrences to fill up this our Paper with at present."

In 1722, Bradford printed a few of John Trenchard's early Cato letters from the *London Journal*, and on May 31 of that year indulged a correspondent who called himself "Americo-Britannus" by printing a supplementary letter signed "Plato." The *Mercury* kept track of the smallpox inoculation controversy in Boston during the early years of the *Courant*, and took pains to notice James Franklin's troubles with the General Court. On February 26, 1723, after a long account of the order prohibiting Franklin from further publishing without official supervision, Bradford inserted as a postscript his own satirical comment on this attempt at prior restraint: "By private Letters from Boston we are informed, That the Bakers there are under great Apprehensions of being forbid baking any more Bread, unless they will submit to the Secretary, as Supervisor General and Weigher of the Dough, before it is baked into Bread and offer'd to Sale."

Bradford, obviously, was politically aware and even alert at this early stage to possible infringements on colonial rights and English liberties. This, in fact, was one of the main themes of his editorial tirade of 1721 against the transportation of criminals.[12] As interesting as they certainly are, however, items such as these were a rare occurrence in the *Mercury* throughout most of the 1720s. The main fare by far was hard news garnished with transcripts of public documents, shipping lists, price lists, and advertisements.

When Samuel Keimer decided in his inexpert way to begin a second Philadelphia newspaper at the end of 1728, he apparently strove to create a journal that would be as much unlike the *Mercury* as possible. "The *Mercury*," he announced boldly in a two-page prospectus dated October 1, "has been so wretchedly perform'd, that it has been not only a Reproach to the Province, but such a Scandal to the very Name of Printing, that it may, for its unparallel'd Blunders and Incorectness, be truly stiled *Nonsense in Folio*, instead of a Serviceable News-Paper."[13] Keimer's *Universal Instructor in All Arts and Sciences; And Pennsylvania Gazette*, which appeared a month later than his "Advertisement" promised, was anything but a straight news sheet. Throughout the thirty-nine weeks that he published his paper, Keimer invariably devoted the entire first page of each four-page number to an excerpt from Ephraim Chambers's new *Cyclopaedia*, published in London the same year the *Gazette* began. News from the London newspapers occupied pages two and three, and page four was given over to a combination of news, advertisements, and miscellaneous material.[14]

It is here, actually a bit before here, that Benjamin Franklin enters the newspaper scene in Philadelphia. Not long after returning from London in 1726, he had gone back to work for Keimer. In 1728, he and Hugh Meredith, a fellow journeyman in Keimer's shop and for a time a close friend of Franklin's, accepted the backing of Meredith's father and set up a third printing business in Philadelphia at "The New Printing Office" in Market Street. The key to their success, Franklin hoped, would be to publish a "good" newspaper, since he considered the *Mercury* "a paltry thing, wretchedly manag'd, and no way entertaining; and yet was profitable to him (Bradford)." News of Franklin's and Meredith's plan leaked to Keimer, which is what led him to step in with his ill-considered *Universal Instructor* to head it off.[15]

Franklin now employed his business instincts and his writing talent (as well as his resentment, which in retrospect he freely admitted)[16] to beat the man who had temporarily beaten him. In the process, he accomplished not one but two transformations. Not only did he work his way into becoming Bradford's sole competitor by acquiring and drastically changing Keimer's new newspaper, but he actually transformed Bradford's *Mercury* as well. "To counteract them," Franklin recalled, "as I could not yet begin our Paper, I wrote several Pieces of Entertainment for Bradford's Paper." The "them" were Keimer and his associate George Webb, who had spilled Franklin's secret to the old printer. "By this means," he added, "the Attention of the Public was fix'd on that Paper, and Keimers Proposals which we burlesqu'd and ridicul'd, were disregarded."[17]

In fact, not only was the attention of the public fixed on the *Mercury*, but that paper was never again the same. From the day that letters signed Martha Careful and Celia Shortface appeared on page one, January 28, 1729, Bradford made his paper more interesting and diverse. While never abandoning his emphasis upon news, he was more likely than not from then through the 1730s to begin the paper with an essay or letter or literary excerpt from one of the English journals, more in the mode of Boydell's *Boston Gazette* than of the *Boston News-Letter*. For several months, that leading piece was the Busy-Body papers.

The occasion for Martha's and Celia's printed outbursts against Keimer was the fifth number of the *Universal Instructor*, by which time the methodical publisher had reached the point in his alphabetical scheme that he reprinted, under the letters "ABO," Chambers's treatment of "Abortion." Though mildly clinical, with a few of the essential anatomical references, this small essay was not what a modern reader might expect. It made no allusions at all to intentional abortive practices, but dealt entirely with the nature, causes, and symptoms of accidental miscarriage, and what ought to be done to treat the mother when such a misfortune occurred.[18] Nevertheless, the piece provided a sufficient excuse for satirical responses in Bradford's *Mercury*, almost certainly contributed by Franklin.[19]

Continuing the proven formula by which he had posed as the Widow Dogood a few years earlier in Boston, Franklin assumed the personae of two offended women who in separate letters complained of Keimer's "immodesty" in "Expos[ing] the Secrets of our Sex . . . To be read in all *Taverns* and *Coffee-Houses*, and by the Vulgar." Any more such "Indecencies" would prompt Martha Careful and her friends "to run the Hazard of taking him by the Beard" and Celia Shortface and her acquaintances "to have thy right Ear for it." Celia added in Quakerese, ". . . if though canst make no better Use of Thy Dictionary, Sell it at Thy next *Luck in the Bag;* and if Thou hath nothing else to put in Thy *Gazette*, lay it down."[20]

The first Busy-Body essay appeared in the very next week's *Mercury*. In this series of pieces, the first four of which and parts of two others were contributed by Franklin,[21] the writer neither posed as a woman nor pursued the attack against Keimer.[22] A short paragraph in the first essay, in fact, took Bradford himself to task for not making his paper more interesting—a deficiency that the Busy-Body now proposed to help him overcome:

> I have often observ'd with Concern, that your *Mercury* is not always equally entertaining. The Delay of Ships expected in, and want of fresh Advices from Europe, make it frequently very Dull; and I find the Freezing of our river has the same Effect on News as on Trade. With more concern have I continually observ'd the growing vices and follies of my Country-folk. . . . I, therefore, upon mature Deliberation, think fit to take *no Body's Business* wholly into my own Hands; and, out of zeal for the Publick Good, design to erect my Self into a Kind of *Censor Morum;* proposing with your Allowance, to make Use of the *Weekly Mercury* as a Vehicle. . . .

What followed in almost every *Mercury* for the next nine months, prominently displayed on page one, was a series of Addisonian essays complete with an urbane style and learned allusions reminiscent of the Janus letters of the later *New-England Courant* and the Proteus Echo columns that had finished their year's course in the *New-England Weekly Journal* just the previous April. Franklin's place as author of these contributions, of which there were thirty-two in all, was taken after a few weeks by Joseph Breintnall, a fellow member of Franklin's Junto.[23]

This sparkling new life in the *Mercury*, combined with the fumbling inadequacies of Keimer's ponderous *Universal Instructor* and his endemic business difficulties, brought Keimer's experiment in publishing to a speedy close.[24] "[A]fter carrying it on three Quarters of a Year, with at most only 90 Subscribers," Franklin recollected laconically, "he [Keimer] offer'd it to me for a Trifle, and I having been ready some time to go on with it, took it in hand directly, and it prov'd in a few Years extreamly profitable to me."[25]

Having helped undermine any chance of Keimer's success by enhancing the *Mercury*, Franklin and his friend Breintnall now pulled the rug out from under Bradford. They simply stopped feeding Bradford the Busy-Body papers, the chief source of the *Mercury*'s new luster. The column stopped abruptly with the essay Bradford printed on September 25, 1729, the same day the *Universal Instructor* carried Keimer's announcement that he had sold his paper to Franklin and Meredith. Bradford continued to put out the *Mercury* with some essay or letter or at least a public document given prominent play where Busy-Body had been, but he could no longer consistently offer an original piece of writing crafted for a Philadelphia audience. The October 2 number of Keimer's former paper, its title greatly simplified to *The Pennsylvania Gazette*, carried an elaborate explanation of the new publishers' plans. The announcement contained a sly suggestion that the *Mercury* was not all a newspaper should be: "There are many who have long desired to see a good News-Paper in Pennsylvania."

Franklin and Meredith spelled out their scheme for an entirely revamped competition newspaper in some detail. The encyclopedia excerpts would be scrapped ("it will probably be fifty Years before the Whole can be gone thro' in this Manner of Publication") because "we believe our Readers will not think such a Method of communicating Knowledge to be a proper One." The new publishers would likewise abandon a serialization of Defoe's *Religious Courtship* on the ground "that the whole Book will probably in a little Time be printed and bound up by it self; and those who approve of it, will doubtless be better pleas'd to have it entire, than in this broken interrupted Manner." News of public affairs—"of War both by Land and Sea; . . . the several Interests of Princes and States, the Secrets of Courts"—would be central to the design, but not to the exclusion of the sort of knowledge that "may contribute either to the Improvement of our present Manufactures, or towards the Invention of new Ones."

Franklin at last had a newspaper of his own. (We may pretty much ignore Meredith, whose ineptitude as a printer and drinking habit made him by far the weaker member of what turned out to be only a short-lived partnership.)[26] At twenty-three, James Franklin's former apprentice was far better equipped for publishing than anyone who had yet begun an American newspaper. He brought to the job his youthful experience with the *Courant*, his training in improved typography in London, his close observation of the printing business and actual manipulation of competitive newspaper publishing in Philadelphia, and his proven abilities as an eminently publishable writer in Boston, London, and Philadelphia. His statement of purpose discloses a mind much more alert than his predecessor's to the particular advantages and limitations of his medium, a small weekly periodical, and a practical inclination toward the dissemination of "useful knowledge" that anticipates his founding statement for the American Philosophical Society in 1743.[27] He had gained influential friends and supporters through his Junto and by gaining an early reputation as a competent printer, good writer, diligent worker, and responsible businessman.[28] It is hard at this point not to recite the moral of the Franklin myth because it is grounded in reality.

Under Franklin, who ran his printing business and the paper by himself from the departure of Meredith in July 1730 until he formed a new partnership with David Hall eighteen years later, the *Gazette* blossomed and prospered. Franklin's own assertion that the paper "prov'd in a few Years extreamly profitable" is not verifiable, but his and Hall's settlement of the firm's accounts at the end of their eighteen-year partnership in 1766 confirms the importance of the *Gazette* in the overall scheme of the printing office. During that period, the £16,630 that Hall took in from the *Gazette* amounted to 59 percent of the gross revenue of the partnership.[29]

Franklin marshaled all his experience and considerable talent to produce a newspaper that was instantly far neater, livelier, and more informative than either its predecessor or its rival. By no means did he transform it into a literary newspaper on the model of the *Courant* or the *Weekly Journal*. Hard news, even European news, became a more significant component of the *Gazette* during Franklin's tenure than during Keimer's ownership, primarily because Keimer had squandered so much of the paper's limited space on reprinting an encyclopedia.[30] Throughout the 1730s he retained the 8- by 12-inch leaf size with which Keimer had begun, enlarging the sheet in mid-1740 and switching from two to three columns in 1742. As he gained readership and circulation, he also gained advertising, so that by 1735 advertisements were taking up about 20 percent of the paper's total space (about four-fifths of the fourth page on average) and more than 38 percent of the space by 1740, three years after his appointment as Philadelphia postmaster. The *Mercury* boasted a considerably heavier advertising budget than the *Gazette* in 1735, but held just about steady during the next five years at a proportion of space slightly less than what the *Gazette* had achieved by 1740.[31] Both these Philadelphia papers carried significantly more advertising than any of the five Boston newspapers that were in business in 1740.

For the most part, perhaps because he had *Poor Richard's Almanack* as an outlet beginning in 1732, Franklin confined his creative writing in the *Gazette* to news summaries, clever snippets, and occasional hoaxes and false letters after the example of the *Courant* (such as those from Anthony Afterwit, Celia Single, and Alice Addertongue in 1732),[32] to be answered by himself. He also occasionally printed verse, probably contributed by others. News dominated the content of the *Gazette* by far, but Franklin's uncommonly clever pen as well as the increasing public usefulness of the paper under his ownership contributed to its popularity.

Franklin and Bradford carried on competitive skirmishes in print just as the rival newspapers were doing in Boston. One exchange between the two papers in 1733 reveals something about the local reputation Franklin was already making for himself as a writer, wit, and adversary whose clever-ness at this youthful stage may have exceeded his judgment. An unsigned piece in the *Gazette* of October 11, 1733, responded to a political essay in the *Mercury* by deploring the convention that all the "venerable Names of Antiquity" have been "prostituted by every paltry Scribbler." Even the "sacred name" of Cato, he lamented, had recently "been subscribed to a weekly Paper, the unhappy Birth of a sickly Brain, born in *Pennsylvania*, and delivered into the World, by that most Sage Matron and accomplish'd Midwife A.[ndrew] B.[radford]." It also cast some sharp stones in the direction of "black gowns," that is, the clergy. In a poetic reply that led the *Mercury* the next week, "J.D." gave Franklin both a back-handed compli-ment and some wise advice. The identity of the author, the poet makes clear, was obvious because the essay had been written so well; it was none other than "Janus," Franklin's persona during the latter days of the *New-England Courant:* "No Mask so dark, but *Janus* must shine thro'," to be known by his "swelling Periods." But Janus, declares the poet, has used his talent badly: "But thou a brave neglect of Fame hast shewn, / Of *Other's* Fame, Great *Genius!* and thy *own.*" Through several more lines, "J.D." urges the young writer to moderate his harsh language, employ his wit sparely, and cool his "fervent petulance," lest he find himself without friends or respect in Philadelphia. The poem ends with some fatherly advice:

> In time, pray, learn, to *use* not *waste* they Sense;
> Nor make a frailty of Excellence;
> Or else write on *unheeded*, since we know,
> That Men, who pardon, disappoint, their Foe.[33]

In 1735 and 1736 the rival papers contested at length over the establish-ment of a chancery court in Pennsylvania, which Bradford championed and Franklin opposed.[34] The bitterest controversy came late in 1740, a time when the hottest newspaper debate everywhere in America was over George Whitefield. On November 6, the *Mercury* printed a long pros-pectus signed by Bradford for the *American Magazine*, a monthly to be printed by Bradford and edited (though that was not revealed until subse-quently) by John Webbe. The announcement brought forth a counter-proposal in the next week's *Gazette* for the *General Magazine*, to be pub-lished by Franklin. The proposal included the disclosure that Webbe, still unnamed, had betrayed Franklin's idea, shared with him in confidence, to

Bradford. There followed an exchange of printed recriminations between Franklin and Webbe, during which the ground was eventually shifted to the question of Franklin's treatment of Bradford's newspaper in his capacity as postmaster. The outcome of this little paper war was inconclusive; both printers started their prospective magazines within three days of each other the next February. Franklin's lasted six months, Bradford's three.[35]

Nowhere was there yet an American reading market sufficient to absorb a diet composed of both weekly newspapers and a monthly such as the *Gentleman's Magazine* or the *London Magazine*, upon which both Philadelphia printers' proposals were modeled. Like Boston, however, Philadelphia easily sustained a lively competing newspaper press that by 1740 was occupying an essential niche in the commercial and political life of the city and province. Through the dynamics of its own competition it was also enriching the culture of the community by supplying both intellectual ferment and simple entertainment.

New York

"This habitual factionalism, this politics for its own sake," writes one of our most respected historians of colonial New York, may provide the key to understanding this most factious of American provinces.[36] Politics indeed is what moved William Bradford from Philadelphia to New York in the first place, and political factionalism of the most raucous kind was the driving force behind the heated newspaper competition that emerged there in the 1730s.

If Benjamin Franklin entered newspaper entrepreneurship better prepared for the business than any other American publisher, William Bradford entered it with the longest memory. When the elder Bradford began the *New-York Gazette* in 1725, six years after his son had started the *American Weekly Mercury*, he had already lived, by our definition, through the entire newspaper-publishing history of England and America. According to family tradition, he was living with relatives in London at the time of the plague,[37] though he could neither have remembered that experience nor been aware of the founding of the *Oxford Gazette* at the same time, since he would have been only two. Certainly, however, he had witnessed part of the building of Christopher Wren's London after the Great Fire and the flurry of unlicensed publications during the brief suspension of the printing act in the latter years of Charles II because he was then serving his printing apprenticeship with Andrew Sowle. In 1685, his apprenticeship completed, he had married his former master's daughter and, with the specific endorsement of William Penn, sailed to Pennsylvania with her and his printing materials.[38] That was the same year Benjamin Harris had fled James II for Massachusetts.

After several episodes of repression in Pennsylvania and upon the invitation of a proud governor, Bradford had moved to New York in 1693, only three years after the *Publick Occurrences* episode. By 1725, when he finally began the *New-York Gazette*, John Campbell, only ten years Bradford's senior, had already ended his twenty-year career as founding publisher of the *Boston News-Letter*. Bradford was sixty-two when he entered the newspaper business. Of the other four men publishing American newspapers in November 1725, only Bartholomew Green, who at fifty-six had taken over the *News-Letter* from Campbell early in 1723, was of his generation.[39]

As might be expected, therefore, the *New-York Gazette* shared the *Boston News-Letter*'s conventionality. Bradford had been brought to New York more than three decades earlier not only to claim the salaried job of official printer but also to satisfy the vanity of a governor who wanted to see his military exploits recorded in print.[40] It could never have occurred to such a printer to be anything other than a supporter of official authority. His approach to journalism, grounded in the assumptions of his own generation, was as unimaginative as Campbell's and Green's, at least at the beginning. The paper's title was surrounded by two woodcuts, one the provincial arms of New York, the other the inevitable mounted postman. Its content for the first several years consisted largely of European news copied from London and shipping lists from New York, Boston, and Philadelphia. Bradford's selection of European news ran heavily to transcripts of letters, addresses, and official documents. In contrast to John Campbell's primary impulses, he clearly preferred copying extended transcripts and news accounts to giving his readers a greater number of briefer items.

The first of any of the surviving numbers of the *Gazette* in which a local item leads the paper is the twenty-fifth (April 25, 1726), which printed a brief address of the New York General Assembly to Governor William Burnet. Six months later, on October 3, the *Gazette* printed, in order, the province election results, Governor Burnet's long speech to the Assembly, the Assembly's address, and the governor's response. The whole occupied just over half of the paper that week. Two other *Gazettes* of 1726 contained similar proceedings from Pennsylvania,[41] but every other number that year led with news or a document from Europe.

From the beginning of publication until well into the 1730s, the *Gazette* carried little advertising, even by Boston standards. Most numbers contained from one to five advertisements, and some none at all. By comparison with Boston and Philadelphia, New York merchants and retailers were extremely slow to use newspaper advertising; most of the *Gazette*'s few advertisements were for real estate, a substantial portion placed by advertisers in New Jersey, where the *Gazette* also circulated. In 1726, the paper's first full year of publication, it ran twenty-six advertisements from New Jersey, mostly from Perth Amboy, and one from Pennsylvania, as compared with only fourteen from New York.[42]

By 1733, the year both Bradford and New York's current political regime had to face the challenge of John Peter Zenger's vigorous new opposition paper, the *Gazette* had developed both greater variety and greater relevance to its New York readers. It contained many more locally generated essays and letters of opinion than in previous years, even during the months before the dispute between Governor William Cosby and the Morrisite faction burst into the open. It was still not publishing much actual local news compared with the Boston papers in the 1730s, and its advertisements, while more numerous than during the *Gazette*'s earliest years, seldom added up to more than a column's worth. But by this time Bradford was making substantially greater and much more regular use of the newspapers from other American towns—the four then being printed in Boston, the two in Philadelphia, and the *Gazettes* of Maryland, South Carolina, and (for a very few months) Rhode Island. His interest in Boston appears to have been especially lively, sufficient even to engage him in a brief intercolonial debate, to be discussed later in the chapter, with John Boydell. This same extensive copying from Boston, with occasional commentary and exchanges, continued through the rest of the decade even during the local dispute of 1734 and 1735 with which one presumes most of the New York readership was preoccupied.

So far we have seen Bradford's *Gazette* in the role of a conventional dispenser of news and entertainment, mostly foreign, and domestic data designed for the use of a commercial readership—not far different from the *Boston News-Letter* and Andrew Bradford's *American Weekly Mercury* before 1728. Its support of the successive administrations in New York and New Jersey was usually implicit rather than explicit, characterized in the main by a simple refusal to recognize opposition voices and enter into local political disputes.[43] As the chief printer in the city, a noted citizen, churchman, and businessman, and government printer for both provinces, Bradford had nothing to gain and much to lose by printed domestic politics.

Yet politics—in the narrow sense of partisan wrangling and maneuvering—was central to New York's public ethos. Factions had jousted for fortune and power long before August 1732, when the arrival of Governor William Cosby set off yet another explosive chain of political events.[44] Cosby's claim on half the salary of his acting predecessor, Rip Van Dam, quickly brought about the formation of a vocal opposition in accordance with New York tradition. Cosby's decision to press a suit against Van Dam by conferring equity jurisdiction on the Supreme Court intensified the resentment against Cosby and thrust into a central role Chief Justice Lewis Morris, who railed against this enlargement of the Court's power and who was sufficiently wealthy and influential to form the natural center of a powerful opposition faction. Cosby dismissed Morris, and the fight by what swiftly became an organized Morrisite party to destroy the greedy and otherwise unattractive new governor was on.[45]

Except for the presence of a competitor, Bradford might never have been compelled to introduce any of this conflict into print. Certainly it was against his inclination to do so; up to that point, the overlap between the oral and the print culture of city and province had been much narrower than it was about to become. For whatever reasons—as Stephen Botein has cogently argued, it is by no means obvious what Cosby's opponents hoped to achieve in this small political arena by resorting to print[46]—the Morrisites decided to enlist in their battle against Cosby the very available printing press of John Peter Zenger. Eventually, Bradford had no choice but to lend his own newspaper to the response.

Zenger, a former apprentice of Bradford's, had first tried his luck in Annapolis, but in 1722, after the early death of his first wife, he returned to New York, a young widower of twenty-five. In 1725, the year of the founding of the *Gazette*, he and Bradford entered into a partnership that lasted only until Zenger set up on his own the next year.[47] Until he and the Morrisites discovered each other, the young printer was clearly struggling. In the years 1726 through 1733, he produced forty-one books, pamphlets, and broadsides compared with the seventy such works that came off Bradford's press in those years in addition to his newspaper and the many small contract printing jobs that never find their way into bibliographies.[48]

That left opposition politics. In his first five years of running his own press, Zenger did find a small niche for himself in Dutch-language sermons and religious tracts, which accounted for eight of his seventeen imprints in the years 1726–30, not counting an English translation of one of them and a Dutch-language arithmetic book. But this small specialty was not nearly enough to sustain a printing business. Zenger's production rose dramatically in 1732, when his imprints actually outnumbered Bradford's. That was the year of Cosby's arrival and the mutual discovery of Zenger and the developing opposition. Nine of Zenger's eleven imprints of 1732 were pamphlets urging changes in the structure of government, most of them focusing on the need for more frequent elections to the Assembly.[49] In 1733, he printed several pieces consisting of transcripts from the trial at which Morris had frustrated Cosby's attempt to extract the half-salary from Van Dam, including the chief justice's long diatribe against equity proceedings that had brought about his removal.[50]

Even though the exact motives of the Morrisites in carrying their fight into print may not be as clear as some have presumed, the availability of Zenger's press certainly invited the use of this option. If Bradford had still been the only printer in the province, such a choice would have been far more difficult to put into effect.[51] Over pondering the attractiveness to Zenger of the now-cemented alliance between himself and the Morrisites, there is no need to linger. For the first time in a discouraging career, he had found here a possible key to carrying on a viable printing business in New York. Simply stated, he needed the money. The next fruit of the alliance was the *New-York Weekly Journal*, which made its first appearance (under the misprinted date of October 5) on November 5, 1733.

THE
New-York Gazette,

Numb 378

From *January* 16 to Tuesday *January* 23. 1732,

William Bradford's *New-York Gazette*, bearing the arms of the province to the left of the title and on the right, according to Isaiah Thomas's mischievous description in his 1810 *History of Printing in America*, "a postman, on an animal somewhat resembling a horse." This number of January 23, 1732/3, copies an official report of Crown action on a dispute between Massachusetts claimants and a royal official over Maine woodlands, a rare bit of published colonial news from the London press. (*Courtesy, American Antiquarian Society*)

Numb. XIII.

THE

New-York Weekly JOURNAL.

Containing the freshest Advices, Foreign, and Domestick.

MUNDAY January 28, 1733.

Lege sceuata omnis poteftas Efto;
BRACTON.

SIR,

MEN in a Torrent of Profperity fel-dom think of a Day of Diftrefs, or Great Men that their greatnefs will ever Ceafe. This feems to be a Sort of a Curfe upon Power, a Vanity and Infatuation blended with the Nature of it : As if it were Poffible nay eafy to bind the Fick-lenefs of Fortune, and enfure Happynefs for a Term of Years. 'Tis from this Af-fureance, often cleaving to very able Men that thofe in Authority often act with fuch Boldnefs and, Infolence, as, if their Reign were never to End, and they were for ever fecure againft all After-reckonings, all cafualties and difgrace. From whence elfe comes it, but from fuch blindSecurity in the Permanence of their Condition, and in the Impunity of their Actions, that Minifters have fometimes concerted SCHEMES OF GENERAL OPPRESSION AND PIL-LAGE, SCHEMES TO DEPRECIATE OR EVADE THE LAWS, RESTRAINTS UPON LIBERTY AND PROJECTS FOR ARBITRARY WILL? Had they thought that ever they themfelves fhould fuffer in the common Oppreffion would they have advifed *Methods of Oppreffing*? Should they have been for *Weakning or abrogating the Laws*, had they Dreamed that they fhould come to want THE PROTECTI-ON OF THE LAW? Would they have aimed at *Abolifhing Liberty*, had they ap-prehended that they were at any time to fall from Power; or at eftablifhing *defpo-tick Rule*, but for the Sake of *having the Direction of it* againft others, without fee-ling ITS Weight and Terrors in their own Particulars?

How few Men in Power have fecured to themfelves a Refource of Friendfhip and Affection from the Publick, in Cafe of a Storm at Court and the Frowns of a Crown? Nay what fome of them have done to ferve the Crown againft the Peo-ple, has been a Motive with the Crown (and a politic Motive, tho not always a juft one, at leaft not generous) to Sacri-fice them to the Pleafure and Revenge of the People, thus *Cefar Borgio*, ufed *Romiro D'orco* Governour of *Ramagna*, one firft employed to commit Cruelties then executed for having committed them. Thus were EMPSON and DUDLEY ufed, and thus the great Turk often ufes his Bafhaws.

The GENERAL SECURITY, is the on-ly certain Security of particulars; and tho'DefperateMen often find fafety in pub-lick Deftruction, yet they cannot infure the fame fafety to their Children, who muft fuffer with the reft in the mifery of all. If Great wicked Men would confider this, the World would not be plagued with their Ambition, their Pofterity fcarce ever mifs to reap the bitter Fruits of their Actions, and the Curfe of their iniquities rarely fails to follow them to the third and fourth Generation.

The INSTRUMENTS OF PUBLICK RUIN, have generally at once intailed mifery upon their Country and their own Race. Thofe who were the Inftruments and Minifters of *Cefar* and *Auguftus*, and put the Common Wealth under their Feet, AND THEM ABOVE THE LAWS, did not confider that they were not only forging Chains for their Country, but whetting Swords againft their own Fami-lies; who were all cut off under fucceeding Tyrants: Nay, moft of their Children fell early

An early number of John Peter Zenger's *New-York Weekly Journal*, January 28, 1733/4, one of those cited in the government's charge against Zenger a year later for seditious libel, which led to Zenger's famous trial and acquittal in August 1735. The first page of this four-page number illustrates the growing tendency among the American newspapers in the 1730s to print letters and essays on political and other subjects at the beginning of the paper. It was not this particular letter (continued inside and signed "Cato") that got Zenger in trouble but an unsigned letter on page 3, strongly critical of Governor William Cosby's administration. (*Courtesy, American Antiquarian Society*)

Just as James Franklin had put out the *New-England Courant* under his own name twelve years earlier, Zenger now produced this opposition paper under his own name. Like Franklin, Zenger went to jail. The difference was that Franklin had been an active and contributing member of the group of opposition writers that sponsored the *Courant*, and the snippet that got him into trouble with the authorities may actually have been a product of his own pen. In a much more complete sense than could be said of Franklin, Zenger was the hired tool of his sponsors.

If, however, we ignore for the moment all the real differences in circumstances that brought the two papers into being, we can readily see that the *Journal*'s role in the rapidly broadening print culture of New York was exactly the same as that of the *Courant* the previous decade in Boston. These two opposition newspapers, in the first place, introduced the voice of contention into the local world of printed discourse. In both cases, such voices had been heard but not previously (or, in the case of New York, not until recently) read. In the second place, they both provoked printed responses—in both cases reluctant responses. The development of a printed dialogue between opposition and establishment—a "paper war" with combatants on each side—could signify to readers and even to participants the equal claim of both sides to a hearing: the legitimacy, in short, of the opposition.[52] At the same time that these rather profound political implications were insinuating themselves into the local culture of both places, a new function, that of controversial debate, was being assumed by the printed word, and specifically by the newspaper.

One more point of comparison between the *Courant* and the *Weekly Journal* needs to be made. Both newspapers outlived the cause of the moment that brought them into being. Once the inoculation controversy had run its course, the *Courant* went on for several years making itself generally annoying to those in the traditional places of power and developing for a brief moment into a fresh and nearly brilliant vehicle of provincial literature. In the case of the *New-York Weekly Journal*, the Morrisites' "paper war" with the Cosbyites, whose outlet came to be Bradford's *Gazette* despite his discomfort in the role of combatant, lasted only through 1734. There is a sort of postscript in the *Weekly Journal* of August 11 and 18, 1735, in which Zenger, understandably, printed an exhaustive account of his trial for seditious libel, his acquittal, the end of his eight-month incarceration, the entertainment of his victorious defense attorney Andrew Hamilton, and the saluting of the lionized lawyer's ship as he sailed for Philadelphia the next day. From then until his death in 1746, when the *Journal* was taken over first by his widow Catharine and then by his stepson, Zenger continued to operate simply another newspaper. He and Bradford conducted a rivalry like that of competing newspapers in Boston and Philadelphia, but the war was over.[53]

An Inter-City Debate

There are plenty of sufficient reasons for historians to concentrate, as they have, on the Cosby-Morrisite affair and the Zenger trial in assessing the role of newspaper dispute in provincial New York. The spectacular nature of these events, however, and especially the continuing inclination of each generation to pursue the debate over the implications of the latter, obscure some culturally significant developments of another kind.

We have already noticed that by the early 1730s, the newspapers of all the publishing towns in America were engaging fairly vigorously in mutual copying. This practice, of course, would become more systematic and widespread as printers in more places undertook the publication of newspapers and as a growing readers' appetite for news and opinion from adjoining colonies supplied the motive for providing more local items worthy of exchange. The main significance of this movement lies in the newspapers' role in helping to create an intercolonial consciousness, a sense among the readership of shared experiences and concerns. This same primitive news network and developing consciousness could result in conflict as well as simple mutual copying. On November 20, 1732, in the first number of the *Boston Gazette* now extant in which John Boydell showed off his paper's more attractive new format, the Boston publisher set off what appears to be the first *intercolonial* newspaper controversy. The theme was one that would last well into the twentieth century: New York impatience with Bostonian prudery and self-righteousness. The subject in this case was dancing—specifically, that newly popular institution that early in the eighteenth century had made its way into the favor of the genteel classes of all the larger colonial seaports: the "assembly," or public ball. It had come last of all to Boston.[54] It is a little surprising, perhaps, to find Boydell lending his paper to the conservative side of this particular debate, since neither his origins nor what we know of his political sympathies and social connections link him in any way with whatever religious or secular remnants of Puritanism might have been found in the Boston of 1732. We might better have expected the *Gazette*, as a self-conscious promoter of Augustan culture in the provinces, to have taken a sympathetic view of this contribution to manners and the social graces. But Boydell published a newspaper in order to sell it, and the opinion he entertained in this instance no doubt went down well with a majority of his readers. So much the better if it stirred up a controversy, which sells better than anything.

The long page-one attack on the introduction in Boston of a monthly "Entertainment of Musick and Dancing, (call'd by the fashionable name of an Assembly)" was not simply a letter from a reader inserted by a neutral publisher in an open forum. Boydell lent his own strong endorsement to it by introducing it with an editor's note: "*The following Observations should have been inserted in last Monday's* Gazette, *but came too late for the Press; yet I hope not too late to prevent the Growth of an Evil too dangerous to be overlookt by any Person who has either a Value for Religion, or Love for his Country.*" The author of the ensuing article expressed alarm "at the Birth of so formidable a Monster in this part of the World" as the dancing assembly, largely because the idea of "so Licentious and Expensive a Divertion" violated the New England economic ethic that in the mind of an eighteenth-century Yankee was woven inextricably into the religious fabric bequeathed by the Puritan "Fore-Fathers," to whose memory he appealed:

> When we . . . read the Wonderful Story of their godly Zeal, their pious Resolution, and their Publick Virtues; how should we blush and lament our present Corruption of Manners, and Decay of Religious & Civil Discipline? They laid the Foundation of their Country in Piety, and a Sanctity of Life. . . . But this their Posterity are too delicate to follow their sober Rules, and wise Maxims, and crying out for Musick, Balls and Assemblies, like Children for their Bells and Rattles; as if our Riches flow'd in so fast upon us, that we wanted ways to dispose of them:
>
> Whereas it is too well known how our Extravagance in Apparel, and Luxury at our Tables, are hastening the ruin of our Country, and are evils which call loudly for a Remedy.

The writer called for "the Interposition of Publick Authority" against this expensive luxury, especially since it was a time of economic hardship, because without the help of the law, an individual husband or father would not be able to deny his wife or daughter "the Liberty of a Pleasure indulged to all their Neighbours and Acquaintances," and "if Madam & Miss are not suffered to shake their Heels Abroad, they will make the House & Family shake at Home."

However much the mainly male Boston readership of the *Gazette* may have appreciated such sentiments, they struck a distinctly discordant note in New York, even for the seventy-two-year-old former Quaker William Bradford, who knew as well as Boydell what his readers wanted to hear.[55] The *New-York Gazette*'s first response, included with the local news under a New York dateline, gives for that among other reasons every appearance of having been by the printer himself, or at least by a close associate. It was, in short, the voice of the paper.[56]

"The Boston Gazette of the 20th November last," Bradford's reply began, "furnishes the Readers of it with a very heavy Dissertation upon the malignity, and dangerous consequences of a chearful Heart, and a polite Behaviour; a Discourse calculated (as it would seem) for that Meridian only, but in Truth publish'd with a more general and worse natur'd View." Not only was the Boston writer obviously hampered by "the Prejudice of Education, the Malice of the Heart, and the Bigotry of the Head" that had already produced instances in Massachusetts of "persecution, Fire and the Sword," but it must be a "very loose" imagination that could project such baleful consequences from an event that the writer had refused to "dignify . . . with his Company."

This would not be the last time that a puritanical disposition would be

equated in a critic's eye with prurience. More to the point, the institution
of the assembly had proven to be productive of good manners and the
taming of party spirit in New York as in England, its place of origin, where
assemblies are "the Promoters and the Patterns of Vertue, Manners, good
Sense, and good Behaviour, the sure Introduction to a general Complai-
sance, to good Neighbourhood, and to a vertuous, genteel, unaffected,
easy Commerce between the well bred of both Sexes, as well as a standing
Discouragement to, and a severe Reproach and Satyr upon the Sot, the
Clown, and the outrageous Party-man of every Denomination."

Since the end of 1732 was precisely when party spirit was heating up in
New York, almost certainly to Bradford's discomfort, the venerable
printer of the *Gazette* may well have had at least one wishful eye on the
local political scene in praising the moderating influences of polite entertainments such as the ones he was defending. But as if to underline the
cultural gap between New York and Boston, which still banned the theater,[57] Bradford inserted immediately after this long reply a brief report of
the opening of "the new Theatre" with a performance of George Far-
quhar's comedy, *The Recruiting Officer*. Boydell promptly copied that item
without comment in his own paper.[58]

The next week's *New-York Gazette* ran yet another long attack on the
Boston writer's response to assemblies in a letter from Perth Amboy, New
Jersey. This one touched most of the same bases that Bradford had, including the vital point of the "Examples in our Mother Country," but
added a discussion of the important educational function of well-con-
ducted assemblies. By sly references to some of the passages from Boston,
the New Jersey writer got across an image of social as well as cultural
backwardness in the Yankee seaport as yet not fully improved by anglicization. The Boston dancing master deserved praise for

> taking the Hint from New-York Assembly, and endeavouring to put to
> Practice among our Brethren at Boston, a Design in his Institution . . .
> of which the good Effects have been experienced in their natural Tendency to
> civilize and polish our Youth, and promote good Society in general amongst
> Neighbourhoods; . . . By our timorous Brother's Representation, I am in-
> duced to think this the more necessary amongst you; for by his Account
> Madams and Misses are apt to be a little termagant and Headstrong, and by
> this Means they might be rendered tractable and good natured, and bear a
> Restraint now and then with less Impatience; and so there would be less
> Danger of their breaking Locks and Bolts, when you have fixed the Padlock on
> their Minds.[59]

Newspapers, obviously, were designed expressly for male consumption in
New York as well as in Boston.

There is no evidence in surviving papers that Boydell ever saw fit to
continue this particular exchange, but there is weekly evidence that all the
colonial publishers now used one another's newspapers as sources along
with those of London. While the most consistently reported items from

other colonies continued to be maritime news, whether in the form of the familiar stark custom-house shipping lists or more elaborate or personalized accounts of particular events, all of the American newspapers in the 1730s took an increasing interest in the actions of the provincial and municipal governments, public events and ceremonies, accidents and fires, crime and its punishment, debates over public issues, news of religion, and curiosities from elsewhere in British America.

Over and above these generalizations, which apply to all the newspapers being printed in America throughout this decade and beyond, a single small but significant achievement of William Bradford stands out. Just on the brink of being drawn against his will into the local political controversy for which he is best remembered, he became the first American newspaperman to engage in inter-city rivalry by drawing attention in print to the cultural differences between another place and his own.

A Decade of Growth

One more newspaper founded during the eventful decade of the 1730s merits brief notice. Ellis Huske's relatively unimaginative *Boston Post-Boy* is significant mainly because it was the last of three Boston papers to be founded by the incumbent postmaster. The *Post-Boy*, of which Huske was largely an absentee proprietor between 1735 and 1754, brought to an end the fifty-year era during which seven Boston postmasters, not a printer among them and none with any real pretensions as a writer or editor, had maintained in the *News-Letter*, the *Gazette*, and the *Post-Boy* the earliest and one of the longest newspaper publishing traditions in Boston. Most of the seven postmaster-publishers were fundamentally politicians, the last of them, Huske, by far the most conspicuous and successful of the lot and, of those we can know something about, by far the least involved in a personal way with his newspaper.[60]

Huske's nominal postmastership in Boston came to an end just as Benjamin Franklin, appointed co-deputy postmaster general for the colonies with William Hunter in 1753, was reorganizing the American postal system. Franklin's choice for the post as Huske's successor in Boston was his brother John Franklin, who alone of Josiah Franklin's surviving sons had remained in Boston and followed his father's trade of tallow chandler.[61] Curiously, the end of the connection between post office and press in Boston that came with the death of the *Post-Boy* was exactly the point at which the new Franklin regime in the colonial postal service was beginning to encourage just such a connection almost everywhere else. Outside of Boston, in provincial England as well as in provincial America, newspapers were always begun and operated by printers, but in America many printer-publishers eventually became postmasters as well.

Through the 1730s, marked by wild experimentation of sponsorship and content in Boston, by the emergence of heated rivalries in the three multi-newspaper towns, and by the development of intercolonial connections through mutual copying and printed debate, the American newspaper moved quite rapidly toward the standardization of a product that in its sponsorship and mix of content would come by 1740 to be much the same everywhere newspapers were printed.

Part III

AMERICA: STRUCTURES AND TRANSITION

Chapter 9

The Printer as Publisher

By the end of the 1730s, with one scarcely significant exception, the newspaper business in British America as in provincial England was entirely in the hands of printers. In the previous two chapters, we have seen how the evolution in ownership occurred in Boston. Elsewhere outside of London, newspapers were a printer's business from the beginning. Because of the centrality of the printer's role not only in developing the shape, design, and content of the newspaper but even in the circulation of information and opinion throughout the provinces, it is time we had a close look at his operation and his product.

The Printer and His Business

"To publish a good News-Paper," wrote Benjamin Franklin when he took over the *Pennsylvania Gazette* from Samuel Keimer in 1729,

> is not so easy an Undertaking as many People imagine it to be. The Author of a Gazette (in the Opinion of the Learned) ought to be qualified with an extensive Acquaintance with Languages, a great Easiness and Command of Writing and Relating things cleanly and intelligibly, and in a few Words; he should be able to speak of War both by Land and Sea; be well acquainted with Geography, with the History of the Time, with the several Interests of Princes and States, the Secrets of Courts, and the Manners and Customs of all Nations. Men thus accomplish'd are very rare in this remote Part of the World; and it would be well if the Writer of these Papers could make up among his Friends what is wanting in himself.[1]

This prescription seems a tall order, especially for one who professed himself, as Franklin did, a "leather apron man"—or, as other American printers would later refer to themselves, a "mere mechanick."[2] To the mechanical skills of compositor and pressman, and to the business concerns of a contractor and retailer, Franklin now proposed to add the requisite literary qualifications and knowledge of world affairs to produce a well-written, intelligently edited "gazette." But under Franklin and David Hall, who would become Franklin's business partner and succeed him as the actual manager of the printing shop and editor of the *Gazette* in 1748, this remarkable Philadelphia newspaper was soon giving evidence in content and quality of writing of just the kind of editorial skills and intelligent reader participation that Franklin thought were requisite for a "good News-Paper."[3]

No one would think of denying that Franklin's talents were exceptional. He was not, however, the only printer in the Anglo-American world who was able to publish what would be by his definition a "good News-Paper." Printing was indeed a trade, but few of the most able printers, despite their leather aprons, were "mere mechanicks." This was, after all, by necessity the most literate of crafts. Handbooks of 1747 and 1771 urged that London compositors have a knowledge of the learned languages as well as their own, and stressed the need for independent judgment in dealing with copy. "A Youth designed for a compositor," says Campbell's *London Tradesman*, "ought to have a tolerable Genius for Letters, an apt Memory to learn the Languages: He must understand Grammar perfectly; and will find a great Advantage in the Course of his Business if he understands *Latin* and *Greek*." A quarter-century later, Philip Luckombe noticed that although the compositor had once been required to "abide by his Copy, and not vary from it," he was now expected to act as copy editor. "Most authors," wrote Luckombe in *The History and Art of Printing*, "[now] expect the Printer to spell, point, and digest their Copy, that it may be intelligible and significant to the Reader; which is what a Compositor and the corrector jointly have regard to." These responsibilities make it necessary "for Master Printers to be deliberate in chusing Apprentices for the Case, and not to fix upon any but such as have either had a liberal education or at least are perfect in writing and reading their own language, besides having a taste of Latin, and some notion of Greek and Hebrew; and, withal, discover a genius that is capable of being cultivated and improved in such knowledge as contributes to exercise the Art with judgment."[4]

The separation of labor between compositor and pressman was found only in London and at the great university presses of Oxbridge. Provincial printers, English and American, were trained in all the jobs of the printing office. While it may well be doubted that many of them had all the classical linguistic qualifications that Campbell and Luckombe urged, or anything like a "liberal education," printing must have attracted many more than one boy with the "Bookish Inclination" that induced Benjamin Franklin's

An interior view of the printing office of Colonial Williamsburg, a working replica of the eighteenth-century original. The cases at the back of the room, from which the compositor works, hold the various fonts of type. Two composing tables (or "imposing stones"), one in front of and one behind the middle press, are visible. Here the pages are made up in "forms." This shop contains three wooden printing presses. A form is in place on the carriage of the middle press, ready for the two pressmen to undertake the various steps that will result in an impression on a sheet of paper. The sheets hanging from overhead wooden bars at the back and right of the room are drying, a necessary step in most cases because the paper was usually moistened in order to take a better impression. Time constraints may have made the process of moistening and drying impractical in the case of newspapers. (*Courtesy, Colonial Williamsburg Foundation*)

father to apprentice him to his brother "to make me a Printer."[5] Likewise, the natural opportunity for literary self-instruction that James Franklin's printing office provided for his apprentice brother, to be repeated in general outline for Horace Greeley and Mark Twain, among other nineteenth-century examples, served many eighteenth-century provincial printers as a more or less effective shirt-sleeved substitute for the university.[6]

Despite the intellectual side benefits that often enabled a printer to become an editor, and sometimes a good one, it must not be forgotten that printing was a handicraft. It was physically demanding work, repetitive and often dreary, usually carried on in uninviting, foul-smelling (the preferred substance for soaking the leather covers of inking balls was human urine), and poorly lighted surroundings. The skills of typesetting, while ideally demanding a high degree of literacy, had as much to do with manual dexterity and mechanical competence as with words. At the wooden "common press," the thirteen separate steps involved in producing a single impression on a sheet of paper, usually performed by a two-man team of "puller" and "beater," were repeated in theory 240 times an hour, though this rate was difficult for even the best pressmen to sustain. Such a team, occasionally alternating positions, might work for as much as ten hours at a stint.[7]

Besides being a mechanic, the printer was a businessman. While a master printer in London could specialize not only in but *within* his craft, the provincial printer in Britain and America usually printed whatever came his way and then supplemented his main activity by retailing books and pamphlets, stationery supplies, and a startling variety of other items, as well as publishing a newspaper. Some American printers also operated bookbinderies, though binding was more usually associated with booksellers than with printers, and Daniel Henchman of Boston, soon to be

A compositor selecting letters from the case to compose lines of type in his composing stick, one end of which is adjustable so that the lines can be set at the proper length. When several lines have been set, the compositor transfers them carefully into a galley tray. After proofs of the entire galley have been taken and corrections made, the type is arranged in the form. (*Courtesy, Colonial Williamsburg Foundation*)

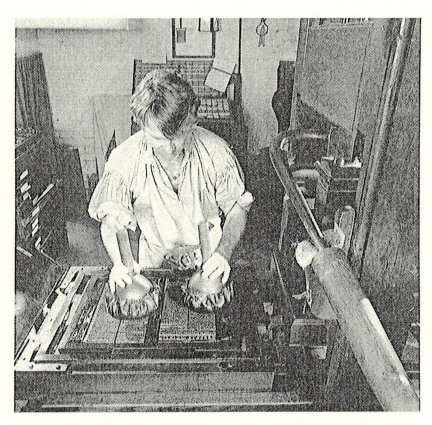

One of the jobs of the "beater," part of the two-man team of pressmen, is distributing ink evenly over the form before each impression with a pair of leather-covered inking balls. Over the inked form, the "puller" will lower the sheet, backed by a padding called the tympan and covered by a light parchment frame called the frisket to protect it from ink in unwanted areas. The whole carriage is then "run in" under the platen, to the pressman's left, by means of a crank device, not visible here, called the rounce. (*Courtesy, Colonial Williamsburg Foundation*)

followed by William Parks of Williamsburg, was continuing a limited printer's tradition begun in 1690 by Philadelphia's William Bradford of initiating and investing in a paper mill.[8] By 1740, printers held most of the postmasterships in the larger colonial towns, and as countless newspaper advertisements ending "enquire of the printer" attest, American printers functioned conveniently as brokers of real estate, indentures, and slaves.

Most printers, despite the complexity of their affairs, were not quite as versatile as Christopher Sauer, the German-language printer of Germantown, Pennsylvania, whom a neighbor thus described in 1739:

Our friend Sauer is a wise and much esteemed man here in this country. He has built a two-story house in Germantown, besides a lathe and a glazier work-shop, which is very spacious. This summer he erected a building for his book-printing establishment, and also a place to burn lampblack, which he needs partly for his printing press, the remainder being sold retail and wholesale. He currently carries on six trades, namely: 1) surgeon and bloodletting, plus a small apothecary shop . . . ; 2) clockmaking . . . ; 3) the lathe shop, where he receives 12 to 13 shillings . . . for a spinning-wheel; 4) the glazier shop . . . ; 5) the printing press . . . ; 6) the lamp-black manufacturing etc.[9]

A master printer was also an employer and a teacher. The number of persons in a printing shop could range from two to as many as perhaps thirty in the largest houses of London. One modern estimate assigns about four printers to a working press in a typical English or Continental printing establishment in the eighteenth century, and most London houses had from three to six presses, very rarely eight or more.[10] Most American printers began with one press and grew to two or three, and because the shortage of labor that was one of the conditions of colonial life affected printing as much as anything else, we can guess that an American printer

Here the "puller" makes the actual impression by turning the spindle, which forces the platen down upon tympan, sheet, and inked form. Two pulls are necessary for each impression, since the platen is not large enough to cover the whole form at once. The carriage thus must be positioned by means of the rounce twice, once for each pull. (*Courtesy, Colonial Williamsburg Foundation*)

typically employed fewer persons per working press than his European counterpart. [11] Nevertheless, nearly every provincial printing-shop proprietor or partner had the responsibility of paying and supervising journeyman printers and training apprentices, who together might amount to as few as one or two to as many as ten. William Parks, who published the *Virginia Gazette* from 1736 to 1750, recorded that during that period he employed in his Williamsburg printing office seven persons besides himself, one of whom was an indentured servant (probably an apprentice) and another a slave. At the height of his business in Philadelphia in the late 1720s, Samuel Keimer employed six besides himself, including one apprentice and the young journeyman Benjamin Franklin. By contrast, when Franklin set up in business with Hugh Meredith in 1728, the two partners worked with the bare minimum, themselves alone. [12]

Relations among American printers were controlled and facilitated, not by the tight regulations and venerable customs of the Stationers' Company that governed the printers of London but by a much less formal intercolonial network of family dynasties and a system of sponsorship and silent partnerships—the former best exemplified by the far-flung tribe of Greens (and its relatives the Kneelands and Drapers), the latter by the business associations of Benjamin Franklin, which in 1740 were already extensive but had hardly begun to achieve their eventual full complexity. [13]

A colonial printer, therefore, as mechanic, businessman, employer, teacher, and participant in web of familial and professional relationships that might cross the boundaries of several colonies, inevitably took a different approach to publishing a newspaper than a government official like John Campbell or Ellis Huske, or an aspiring young college-educated writer like Mather Byles or Jeremy Gridley.

His first concern needed to be profitability; if a newspaper were to constitute a significant share of the work of the printing office, it would have to carry at least its own weight. A printer's commitment to a weekly newspaper would tie up substantial amounts of type and probably permanent space on a composing table for two or four forms, since the general size and column layout of each page and certain parts of the newspaper, such as the nameplate and colophon, could remain in place indefinitely, and many advertisements for several weeks at a time.

Surviving financial records for the years immediately surrounding 1740 are scarce. It is therefore not possible to reconstruct with great confidence the precise economics of colonial newspaper publishing at a time when any actual figures we might use would be subject to distortion by the several severely depreciated provincial currencies then in circulation. But the few figures we do have, some necessarily from the following decade, suggest the sort of calculations a printer had to use in order to determine whether publishing a newspaper on his own account would be economically feasible.

In 1754, for example, Benjamin Franklin reported the price and wage structure he was following in Philadelphia. There a journeyman compositor received six pence for every thousand letters, reckoned by the "em" (the size of the capital M in whatever font was being used). An inside page of the four-page *Boston Gazette* for October 20, 1741, set in what is apparently brevier type, the equivalent of eight points by the modern system, contains in its two columns of 66 lines each a total of approximately 4750 ems—36 to the line. A much more spacious-appearing page one of the same newspaper for April 20, 1741, set in bourgeois or long primer with more leading between lines and beginning two and a half inches down the page to allow for the *Gazette*'s generous nameplate, contains something more than 2500 ems. If there was such a thing as a "typical" number of the *Boston Gazette* in the early 1740s, therefore, we might estimate the work involved in setting its type at perhaps 17,000 ems. For this a journeyman compositor paid according to Franklin's Philadelphia scale of 1754 would have received eight shillings sixpence, or twenty-one pounds two shillings for fifty-two weekly numbers. More to the point, in an office in which much of the work was done either by the master himself or by an apprentice, the job would have taken one good compositor up to twenty-eight hours, or at least two and a half working days, to accomplish.[14] William Hunter's wage structure in Virginia currency in 1751 must have been quite different, for he reckoned the cost of composing a full-sheet number of his weekly *Virginia Gazette* that year at twenty-one shillings three pence, for a total of fifty-five pounds for the year.[15]

To print a newspaper would also mean setting aside a significant weekly block of press time. Six hundred copies of a four-page paper adds up to 2400 pages on 600 sheets, each printed on both sides—a total of 1200 impressions, or five "tokens." That would have meant five hours of work for puller and beater laboring at top efficiency, under ideal conditions, and without interruption—not including the various preparatory steps lumped under the printer's term "make ready." We can guess that the job actually took longer than that. In a small shop there would have been interruptions for other duties. It was necessary to "make ready" for this job not once but twice, once for the side of the sheet containing the two outside pages and once for the inside pages. Chances are high, too, that a good share of the press work was done either by an apprentice, whose skill might not have been sufficiently developed to reach the ideal token-per-hour, or by the master printer himself, who would have been forced to leave the press periodically to attend to the immediate concerns of his varied business. Thus a printer's newspaper must have tied up one press, preventing its use for anything else, at least one full working day a week—obviously a much more serious consideration for a one-press shop with its limited supply of type than for a shop containing two or three presses, one of which might be dedicated primarily to newspaper production.[16]

Under Franklin's scheme of 1754, the wages of two journeymen for printing 600 copies of a four-page newspaper at a shilling each per token would have been ten shillings, or five shillings each.[17] In 1751, Hunter recorded but £13.17.4 for press work for the year, which figures out to about five shillings four pence a week.[18] The contrast is made all the more striking by the evidence we shall soon see that Hunter must have printed considerably more than our hypothetical 600 copies, which would reduce the price for piece work even more below Franklin's scale. The explanation for such an apparently low cost for press work in Williamsburg certainly lies in Hunter's use of unpaid labor. We know that his office contained one slave and one indentured apprentice, and either one or both of them no doubt worked the press much of the time. But of course northern printers used unpaid labor as well, including members of their own families of both sexes, bound apprentices, and at least one black slave, Daniel Fowle's man Primus.[19] Trying to apply Franklin's or any other scale of journeyman's wages to any particular printer's operation, therefore, will provide us with labor costs that are at best only theoretical.

The American printer was not as impeded as his British counterpart by the cost of paper, since the Stamp Acts of 1712 and 1725, enacted specifically to discourage newspapers, applied only in Great Britain. Nor, for the same reason, did he have to devise elaborate publishing stratagems (such as using a large half-sheet instead of a small whole sheet in order to halve the cost of the required stamp, or, before the law was tightened in 1725, printing newspapers as six- to twelve-page pamphlets because the tax on pamphlets was less) in order to avoid being driven from business by government policy.[20] Nevertheless, rag printing paper cost a colonial printer ten to twelve shillings a ream in 1740, and was the printer's greatest expense next to labor.[21] Six hundred copies of a four-page newspaper, assuming one sheet per copy, would have taken one and a quarter reams. Hunter bought 104 reams at thirteen shillings each for the *Virginia Gazette* in 1751, which at 480 sheets per ream means he must have printed not far from a thousand copies of his paper each week.[22]

The printer's theoretical expenses for labor and paper add up to twenty-nine or thirty shillings a week for 600 copies of a four-page newspaper the size of the *Boston Gazette* if we apply Franklin's Philadelphia scale of 1754, while Parker's actual accounts inform us that he spent fifty-two shillings seven pence each week for those items in Williamsburg to print, apparently, 960 weekly copies in 1751. While those were the major costs of printing, they were not the only ones. There were minor costs such as ink and folding and major long-term expenses such as the printer's investment in his shop and its equipment, the possible acquisition of additional expensive type from England in order to make the regular printing of a newspaper feasible, and other overhead. Hunter added to his *Gazette* account a five-pound item under printing forthrightly entitled "Wear & Tear."[23]

All these costs to the printer would have been about the same whether he paid them himself or passed them on to another publisher, adding enough of a mark-up to make a decent profit. For job printing in 1756 Franklin was charging three times the cost for labor (or rather three times standard journeyman's wages for the typesetting and press work, whatever his actual cost) and adding 10 percent to his cost for paper.[24] It seems doubtful, judging from certain sparse accounts, that the printers of Boston were rewarding themselves quite as generously as this in the 1740s and '50s,[25] but that is beside the main point. When confronting the decision of whether to undertake publication of a newspaper on his own, the printer had to calculate the cost of printing it and try to determine whether his likely income from this part of his business would exceed expenses at least to the extent of matching the profit he could earn, whatever the formula he was using at the time, for doing a comparable amount of work for someone else—assuming, that is, that such work was available.

All these familiar elements of the business—labor, paper, incidental printing expenses, overhead, and "wear and tear"—an experienced printer could adeptly figure. There were other considerations in putting out a newspaper, however, that were not part of an ordinary printing job. Among them were new financial risks and a more complicated fiscal structure for his business, new commitments of time, the exercise of new skills, new social responsibilities, and an altered, more highly visible status in the community. The potential rewards of newspaper publishing, however, were sufficiently alluring to most American printers of the era that they were quite ready to take on the necessary new responsibilities, including the risks. To help us understand something of the new economic world in which a printer would have to live once he began publishing a newspaper, let us look at a newspaper's two chief sources of revenue, circulation and advertising.

The publisher had to find ways of getting his newspaper into the hands of his readers. I know of no evidence suggesting that the pre-Revolutionary American weeklies were very often hawked like the London dailies in the streets or that publishers relied very heavily on sales by the single copy. Early in his ownership of the *Boston News-Letter*, Barholomew Green did hope to promote single-copy sales by moving to Thursday lecture-day publication in 1723 and announcing copies for sale at the bookshop of Daniel Henchman. Green's predecessor, John Campbell, had also offered copies of the *News-Letter* for sale.[26]

There is good reason, however, to doubt that sales by the copy ever amounted to a large percentage of newspaper circulation in this period, even in the case of the *News-Letter*. Single-copy prices appear on the papers only rarely, annual subscription rates fairly often. The publisher's periodic plea to his subscribers to pay their bills was a predictable feature of almost every newspaper of the period from John Campbell's time to Thomas Fleet's. Printers' receipts and accounts deal in subscriptions, not individual copies. When Fleet moved the *Rehearsal* to evening publication and changed its name to the *Evening-Post*, he promised that except on "extraordinary Occasions," the paper would be left at the houses of "all the Readers in Town" before dark.[27] Then there are the surviving "carriers' addresses," usually printed in verse on broadside to be presented to the subscribers on New Year's Day. They sang the importance and pleasure of reading the news, pointed out the diligence of the boy who delivered it, and hinted more or less broadly for a tip.[28] Bartholomew Green began his proprietorship of the *News-Letter* in 1723 by suggesting that for convenience subscribers pay their quarterly bills to the carrier.[29] Delivery to in-town subscribers was one place that a printer could save on expenses if he published the paper himself, for it was apparently standard practice for his own young apprentice, son, or daughter to do the job.

Papers sent to "country" readers went by post if the subscriber happened to live along a postal route. Before 1758, when postal regulations became more restrictive, delivery was made under a variety of arrangements between publisher and postmaster or between customer and postrider. The subscriber paid the postage, either directly to the postrider or indirectly under an arrangement by which postal charges were funneled through the publisher and added to the price of subscription.

For the first part of 1740, for example, subscribers to the *Boston Gazette* paid Hannah Boydell's agent 24 shillings per year for delivery in town, and either 28 or 32 shillings for delivery by post depending upon whether the *Gazette* came "uncovered" or "inclosed." In the latter case, the paper would come in wrapping paper addressed to the subscriber, not only making delivery more certain but also providing the customer with a writing surface upon which he could add his own letter to the *Gazette* before forwarding it to a distant correspondent. The resulting package would become a "double letter," which cost twice as much to mail as a "single letter." Beginning on April 28, however, the date on which the *Gazette* announced that it had been granted the same post-free status that John Boydell had enjoyed during his lifetime, out-of-town subscriptions dropped to 24 shillings "uncovered" and 30 shillings "enclosed." At the same time, in-town subscriptions went from 24 to 20 shillings.[30] Thirteen years earlier, when Bartholomew Green took over the *News-Letter* from John Campbell, he added four shillings to the twelve-shilling annual subscription price for sending the paper "Sealed & Directed," but made no mention of postal charges, which must have remained a matter to be settled between subscriber and postal delivery man.[31]

William Hunter's *Virginia Gazette* expenses for 1751 included a five-pound item for "outside Paper" and twenty pounds charged to his binding account for "making up"—apparently meaning wrapping and addressing papers for subscribers who wished to be served in this way.[32] Hunter, however, like Ellis Huske in Boston, was postmaster for his town and therefore could offer his subscribers delivery of the paper post-free.

The greatest actual risk that a printer assumed when he took on publication of a newspaper was the notorious difficulty of collecting subscribers' debts. For American newspapers in the eighteenth century, subscription fees were a more important source of income than advertising. Subscribers were usually expected to pay quarterly, normally at the end of the quarter instead of in advance. There is overwhelming evidence, in the form both of printed newspaper notices and fragmentary publishers' records, that such fees were not easily collected, especially from out-of-town subscribers.

John Campbell sounded the perennial note in his *News-Letter* of December 1, 1718, and in successive numbers throughout December: "It being Customary every where to pay Quarterly for News-Papers, such as have not already paid for . . . the Current Year . . . are hereby desired now to pay or send in the same . . . if they would have it continued. . . ." Some subscribers let their accounts fall dramatically into arrears. Thomas Fleet appealed in 1739 to indebted subscribers to the *Boston Evening-Post*, "*especially such of them as are several Years in Arrears; (most of which live out of Town, and of which the Number is not very small). . . .*" A year later, he was referring to delinquent customers, "*some 7, others 6, 5, 4, 3, and 2 Years in Arrears, and the least one Year the second of this Instant* April."[33] Nine months after John Boydell's death at the end of 1739, Hannah or her agent was prepared to take desperate measures. "ALL Persons Indebted unto, or that have any *Demands on the Estate of* John Boydell," ran an announcement in the *Boston Gazette* of September 22, 1740, ". . . *are desired speedily to come to a Settlement. . . . And whereas sundry Persons (chiefly in the Country) are Indebted for the* Boston Gazette, *and have been so for several years, without paying one Farthing, many of which was dropt by the late Publisher for their bad Pay;* These are therefore to Notify those Persons, that unless they discharge their several Accounts, they will certainly be sued for the same to *October* Court." Not everyone, obviously, had responded to a personal demand such as the one sent to a "country" subscriber to the *Gazette* in far-off Guilford, Connecticut, who responded with a payment of three pounds for two years' back papers and a request to renew his subscription.[34]

By comparison with some of the customers of Benjamin Franklin in Philadelphia and the younger John Zenger in New York, however, Mrs. Boydell's Connecticut subscriber was a model of fiscal responsibility. On October 4, 1739, Franklin announced on the occasion of the *Pennsylvania Gazette*'s eleventh birthday that "*whereas some Persons have taken it from the Beginning, and others for 7 or 8 Years, without paying me one Farthing, I do hereby give Notice to all who are upwards of one Year in Arrear, that if they do not make speedy Payment, I shall discontinue the Papers to them, and take some proper Method of Recovering my Money.*" He added that he would no longer accept new subscriptions without payment for the first half-year in advance, a measure similar to that taken by John Boydell in Boston at the beginning of the same year.[35] In his *New-York Weekly Journal* of February 25, 1751, Zenger added a plaintive plea of personal poverty to his threat to take legal action: "My country subscribers are earnestly desired to pay their arrearages for this Journal, which, if they don't speedily, I shall leave off sending, and seek my money another way. Some of these kind customers are in arrears upwards of seven years! Now as I have served them so long, I think it is time, ay and high time too, that they give me my outset; for they may verily believe that my everyday cloathes are almost worn out."[36] James Parker reported in 1759 that "in the best of my Times," at least a quarter of the subscribers to his *New-York Gazette* failed to pay.[37]

Collecting advertising fees, the newspaper's other main source of revenue, was much easier. Except in the case of the government, to which the printer sent periodic statements of account to be approved by vote of the legislature, placing an advertisement was usually an over-the-counter cash transaction. Publishers charged a fixed amount per advertisement with variations according to length and a reduced price for repeating it in subsequent weeks. John Campbell announced in his first *News-Letter* in 1704 that advertisements would cost between twelve pence and five shillings. By mid-century, four shillings seems to have been the customary charge for an advertisement of "middling" length in Boston. A great majority of the *Evening-Post* advertisements for which Thomas Fleet billed the Massachusetts government for the period June 1756 through January 1758 cost four shillings, and in 1772 and 1773, Edes & Gill were charging Ebenezer Hancock the same amount for advertisements in the *Gazette*.[38] In 1754, Benjamin Franklin spelled out the advertising rates for the *Pennsylvania Gazette* in some detail:

> In the Gazette, small and middling Advertisements at 3/ the first Week, and 1/ per Week after, or 5/ for 3 Weeks. Longer ones to be valued by Comparison with the foregoing; as if 20 Lines be a middling Advertisement, Price 5/ for 3 Weeks, one of 30 will be 7/6d, etc. judging as near you can, by the Light of the Copy, how much it will make.[39]

Judging by the amount and distribution of advertising in the Boston newspapers of the 1730s and early 1740s, it seems doubtful that advertising was any more reliable a source of revenue in that town than subscriptions. The number of advertisements fluctuated wildly from week to week in every paper, though seldom a week went by for any of them without at least one or two. Typically, a newspaper such as the *News-Letter* or the *Gazette* would run six to ten advertisements, occupying half to three-quarters of the last column in the paper, but occasionally would fill up all or nearly all of the last page with twenty advertisements or more. For ten advertisements, which if anything is on the high side, a publisher might collect advertising revenue of forty shillings per week on average, but would not be able to predict his income from that source on any given week. Annual advertising revenue in such a hypothetical case would run about £100, compared with the £360 that a publisher might take in if three-quarters of his 600 subscribers paid their sixteen-shilling subscription rate, which seems to have been about the median in Boston in this period.[40]

The financial uncertainties of publishing a newspaper in the eighteenth century could lead to failure. Ten of the sixty newspapers begun in the thirteen colonies before 1760 lasted less than a year, and another ten less than four years.[41] On the other hand, a printer's newspaper could become the most profitable part of his enterprise. All the calculations of costs and income above, as rough and speculative as they are, suggest substantial potential profitability, especially if a newspaper could exceed the circulation figure of 600 that Isaiah Thomas said was the necessary minimum— and if the printer could collect his bills. In the case of a successful advertising medium such as the *Pennsylvania Gazette*, which beginning in the mid-1740s was using more than half its space for paid advertisements, it might seem that this source of income offered greater possibilities for profit than subscription fees. For the seventeen years after 1748, when Benjamin Franklin stepped down from an active role in his printing business and turned its management over to his partner David Hall, the *Gazette* carried an average of sixty advertisements a week, and often added extra pages to accommodate the demand.[42] At Franklin's five shillings for three "middling" advertisements, 3000 of them would have yielded about £250 in advertising revenue each year. Yet when the partnership disbanded in 1766, the final accounting showed that the £3,639 in advertising revenues over the years amounted to only about 22 percent of the £16,630 of total income attributed to the *Gazette*—a proportion identical to the speculative ratio between advertising and circulation income suggested above for the Boston newspapers of the 1730s and 1740s.[43] It should be added, however, that besides carrying many more advertisements than most of its contemporaries, Franklin's and Hall's *Gazette* could also boast an extraordinary circulation for its time, probably between 1500 and 2000 copies each week.[44]

The Franklin and Hall figures make a larger point about the possible financial role of a newspaper in a printing office. The £16,630 that the *Pennsylvania Gazette* took in over the eighteen years from 1748 to 1766 amounted to nearly 60 percent of the partnership's gross revenues.[45] These figures disclose the important place of a newspaper, albeit an unusually successful one, in the financial structure of an illustrious American printing firm whose other activities included government printing for both Pennsylvania and Delaware, a long list of books and pamphlets, and extensive miscellaneous job printing, not to mention *Poor Richard's Almanack*. This cannot help but suggest the attractiveness to a printer of taking on the publication of a newspaper.[46]

In Boston, with its ten master printers in six firms and another young Green, Kneeland, or Draper being bred up to the craft every few years, putting out a newspaper may have been for some printers a response as much to pressure as to opportunity. Certainly the density of printers created as well as filled a demand for the printed word, but government printing was limited to one competitor at a time, and even in a city of preachers in the midst of a Great Awakening, there was ultimately a limit to the number of sermons that could be printed and sold. Perhaps one explanation for what seems an extraordinary number of newspapers in one provincial town—each, according to Isaiah Thomas, with a circulation barely sufficient for survival—was the need for some printers to create business for themselves in an overly competitive environment for job printing. Some might happily have gone on printing a journal for a club of writers or some other kind of entrepreneur, but as we have seen already, that kind of sponsor usually ran out of steam. If after the period of experimentation in the 1720s and '30s there were to be newspapers in Boston at all, it was up to the printers (with one exception) to take on publication themselves. For Bartholomew Green, John Draper, Samuel Kneeland, Timothy Green, and Thomas Fleet, a newspaper may have been not simply an attractive addition but a necessary supplement to printing jobs that were being spread too thinly among too many competitors.

The Printer's Newspaper

Whether a printer took on a newspaper out of desire or out of necessity, his product reflected its sponsorship. By and large, original creative material was subordinated to the news. When literary or political essays did appear, they were usually in the same place of honor used for such pieces by the *Courant*, the *Weekly Journal*, and the *Rehearsal*—at the top left of page one. But since most printers lacked both the time and the inclination to imitate the essayists of London, material of this sort was almost always in the form either of extracts from English journals or of letters from readers.

While letters and essays of this kind could still be on such topics as education, marriage, medicine, and fashion, readers had by 1740 developed the habit of writing letters of opinion on controversial issues. The extent to which letters of opinion became a conspicuous part of a newspaper varied from printer to printer and according to the issues of the day, but such "newspaper wars" as were waged over questions of the 1740s such as the land bank scheme, bills of credit, and the visits of George Whitefield were conducted mainly by newspaper readers, not editors. This is not to say that some printers could not be more hospitable to one side of a controversy than the other, but they did so by allowing their newspapers to be used as vehicles for partisan expression, not by entering the argument with their own voices.[47]

When Thomas Fleet took over the *Weekly Rehearsal* from Jeremy Gridley in 1733, he took special pains to invite controversial political writings:

> *The Publisher declares himself of no Party, and invites all Gentlemen of Leisure and Capacity, inclined on either side, to write any thing of a political Nature, that tends to enlighten and serve the Public, to communicate their Productions, provided they are not over long, and confin'd within Modesty and Good Manners; for all possible Care will be taken that nothing contrary to these shall ever here be published.*[48]

Fleet's stated policy on the limits of discourse, then, was identical to that of his predecessor, Gridley, who had announced two years earlier that contributions to the *Rehearsal* would be "circumscrib'd by nothing, but discretion, Duty and good Manners."[49]

Such a policy, either stated as such at the outset or implied in various published refusals to print proferred letters that were deemed outside the limits, can be taken as close to the norm for American printers in the 1730s and '40s, with the possible exception of those in New York during the most intense paper warfare. Historians such as Stephen Botein and Thomas Leonard have remarked on the printers' "open press" policies prior to the Stamp Act as techniques for survival.[50] The argument is hard to fault: overt partisanship might have compromised a paper's—and its printer's—acceptability to one faction or another, and every printer was more interested in preserving a viable business than in advancing a political cause. (In this light, John Peter Zenger's *New-York Weekly Journal* is less exceptional than at first appears, since for Zenger political partisanship served as a *means* to the more important end of business.)

The obvious need to retain the patronage of as broad a clientele as possible, therefore, was the paramount concern in a printer's acceptance or rejection of controversial contributions. In the case of many of the printers, that necessary clientele included the province government. The statements of some of the best printer-editors, however, also disclose other concerns at work in this sensitive area of the printer's operation. With such statements, in fact, and by the editorial choices they made, the printers were defining the nature and extent of the provincial public sphere. Even more, they were providing rubrics for the ritual of which the public sphere essentially consisted: producing, consuming, and responding to the printed word.

Early in 1735, Fleet excused himself from printing "certain abusive verses" on the ground that he had "long ago taken up a Resolution never to publish any thing wherein the Character or Interest of any particular Person is concerned or pointed at, whether it be Friend or Foe." He added that he welcomed contributions aimed "as sharply as they will against the prevailing Sins and corruptions of the times, provided they point not at particular Persons."[51] About a decade earlier in Philadelphia, Franklin had refused to print in the *Pennsylvania Gazette* a letter he found to be "scurrilous and defamatory,"[52] and in 1732 Thomas Whitmarsh, founder of the *South-Carolina Gazette*, rejected some anonymous essays on the same grounds.[53]

To modern sensibilities, the most obvious reason for such care is a possible concern about libel, but printers of Fleet's and Franklin's day had more to fear from accusations of "seditious libel"—attacks upon government—than from suits for personal defamation. The principled rejection of "abusive," "scurrilous," and "defamatory" letters does, however, fit with Fleet's (and his non-printer predecessor's) concern to maintain the values of "politeness." Fleet's opening invitation for political letters, it will be remembered, was addressed to "Gentlemen of Leisure and Capacity," the class of writer that the age presumed would convey in style and substance the admirable qualities of modesty, civility, and good manners.[54]

There were therefore two sides to the printers' nearly universal espousal of "liberty of the press," in its eighteenth-century meaning of openness to the expression of competing views on public matters. On the one hand, the printers welcomed such expressions, or at least said they did, because in so doing they not only were making their papers available for useful discussion in the public sphere and thus performing a laudable service to the community but also were protecting themselves from charges of partisanship by keeping them open to all sides. On the other hand, the "liberty" that the printers extended had rather strict limits. Attacks on individuals, as we have just seen, were out of bounds, as were other violations of "modesty and good manners." By 1766, at least, Alexander Purdie of Williamsburg was even applying literary judgment when he rejected some verses submitted to the *Virginia Gazette* because they were "below mediocrity and . . . quite unfit for publication."[55]

Some if not most printers obviously believed that to maintain an "open" or "free" press did not absolve them of responsibility for their papers' contents. As Benjamin Franklin recollected late in his life, at a time when the paper wars were heating up over the ratification of the Constitution, he had never considered his newspaper "a Stage Coach in which any one who would pay had a Right to a Place." Instead, he recalled, "I carefully excluded all Libelling and Personal Abuse, which is of late Years become so disgraceful to our Country. Whenever I was solicited to insert any thing of that kind, . . . my Answer was . . . that, having contracted with my subscribers to furnish them with what might be useful or entertaining, I could not fill their Papers with private Altercation in which they had no Concern without doing them manifest Injustice."[56] Franklin's recollections, set beside the statements and behavior of Fleet, Whitmarsh, Purdie, and others, suggest an incipient ethic of journalistic responsibility distinct from considerations either of business advantage or fear of the law, though obviously they developed in conjunction with both.

This was not an ethic, however, that was fully shared or even fully understood in the 1730s and '40s, for American printers were arriving at their own policies and practices individually, not as members of any sort of guild. Nor did the ethic exclude the acceptance of pay for printing letters and articles of opinion. This realization perhaps comes as a surprise to us who are accustomed to at least the ostensible separation of editorial judgments from the business and advertising sides of the modern newspaper, especially in the view of the various moralistic utterances we have just noticed. Alexander Purdie, for one, rejected the principle of pay for publishing "pieces of amusement" because "I esteem their being sent to me as a favour."[57]

Purdie's pronouncement on that issue, however, was made in 1766. He may have been an exception to the general rule even in his own day, and in any case he included no hint of the modern idea that the point of keeping editorial and business judgments separate is to ensure the independence and integrity of the former. Obviously, it had not occurred to the printers of two and three decades earlier to be even as scrupulous as Purdie on this point.

Fleet's rejection of "abusive verses" in 1735 was accompanied by an offer to return both the letters and the "handsome Bills" that had come with them, but it was not a rejection of payment on principle. Indeed, he announced that if letters and money were not claimed within a week, he would "look upon the Money as due to him for his present Trouble."[58] On July 24, 1740, during the height on the controversy over George Whitefield, Benjamin Franklin articulated an "open press" philosophy that seems to have taken the practice of pay-for-print for granted. "It is a Principle among Printers," he wrote, "that when Truth has fair Play, it will always prevail over Falshood; therefore, though they have an undoubted Property in their own Press, yet they willingly allow, that any one is entitled to the Use of it, who thinks it necessary to offer his Sentiments on disputable Points to the Public, and will be at the Expence of it." Obviously, in view of Franklin's concern to avoid "personal abuse," he did not consider the entitlement to use his press an unlimited one. But he did expect those who used it for public debate to pay for it.[59]

In 1747, Peter Timothy acknowledged in print the receipt of several letters for his *South-Carolina Gazette* but said he was not printing them "as certain Persuasives were wanting with each." The next year, Timothy even resorted to a kind of blackmail by warning an anonymous political writer who had failed to pay promptly that "unless he pays the Price notified for publishing the same, on or before the first of next Month, the said Letter will be nailed up in the Printing Office for publick Inspection." Anyone examining the letter, Timothy suggested, would be able to identify the writer.[60]

Timothy's blatant tactics may have been exceptional, though certainly not much different in principle than the practices of Hugh Gaine and John Peter Zenger, who essentially hired out space in their New York newspapers for the use of competing political factions. There is no doubt, however, that the general practice among American printers prior to the Revolutionary crisis was to accept, if not solicit, fees for the publication of controversial pieces in their newspapers.

On any given week, public documents, both imperial and provincial, could take their place at the head of any printer's paper instead of an essay or letter. So could news, either foreign or domestic but more usually foreign. In short, though all printers adopted common principles of format and arrangement of content, none of them tried to follow a rigid formula. Printers as publishers, while achieving a greater uniformity of product among themselves, also took advantage of the flexibility and variety that their format allowed.

In their selection of news, printers as editors tended to be far less systematic than, for example, John Campbell had tried to be, and to print what they thought would appeal to readers on the grounds of freshness, importance, or amusement. After Bartholomew Green had published the *Boston News-Letter* for four years, more or less following Campbell's original plan, he explicitly rejected the old model and tried for a fresh start. Renaming the paper *The Weekly News-Letter* and beginning anew with Number 1, Green acknowledged in his first number of 1727 that the "Thread of Occurrences of an Old Date, and a Summary of the most Remarkable News of *Europe*" had "not been very acceptable to the Publick, nor satisfactory to it's [the *News-Letter*'s] Encouragers." He now proposed, therefore, to print "the latest and most remarkable News, both Foreign and Domestick, that comes to hand well Attested."[61] This was only a step toward the quite standardized procedures of news selection and presentation that most American printers would be following by about mid-century, but discarding Campbell's "thread of occurrences" and his virtual concentration upon Europe alone was a giant step. Instead of continuing to offer the *News-Letter* under its original concept, as an alternative to the rather different presentations of the *Gazette* and the dying *Courant*, Green elected to follow their example, at least to the extent of selecting news according to a deliberate judgment about what would be most "acceptable to the Publick." Green recognized that market forces had already effected the obsolescence of the *News-Letter*'s original approach to reporting—or rather recording—the news.

With a printer in charge of a newspaper, the collection of news was still largely a passive affair. Whether copying from the London colonial prints, printing letters containing news from the "country" in his own province, or writing up what he heard from the local grapevine, the printer took, by and large, what came to him. Thomas Fleet, however, took special steps to achieve a comprehensiveness and variety that he hoped would set off his *Weekly Rehearsal* and its successor, the *Evening-Post*, from the competition. He announced when he took over the *Rehearsal* in 1733 that he had "settled a Correspondence" not only in "most of the principal Towns" in New England, which the sponsors of the *Weekly Journal* had claimed to have done back in 1727, but even with "gentlemen in London." He also noted that he was "favoured with the Acquaintance of many intelligent Persons in Boston," the better to make the *Rehearsal* "as Useful and Entertaining as any of the Papers now published." He next invited "all Gentlemen in town and Country" to communicate "any thing new or curious, whether in the Way of News or Speculation, worthy the public View," and promised a free subscription to the *Rehearsal* to any regular correspondent who would "frequently favour him with any thing that may tend to the Embellishment of the Paper."[62]

It was perhaps natural that the most noticeable advances that the printers brought to the newspapers of Boston was not in literary content or in their treatment of foreign affairs, but in the news of town, province, and the other American colonies. Familial and business networks in the trade extended all along the Atlantic seaboard. The resulting system of newspaper exchanges and personal correspondence was reinforced by the increasing tendency everywhere except in Boston toward combining the printing office and the post office. Migrant journeymen brought to a succession of printing houses not only the skills but also the assumptions about the newspaper printing that they had learned from another, perhaps distant, master. The binding of the printing fraternity in these and other ways contributed to a systematizing of intercolonial news exchanges and an increasing standardization of the American newspaper.

At the level of his local community, the printer's associations and working conditions were also such as to stimulate a particular kind of development. A Byles or a Gridley, perceiving himself as a writer and his role that of a detached and genteel commentator on the passing scene, tended to emulate what he imagined would be the manner and modus operandi of his favorite British essayist. A printer, on the other hand, such as Draper, Kneeland, or Fleet, spent his long workday in a crowded, busy shop opening onto one of the principal business streets of the town. His newspaper was only one of a dozen different concerns of his own business to which he constantly had to attend. Though he may have had a back room to which he could retreat briefly, his editorial decisions were made at the imposing stone. Much of his writing, no doubt, was a more or less spontaneous matter of standing at his case and deftly placing letters into his compositor's stick while he pondered how he would phrase the next sentence, just as Benjamin Franklin recollected Samuel Keimer's doing during his early years in Philadelphia.[63] Into his shop came public officials to arrange for government printing, merchants and tradesmen to place advertisements or order handbills, booksellers and ministers and Harvard tutors to purchase stationery items or discuss the publication of a pamphlet, the contributors of letters of opinion to the newspaper, and busybodies of various kinds who came to read the posted broadsides and share their gossip with the printer in the hope that they might have the satisfaction the next publication day of seeing it dignified by print.

In this unsystematic way, the printer collected the news of his community, or at least a part of it. He did not then reflect upon it or write highly crafted "lucubrations" in response to it, or embellish it or search out its background. But he did report it. In summarizing this locally received news in his own words in that portion of his paper that was headed by his own city's dateline, he added to his function of selector or editor the function—though nobody had yet thought of the word—of reporter. Of the printers of the three multi-newspaper towns, Bejamin Franklin of Philadelphia and Thomas Fleet of Boston performed this new function most effectively. Fleet, in fact, made a specific allusion to the gradual shift toward more local and American news when he announced the change in his paper's name and publication time in 1735. In the new *Boston Evening-Post*, he promised, he would "take Care to collect and publish not only the most fresh and authentick Advices from abroad, but also what occurs among our selves or Neighbours, worthy the publick View."[64] This printer recognized explicitly that an American reading audience was ready to break the habit of assuming that intelligence "worthy the public View" could come only from Europe.

The printers, however, moved their collection of news, whether foreign or local, no further than their predecessors beyond the essentially passive activity that it had been since John Campbell entered the printed news business in 1704. The point is vividly made by contrasting the editorial content of Fleet's *Boston Evening-Post*, one of the very best printer's papers, with two especially provocative advertisements in the paper on September 29, 1740.

Among the nine advertisements that the *Evening-Post* carried that day, four were for real estate, one was a proprietors' notice, one offered goods for sale in Boston, one announced a runaway "Indian Man servant" from Rhode Island, and one offered to give away, upon inquiry of the printer, "A Fine Negro Male Child." The ninth was a notice warning prospective buyers away from part of the real estate advertised for sale by the heirs of William Tailer in the announcement that appeared directly under it. The unsigned notice ran as follows:

> *WHEREAS there is one half of an Island called* Little Chebasquadegan *in* North-Yarmouth, *in the County of York, advertised to be sold by the Heirs of the late Honourable* William Tailer, *Esq; deceased. This is therefore to caution all Persons from purchasing the same of them, for that the* Town of North-Yarmouth, *who formerly granted it to the Hon.* William Tailer *and* Elisha Cooke, *Esqrs. had no Right so to do.*

One can easily imagine that the two juxtaposed advertisements, this one and the offer directly underneath to sell the North Yarmouth property among other frontier lands, attracted greater notice and occasioned more conversation within Boston's public sphere than many of the more routine—and remote—matters that the *Evening-Post* reported that day. The absence of any reference to this intriguing situation in the editorial matter of the newspaper reminds us of the great distance that still separated the newspaper practices of Thomas Fleet and his contemporaries from an approach to the news that we would call "modern." A twentieth-century editor, of course, having spotted this evidence of an interesting and possibly significant dispute involving two recently deceased prominent politicians and the hot topic, as it was, of Maine lands, would immediately assign a reporter to interview the contending parties, check the deeds, and search out the "background." The result would likely be a bylined investigative piece displayed prominently for readers whose only awareness of the situation would come to them by this means.

This use of the newspaper would not have occurred to anyone in the middle of the eighteenth century even if a publisher could have found the necessary time and resources. No doubt many Boston readers were able to fit the North Yarmouth advertisements into a larger story that they knew and understood, and perhaps found entertaining, but it was not one that they had learned from their newspapers. Under the ownership and direction of their printers, the colonial newspapers of 1740 had come a long way from the pioneering efforts of John Campbell. But providing the context and fitting the pieces together was still a function of the oral culture, not the public prints.

Chapter 10

The Ritual:
The Reader's World

Space and Time

When a subscriber to one of America's earliest newspapers sat down for communion with the fellowship of readers that had been gathered by print, he entered a very much larger mental world than the one in which he was likely to live from day to day. It was, nevertheless, a world with definite limits, both geographic and perceptual. From east to west, it extended from St. Petersburg and Constantinople to the western limits of the thirteen continental American colonies. From north to south, it reached from Sweden to the islands of the Mediterranean in the Old World and from Cape Breton to the Spanish Main in the New. Only rarely, and then only if accompanied by a printed warning of exoticism, was a reader able to venture beyond these limits of the world that mattered to most literate eighteenth-century Englishmen. Not even India, where British interests were already well entrenched but would not rise to prominence in the imperial scheme until later in the century, found its way very often onto the pages of an American newspaper.

What a subscriber read about mostly was events that had taken place from six weeks to six months previously on the continent of Europe. A statistical breakdown by geographic location of the news in the *Pennsylvania Gazette* from 1723 to 1765 is indicative:[1]

Place of Occurrence	Percentage of News Items	Percentage of News Space
Continental Europe	45.3	48.9
British Isles	23.2	18.4
British North America (excluding Pennsylvania)	15.6	16.4
W. Indies & Latin America	9.1	10.8
Pennsylvania, including Philadelphia	6.0	4.8
Asia, Africa, Middle East	0.8	0.8

While every publisher selected somewhat differently and the *Pennsylvania Gazette* figures thus cannot safely be applied across the board, one could expect to find a similar distribution in most American newspapers before 1750. The chief exception would be John Campbell's eighteen-year proprietorship (1704–22) of the *Boston News-Letter*, during which the allotment of European news was almost certainly even greater than that found in the thirty-seven-year span of the *Pennsylvania Gazette* because Campbell's use of local and other American materials was so very limited. Another exception might be the *New-England Courant*, which during its six-year life (1721–27) devoted an atypical proportion of its space—though not all of it was *news* space—to local affairs. Thus the American provincial reader's news diet was weighted heavily toward Europe. In that respect, his mental map was little different from that of a habitual newspaper reader in London, Norwich, or Bristol.[2]

The conventions of news writing and newspaper layout presented the eighteenth-century reader with a world that in addition to having rather specific geographic limits was a world of sequential events. John Campbell's "thread of occurrences" is an extreme example of the chronological presentation of the news, an example that his competitors and successors modified in various ways. The main difference between Campbell and the others, however, was in his eagerness to construct a record that was in some measure complete as well as systematic, not in his use of a chronological format.

The eighteenth-century world was an orderly one, or at least so it was perceived by those who lived in it. The rationalistic currents of the time had encouraged the classification of phenomena, the contemplation of secular cause and effect, the closer scrutiny of governments and the theories behind them, the invention of the novel, and new strides in the writing of history. In every case the effort was to impose the order that was necessary for an eighteenth-century understanding of things and events both natural and human. The makers of newspapers, whether consciously or unconsciously, adopted as their main ordering device the same one used by the novelists and historians of the day, the device of narrative.[3]

It was an obvious choice, for several reasons. The printed word itself, with its linear succession of symbols, must have had some influence in encouraging a writer of fiction, history, or news to use a linear ordering of events.[4] The presentation of events in chronological order, however, was the most obvious way to do it even without the reinforcing mechanism of print. This was the method of the newsletter tradition, the most important precedent for the newspaper, which in turn had been the method of the least sophisticated of historical writings, the centuries-old chronicles. Seventeenth-century improvements in clock-making and the wider distribution of timepieces, the acute English consciousness of the calendar resulting from the ever-widening discrepancy between the unreformed Julian version and the Continental Gregorian version to which England would finally capitulate in 1752, and the immense popularity of almanacs on both sides of the Atlantic all helped contribute to a fascination with "time" as an objective, measurable, uniformly flowing stream in which events occurred. Newton, building upon Descartes, wrote that "Absolute, true, and mathematical time, of itself, and from its own nature flows equably without regard to anything external, and by another name is called duration."[5] It was with just this notion of time that Isaac Watts wrote in 1719, "Time, like an ever-rolling stream,/Bears all its sons away."[6]

Such an understanding of time and events not only was compatible with the newly explained universe of Newton but suited the eighteenth-century passion for measurable order. In fact, the newspapers themselves, in measuring out the flow of time into weekly or daily segments by their periodic appearance, contributed in no small part to the imposition of that order.[7]

Newspapers used a chronological presentation in two ways: in the order in which items appeared on the page, and in the narrative form in which the items were written. Even without the strenuous effort to preserve a strict continuity of events from number to number, which is what distinguishes Campbell's "thread of occurrences" from the rest, almost all the newspapers of our period consistently ran reports of events that had occurred earlier in time before reports of events that had occurred later. American newspapers, even those few that customarily printed literary or polemic materials ahead of the news, nearly always categorized the news by place of occurrence, and grouped news items accordingly: Europe or "Foreign"; sometimes a separate category for England; America; and finally the newspaper's home city. The reader worked his way from the most remote places in the week's news to his own home, and in so doing read the news in order of traveling time. Just as the ordering of categories itself was as much a chronological as a geographic arrangement, items within each category were always listed in order of occurrence.

There would perhaps be no reason to consider this arrangement in any way remarkable were it not for our own daily familiarity with the newspaper conventions of the twentieth century. Today an editor attaches to each item a judgment about its importance or interest, and assigns it a more or less prominent place in the paper, along with a more or less conspicuous headline, accordingly. Far from appearing in order of occurrence, news items are likely to be selected for importance at least in part on the grounds of freshness, and often according to their immediate interest to the local readership. Thus what the standard practice of the eighteenth century placed absolutely at the end of the news, an editor operating under twentieth-century assumptions might place instead in the most prominent place on page one.

The same applies to the writing of the news. The standards of newswriting continue to evolve, but the canons that have dominated most of the twentieth century call for the compression of the most essential details of the story at the very beginning. Elaboration then follows, with details in roughly diminishing order of importance. The "inverted pyramid" formula, originating with the introduction of the telegraph and no longer adhered to as strictly as it was once, is nevertheless still conceived not only as a service to busy readers who might want only to skim the "top" of the story, but also as a practical hedge against rendering the story incomplete or meaningless if the end of it must be hastily scrapped in the composing room.

In the eighteenth century, however, this writer's device was a very long way from invention. Many of the news items that were arranged in chronological order were only short paragraphs, perhaps one to three sentences long. This was the standard format of the newsletter tradition. With a frequency that increased between 1704 and 1740, however, occasional accounts of happenings at home or abroad were of a more substantial length. The shape of such articles was invariably that of a narrative, leading the reader through a sequence of events to a climax that in a modern reporter's rendition would have served as the story's "lead."

Take as an especially dramatic example of this technique the *Boston News-Letter*'s laconic narrative of the capture of Blackbeard the pirate, reported on February 23, 1719, more than two months after the event:

> By Letters of the 17th of December last from North Carolina, we are informed, that Lieutenant Robert Maynard of His Majesty's Ship Pearl (Commanded by Capt. Gordon) being fitted out at Virginia, with two Sloops mann'd with Fifty Men, and small Arms but no great Guns, in quest of Capt. Teach the Pirate, called Blackbeard, who made his Escape from thence, was overtaken at North Carolina, and had ten great Guns and Twenty one Men on board his Sloop. Teach when he began the Dispute Drank Damnation to Lieutenant Maynard if he gave Quarter. Maynard replyed he would neither give nor take Quarter, whereupon he boarded the Pirate and fought it out, hand to hand, with Pistol and Sword; the Engagement was very desperate and

bloody on both sides wherein Lieutenant Maynard had thirty five of his Men
killed and wounded in the Action, himself slightly wounded. Teach and most
of his Men were Killed, the rest carryed Prisoners to Virginia by Lieut.
Maynard to be tryed there, who also carryd with him Teach's Head which he
cut off, in order to get the Reward granted by the said Colony.

Or this from William Bradford's *New-York Gazette*, copied from a London paper some fifteen years later:

> Oct. 16. On Monday last as two young Lads were fighting on Clerkenwell-
> Green, a large Dog, belonging to a Brewer's Dray, passing by, seized one of
> the Boys by the Hand, and not only bit him in a cruel manner, but held so fast
> that it was with Difficulty the Boy's Hand could be got loose; after which the
> Dog seized another Dog, and fought for some Time, . . . and the Dog being
> parted from the other returned and seized the same Boy about the Groin, and
> held on so fast that he could not be separated, whereupon one of the Company
> . . . cut the Dog's Throat, . . . but in the Hurry and Surprize cut the
> Sinews on the back side of a Man's Hand who was assisting, and 'tis thought
> he will lose the Use thereof; The Boy being taken away, in order to be carried
> to St. Thomas's Hospital, Died on the Way.[8]

If the narrative were to have a tragic or a comic ending, the reader might
be prepared for such an outcome by the use of a formulaic opening, such as
"On Monday last . . . an awful and Lamentable Providence fell out
here" (the *News-Letter*'s introduction to the narrative of a multiple drowning)[9] or by the use of that favorite eighteenth-century adjective "melan-
choly," as in the following report from London, copied in the *Boston Gazette* of January 2, 1717:

> *London, Octob. 8.* On Saturday last, a melancholy Accident happen'd at the
> Seat of Sir John Shelly Bart. at Mitchel Grove in Sussex, where Sir John, his
> Lady, and Mr. Shelly, his Brother, after having diverted themselves with
> Fishing, rode together in the Park. The lady's Horse taking a sudden Fright,
> ran away with her between two Thorn Bushes, so that Sir John and his
> Brother could not readily pursue. After much Search about the park, the
> unfortunate Lady was found by her Husband lying on the Ground, with her
> Face dreadfully cut; Surgeons were sent for from Chichester, and all possible
> Means used for her Recovery; but on Monday Morning she expired. She was
> Daughter to Sir Thomas Scawen, one of the Aldermen of this City, and Sister
> to Thomas Scawen, of St. James's Square, Esq.

This piece raises a question that such items often do: why did a publisher, Henry Marshall in this instance, consider this bit of intelligence
deserving of some of the sparse space in an American newspaper? The
question has no easy answer, perhaps because the decision to copy it may
not have been an especially deliberate one. It may simply have taken its
place in a column of news in a London paper that the publisher or his
printer decided somewhat arbitrarily to copy out whole. But the account
of Lady Shelly's accident, like that of the defeat and beheading of Black-

beard, helps make the point that the newswriting style of the day was a simple narrative that made no distinction of emphasis among the various facts in the story. The prosaic details of the fitting-out of Lieutenant Maynard's expedition and the leisurely sequence of fishing and riding in Mitchel Grove are related in their proper sequence, and in the same tone, as the grisly climax of the one story and the protracted tragedy of the other.

The same style of news presentation applied to events less complex and less grave, as in this brief account of a destructive storm as reported in the *Boston Weekly Post-Boy* of August 4, 1735:

> Last Monday Afternoon an exceeding black Cloud gather'd over this town, from whence fell a great shower of Rain, attended with a fresh Gale of Wind, several hard Claps of Thunder and Sharp Lightning, whereby two Houses were much damaged: One was the house of the Honourable *Thomas Palmer*, Esq; near Fort-Hill where it struck the Chimney, as the S.W. Corner of the House; and descended thro' the Roof and Wall even to the lower room, starting the Window Cases out of their Places, and breaking the Windows as it went, with much other Damage: The other was the House of Mr. *Williams* in the common, with [sic] was likewise much hurt.

In this case the writer thought it necessary to start with the rain cloud with which the storm began, and, with respect to the Palmer house, to follow the progress of the lightning bolt just in the order in which it presumably did its damage, from the chimney to the lower room.

A variation on the narrative format is to be found in the frequent reporting of the accounts of arriving ship captains, who told publishers and printers not only what they had seen but what they had heard during their voyages. Such reports invariably began with the arrival of the ship, followed by the captain's narrative as taken down by his interviewer in writing. Alternatively, a newspaper might publish a captain's own written narrative, often made available to the printer by the person who had received it as a letter.[10]

What all these variations have in common is a chronological sequence of events, none of which is distinguished from the rest in tone or emphasis. It is the method of the diary, and of the ship's log. Methodical presentation and orderly sequence were of more importance both in the writing and the arrangement of the news than either interpretation or the making of what today would be understood as "news judgment."

What Was News?

The fact that the eighteenth-century publisher subordinated news judgment to another kind of order in the presentation of the news does not mean that he exercised no judgment at all. He made a choice every time he decided to print an item in his newspaper. To be sure, many of these decisions were unconscious, or at least automatic. Since he copied nearly all of the 60 to 70 percent of the news in his paper that came from across the Atlantic directly from one or more of the London newspapers, his main act of judgment in many cases was simply to choose his favorite source newspaper from the most recent bundle of mail and copy out a column or more of news items just as they had appeared in London.

The American reader, in fact, was seeing Europe specifically through London eyes. Almost always his news of the Old World came to him embodied in the very words in which it had appeared in the London newspapers from which his American publisher copied it. Since this meant in many cases that he was reading what had originally been an official intelligence report or an imitation of one, it not only came to him in the formulaic language of the newsletter tradition but dealt over-whelmingly with a very narrow range of subjects. Of all the news printed in the *Pennsylvania Gazette* from 1728 to 1765, 55 percent of the items and 58 percent of the space dealt with diplomacy, war, and military matters. Two other categories made up another 20 percent: items describing the personal and ceremonial lives of royalty, nobility, and other illustrious persons, with 11 percent of the items and 9 percent of the space; and accidents, fires, crimes, and punishments, with 11 percent of both items and space. Thus these three categories of subject alone accounted for nearly four-fifths of the news, and war and diplomacy made up well over half.[11]

The American provincial reader was invited by his newspaper to share a perception of the world that was very similar to the one held by his metropolitan counterpart. Both the geographic limits and the important subjects of that world were the same. What was different was the slight alteration in emphasis resulting from the inclusion in the colonial press of a small but steadily growing measure of American news, an element con-spicuously lacking in the newspapers of Britain in this period. That small exception aside, American newspaper readers viewed the world, which was primarily a European world, through the eyes of official London.

This was not just an "English" perception, whatever such a generalized and diverse perception might have been, nor was it just a "metropolitan" perception. It was the perception, by and large, of the men in charge of the political and business life of the realm. It was a perception framed for public consumption by government bureaucrats, by professional writers hired by combinations of booksellers, and by men of fashion or oppor-tunity who haunted the clubs, the coffee houses, and the exchanges to learn the gossip and the opinions of those who mattered or who hoped to matter. It was a perception shaped by national interests, religious preju-dices, traditional attitudes toward class and gender, eighteenth-century intellectual currents, a strong measure of ethnocentrism, and much more. By and large, it was the perception of the upper-class, cultivated, fiercely patriotic and doggedly ethnocentric Protestant English male.

It was by no means necessary to be a member of this dominant group to share the perception; indeed, it was probably best articulated by government employees and professional writers, most of whom would not have been members of this privileged fraternity. And it was embedded in this view of things, to which they silently assented whatever their social standing or economic function in the world, that most literate Englishmen and Anglo-Americans found the news. This was as true of the small but growing portion of news written locally for the American newspapers as for the much larger amount these papers copied from London. The resulting consensus, at least as it was reflected in the public prints over the first half of the eighteenth century, covered a remarkable range of attitudes. They included the following:

> An assumption of the superiority of "gentility" over the more common orders.[12]
> An assumption of the superiority of the white over the colored races.
> A belief in the superiority of the English over other nationalities, especially the French, and of Protestantism over Catholicism and non-Christian faiths.
> A condemnation of the Spanish Inquisition.
> A joyous approval of the revolutionary settlement of 1689 and a fervent devotion to the House of Hanover, the legitimacy of which was unquestioned.
> A belief in the liberty of speech and press and private property as guards against tyranny.
> A commitment to "liberty," meaning the opposite of tyranny, as a high political value.
> A commitment to social order as a political value higher even than "liberty."
> A belief in effective male governance of the family as essential to social order.
> A belief in the certain, swift, and severe punishment of crime, including the frequent use of public capital punishment, as a deterrent to criminal behavior.
> A greater interest in the protection of society from criminals than in the protection of the accused from possible unjust punishment, partly because the accused were usually of the lower social orders and therefore likely to be guilty.
> A belief in the virtues of industry, frugality, honesty, and piety.
> The assumption that material success (despite occasional protestations to the contrary) was a measure of good moral character.
> A belief in science and reason and a curiosity about the natural world, combined in varying degrees with a continued belief in the providential governance of both natural and human affairs.

Individual American newspapers differed among themselves over the details of public policy such as the currency issue and land banks, and over details of religious attitudes, such as whether to support George

Whitefield. On the more general beliefs and attitudes, however, of which the above list is a partial compilation, there was near unanimity.

Who Counted

The selection of items of news and comment, and the manner in which events and people were reported on, tells us much about prevailing attitudes toward categories of people. Like their London counterparts, the American publishers distinguished between those who were newsworthy because of who they were and those who happened to figure in newsworthy events. The former, of course, were always named. The latter, if they lacked any other claim to prominence, were as likely as not to retain in print the same anonymity with which they were regarded in the most respectable circles of their communities. A string of summer deaths copied from Philadelphia in the *Boston Gazette* of July 15, 1734, makes the point:

> *Philadelphia, July 5.* Yesterday a Labourer died suddenly at his Work, as is supposed of the excessive Heat.
> And several others have this Day been taken ill from the same Cause.
> Monday last was found in our River the Corps of *Edmund Alder*, who accidentally fell out of a Shalop the [illeg.] past and was drowned.
> *Philadelphia, July 22.* On the 6th Instant at *Byberry*, one *James Worthington*, as he was Reaping, was so overcome with the excessive hot Weather that he fell down, was carried into the shade in hopes he would recover, but he died immediately.
> *N.B.* He was the Person mentioned in our Paper last Winter that Eat the Forty one Eggs and a half after a hearty Dinner.
> On the 9th Instant *Jacob Lee* a Gardiner, as he was at Work in this City dropt down and died in a few Minutes, by reason of the excessive Heat.
> On Monday last a Person belonging to the Bristol Hope, *Author Tough* Commander, went to swim in our River with some of his Shipmates, and was accidentally drowned.
> The same Day a child was drowned in a tub of Water.

Of the six ordinary people whose deaths are reported in this sequence of items, three are named, and of those one had already achieved an odd kind of local notoriety half a year earlier.[13] The inclusion of the names of some and not of the others, however, is arbitrary. It is a testimony not only to what by modern standards were the rather slipshod reportorial and editorial practices of the day, but also to the assumption that to the readers of the public prints, the actual identity of these victims of a vicious heat wave was a matter of indifference. The news was that the deaths had occurred, not who had died. If the informal procedures of local news gathering, which most likely consisted in this case of recording the simple street talk that had made its way inside the print shop, happened to yield some names to match with the events, the printer would happily print them. If not, he would not go in search of them, nor would he presume that his readers would on that account feel deprived. This was the assumption not only of the Philadelphia publisher who compiled and printed this news in the first place, but also of the Boston publisher who copied it.

The quite substantial column and a quarter of nine local items listed under "Boston" in the *Boston Gazette* of January 1, 1739, reported eight deaths, one marriage, two house fires, a highway accident, and a serious burning injury to a child. The deaths were those of Samuel Checkley, a Boston deacon, militia colonel, and holder of numerous local offices during his life; Jonathan Remington, son of a judge, a "promising youth" who had recently graduated from Harvard; Captain James Webster, master of a Boston sloop then in North Carolina; "one Mr. Sumner of Milton," who died in a seizure after stopping at a house in Roxbury to warm himself; and the four unnamed Boston seamen, including the mate, who had died of the same disease as Captain Webster during a southern voyage.

The marriage was of Nathaniel Cunningham, identified only as "Merchant in this Town," to the widow Mrs. Susanna Gerrish, "(only Daughter of *Wentworth Paxton*, Esq. formerly Commander of one of his Majesty's Ships of War) a Gentlewoman of an unspotted Reputation, and great Merit."

The highway accident was reported this way:

> Saturday last Mrs. *Peagram*, the Surveyor General's lady, with Miss *Malbone*, passing through the Town of *Roxbury* in a Chaise with one Horse, drove by a Negro; the Horse made up to the *Greyhound* Tavern against the Negro's Will, whereupon he pull'd about the Horse suddenly, as it happen'd by the wrong Rein, and being a Horse of Spirit and frightened, he ran full breast against Mr. *Pue*'s Garden Wall of Stone, drove it before him, and tumbled over it into the Garden with the Negro, Chaise, and Ladies, a Descent of several Feet below the Road. The Chaise was turned upside down, and the Ladies thrown out in the Sight of many Spectators . . . , yet by the Providence of God they were so remarkably preserved that no Damage was sustain'd by the Gentlewomen, or even by the Horse or Chaise. The Negro Fellow met with a slight Bruise from the Horse in the Fall.

And the burning accident like this:

> Some Time since a Woman at the South End, having sat her young child before the Fire and left it alone while she step'd out to fetch some Water, in which Time a Spark of Fire flew upon the Child's Cloaths, and before it's Mother return'd, it had spread and got thro' to the Flesh, so that the Child's Legs were burnt in a terrible Manner, and 'tis tho't they must both be cut off in order to save it's Life.

The *Gazette* followed up the next week by reporting that "The child whose Legs were so terribly burnt, as mentioned in our Last, . . . dyed last Monday Morning; Part of one Foot having been cut off the Day before, and the whole of the other was to have been cut off to the Ankle the next

Day, if the Child had liv'd."[14] The name of neither the child nor its parents, however, ever found its way into print.

The people who counted in this unusually large burst of Boston news, therefore, were those who were noteworthy because of family or because of conspicuous position. In the brief wedding announcement, the bride got more space than the groom because she was the daughter of a naval commander and a noted "gentlewoman." All of the named decedents save one were either prominent persons or the promising son of a prominent person.

The account of the chaise accident is revealing on several counts. There was great fear for the ladies' lives, and relief that they had escaped uninjured and the horse and chaise undamaged. The unnamed Negro "fellow," one of many meanings of which at the time was "a person of no esteem or worth,"[15] had survived with perhaps less pain than he deserved, since he was clearly at fault in having mishandled a fine "Horse of Spirit." As for the horrible burning accident, the interest of the publisher, and presumably the reader, is in the distressing and in some respects sensational details of the event rather than in the identity of the child or its family, and perhaps even in the carelessness of the unnamed and obviously common young mother whose momentary neglect had brought on the tragedy. The *Boston Evening-Post* of January 1, which reported the same event using some of the same language, included an explicit judgment of the mother, along with a plea for a certain kind of patriotism:

> This is a fresh Instance of the Folly and Pride of our Women, who will continue the Custom of cloathing their poor helpless Infants in *Callicoe* or *Linen*, which is so susceptible of Fire, and by which so many terrible Accidents have happened, rather than make use . . . of the . . . decent and durable Woollens, with which our Shops abound, and which are for the most part the Manufacture of our Nation or our selves.

Judgmental undertones are also present in the *Weekly Post-Boy*'s short sentence of August 4, 1735, reporting an anonymous suicide: "We hear from *Needham*, 18 Miles from this town, that last Monday a young Woman, who had for some time been disordered in her Senses and troubled in Mind, hang'd her self with the Stirrup of a Saddle." Again, the details of the hanging and the clinical symptoms leading to the event are of interest, while the identity of the morose and now deceased young woman is not. Nor is that of the New Hampshire horseman whose abrupt death was reported with consummate efficiency in the *Evening-Post* of October 13, 1735: "Last Week a Man belonging to *Rye* in *New-Hampshire*, was thrown from his Horse, and kill'd on the Spot."

The people who did count in the judgment of American provincial publishers were of the same sort who counted in the London prints. Naturally, there were differences resulting from the far smaller size and complexity of American communities and the consequent ability of persons of smaller means and accomplishment to gain a measure of prominence. But newsworthiness *was* based on prominence in America as it was in Britain, and prominence on both sides of the Atlantic had largely to do with position, wealth, and accomplishment—roughly in that order of importance. Obituaries of the day, both in England and in America, also stressed the "character," or moral and mental qualities of the deceased. It is nearly always evident, however, that character alone would have gained a person neither prominence nor an obituary.

Those who counted began with the reigning sovereign, whose slightest movements and most routine ceremonies of state were noted in the *London Gazette* and most of the private London papers, to be copied out in due course by their provincial counterparts on both sides of the Atlantic. If a proclamation or an exchange of compliments with both houses of Parliament or other groups was involved, the formal language of all the relevant documents was repeated without omissions in the newspapers; if a procession, the complete order of march. Publishers who had to manage their limited space as best they could faced their most critical challenge on the occasion of a royal death or a coronation, a declaration of war, an important military victory, or the conclusion of a major treaty. All such occasions produced a mountain of official verbiage, the reporting of which was done almost entirely by verbatim copying. The point of all this, we need to keep reminding ourselves, was not to transmit the news that a royal accession or declaration of war had occurred, but to provide the means of ritual participation in the public life of the monarch, with whom all identified. While it was the reigning British sovereign who counted most in the public prints, members of the royal family and court and even foreign royalty got plenty of space as well.

Since the provincial newspapers operated as a kind of analogue to those of London, they paid significant attention to the King's representative or counterpart in their own province—to the royal governor in the case of Boston and New York and the proprietary governor of Pennsylvania in the case of Philadelphia. The governors' travels, entertainments, ceremonial appearances, and formal communications and proclamations received the same kind of reportage and placement in the newspapers of their respective provinces that the comparable activities of the King received in the *London Gazette*.

The death of Governor Joseph Dudley in 1720 prompted the longest and most elaborate obituary yet seen in an American newspaper. Campbell lavished nine inches of space on an effusive and utterly complimentary account of the career and character of one of the most unpopular public figures in Massachusetts before Thomas Hutchinson. The Mathers, among others, must have cringed as they read, "He was a Man of rare Endowments and shining Accomplishments, a singular Honour to his Country, and in many Respects the Glory of it."[16] The *Boston Weekly Post-Boy* and the *American Weekly Mercury* of Philadelphia copied from the

Barbadoes Gazette the even longer and more extravagant obituary of Lord Howe, governor of that island, who died prematurely in March 1735. Samuel Keimer, the transplanted Philadelphia printer who now published the *Gazette*, began his piece: "I am now to mention the worst Piece of News that ever had a Place in this Paper, or probably ever will, and which therefore I insert with a trembling Hand and aching Heart. . . ." There follows a lachrymose account of the young governor's death of a fever, his funeral, his family, and the observation that an estimate of "the Character of this great and valuable Man" must await the services of "the best Pen that ever wrote," since for the moment all are so overcome with grief that "they can only say, HE WAS, but that HE IS no more!"[17]

While no other members of American provincial society received quite the attention accorded the governors, men and women in other categories figured occasionally and favorably in the news during their lives and received more or less fulsome obituaries after death. Among those so regularly favored were the richer merchants, sea captains, and clergymen. Wives and widows of men in all of these categories could count on being remembered with a fairly lavish obituary in one or more of the local newspapers, though they did not share their husbands' prominence in print during life. The Boston newspapers routinely printed elaborate accounts, with names, of Congregational ordinations from all over New England, and of all the ceremonials of Harvard College from the inauguration of presidents and professors to the annual conferral of degrees.

The death of Cotton Mather on Tuesday, February 13, 1728, occasioned nearly identical obituaries in Thursday's *Weekly News-Letter* and the next Monday's *Weekly Journal*, either supplied by a common source or copied by the *Journal* from the *News-Letter*. The obituary celebrated Mather as "perhaps the *principal Ornament* of this Countrey, & the *greatest Scholar* that was ever bred in it," and reported that he had "finished his Course with a *Divine Composure and Joy*" after forty-seven years in the "faithful and unwearied Discharge of a lively, zealous and awaking *Ministry.*"

The other newspaper then in Boston, the *Gazette*, was published Mondays like the *Weekly Journal*, but did not print the obituary. It compensated by running on the *following* Monday, the 26th, a long page-one proposal by Peter Pelham, a printmaker, soliciting subscriptions for a mezzotint of Mather—the sort of thing ordinarily found among the paid advertisements at the end of the paper. All three papers printed similar and rather elaborate descriptions, again apparently supplied by a single source, of Mather's funeral procession and burial, which took place on February 19.[18]

As it happened, all three Boston newspapers at that point were either printed or published by a Green or a Kneeland, and young Mather Byles was probably still somewhat involved with Samuel Kneeland's *Weekly Journal*. The *Courant* had come and gone, and the *Weekly Rehearsal* was not yet on the scene. Thus the press was entirely "establishment," not to say "Matherian." It is not surprising, therefore, to find such a unanimous celebration of the great man. Whether the Franklin brothers would graciously have joined in had the *Courant* survived another year, we shall never know.

While the obituaries of the illustrious were often more in the nature of printed eulogies than of the more informative *curricula vitae* of our own day, colonial publishers became capable in the 1730s of presenting full-fledged biographical treatments of persons with important local reputations but whose names were not household currency throughout the province. Among such examples are the lengthy Boston obituaries in several 1739 newspapers of Isaac Winslow of Marshfield, who was illustrious as much for his ancestry as for his own accomplishments; the Reverend James Gardiner of Marshfield; and Samuel Checkley of Boston, already mentioned, a former militia colonel, Boston selectman, town clerk, county treasurer, and justice of the peace. It was not irrelevant to Checkley's dignity, however, that he was the son-in-law of the eminent Judge Joshua Scottow and father of the Reverend Samuel Checkley of Boston's South Church. The *News-Letter*'s equally long obituary that year of the Reverend Peter Thacher of Boston, unlike the mainly biographical treatments of these three, was devoted almost entirely to an adoring description of the man's "character."[19]

Here, by contrast, is the *News-Letter*'s terse notice of the accidental death of a young seaman whose money was more notable than his name: "Last Week, at Marblehead, a Young Man (the Mate of Capt Frost's Ship) Firing off a great Gun, which split, and Kill'd him. He is said to have good Friends in England, and was worth 1500 l."[20]

The Lower Orders

It was not only the people who counted, however, who figured in the news. American publishers, like those of London whose papers they copied, were sensitive to both the moral and entertainment value of ordinary human events. Such matters commanded only a small proportion of newspaper space, but no newspaper did without an occasional item illustrating the misfortunes, foibles, and shortcomings of those whose place in the stratified society of the day did not entitle them to the dignified treatment accorded those who counted. People of this sort usually found their way into the news as the unnamed subject of an anecdote intended to evoke sympathy, scorn, amazement, or, more frequently, amusement.[21]

"We have Advice from *Charlestown*," wrote Thomas Fleet for the *Weekly Rehearsal* of June 16, 1735,

> That one Night the beginning of last Week, a very unlucky and dirty Accident happened there, *viz.* A young Man just come in from Sea, being in a *necessary House* with a young Woman, about Twelve or One o'Clock, the Floor unhappily gave Way, and the Woman slumped up to her Neck in Ordure; but her Paramour immediately calling for Help, she was extracted from her Confine-

ment with little or no Damage but what her Cloaths received. 'Tis hoped however, that this Misfortune will put them upon the choice of a more *sweet* and *safe* Place for their Amours for the future.[22]

To relate this local item of no public significance whatever, Fleet employed the jocular, mock-serious tone that was common in English stories about sex, non-fatal fights and accidents, and sometimes crime. The code words "unlucky and dirty Accident" alert the reader to an amusing rather than serious outcome. The use of elegant euphemisms like "ordure," "paramour," and "extracted from her Confinement," and the brief moral with which the story ends are intended to provide comic incongruity not only with the simple and mildly sordid little episode itself but also with its main characters. The young couple who are the objects of all this hilarity, an ordinary seaman and a woman presumed to be of equal dignity or less, are of course unnamed.

The same tone pervades the following much more complicated account of the spectacular humiliation of an anonymous Scottish inventor. For the entertainment of his Philadelphia readers, Andrew Bradford copied it from London in the October 20, 1726, *American Weekly Mercury*.

> They write from Canterbury, That a Scotsman having projected a Leather Boat, to be carried in a Hankerchief, in which he lately went off to Sea at Deal near a League, to the Amazement of all the spectators, came last Week to that City, to shew so great a Curiosity; and last Friday in the Afternoon . . . , abundance of People assembled . . . ; but were unluckily disappointed by the following Accident, viz. The Projector being on Coal Harbour-Bridge, blowing up his Boat with a Pair of Bellows, . . . and being much crowded, the middle Part of the Bridge fell in, . . . by which means about 50 Men, Women, and Boys tumbled into the river, as well as the Projector and his Boat; . . . by good Providence, all got safe out, suffering no other Hurt, than being extreamly supriz'd, well Duck'd, and the Loss of some Hats, Wiggs, &c. The Projector said, It was an English Trick; others in return, took him to be a Conjurer.

It is even present in this rather insensitive narrative of a chain of personal tragedies, offered to its original London audience as an amusing curiosity and copied in the *Boston Weekly News-Letter* for April 8, 1738:

> *London, Feb. 14.* By Letters from Lanerk in Scotland, we have an account of a very uncommon Chain of Events which happened there t'other Week, viz. Elizabeth Firy was proclaim'd (in order to Marriage) on Sunday, was accordingly married on Monday, bore a Child on Tuesday, her Husband stole a Horse on Wednesday, for which he was banish'd on Thursday, the Heir of this Marriage died on Friday, and was decently interred on Saturday all in one Week.

It was probably nothing more than an accident of reporting by which poor Elizabeth's name made its way into the story; the publishers would have printed these Fieldingesque materials from real life either with or without it. It is permissible to chuckle as well as to sigh over the events of her tragic week because of the social and moral status of the people involved, people with whom the intended readers of the story cannot be expected to identify. The crimes of fornication and horse-stealing presumably indicate a pattern of Scottish low life that is amusingly at odds with the intentionally ironic and pompous phrase, "the Heir of this Marriage." No publisher, save perhaps the Franklin brothers during the brief heyday of the *Courant*, would have thought of employing the same tone in reporting the affairs of a family that was producing real heirs.

Detached amusement, however, was not the only angle from which newspaper writers perceived and reported the doings of the lowly. They could also be judgmental, especially when dealing with racial and ethnic minorities.

Notices of runaway servants, much more numerous in the newspapers of Philadelphia than in those of New York or Boston, often contained some disparaging comment related to the fugitives' non-English origins. Phrases such as these convey the idea: ". . . a squat Fellow with a down look, has the *Irish* Brogue pretty strong"; "He seems mighty Religious, but on a small Provocation will curse and Swear, he speaks Swede, High German and English, but so as easily discover'd to be a Foreigner, his Voice low"; "a Negro Man . . . , a tall slender Fellow, not very black, he has thick Lips and by his Speech it may be known he is a *Bermudian*."[23]

Identification by race or nationality was also a common feature of items reporting crimes, disorders, or accidents. In Philadelphia and New York, with their relatively diverse white populations, terms such as "Irishman" and "Dutchman" figure in the news along with racial identifications. In Boston, it is usually only race that calls for special notice, though one of the three "ordinary Fellows" who killed a Boston shopkeeper during an argument in 1739 was "one *Cosseran, an Irish Pedler, that has a Cast in his Eye*."[24] On at least one occasion, not content with reporting the suspicion that it was two Negro slaves who were responsible for the attempted poisoning of a Boston family, the *Gazette* offered an opinion on the matter: "'tis hoped they will both be made Examples of, by some severe Punishment, for deterring other such Wretches from the like abominable Attempts for the future."[25] None of these examples, perhaps, quite matches the callousness with which Benjamin Franklin accounted the cost of a smallpox epidemic in the Quaker city of Philadelphia:

> The Small-pox has now quite left this City. The Number of those that died here of that Distemper, is exactly 288, and no more. 64 of the Number were Negroes; If these may be valued one with another at £30 per Head, the Loss to the City in that Article is near £2000.[26]

Or of the cruel jocularity with which the *Maryland Gazette* reported a small but painful incident from the point of view of a horse rather than a human being. One of the plow-horses being led by "a Negro Boy, belonging to Mr.

Sellers," according to the item from Annapolis copied in the *Boston Gazette* on June 17, 1734, "being . . . *hungry,* took hold the Boy's Ear, and bit it off, close to his Head. *But I cannot tell whether he eat it afterwards, or not."*

Women

In 1739 the Boston press noted the deaths of two prominent women. Mary Hazard, whose "500 Children, Grand Children and Great Grand Children" included in the second category the late deputy governor of Rhode Island, died in that colony in her hundredth year. The *Boston Gazette* of February 12 published under a Newport dateline a brief account of her life and death which, besides noting her impressive fecundity and longevity, included the following appreciation: "She was accounted a very useful Gentlewoman both to Poor and Rich on many accounts, and particularly amongst Sick Persons for her Skill & Judgment, which she did Gratis." In the *Weekly Journal* of June 19 appeared a considerably longer obituary of Mary Partridge, widow of the late lieutenant governor of New Hampshire and mother-in-law of Jonathan Belcher, the sitting governor of Massachusetts. The portrayal of her "character," with its stress on piety, virtue, intellect and her exemplary life and death, stands as an adequate summary of the eighteenth century's image of the ideal woman:[27]

> Madam PARTRIDGE must be mentioned as a Gentlewoman whose Memory will be always fragrant and blessed; having merited by her extraordinary Piety and Devotion, as well as by every Virtue solitary and social, one of the brightest Characters among her Sex, which was justly acknowledged in both those Provinces, in which she lived many Years.
>
> Her superiour natural Powers of Mind, and her intellectual Accomplishments were obvious to all who had the Honour and Happiness to be at any time conversant with her, which Endowments continued in great Perfection to the last Hours of her Life.
>
> Her Person was very graceful and amiable, and the Serenity of her Countenance was such at all Times, and thro' the various Stages and Scenes of Life, as spoke a constant calmness of Soul within, which Death it self could not interrupt, for in perfect Peace she received his Message, and departed this life without a Groan, as knowing that she was called to enter upon her everlasting Sabbath in a better World.

While the account of Madam Partridge's sublime departure combines the seventeenth-century ideal of female piety with the eighteenth-century ideal of the "genteel lady," a development fostered in New England especially by Cotton Mather, it does not look ahead still further to the sentimental nineteenth-century image of the "tender mother."[28] Yet that is precisely the phrase that the publishers of the *New-England Weekly Journal* invoked in 1733 when they introduced a carefully crafted poem by an anonymous young mother on the death of her child. It was not so much the assertion of "tender motherhood" that concerned Kneeland and Green, however, as the assurance that the author had not been so forward as to offer the piece for publication herself. The brief introduction thus testifies both to the young woman's appropriately feminine modesty and, somewhat patronizingly, to her poetic achievement: "The following Lines, (compos'd by a tender Mother, not far from this Place,) on the Death of a most forward, amiable and hopeful Child, was lately left with us for a Publication, without her Knowledge, and without the least Alteration." Here are the last eleven of the thirty-one lines of "A Lamentation &c. On the Death of a CHILD":

> Then go sweet BIRD, mount up, and sing on high,
> Whilst winged Seraphs bear thee thro' the Sky.
> There clad with Glory and with Joy sereen,
> On Boughs Immortal ever fresh and green,
> Chant forth high Praises, with the lovely Train
> Of spotless Doves, for whom the Lamb was slain.
> Touch *David*'s Harp with wonder and suprize,
> While ours neglected, on the Willows lies.
> Hosanna's sound on each exalted String,
> There join the Cherubim and Seraphim,
> In endless Songs of Triumph to this KING.[29]

One attitude toward women that the newspapers reflected, therefore, is the respect due a "gentlewoman" of high status, and respect for the marks of womanly character and accomplishment that the age admired. In addition, at least one newspaper on at least one occasion presented a female literary production for the serious contemplation and admiration of its readership. Before we explore some other attitudes that the newspapers reflected, one further and even more atypical instance of female participation in the printed public sphere deserves our attention.

When Thomas Whitmarsh started the *South-Carolina Gazette* in 1732, sixteen-year-old "Martia" immediately breached the gender barrier that usually excluded female writings from the newspapers. The precocious and obviously genteel young woman responded to Whitmarsh's invitation to correspondents by noting that although the printer had "not applied your self to our Sex particularly, for our Correspondence, yet I doubt not, but we are of Course implied, among those, whose Genius (as you express yourself) reaches no further than Amusement." She also admitted that "you'll think [it] comes awkwardly from a Female Pen." Beyond mere "Amusement," however, Martia criticized the "Choice of Company" and "frivolous behavior" of a "set of young Gentlemen" who, she feared, were spoiling the reputations that would be necessary for "making any considerable Figure or Advantage in Trade." She was particularly distressed that "one of these Sparks is my Brother, and . . . another of 'em stands so fair in my Opinion, that I can see no other Blemish in his Conduct, than what has been here hinted at."[30]

The next week's response from "Rattle" was addressed not to Martia but to her "Papa." It is full of sexual innuendos, suggesting that such a forward young lady risks seduction if she is not kept in check by her father, to whom Martia had attributed her education. The writer next implies that a young woman ought to have been given instruction more appropriate to her sex, and then offers himself as a possible husband "Provided you throw some material additional Requisites into her *Portion*, besides that of her *Education*." "Rattle" concludes by suggesting that someone of his own qualifications needs to step in and assert authority: "When, with all due Respect to your good old Bladeship, I may, perhaps, be in the Humour to save her Longing, and rid you of a *Charge*, that, in all probability, may, by that Time, be too much for you to manage."[31] Martia's response defends her father, dismisses "Rattle" as a bore, and urges the printer to suppress two other letters (one of which came with money enclosed) that he has apparently shown the young woman rather than print without her permission.[32] Most readers must have agreed that in this instance it was the woman who came away not only with the last word but the best of the exchange. In entertaining such an unusual confrontation, as in welcoming even a debate in prose and verse over miscegenation,[33] the Charleston paper under its first publisher allowed a freer debate over sexual matters, including the expression of unorthodox views, than was ordinarily found in the northern papers.

By a startling coincidence, in the very week that Martia's initial foray appeared in the *South-Carolina Gazette*, another young woman ventured into print in Boston. "Betty Pert"'s purpose was to take issue with a satirical essay on female fashions, rather typical for its time, that had filled the front page of the *Weekly Rehearsal* the previous week. "You seem to blame us," she wrote in reply to the essayist, "for our Innovations and fleeting Fancy in Dress, which you are most notoriously guilty of." A gentleman's long coat, she proclaimed, was sillier than the much-maligned hoop skirt, and as for other fashions:

> You complain of our masculine Appearence in our Riding Habit, and indeed we think it is but reasonable that we should make Reprisals upon you, for the Invasion of our Dress, and Figure, and the Advances you make in Effeminacy, and your Degeneracy from the figure of Man. Can there be a more ridiculous Appearance than to see a smart Fellow within the compass of five Feet *immers'd* in a *beige long Coat* to his *Heels*, with *Cuffs*, to the *Armpits*, the *Shoulders and Breast* fenc'd against the Inclemencys of the Weather (with as much Care as a *Wet Nurse*) by a *monstrous Cape*, or rather *short Cloak*, *Shoe toes* pointed to the Heavens, in imitation of the *Laplanders*, with *Buckles* of a *Harness Size*. I confess the *Beaux* with their Toupee *Wigs* make us extreamly merry, and frequently puts me in mind of my Favourite Monkey, both in Figure and Apishness. . . .[34]

Thus the battle of the sexes, only one side of which was customarily waged in print, occasionally broadened into an actual debate in the columns of the newspapers. It should be noted, however, that the female combatants in both the South Carolina and New England skirmishes of January 1732 were obviously not only of the rising generation but also of a privileged social station.

Newspapers both north and south, besides entertaining a rare exchange such as those just noted, either expressed or lent their pages to ideas about women that covered quite a broad spectrum. The newspapers, as we have already seen, could function as an equivalent to a funeral sermon or elegy in their solemn treatments of deceased ladies. They could also, occasionally, raise up a more ordinary female for admiration. But in this century that could juxtapose "the gross and the elegant" with such little difficulty, it was inevitable that a variety of other male attitudes toward women should find expression in newspaper type.

One was amusement, especially when females stepped out of their customary sphere and took on male roles. Incongruity is always a basis for humor; in the Anglo-American culture of the eighteenth century, imaginary or actual violations of firm gender roles could result in surprisingly incongruous, and therefore funny, departures from the expected. That was obviously part of Benjamin Franklin's joke when he cast Mrs. Silence Dogood into the role of *censor morum*. About the time Franklin went to Philadelphia, the *American Weekly Mercury* copied from an unnamed English paper an account from the fashionable watering place of Bath of a real-life role reversal, reported in a tone and style that left little doubt as to how the reader was expected to react: "Yesterday a new and extraordinary Entertainment was set on Foot for the Diversion of our polite Gentry; and what should it be but a Match at Foot-ball, play'd by six young Women of a Side."[35]

Another was the romantic. When Mather Byles closed out the "Proteus Echo" series in the *New-England Weekly Journal* with a poetic tribute to "Belinda,"[36] it was in the same April of 1728, when the sap must have been flowing with special vigor, that another young blood living in Boston's North End used the front of the *Boston Gazette* to woo the object of his desires. In an introductory letter, "Timothy Vainlove" bewails the cruelty of "the Beautifull'st Young Lady my Eyes ever beheld," with whom he had "been most passionate in Love" since first setting eyes on her nearly seventeen months before. The letter prefaces a poem of the same genre as Byles's, this one addressed to "Florinda." Making clever allusions to the Greek myth of Aurora, goddess of the dawn whose lover grows old, weary, and impotent at day's end, the poet, in the tradition of Andrew Marvell, urges his favored one to make hay while the sun shines, so to speak:

> Tho' ne'er so Lovely, ne'er so form'd for Bliss,
> Florinda *shall be, what* Aurelia *Is;*
> *Vast Graces did that haughty Fair adorn,*

How sighted Man enjoys his turn of Scorn.
    By sorrows, not your own, learn fatal truth
Yeild [sic], *while you Triumph, and Consent in Youth;*
Time Cools our Passions, and your Power disarms
Lovers are Fugitive, as well as Charms.[37]

In the midst of the raging political controversy of 1734 that would soon land New York's John Peter Zenger in jail, he heeded an anonymous contributor's request to give his readers *"a little Relaxation from those more weighty Affairs"* and printed a longish poem addressed, like Byles's, to "Belinda." Its essential message is captured in these two lines: "One only Care your gentle Breasts should move,/ The important Business of your Life is Love."[38]

Love letters of course provided much more obvious material for spoofs than the New England funeral elegy that young Benjamin Franklin had satirized in the *Courant* in 1722. Franklin himself, as the more mature publisher of the *Pennsylvania Gazette*, played with the variety of possible responses to an anonymous letter addressed to the "prettiest Creature in this Place" who, "if it was not for her Affectation, . . . would be absolutely irresistible." Having published the initial one-sentence teaser in the *Gazette* of November 20, 1735, he provided six responses, ranging from the ponderously serious ("I Cannot conceive who your Correspondent means by *the prettiest Creature* in this Place; but . . . she who is truly so, has no Affectation at all") to the outrageous ("They who call me affected are greatly mistaken; for I don't know that I ever refus'd a Kiss to any Body but a Fool.")[39] In the same year the *Boston Evening-Post* copied from a London journal *"The true original Receipt for composing a modern Love-Letter,"* very much along the lines of Franklin's treatment of the elegy thirteen years before.[40]

Published love letters and satires upon them were sometimes ambiguous in their intent, or at least appear so at this distance. Newspaper essays occasionally confronted more or less explicitly the perennial question of whether the suitor was seeking marriage or merely seduction, and the very real social and sexual dilemmas facing the young unmarried woman of the age. "Instructions to unmarried Ladies," for example, an essay in the *New-England Weekly Journal* in 1739, alludes to "the strong Temptations the Fair Sex are exposed to, from the *warm* Addresses of *ours*." The author then develops at length the distinction between "virtue" and "reputation," the former meaning the actual preservation of virginity and the latter its apparent preservation. Since the world is prejudiced unfairly in favor of reputation, the main thing is to avoid publicly compromising situations that cast doubt on a lady's virtue, however pure she may actually be.[41] The same theme is taken up in an essay copied from the *London Magazine* by the *Boston Evening-Post*, also in 1739, but the conclusion is different: "Such is the Difference between a *Hypocritical Prude* and a truly *virtuous Woman;*

The first fears the common Reflexions of the World, and, if she can secretly err, feels no Compunction at the Crime; the latter, conscious of not erring at all, feels no Pain at the common Censure of the Publick."[42]

Most speculative writing that addressed the issue, whether seriously or in the form of satire, valued virginity in unmarried women, early and fruitful marriage, and faithfulness and obedience in marriage. Conversely, the writers expressed the conventional pity for the ruined maiden who had been the victim of male deceit on the one hand, and complained of young women who refused or postponed marriage on the other.

In a variation on the usual themes relating to marriage, a correspondent to the *American Weekly Mercury* complained in 1735 of the injustice and misery caused by parents who arrange unwanted marriages for their children. The context of his complaint suggests that in Philadelphia, as it seems to have been in Boston, marriage for love was more usual than marriage by parental arrangement. It also reveals some insight into the private shortcomings even of some marriages that had begun happily: "This fatal Necessity, of Marrying whom their Parents arbitrarily chuse for them, leaves no Room for the Pleasure of Choice, for the Delicacy of Courtship, or the Fondness of Passion. Knowing it must be so, they are both as indifferent before-hand, as many others are afterwards."[43]

The newspapers' sharpest barbs by far were reserved for neither fallen women nor reluctant brides, but for female misbehavior within marriage and for the husbandly shortcomings that allowed such transgressions to occur. Any resistance to male family governance was considered a breach of normal civility and a symptom both of female contrariness and of the husband's ineffectiveness. Commentators took such resistance seriously because the Anglo-American household, a "little republic," was the fundamental building block of society, and disorders in the household seemed to threaten order in the society at large. Commentators also aimed derisive laughter at such resistance, perhaps because even small instances of rebellion or the flaunting of undue freedom seemed to be symbolic steps, at least, in the direction of that ultimate male disgrace, cuckoldry—the final mark of a failed husband.

"Last Saturday a certain Moabite in the Burrough," the *American Weekly Mercury* copied from London in 1721, "engaging with his Wife in the Dispute of ancient Fame for the Breeches, was so warmly handled by his Antagonist, that in vengeful Wrath he fell'd her to the Ground, broke one of her Legs, and bruised her Body in such a Manner, that she will hardly ever be in a Capacity to enter the Lists with him again." Three weeks later, the same paper was reporting, again with the help of a London paper, "On Tuesday a Woman was committed to Bridewell . . . for Tying her Husband to a Bedpost, and whipping him almost to Death, being assisted therein by several of her Gossips."[44]

These examples of domestic conflict, of course, are both extreme and violent, and they are from London. I have not encountered the reporting of similar American cases in the newspapers. Nevertheless, Andrew Bradford copied both reports for the appreciation of his American readers. The language is revealing, especially in the first case. Even though the wife was severely beaten, the tone of the piece is humorous and mock-heroic. The woman is to blame for her own bruises and broken bone for challenging her husband's authority and starting the fight in the first place. The term "her Gossips" in the second item is obviously pejorative, and of course of the two victorious combatants in the two stories, only the female one is jailed.

One of several issues in the exchange of 1732 between the *Boston Gazette* and the *New-York Gazette* over dancing schools was whether the assemblies were a hindrance or a help to maintaining paternal family governance. The Boston writer, whose views John Boydell warmly endorsed, warned that without official intervention, heads of families would be hard put to deny wives and daughters "the Liberty of a Pleasure indulged to all their Neighbours and Acquaintances." If everyone else is doing it and "Madam and Miss are not suffered to shake their Heels Abroad, they will make the House & Family shake at Home."[45] Better to call in province law in aid of frugality and Puritan good order than to place husbands and fathers in a position to be thus challenged.

Part of the protracted New York response picked up on the concern thus raised by "our timorous Brother," since it gave the impression that in Boston "Madams and Misses are apt to be a little termagant and Headstrong." Dancing assemblies will help in that distressing situation, because "by this Means they might be rendered tractable and good natured, and bear a Restraint now and then with less Impatience; and so there would be less Danger of their breaking Locks and Bolts, when you have fixed the Padlock on their Minds."[46] Thus not only could the writer accuse his New England antagonist of prudery and of being out of fashion, but he could discredit the Yankee's argument still more by suggesting that he had admitted that the men of Boston were having trouble ruling the roost.

Seven years later, New York's other newspaper, the *Weekly Journal*, turned what might have been simply a report of a "remarkable occurrence" into a comment on husbandly sufficiency, complete with an assumption about the male role in reproduction that has not stood the scientific test of time: "*Middletown* in *Monmouth County, October 26th.* 1739. The Wife of one *John Mackenster* was brought to Bed of three Girls and all likely to live, being her first Children, and she upwards of 40 Years of Age, the Neighbouring Women of all Ages, both far and near come Daily to see them; And it is thought there will be a great Discontent amongst the Marry'd Women that their Husbands can't Perform the same piece of Manhood."[47]

In 1740, the *American Weekly Mercury* satirized either ineffective husbands or female assertiveness, depending on how the reader received it, by reprinting from the new anti-Walpole *Champion* the mock proceedings of a council of the "Censor of Great-Britain." Part of the agenda was a resolution concerning "wearing the breeches":

> Mrs. Joan Vinegar read a Petition from Dame *Catherine High-Blood*, in Behalf of herself and several others, setting forth the utter Incapacity of many Husbands in this Kingdom for Government, that Male-Administration is an equivocal Term, and signifies both a Man's governing and governing ill: That, whereas we admit of no Salique Law, the Families may be no more shut out from private than publick Power.
>
> Resolv'd, That in certain Cases hereundermentioned, it may be lawful for a Woman to wear the Breeches.

The "Cases" were then enumerated, and included "Every Woman of great Fortune marrying a Man of none," "Every Woman who shall approve herself able to conquer her Husband in fair Battle," "Every prudent Woman above the Age of fifty, who marries a Boy," and "every Woman of Sense whose Husband is a Fool, infirm, a Child, or a Dotard."[48] Whether the piece just quoted constitutes a satirical expression *of* that view or a misogynist satire *on* that view—either reading is possible— eighteenth-century sympathies were often with the woman when a husband failed to do his duty. In dealing with material of this sort, at least so far as my reading has disclosed, the American newspapers stopped short of the outright ribaldry that occasionally found its way into the English press, both metropolitan and provincial. Just as the American press lacked the grosser Grub Street elements of many of the London newspapers, so too did it refrain from the blatant sexual content of, for example, this item from the *Weekly Courant* of Nottingham, one of the earlier and longer-lived provincial papers of England:

> any able young Man, strong in the Back, and endow'd with a good Carnal Weapon, with all the Appurtenances thereunto belonging in good Repair, may have Half a Crown per Night, a Pair of clean Sheets, and other Necessaries, to perform Nocturnal Services on one Sarah Y-tes, whose Husband having for these 9 Months past lost the Use of his Peace-Maker, the unhappy Woman is thereby driven to the last Extremity.[49]

Obviously, there was a difference between both metropolitan and provincial England on the one hand and provincial America on the other in the extent to which the print culture admitted to taboos in certain areas. The dissenting religious sensibilities that prevailed in most parts of America are undoubtedly part of the explanation. So, one suspects, is the familiar distinction between Old World sophistication and the fresh naïveté and optimism of the New. The relative absence in America of social strata either above or below the conventional "middle class" may also be a factor. Whatever the reasons, of which there are probably several, American publishers drew the line that separated the printable from the unprintable more narrowly than their English counterparts. In doing so, to use a modern legal concept that had at least as much practical application in the eighteenth century as it does today, the publishers were conforming to prevailing community standards.

The Remarkable and the Sensational

News publishers on both sides of the Atlantic often used the phrase "remarkable events" or "remarkable occurrences" to describe the contents of their papers. The *New-England Weekly Journal* even invited the communication of "Remarkable Judgments or Singular Mercies,"[50] adding a providential cast to the general assumption of the day that the very concept of "news" implied the reporting of events that were out of the ordinary.

In actual practice, of course, the newspapers of the eighteenth century, like those of our own day, reported much that was routine and unremarkable. The shipping lists, the periodic convening of legislative assemblies, the ordinary travels of kings and governors, the regular rituals of church and state and of life and death—none of these categories of news actually involved "remarkable" events in the strictest sense, though some of them involved remarkable people. Every publisher, however, also welcomed the chance to record the unusual, the curious, the mysterious, the sensational, and indeed the providential.

Naturally there was a difference between the merely curious and the truly remarkable and serious. Of the latter, no event except the earthquake of October 29, 1727, commanded as much newspaper attention as an incident the previous July in which two men, the second intending to rescue the first, died upon being lowered into a 28-foot dried-up well near the Boston town dock.

The original report of the incident, followed by a scientific discussion speculating upon the cause of the deaths, occupied many inches of print in no fewer than seven numbers of the *New-England Weekly Journal*. The event and part of the discussion was copied soon afterward in the *New-York Gazette.*[51]

Shipwrecks, storms at sea, West Indian slave revolts, and disastrous fires all provided "remarkable" materials that American publishers were only too glad to print on the rare occasions that reports of such events came into their hands. Equally deserving of newspaper type, however, were the little curiosities and coincidences that occurred either abroad or close to home. The cheating Irish tenant who was struck blind at the same instant the man he got to perjure for him fell down dead, the simultaneous deaths from smallpox of two engaged persons on the day following what was to have been their wedding day, a two-headed calf in Virginia, a shift wedding and an extraordinary eating performance in Pennsylvania, and a "most surprizing Appearance of the *Aurora Borealis*" in Boston all qualified as remarkable occurrences. Both New York newspapers carried the same account, copied verbatim from the same London source, of a "dusky Blood"-colored moonrise near Dublin.[52]

A special kind of remarkable occurrence, often getting sensational treatment in the newspapers, was the public execution. The tough-minded attitude of the age toward capital crimes is nowhere more plainly stated than in a 1737 report from Naples, printed in London and reprinted in Boston, of the alarming tendencies toward clemency being exhibited by Charles IV, the reformist King of Naples and Sicily:

> From Naples they write, that the frequent Murders in that City these three or four Months past having oblig'd his Sicilian Majesty to sign several Warrants for executing the Murderers, after Sentence of Death had been pass'd upon them, he lately refus'd to sign one that was presented to him. *What*, says he, *must I always sign Sentences of Death, I that would willingly sign nothing but Pardons? And can I not make my Subjects better but by destroying them?* That Prince has given such re-iterated Marks of his Clemency and Tenderness to his People, that the several Courts of Justice have been oblig'd to make Remonstrances to him upon that Head, and to represent to him that his Mercy would only give Room to the commission of greater Crimes and more frequent Disorders.[53]

The ritual of execution in the eighteenth century was perceived by its participants, its spectators, and its reporters as more than simply a grisly public warning against crime. When ideally performed upon a cooperative subject, it became a solemn testimonial to human frailty, civic justice, and divine mercy. The condemned person was expected to make a public statement lamenting the errors of his (or her) usually short life, warning the onlookers against doing the same, professing the justice of his sentence, thanking his spiritual advisors and asking for their continued prayers, and committing his penitent soul to God. The ceremony also turned into a test of human character. What the spectators especially wanted to see, and what the newspapers usually reported, was whether the condemned person died with dignity and repentance. "*Cole & Greenvill* appear'd very Penitent," reported the *Boston Gazette* of two of the three pirates hanged at Charlestown Ferry on July 12, 1726, "But *Fly* shew'd no manner of reluctancy for the Crimes for which he suffer'd; He was the same Day hung in Chains upon an Island call'd *Nick's Mate*." An advertisement in the same paper offered for sale Cotton Mather's sermon on the occasion, including "*an exact Account of their Behaviour at their Execution.*"[54]

Two contrasting execution items in the same April 11, 1738, number of the *New-England Weekly Journal* illustrate the importance that was attached in the public mind to the behavior of the criminal. They also betray the common disdainful attitude of the age toward a person whose ethnicity and religion was not English—in this case, a Jew.

The first item reports the hanging in London of "Carr the Attorney, and Mrs. Adams," who went composedly to their execution "in two Mourning Coaches . . . and the other 11 Malefactors in Carts." Both principals had "behaved very Decent" and "received the Sacrament" before their deaths. The contrasting story, also copied from London, originated in the German city of Stuttgart, where "Suss the Jew," formerly a financial official under the Duke of Württemberg, was hanged for treason. Though his crime is not thoroughly explained, his conviction and execution are rehearsed in gloating detail:

> The following Circumstances are told of him: That having been conducted before the Commissaries, which were to pronounce Judgment against him, he threw himself at their Feet, and made the most earnest Supplications to obtain Pardon, but was silenced that he might hear his Sentence. When they came to that Part of it which says, *that he was condemn'd to be hang'd for having endeavour'd to ruin his Country*, he gave Tokens of the most violent Dispair: They were obliged to hold him, and to stop his Mouth. He was carried to Execution cloathed in Scarlet embroidered with Gold. He struggled so much, and made such violent a Resistance, that it was with great difficulty he was executed. He would fain have spoke to the People when he was upon the Ladder, but was hindred by the Noise of Drums.

The *American Weekly Mercury* devoted most of its first page on January 21, 1729, to two separate accounts of the dismemberment and strangling in Brussels of an anonymous man "of Prodigious Parts and a superior Genius" who had been convicted of "forging the Hands of Sovereign Princes." He had made such a hit with all the city, and especially with the archduchess, that his execution was delayed two days to give him time for preparation, and continual Masses were said on his behalf in the royal chapel and in all the convents. "He bore the Stroke with the greatest Undauntedness, and a perfect Resignation to the Will of God. His Right Hand was first chopped off with an Ax; and then he mounted the Scaffold, on which he was strangled. . . . Thus died this notable Man, whose Origine and nation all the World are ten times more impatient to know, than the Nature of his Crimes."

No acts of juridical killing were more offensive to an Anglo-American readership, nor treated more luridly in the press, than those at the hands of the Inquisition. The *New-York Gazette* for February 13, 1726, gave more than a quarter of its two pages of print to an especially detailed account of an *auto-da fé* in Lisbon and the subsequent burning at the stake of a priest who refused to recant under torture from his heretical belief *"That Christ came to Perfect, not Abolish the Law of Moses, and that therefore Circumcision and Baptism ought both to be observed."*

One correspondent reported, "During the twenty Minutes that he was alive at the Stake, He did not once Change his Countenance, nor give the least loud Cry, He only some times shrunk up his Leggs, and put his Handkerchief to his Scull and Chin, till it was burn't away. . . . I never saw a Creature in their Bed dye in so calm resign'd and intrepid a Manner."

Though publishers did not usually make it explicit, their recording of remarkable occurrences nevertheless did have a point. In a part of the eighteenth century when scientific curiosity had begun to merge with the habitual tendency to look for divine portents in nature and human affairs, the point could sometimes be obscure or ambiguous. But whether the event was a monstrous birth, an astronomical oddity, or the heroic death of a martyr to his faith, the reader was expected to draw from its recording a lesson of divine governance, of scientific truth, or of human character.

Persistence and Change

The Anglo-American newspaper reader's world during the thirty-five years after the founding of the *Boston News-Letter*, described in its essentials in the chapter now ending, retained much of its character for the next quarter-century. "Provincial" culture persisted through the provincial period (the approximate end of which, it is presumed here, can be dated with reasonable precision at the rise of a more militant and eventually separatist Americanism near the beginning of the Revolutionary crisis), and the newspapers continued to provide the means for ritual participation in that culture. The underlying attitudes in which the news was embodied did not change throughout that period. Nor, in most respects, did the stuff of printed news—the actions of governments and armies, the curious and the entertaining, the remarkable and the sensational.

In one important respect, however, the newspapers and their readers experienced a profound turning point about 1740. The press of American events turned American eyes toward their own continent, and the newspapers responded by leading the way toward a new American consciousness. The new attention to American affairs and events by no means involved a rejection of Britain at this stage; the war against Spain and France, which was one of the stimuli to the new consciousness, if anything reinforced loyalty and British patriotism. The transition, nevertheless, was of far-reaching importance. It is the subject with which this book concludes after considering the place of the newspaper in the provincial culture of British America.

Chapter 11

The Newspaper in Culture

Creative Consumption

It is fitting that a book that began with an episode from the diary of Samuel Sewall should return to that worthy person to open the final full chapter. Even before the coming of the *Boston News-Letter*, both he and that other stalwart of the traditional Boston establishment, Increase Mather, were readers of newspapers. For them, the events of human history and the natural world were more than just events. In them were to be sought portents, evidence of the fulfillment of divine prophecy.[1] In New England, as David Paul Nord has well argued, this was the first meaning of news and the first purpose of recording and reporting it.[2]

Sewall's diary is a record of public as well as personal happenings, and discloses a sharp sensitivity to "news" even before the coming of the *Boston News-Letter* made it more readily available. The "Gazett," no doubt the *London Gazette*, that Sewall read aloud to the Massachusetts Council on February 11, 1702, "comes," Sewall wrote, "by way of New-York." In September 1703, he received by word of mouth the false news that Louis XIV had died: "As I was going, Mr. Oakes met me and ask'd if I had not heard the News? He said French King; he had his Neck broken by a fall from his Horse. . . . . One Bodwin brings the Report, who comes from New Castle, and had it at Sea from Commodore Taylor." Thirteen days later, however, a ship arrived in Boston directly from Europe: "Wadsworth arrives from Dublin 7 weeks: Brings no News of the French King's death, so that conclude he is alive."[3] Even in 1703, until confirmed by the authority of the printed word an oral report was only a rumor, presumed in the continued absence of such confirmation to be false.

We already know that on the very day that Campbell's first *News-Letter* came off the press, Sewall recorded the importance of the event by noting that he had "carried" it to President Willard. His surviving annotated files of the *News-Letter*, some of them accompanied by a calendar of the paper's contents, disclose that he kept his copies systematically for use as a permanent record for his own reference. He also sent them to distant friends and relatives and presented them as gifts to widows he was courting.[4]

Soon after the *News-Letter* began, Sewall quickly became not only a reader but a contributor to the new journal. In 1705, he noted Campbell's reluctance and subsequent agreement to print a supplement, including a bit of Latin verse of Sewall's composition, to a previous item on the burning of the college in Quebec. Sewall's Protestant sensibilities had been piqued by the report of the fire during the visit to the French capital of two returning New England commissioners. The crucifix atop the chapel to which the flames spread, wrote Sewall in his diary, "bowed and fell down." The *News-Letter* of November 26 had carried a brief account of the return of the delegation, including a reference to the fire. Campbell evidently at first refused to print Sewall's elaboration and poetic gloss on the event, which its author intended for the December 17 number, but gave in the next week.[5] It is impossible to suppose that this was the only occasion upon which Sewall, an inveterate writer and publisher, provided news or comment to Campbell or his rivals.

Increase Mather, like Benedict Anderson's hypothetical Spanish official in Caracas who if possible would avoid the local newspaper in favor of the one from Madrid,[6] apparently preferred the London prints to the provincial ones, even though there were three in Boston and another in Philadelphia by the time of his death in 1723. Mather's personal routine, recorded in his diary as diligently as his frequent sessions of secret prayer, involved reading the pamphlets and newspapers that had arrived on the most recent ship from England. He then included the intelligence gained in this way in his "causes for humble Thanksgivings before the Lord" or, more frequently, "grounds for Humiliation and supplication."[7]

The interaction of Samuel Sewall and Increase Mather with newspapers disclose several forms of creative consumption early in the provincial period. For both, newspapers formalized and systematized the record of God's dealings with His people, His intrusion into human history. Thus this almost definitively secular genre served as a religious resource, providing for Mather the specific substance of prayer. For both men, in addition, the newspapers helped define their social roles. Sewall was able to gauge his centrality in the newly enlarged public sphere in part by his involvement with the *Boston News-Letter*, whether as the bearer of the first issue to Harvard or as a contributor, a status he apparently worked hard to achieve. For Mather, it was apparently the newspapers he read as distinct from those he did not admit to reading that to his own satisfaction measured his status in the provincial community. Finally, Sewall accepted the authority of print, in this case British print, as a test of truth for information imparted orally.

Sewall and Mather were by no means alone in making individual creative use of the newspapers they read. The few surviving files of most of the earliest American newspapers indicate by their arrangement that some readers, at least, kept and even bound their copies by consecutive numbers, a practice both expected and encouraged by publishers who made references to previous numbers in the course of recording current events. This is a habit we should expect from the possessor of at least a modest private library, one with more than a passing interest in public affairs. For such subscribers, the newspapers were not only a source of fairly current information, to be discarded after their reader or readers had been brought up to date, but a permanent record of events—a history. This is exactly how John Campbell conceived of his *Boston News-Letter*, and some of his readers, including Samuel Sewall, followed his intent by making the record permanent in their personal libraries.

Another subscriber and collector annotated his files of the *News-Letter*, the *Boston Gazette*, and the *New-England Weekly Journal* in 1739 and the early 1740s, correcting serial numbers when they were wrong, making marginal comments, and drawing attention to certain articles that interested him. He may have been doing this for the benefit of someone other than himself, since his annotations occasionally seem more like a command than a reminder: "Letter from Capt. Vaughan being taken by Spaniards. Read it." "Some acco: of South Sea Company. Read it." "Acct. of Fever in N. Engld. the remainder to be in Next. See large answer in N 647." "Two Schemes for A Medium or Paper Currancy [sic]. Read them." On one occasion, he supplied a detail that had not been committed to print. "Capt. Howard of Marblehead Dead Cut his throat," this reader wrote at the bottom of the third page of a 1739 *Boston Gazette*. The adjoining newspaper item does report Howard's death but not its cause.[8] Many articles, rather than being annotated in this fashion, are simply marked with a marginal "X," much in the way a student marks his textbook as he reads through it. For this reader, the record of current history, thus embodied in print, was to be taken with the same seriousness and considered of the same permanence as the printed word in other formats. The embellishment of the report of Captain Howard's death serves as evidence that the event, including its unrecorded details, was already circulating in the oral culture at the time of its appearance in print. The printed report, therefore, was not so much "news" as a kind of official confirmation, and for one who kept a record of the events of his day, it served as a permanent entry in what amounted to a printed journal.

Not many years later, the Swedish naturalist Peter Kalm traveled in America on a scientific mission for the Swedish Academy of Sciences. His report on American phenomena to the Academy was based on newspapers as well as on personal observations. During his protracted stay in Philadelphia from late 1749 to the autumn of 1750, Kalm was in close contact with Benjamin Franklin, an association which as well as being scientifically stimulating no doubt introduced him to the world of American newspapers. He took obvious pride in recording in his journal that Franklin had "published under my name my whole article on Niagara Falls" in the *Pennsylvania Gazette* of September 20, 1750, which was almost three years after Franklin had turned over the active guidance of the paper to his partner David Hall. The *Gazette* and *American Weekly Mercury* provided Kalm with reports of natural phenomena and curiosities such as violent storms, instances of longevity, the destructiveness of squirrels, animal diseases, and earthquakes. The fluctuation of prices, lists of births and deaths, and the long obituary of a German pastor of Philadelphia also found their way into his journal. In December 1749, he took home from the Library Company of Philadelphia "the first old newspapers of Philadelphia to make extracts about North American events that might have special interest," and spent three days recording miscellaneous items from the *Weekly Mercury* from 1720 to 1728.[9]

While the Philadelphia newspapers served Kalm primarily as sources for his report to the Swedish Academy, and thus were valuable to him mainly as a permanent record of human and natural history into which he could delve as into an archive, there was one occasion when as a Swedish patriot he was affected overwhelmingly by current news. "A few moments ago I received the newspapers that were published to-day," Kalm wrote on February 3, 1750. "In these I learned, from a dispatch of September 30, 1749, that the minister of the Russian Czarina in Stockholm had delivered a memorial to the Royal Swedish Court requesting the permission to station troops in Finland, since she was a guarantee of Swedish freedom. As soon as I had read but half of the Czarina's insolent, damnable and super-immoral demand, I became so angry . . . and my blood circulation so violent, that every limb in my body shook for an hour . . . , and I could not read or write a word.[10]

Still later in the century, the Geneva-born artist Pierre Eugene Du Simitiere, having settled in Philadelphia after sojourns in the West Indies, New York, New Jersey, and Boston, took the newspaper record a step further than either Kalm or the unknown collector and annotator in Massachusetts. In a notebook entitled "Notes on Publications 1748–1769," Du Simitiere undertook to construct a systematic account of American history, geography, and natural history which would serve at the same time as an index to his newspaper collections. Under headings such as Boundaries of Several Colonies of No. America," "Public Institutions in North America," "Comets, Meteors & uncommon appearances in the Skies," "Essays relating to the No. American Colonies," "Remarkable Deaths and Other Unfortunate incidents," "Religious and enthusiastical Matters,"

"Essays relating to American Customs," "American Husbandry," several categories of natural history, and "Essays on Various Subjects, humorous and entertaining," Du Simitiere made chronologically ordered entries, each citing the title and date of the newspaper from which the item was taken. His main source was the *Pennsylvania Gazette*, of which he must have kept a complete file, but his entries also include citations of the *Pennsylvania Journal*, *American Magazine*, *Pennsylvania Evening Post*, *Pennsylvania Chronicle*, *New-York Journal*, *New-York Mercury*, *New-York Gazette*, and *New-York Evening Post*. Curiously, it was from this last New York paper, dated October 23, 1752, rather than the previous week's *Pennsylvania Gazette* from which it was copied, that Du Simitier made his lone entry under "Experiments in Natural philosophy in America": "Experiment of the *Silk Kite* made in Philadelphia to draw the electric fluid from the Clouds, during a thundergust."[11] Du Simitiere also kept a second book, dated 1762–82, which was essentially a chronology, taken from the newspapers, of the American Revolution.[12] In 1776, John Adams was much taken with Du Simitiere's systematic use of the newspaper record. Here he describes to his wife a project to which the 1762–82 notebook was evidently a supplement:

> This M. Du Simitiere is a very curious man. He has begun a collection of materials for a history of the revolution. He begins with the first advices of the tea ships. He cuts out of the newspapers every scrap of intelligence, and every piece of speculation, and pastes it upon clean paper, arranging them under the head of that State to which they belong, and intends to bind them in volumes.[13]

Seriously though a collector and chronicler like Du Simitiere might take the newspapers as sources of history, he was not too solemn to appreciate the levity that they might inspire in others. Among his descriptions of "Essays on Various Subjects" was "a humourous essay upon the blunders committed by printers, with this motto prefixed, *Printorum est errare*," from the *Pennsylvania Gazette* of March 13, 1730. He also cited *"Papyrius Cursor*, his new way of Reading the News-paper" from the *Pennsylvania Chronicle* of March 2, 1767. This entry referred to an essay by an irreverent English wit reprinted from the *General Evening Post* of London in which the content of newspapers was satirized as "an *olio*, or mixt composition of politics, religion, picking of pockets, puffs, casualties, deaths, marriages, bankruptcies, preferments, resignations, executions, lottery tickets, India bonds, Scotch pebbles, Canada bills, French chicken gloves, Auctioneers, and Quack doctors." The reader's remedy is to treat a newspaper as he would a pack of cards, shuffling the pieces in order to provide constant variety:

> At present I shall only mention one improvement in reading the papers, which we practised in the country with great success; and that was, after we had read the General Evening-Post in the old trite vulgar way, *i.e.*, each column by

itself *downwards*, we next read two columns together *onwards*, as if the lines
had been continued through both columns; and by this *new* method found
much more entertainment than in the *common* way of reading. . . .

Here are some of the many results of the "new method" that "Papyrius
Cursor" communicated:

Yesterday Dr. Jones preach'd at St. James's,
and performed it with ease in less than 16 minutes.
   Last night the Princess Royal was baptized;
Mary, alias Moll Hacket, alias Black Moll.
This Day his M——— will go in state to
fifteen notorious common Prostitutes.
   To be let, and entered upon immediately,
A young Woman, that will put her Hand to anything.

These are a few examples of the uses of newspapers by conspicuous
members of the mainly privileged audience at which they were aimed.
Some of them are from beyond the terminal date of this study, but not
greatly beyond, and can certainly be taken as characteristic of the provincial period in general. This evidence shows us that indeed the papers were
read by the dominant class of people at whom almost all the newspapers
ostensibly were aimed, but it also shows us that not all readers used the
newspapers in exactly the same way. Some of the uses would have come as
a considerable surprise to the publishers.

For nearly all of these readers, the newspapers were sources of current
intelligence, but the usefulness of that intelligence varied according to the
position and interests of the reader. For some it was useful for business or
the conduct of public life. For a visiting Swede, it was useful for the
stimulation of patriotic ardor during an absence from his home soil. For at
least two of these readers, the newspapers were sources of amusement and
entertainment, but in one case it was amusement at the expense of the
publishers and their genre, not at all in accordance with what the publisher
had intended. What stands out more than anything in all this evidence is
the use that these readers made of the newspapers as a permanent printed
record of events and ideas, in the case of Du Simitiere probably much
more elaborate and sophisticated than any newspaper publisher would
have imagined. In the words of Roger Chartier, "Cultural consumption,
such as reading, is always a form of production that creates ways of using
that cannot be limited to the intentions of the producers or manipulators.
Cultural consumption is not passive, or dependent, or submissive, but a
creative activity, an 'art of doing' and 'doing with' imposed materials."[14]

The Ritual as Message

All the preceding examples of the private creative consumption of newspapers have been provided, as we have just noticed, from among the

intended audience of the American provincial press. In London, there was room for specialization and a targeting of audiences according to political faction, literary tastes, and even, in the case of those aimed explicitly at a commercial readership, occupational interests. Such differentiation of audiences was obviously impractical elsewhere.

Provincial newspapers—excepting, as usual, the *New-England Courant*—were aimed at those who did business or practiced professions, owned property, paid taxes, and cast votes in their communities and provinces. It was they who were assumed to have sufficient interest in public affairs, business, and general culture to buy the journals in which these matters were reported, discussed, and advertised. Axiomatically, this was a group of white, mostly Anglo-Saxon, overwhelmingly male, propertied heads of families. Not only was the target audience literate, but it was at least somewhat and in many individual cases highly educated. It was politically active and presumed to consist generally of Protestant church-goers. With few exceptions, publishers addressed their papers to "gentlemen" or in some cases "gentlemen and others." Since printers and publishers, though they may not usually have met the technical requirements of "gentleman," shared most of the characteristics of their "implied readership," to borrow a term from literary criticism,[15] communication by newspaper took place, or so it was presumed, almost entirely within a fairly narrowly defined in-group.

It is true that at least one of Boston's literary newspapers, the *New-England Weekly Journal*, aimed at a female as well as a male audience. This may also have been true of the other literary newspaper of the 1730s, the *Weekly Rehearsal*, though there is little direct evidence to prove it. The first Proteus Echo essay in the *Weekly Journal* invited contributions from "Gentlemen or Ladies," and it is fairly obvious that Mather Byles's parting verses to "Belinda" a year later would not have found a place in the *Journal* had the author not expected Belinda to have read them there.[16] The *Journal*'s inclusion of the poem by a young bereaved mother in 1733, well after the editorial direction of the paper had been taken over by its printers,[17] offers further testimony to the understanding of the day that the culture of letters was open to women of a certain social standing, and of course the *South-Carolina Gazette* welcomed the contribution of sixteen-year-old "Martia" and the exchange that followed in 1732.[18]

But although there are certainly exceptions and anomalies to be noted, publishers as a whole aimed their journals mainly at those with votes to cast, money to spend, and the same dominant vision of the moral universe and social order that the newspapers almost unanimously conveyed and reinforced. It was mainly members of this group, beginning with John Campbell's small cluster of readers in 1704, who shared with one another the communal celebration of culture and nationality in the ritual of reading.

This was not, however, a closed communion. Anyone who could read might participate. If our small collection of evidence confirms that the consumption of newspapers was creative, taking place in ways not limited to their producers' intentions, may we not also speculate that the audience itself overflowed the rather narrow readership that was implied by the papers' contents? While acknowledging that eighteenth-century audiences were in no way comparable to the "mass" audiences for the print and electronic journalism of our own day, we still cannot help noticing: 1) that the bounds of literacy were considerably broader than the publishers' intended audience; 2) that accessibility to the newspapers in homes and public places, especially by comparison with accessibility to most other printed genres, must have been quite simple and widespread; and 3) that the content of the newspapers, despite the elite audience that it was presumed would most profit from it, was intelligible and potentially enjoyable to almost anyone who could read. This was not, in other words, "high" culture, whatever such a term might signify when applied to eighteenth-century Anglo-American society.

So it was that the "ritual" role of the provincial newspaper, to return to the two-fold conception of communication proposed by James Carey, took on the additional role of "transmission"—in this case, the transmission of culture. The celebration of communal identity that was involved in reading newspaper print became an invitation for broader participation. The ritual, in short, became a missionary message to those outside the restricted and privileged circle of communicants that the press, by implication, described.[19] Records do not disclose the extent to which the readership exceeded the bounds of male gentility, but common sense does.

Try, for example, to imagine a New York or a Boston household exposed by the public prints in 1732 to the running controversy over dancing assemblies. Or a Philadelphia family intensely aware in 1740 of the presence in their city of George Whitefield. It stretches credulity to suggest that the mistress of the family along with the young of both sexes would not contribute to the family debate over the former, or that servants and older children alike would not be avidly scanning the family copies of the *Pennsylvania Gazette* and *American Weekly Mercury* for the latest news and opinion on the charismatic and controversial evangelist.

Again, consider the very printing offices in which all newspapers, whether owned by the great booksellers' combinations of London or by the sole proprietors of the provinces, were produced. But since we are focusing here on America, I am thinking especially of the six mainland colonial towns that were putting out newspapers in 1740—Williamsburg, Charleston, and Germantown in addition to the big three that have been our main concern. Journeyman printers, bound apprentices, African-American slaves, and master printers' wives, sons, and daughters were among the categories of humanity, all obviously literate, that were involved here and there in the production of newspapers. In most cases this meant reading copy, setting and correcting type, interacting at some level with contributors, advertisers, and subscribers, scanning and perhaps criticizing the weekly product, and in general learning all about newspapers. One of the "master" printers, Elizabeth Timothy of Charleston, was female, and the principal language of another, Christopher Sauer, was German. If the wives, children, and apprentices of other tradesmen were not drawn as directly as those of the printer's household into the world the newspapers portrayed, they were nevertheless part of the community that did business with the printers and whose exposure to their peers who lived and worked down the street in the printing office, and to the weekly prints themselves, must have been routine.[20]

In short, through channels formal and informal, intended and unintended, expected and unexpected, the newspapers' message almost certainly reached well beyond the audience most publishers had in mind. And if in the mid-eighteenth century, as I believe, newspapers were still serving as extensions and reinforcers of the oral culture rather than as substitutes for it, the likelihood of a broadened audience is even greater. The mental world that one encountered in the newspapers was not one apart from other expressions of eighteenth-century life and consciousness. On the one hand, with its learned political essays, its Latin garnishings, its appropriation of current (or at least recent) English literary modes, and its classical and Biblical allusions, the world of the newspapers brushed against the realm of what might be called "formal," or "academic," culture. On the other hand, it dignified and made permanent—and in the form of advertisements made usable—the daily gossip and worldly concerns that were common to shops and counting houses, taverns and clubs, wharves and garrisons, legislative halls and council chambers. The newspapers contained no barriers separating the formal from the workaday, the "elite" from the "popular," but instead invited anyone who could read to extend and confirm by print the everyday world already known by ear, and in the process to gain access to that other, more formal world of letters heretofore familiar mainly to the educated and the powerful.

The Newspaper in Provincial Culture

First a word about "influence." The urge to assess the influence of the information media on opinion and politics in any era is a natural one, especially in light of everyone's acute awareness of the complicated and to a large extent even measurable relationship between media and politics (and politicians) in modern societies. It is also natural to see the eighteenth-century American press as a possible agent of causation either when one's subject is the American Revolution or when it is the colonial period, viewed as "prelude to independence." If all of American history from European settlement to 1776 is to be studied and assessed with a view to explaining its Fourth of July climax, the provincial press becomes interesting mainly for the ways in which it may have helped set off the fireworks.

Alternatively, if one wishes to use a broader concept of "prelude," the newspapers of that period deserve scrutiny as ancestors or primitive and probably relatively powerless precursors of more highly developed versions that flourished in times when, it can be confidently asserted, they really made things happen.

The link between the press and society, and particularly that between the press and politics, is a general theme that has challenged scholarly energies at least for several generations.[21] Most recently, Jeremy Black has argued the lack of a political edge and the failure of the newspapers of eighteenth-century England to influence change. The late Stephen Botein, in different terms, has made essentially the same argument concerning the newspapers of pre-revolutionary America[22] American scholars from Arthur Schlesinger to Jeffery Smith have tried to assess the role of the newspaper press in the American Revolution, concentrating among other special topics on the consensual development of an ideology "in defense of their own liberty."[23] Such studies, interesting and valid as they are, tend to reinforce the assumption that the colonial press is worth examining mainly in the light of contemporary questions about the relationship between press and society, and especially between press and politics.

The main effort here, however, is to comprehend on their own terms the American newspapers of the provincial period in the hope, more generally, of discovering something worthwhile about British-American provincial culture itself. My purpose, in other words, is less a quest for antecedents than for context. In such an effort, the question of "influence" may be less useful. Not only is it likely to lead to despair over discovering the answer, but it may also be that the question diverts attention from some truly answerable ones that can lead to a better understanding of the newspapers' significance in their own culture.

The newspapers, once begun, quickly achieved permanent status as an accepted and demonstrably utilized phenomenon of provincial life. Their contents regularly offered readers a broader view of the world than was available elsewhere. From the relative insularity of the seventeenth century, American colonials were moving into a more acute consciousness of their place in an ever more glorious empire in which they were proud participants, and of partisans and sometimes combatants enlisted in the service of a constitutional sovereign whom they adored against the despotism and popery of France and Spain. News from Europe and the Caribbean nourished this anglicized consciousness and inspired martial zeal, while the cultural products of Augustan England—and their American imitations—instilled a sense of Englishness, of sharing the tastes and sensibilities of their world's metropolitan center, remote from them though it was.

And at the same time the readers' world was becoming broader and more "anglicized," it was becoming more "Americanized." With the establishment of every new newspaper, the older ones had a new source from

which to copy news and opinion from elsewhere in the colonies. Newspapers and their readers did not at any time in the provincial period refer to
themselves as "Americans," and would not do so until a revolutionary
situation and its accompanying consciousness gave them cause to do so,
nor do we find any other kind of evidence of anything that could be
described as an incipient American national identity.[24] The newspaper
readers of about 1740, however, were becoming increasingly aware of
what were often called their "neighboring provinces." Shared experiences
such as King George's War and the Great Awakening provided materials
for mutual copying that were of guaranteed interest across provincial lines.
"Remarkable occurrences" from other parts of British America as well as
from Britain and one's own locality were now a part of every reader's
steady diet. Reports of political conflicts, epidemics, incidents of crime,
droughts, and storms in any province all made for sympathetic reading
everywhere newspapers were printed, and helped foster a sense of kinship
with fellow colonials elsewhere. In addition to reporting more than ever
before about other British colonies, the newspapers inevitably drew attention to other parts of the New World by printing direct reports of expeditions and hostile encounters in the American theater of the war. The last
international conflict had ended in 1713, when Campbell's *Boston News-
Letter* was the only newspaper in America. Campbell's transcribed news
from London had left the impression that the War of the Spanish Succession was exclusively a European conflict unrelated to his occasional incomplete reports of Indian raids and skirmishes on the New England frontier.
The coming of the war with Spain in 1739 and its broadening into the War
of the Austrian Succession stimulated a very different kind of coverage, to
the point even in 1745 that the *Pennsylvania Gazette* printed a large woodcut
plan of the fortress at Louisbourg then under siege by New England
troops, thus "render[ing] the News we receive from thence more intelligible" and allowing an American readership to participate vicariously in
what was from the colonial point of view the most dramatic moment of the
war.[25] Like other war news, of course, this served at the same time as a
stimulus to British patriotism. The American reader's expanded horizons
thus included a newly broadened awareness of the colonial hemisphere
and his place in it as well as a heightened sense of his identity as a Briton.

Finally, the newspapers narrowed the cultural gap between the learned
and the merely literate, and the information gap between the privileged
and the merely competent. If "knowledge is power," to borrow the title of
Richard D. Brown's important social history of information in early
America, this obviously was an accomplishment of considerable long-term
significance.

The coming of the *Boston News-Letter* made available to the readers of its
250 copies much of the same news that Samuel Sewall and other insiders
had been getting directly from journals imported from overseas or from
participating in the councils of government. Even if a fair proportion of the

PHILADELPHIA, June 6, 1745.

As the CAPE-BRETON Expedition is at present the Subject of most Conversations, we hope the following Draught (rough as it is, for want of good Engravers here) will be acceptable to our Readers; as it may serve to give them an Idea of the Strength and Situation of the Town now besieged by our Forces, and render the News we receive from thence more intelligible.

PLAN of the Town and Harbour of LOUISBURGH.

The Harbour

Furlongs
1 2 3 4 5 6 7

EXPLANATION.

1. The Island Battery, at the Mouth of the Harbour, mounting 14 Guns, 28 Pounders. This Battery can rake Ships fore and aft before they come to the Harbour's Mouth, and take them in the Side as they are passing in.
2. The Grand Battery, of 36 Forty-two Pounders, planted right against the Mouth of the Harbour, and can rake Ships fore and aft as they enter.
3. The Town N. East Battery, which mounts 18 Twenty-four Pounders on two Faces, which can play on the Ships as soon as they have entered the Harbour.
4. The Circular Battery, which mounts 16 Twenty-four Pounders, stands on high Ground, and overlooks all the Works. This Battery can also gaul Ships, as soon as they enter the Harbour.
5. Three Flanks, mounting 2 Eighteen Pounders each.
6. A small Battery, which mounts 8 Nine Pounders. All these Guns command any Ship in the Harbour.
7. The Fort or Citadel, fortified distinctly from the Town, in which the Governor lives.
8. A Rock, called the Barrel.
T The Center of the Town. L The Light-House.
Every Bastion of the Town Wall has Embrasures or Ports for a Number of Guns to defend the Land Side.
The black Strokes drawn from the several Batteries, shew the Lines in which the Shot may be directed.

CAPE-BRETON Island, on which Louisburgh is built, lies on the South of the Gulph of St. Lawrence, and commands the Entrance into that River, and the Country of Canada. It is reckon'd 140 Leagues in Circuit, full of fine Bays and Harbours, extremely convenient for Fishing Stages. It was always reckon'd a Part of Nova-Scotia. For the Importance of this Place see our Gazette, No. 858. As soon as the French King had begun the present unjust War against the English, the People of Louisburgh attack'd the New-England Town of Canfo, consisting of about 150 Houses and a Fort, took it, burnt it to the Ground, and carried away the People, Men, Women and Children, Prisoners. They then laid Siege to Annapolis Royal, and would have taken it, if seasonable Assistance had not been sent from Boston. Mr. Duvivier went home to France last Fall for more Soldiers, &c. to renew the Attempt, and for Stores for Privateers, of which they proposed to fit out a great Number this Summer, being the last Year unprovided: Yet one of their Cruisers only, took 4 Sail in a few Days, off our Capes, to a very considerable Value. What might we have expected from a dozen Sail, making each 3 or 4 Cruises a Year? They boasted that during the War they should have no Occasion to cut Fire-Wood, for that the Jackstaves of English Vessels would be a Supply sufficient. It is therefore in their own NECESSARY DEFENCE, as well as that of all the other British Colonies, that the People of New-England have undertaken the present Expedition against that Place, to which may the GOD OF HOSTS grant Success. Amen.

first newspaper's subscribers already had access in other ways to most of
the information it printed, the reasonably prompt sharing of news, undis-
torted by repeated transmissions by word of mouth, was now extended far
more broadly than before. The process obviously became intensified with
the introduction of every new journal, most of which exceeded the *News-
Letter*'s circulation. Advertisements make it clear that by 1740 the use of
newspapers had extended well into the hinterlands of the publishing cities.
Communications to the *New-England Courant* as early as the 1720s and
fragments of subscribers' billing information for nearly all the newspapers
convey the same message. The likelihood that the newspapers were being
regularly read by an audience substantially broader demographically and
socially than their targeted readership has already been argued, and the
diversity of advertisements in the 1730s and 1740s, especially in Philadelphia and New York, implies that neither advertisers nor prospective
clients were confined to social or economic elites.

There is no question, therefore, that American provincial society as a
whole was enormously more broadly informed about current public events
and opinion in 1740, when no part of the mainland colonies was outside the
reach of at least one of the 12 newspapers, than had been the case in 1704.
To suggest that such a society was therefore a more "democratic" society
in any sense would be to state a proposition that cannot be tested by any of
the evidence in this book. The question, however, is not beyond the reach
of numerous research strategies that might be devised. Certainly an enlarged accessibility to information of this kind is one of the preconditions
of a wider participation in government and a more broadly based public
opinion. Certainly, too, there were psychological effects on readers who
would once have considered themselves forever outside the small,
privileged—and powerful—circle of the informed. Whatever empirical
measures of "equality" one might use, the possession of current news and
information by such persons cannot help but have been a source of self-
esteem and sense of belonging to a community that was becoming in
Benedict Anderson's terms, more distinctly, and more commonly, imagined.

The newspapers, however, contained more than reports of public
events. In comfortable juxtaposition with the "intelligence" from Europe
and the often humdrum record of local legislative acts, ship arrivals, remarkable occurrences, and street gossip, there resided the essays, poetry,
and learned letters that linked the newspaper world of ordinary affairs
with that of formal learning. We have already suggested that content of the
familiar, comfortable kind could and probably did provide an easy access
route for readers who were merely literate to the more polished writings
intended to appeal mainly to a genteel and educated audience. Such writings, it is important to notice, included political essays. The *New-England
Courant*, which satirized both higher education and gentility, hoped to
appeal in part to readers who shared neither of those advantages. But such

a readership would have missed the point had it not also possessed at least some familiarity with the institutions and literary forms that were being satirized. One source of that familiarity had surely been Brooker's and Musgrave's *Boston Gazette*. By 1727 the *Courant* was gone, and subsequent American newspapers, with the partial exception of the very catholic *Pennsylvania Gazette*, printed literary materials that were in large measure intended to be either taken seriously or appreciated for wit that was a product of the dominant culture rather than a detached criticism of it.

Thus the merely literate readers of newspapers, while being offered the advantages not only of public information but also of exposure to a richer cultural world than they had previously known, were also being drawn into a system of shared values and essentially elite attitudes that were part of the fabric in which news and literature alike were almost universally embedded. We have encountered before the cluster of assumptions that underlay the presentation of news, instruction, and entertainment in the newspapers on both sides of the English Atlantic. They included racial, ethnic, and sexual attitudes, assumptions about patriotism and religion, devotion to the Crown, notions about crime and punishment, and ideas about better and inferior sorts of people. In the early and middle parts of the eighteenth century, these attitudes were supplemented, though not changed, by an unqualified attachment to the revolutionary settlement of 1689, a horror of Jacobitism, and an embrace—unanimous in America though not in England—of the whiggish doctrines of limited government and personal liberties. Whether consciously or not, anyone who read a newspaper in provincial America came under the influence of this cluster of attitudes. It was implicit in the news and explicit in essays and poetry. To be offered the advantages of reading was also to become a partisan of the ideology that was embedded in the text.

And just as there was no division in the ideology underlying the several kinds of content in the newspapers, there was no intended division in the readership—no dividing up the paper as in a contemporary American family or lunchroom among devotees of the editorial page, the sports section, the comics, and the crossword puzzle; no selection of reading according to "highbrow" or "lowbrow" tastes. The newspapers had made the news and "cultural" content, to make a false distinction, all of a piece.[26]

This eclectic world of print that the newspapers presented to their readers was, to be sure, an imagined world. It was a world of only selected events, presented in such a way as to infer connectedness—a world structured from the habits of reporting, the accidents of transmission, the mechanics of printing, and the largely unconscious assumptions of those who did the selecting and arranging. Benedict Anderson has remarked upon the newspaper's "profound fictiveness," by which he means the "imagined linkage" between the juxtaposed items in a modern newspaper.[27] This observation is as just when applied to the newspapers of the eighteenth century as to those of the twentieth. And since the linkage was largely unarticulated and usually constructed unconsciously, and because the materials of news, opinion, entertainment, and advertising were so diverse and casually collected, the newspapers reflected more thoroughly and more accurately than any other printed medium the varied concerns of the day. For us who study them in retrospect, they provide a richly textured if not fully coherent expression of the culture of which they were a part. For those who read them in their own time, they built community solidarity and affirmed common values by combining materials from all walks and levels of life and binding them with the ideology that was articulated only in the more formal essays and letters that took an easy place amongst reports of ordinary affairs. Books, broadsides, and pamphlets, every one of which was produced with far more single-minded intent than any number of any newspaper (excluding, again, certain numbers of the *New-England Courant*), could not have had the same effect.

Thus the newspapers more than any other single printed vehicle of the eighteenth century reflected the "collective mentality" of the age.[28] In America, they served no more important function than to collect, embody, and diffuse to a broader and receptive population the shared beliefs that gave coherence to provincial culture.

Chapter 12

The Transition

By about 1740, the provincial newspaper in America had concluded its first period of development. Successive experiments in sponsorship and content had eventuated in a product published almost exclusively by their printers and consisting of a standardized mixture of European and domestic news, essays, letters, and advertising. During the three and a half decades following the appearance of John Campbell's *Boston News-Letter*, the American newspaper became both "anglicized" and "Americanized," and in the process served with increasing accuracy and relevance the commercial and political demands of its society as well as the ritual needs of a people moving toward an understanding and expression of its provincial identity. They were still very much a part of the larger British world of print, a branch of the English provincial press on the western Atlantic rim. A glance at that transatlantic context at the end of our period will help to remind us of how very "provincial," certainly in a quantitative sense, the American newspapers still were.

In 1740, the British empire contained sixty newspapers, more or less. All but about a dozen came out weekly, and probably two-thirds of the total circulated to fewer than a thousand purchasers each. The exception was in London, where of about seventeen newspapers, at least six were dailies and five or six were thrice-weeklies. The circulation of each major London daily, intended for local distribution, averaged about 2000 copies. The thrice-weeklies, timed for the Tuesday, Thursday, and Saturday post departures and aimed at a national circulation, averaged between 3000 and

5000 copies for each press run. This compared with a maximum of 600 for most American newspapers.[1]

The dominance of the metropolis as the publishing center of the empire, upon which the relatively tiny provincial press on both sides of the Atlantic still depended, can be roughly gauged as follows: using known newspapers and frequencies of publication in Great Britain and the Atlantic empire, and rough estimates of circulation for London, English provincial, and American newspapers, we can estimate that in 1740 something over 200,000 copies of sixty newspapers were being printed in the British world each week. Of those, perhaps 164,000 copies, or 81 percent, were being run off weekly by the printers of London's 17 newspapers. Another 30,000 or so, roughly 15 percent, can be attributed to England's 29 weekly provincial papers and the thrice-weekly *Edinburgh Evening Courant*, and about 8000, or 4 percent, to the 12 newspapers being published weekly in the mainland North American colonies and the one in the West Indies.[2] In London, with its 675,000 people, one copy of a newspaper was being printed each week for every four inhabitants; in Great Britain as a whole, a copy for every 67; and in the American colonies a copy for each 125. Boston, one of the best-informed places in the empire by this particular measure, was printing a copy of one of its five newspapers each week for every five or six of its inhabitants—or, if the same conjectured circulation is applied to Massachusetts as a whole, a copy for every 67, exactly the same as in Great Britain.[3]

These figures, rough as they are, show the American colonies to have been remarkably well served by newspapers, especially when one considers multiple readership. Most of the 8000 or so copies of the thirteen weekly colonial newspapers were delivered on a subscription basis to households rather than being sold, as many of the London papers were, on the street. The readership of some home-delivered copies might be multiplied by as many as four or five, somewhat more north of the Chesapeake than in points south because of differences in the literacy rate. Because at this time the gap between male and female literacy was rapidly closing, it seems likely that the home readership of most newspapers, as suggested in the last chapter, included women and girls as well as men and boys.[4] The last chapter also suggested that from a cultural standpoint the newspapers formed an especially significant part of reading by Americans. These figures suggest that they were quantitatively significant as well.

In 1739 and 1740, the newspapers changed. Two events, both in 1739, brought it about. England declared war upon Spain, and the twenty-five-year-old George Whitefield, having visited Georgia briefly in 1738, now returned for the most momentous of his several evangelical tours of the American colonies. The newspapers' response to these events was to focus their editorial content increasingly on news and opinion, much of it locally generated, concerning a few large and very pressing issues that had a direct impact on the provincial readership.

THE Numb. 659.

New England Weekly JOURNAL.

Containing the most Remarkable Occurrences Foreign and Domestick.

TUESDAY December 4. 1739.

The following Piece was lately printed at New York, directed to the Inhabitants of that City, Nov. 17.

My Dear Brethren,

IT is with Grief and Pitty that I survey your present exposed State & Practice, by reason of Mr. Whitefield's *erring and preaching among you; I now warn you to treat him as he deserves, i.e. with Neglect and Contempt, as being the most irregular Man in Doctrine and Manners, that I ever knew; Remarkable for Ignorance and Confidence: Tho' he makes large Pretences to* Inspiration *and* Divine Knowledge, *he is unworthy the Honour of the Gown, or the Character of a Clergyman; for he gives himself the Liberty of condemning the whole Body of the* Bishops *and* Clergy *of the* English Church, *and passing unwarrantable* condemnatory Sentences *upon Men, as if he was the Supreme Judge. And when I Reprimanded him last Night at the House of Mr.* Smith *the Lawyer, charging him with* false Doctrine, The most Unchristian Spirit *and* vilest of Manners, *offering to dispute various Points with him, and make good my Charge or do Penance; He refused; giving this Reason,* That I was an unregenerate Man; *which I look upon an Evidence, either of Weakness or Guilt. I therefore Warn you in Christ's Name, in Faithfulness to your Souls,* To shun him as an open Enemy to Religion, *whatever may be his specious Pretences,* A Violator of all Rule and Order, disobeying those who have the Rule over him, and dispising his Betters: *Don't suffer yourselves to be imposed upon or drawn away by this* Deceiver, *but* Watch and Pray that you enter not into Temptation.

Thus Wishes and Prays,
Yours Souls Assured Friend,
and Humble Servant,
Jonathan Arnold,
Itinerant Missionary.

From the New York Gazette, Nov. 26.

Mr. Bradford,

I Have seen two Papers published under the Name of Jonathan Arnold, *wherein my Name is mentioned. I am sorry that I am obliged in my own Defence to take Notice of them. 'Tis true that I invited Mr* Arnold *to come to my House, at the same time that I invited the Rev. Mr.* Whitefield, *and it is as true that I have heartily repented it since. I little thought that Mr.* Arnold, *would have so far transgressed the Laws of Hospitality, as to have* laid me *under the necessity of exposing his Conduct* in such a Place. *After Mr.* Arnold *had published his first Paper, I represented to himself, the ill treatment I had received,* and he asked my Pardon, *and I thought the matter would have ended there. But since that without any Provocation in a second Paper he has represented me as a DECEIVER in first accepting the Office of a* Moderator *between him & Mr.* Whitefield; *and then (I suppose) refusing it, could hardly have expected such Usage from Mr.* Arnold's *Hands! That I refused to be a Moderator, in any Disputes between them, it true, but that I accepted that Office, is* false. *Mr.* Whitefield *did not desire it, and to suppose a Man to accept that Office without the Consent of both, (I think) is impossible & ridiculous. Besides, if both had desired it, would it not have been a Piece of* Arrogance *in me to have accepted it.*

As to the CHARGE against Mr. White*field, if I may judge of it by the same Rule, I must conclude it to be* false. *He own'd no Promise to enter into any Disputation with Mr.* Arnold. *As to any Thing farther that passed at my House, between Mr.* Arnold *& Mr.* Whitefield, *I hope I shall not be obliged to expose it, I am unwillingly brought this length, —— I would not have the* [illegible] *Gen*[illegible] *Gentlemen to Contrast* [illegible] *least their* Characters *should appear thereby as opposite to each other as* Light *and* Darkness. *Mr.* Whitefield *and his Cause, I hope are in better Hands than mine. But as to Mr.* Arnold, *as he has honour'd me with the Title of having been his* Master *and* Tutor, *I still beg leave to advise him to consult a certain* Gentleman *in the* Acts *called the* Town Clerk of Ephesus, *before he takes one step farther* i.e. Do nothing rashly. *As to his Treatment of Mr.* Whitefield, *I would apply to him the Advice of* Gamaliel, Refrain from this Man, and let him alone, for if this Counsel or this Work be of Man, it will come to nought; But if it be of God, you cannot overthrow it, least haply you be found to fight against God. *This is wholesom Advice, and if Mr.* Arnold, *despises it, let him remember the Wo of them* that perished in the gainsaying of Corah.

William Smith.

We have the following Account of the Rev. Mr. White*field's Arrival &c at N York from the said Gazette.*

THE Rev. Mr. *Whitefield* arrived at the City of *New York* on Wednesday the 14th inst. a little before Night. The next Morning he waited on the Rev. Mr. *Vesey*, & desired leave to preach in the English Church, but was refus'd: The Reason assigned for such Refusal was, because Mr *Whitefield* had no Licence to Preach in any Parish but that for which he was ordained; and an old Canon was read. To this Mr. *Whitefield* reply'd, That that Canon was Obsolete, & had not been in Use for above 100 Years, That the whole Body of the Clergy, frequently preach out of the Bounds of their Parishes, without such Licence. — These Arguments not prevailing, some Application was made to the Rev. Mr. *Boel*, for the Use of the *New Dutch Church*, but this also was refus'd. Then Mr. *Whitefield* had the offer of the *Presbyterian Church*, but did not care at first to accept it, not being willing to give any Offence to his Brethren of the Church of *England*; but said, *He chose rather to go without the Camp, bearing his Reproach, and Preach in the Fields.* At length being informed, that in some Parts of this Country, the Meeting Houses had been alternately us'd by the Ministers of the several Communions, & very often borrowed by the Church of the Dissenters, he consented to accept the Offer for the Evening. However, in the Afternoon he preached in the Fields to many Hundreds of People.

Among the Hearers, the Person who gives this Account, was one, I fear Curiosity was the Motive that led me and many others into that Assembly. I had read two or three of Mr. *Whitefield's* Sermons and part of his Journal, and from thence had obtained a setled Opinion, that he was a Good Man. Thus far was I prejudiced in his Favour. But then having heard of much Opposition, and many Clamours against him, I tho't it possible that he might have carried Matters too far. — That some *Enthusiasm* might have mix'd itself with his Piety, and that his Zeal might have exceeded his Knowlege. —— With these Prepossessions I went into the Fields; when I came there, I saw a great Number of People, consisting of *Christians* of all Denominations, some *Jews*, and a few, I believe, that had no Religion at all. When Mr. *Whitefield* came to the Place before designed, which was a little Eminence on the side of a Hill, he stood still, and beckned with his Hand, and dispos'd the Multitude upon the Descent, before, and on each side of him. He then prayed most excellently, in the same manner (I guess) that the first Ministers of the *Christian Church* prayed, before they were shackled with Forms. The Assembly soon appeared to be divided into two Companies, the one of which I considered under the Name of *GOD's Church*, & the other the *Devil's Chappel*. The first were collected round the Minister, and were very serious and attentive. The last had placed themselves in the skirts of the Assembly, and spent most of their Time in Gigling, Scoffing, Talking & Laughing. I believe the Minister saw them, for in his Sermon, observing the Cowardice & Shamefacedness of *Christians* in Christ's Cause, he pointed towards this Assembly, and reproached the former with the boldness and Zeal with which the Devil's Vassals serve him. Towards the last Prayer, the whole Assembly appeared more united, and all became hush'd & still; a solemn Awe & Reverence appeared in the Faces of most, a mighty Energy attended the Word. I heard and felt something astonishing & surprizing, but, I confess, I was not at that Time fully rid of my Scruples. But as I tho't I saw a visible Presence of GOD with Mr. *Whitefield*, I kept my Doubts to my self.

Under this Frame of Mind, I went to hear him in the Evening at the *Presbyterian Church*, where he Expounded to above 2000 People within & without Doors. I never in my Life saw so attentive an Audience: Mr. *Whitefield* spake as one having Authority: All he said was *Demonstration, Life* and *Power*! The Peoples Eyes and Ears hung on his Lips. They greedily devour'd every Word. I came Home astonished! Every Scruple vanished; I never saw nor heard the like, and I said within my self, *Surely God is with this Man of a Truth.* He preach'd & expounded in this manner twice every Day for four Days, & his Evening Assemblies were continually increasing. On Sunday Morning at 8 o'Clock, his Congregation consisted of about 1500 People: But at Night several Thousands came together to hear him, and the Place being too strait for them, many were forced to go away, and some ('tis said) with Tears lamented their Disappointment. After Sermon he left *New York* at Ten at Night, to fulfil a Promise that he had made to preach at *Elizabeth Town*, at 11 A.M. the next Day.

Mr. *Whitefield* was born at *Glocester* ('tis said) in the Month of *December*, 1714. He observes in his Journal, that he was baptized at the Font of one of the Churches in that City, on the 25th Day of that Month. He was bred up in the Bosom of the *Church of England*, and educated at *Oxford*. There he commenced Batchelor of Arts. He was ordained Priest, according to the Orders of the *Church of England*, on the 14th of *January* last, which was almost as soon as it could be, by the Canons of the Church, he being then but little more than *Twenty Four* Years old. He is a Man of a middle Stature, of a slender Body, of a fair Complexion, and of a comely Appearance. He is of a sprightly chearful Temper, acts and moves with great Agility and Life. The Endowments of his Mind are very uncommon; his Wit is quick and peircing; his Imagination lively and florid; and as far as I can discern, both are under the Direction of an exact and solid Judgment. He has a most ready Memory, and I think, speaks entirely without Notes. He has a clear and musical Voice, and a wonderful Command of it. He uses much Gesture, but with great Propriety: Every Accent of his Voice, every Motion of his Body, *speaks*, and both are natural and unaffected. If his Delivery is the Product of Art, 'tis certainly the Perfection of it, for, it is entirely concealed. He has a great Mastery of Words, but studies much Plainness of Speech. His Doctrine is right STERLING, I mean, perfectly agreeable to the Articles of the *Church of England*, to which he frequently appeals for the Truth of it. He loudly proclaims all Men by Nature to be *under Sin* and

obnoxious

The tendency had begun in Boston as early as 1734 with a protracted exchange of lengthy letters in the *Boston Gazette* and the *New-England Weekly Journal* over Rhode Island's bills of credit and a Massachusetts scheme for merchants' "notes of hand." The latter proposal was one of the proffered solutions for the Bay province's endemic shortage of currency and the anticipated crisis that would occur as most of the existing bills of credit in circulation approached their legal cancellation dates.[5] At the same time in New York, the acrimonious paper war between Morrisites and Cosbyites was heating up in the columns of John Peter Zenger's *New-York Weekly Journal* and William Bradford's *New-York Gazette.*

With the coming of war and Whitefield, American newspapers everywhere found two other issues upon which to lavish increasing space while continuing to entertain news and comment on the currency question and local politics. Departing from the more diversified news topics and literary fare that dominated most newspapers of the 1730s, the newspapers of the 1740s tended to present their readers overwhelmingly with news and discussion of the hard issues of the decade: money, war, and the Great Awakening.

News of the War of Jenkins's Ear and the expansion of hostilities into the War of the Austrian Succession at the end of the following year occasioned little printed controversy, but it did occasion much print. Of the *Boston Weekly News-Letter*'s 51 numbers for 1739, 31 led the paper with news, articles, or announcements bearing on international tensions, war, or patriotic themes; this was true for 18 of the 53 numbers of the *Boston Evening-Post* in that year. The newspapers printed the declarations of war, proclamations and gubernatorial messages for raising colonial volunteers and building fortifications, various accounts of the largely unsuccessful expeditions to Florida, Porto Bello, and Cartagena, sporadic reports from privateers, and news of the European conflict copied from the usual London sources. This was as much the case with the newspapers of New York and Philadelphia as with those in Boston, but even a common cause such as this disclosed one fundamental political division. When the Quaker-dominated Pennsylvania assembly refused to appropriate funds for defense in

---

(facing page) The front page of the *New England Weekly Journal*, published by Samuel Kneeland and Timothy Green, in December 1739 during the height of the excitement over George Whitefield, who would not actually arrive in New England until the following autumn. Here the *Weekly Journal* copies at great length from New York, the northern point of Whitefield's tour that winter. A letter from his most conspicuous New York opponent provides the foil for a spirited defense of the evangelist and a favorable narrative of his New York visit. This use of the *Weekly Journal* illustrates how contemporary American events in 1739 and 1740 provoked the beginning of a transition in the nature and fundamental purpose of American newspapers. (*Courtesy, American Antiquarian Society*)

January 1740, Governor George Thomas's lengthy and very critical response occupied nearly half of the *American Weekly Mercury* of January 29.

The currency issue was an especially crucial and heated one in Massachusetts, where all the Boston newspapers carried long letters and essays on the subject in 1739 and 1740. The question, however, became a particular specialty of the *New-England Weekly Journal*, which became host not only to discussions of the proposed land bank, which was actually put briefly into effect late in 1740, but to detailed expositions of, as one correspondent put it, "No less than 6 or 7 *Schemes* . . . [that] have been exhibited in publick Print."[6]

It was indeed the currency issue that most firmly established the newspapers as a forum for debate. It was as hosts to printed exchanges over this complex and to some extent arcane question that the printers functioned more purely than they did in certain other roles in accordance with the "open press" ideal to which they all subscribed. Between 1739 and 1741, the debate consumed a huge amount of newspaper space, especially in Boston.

The opening of the war, on the other hand, was the main force in causing the printers of newspapers to respond to the press of New World events. Time and again the chronologically arranged columns of European news snippets were forced from page one in favor of some breathless report brought by a ship's captain from the Caribbean or the Spanish Main, a local recruiting effort, or the political squabble in Pennsylvania over financing the war. The European news itself, of course, was heavily weighted toward war news in these years. The war even provoked amateur debates about strategy, as in the *Boston Evening-Post*'s fictional dialogue between "John Tar" and "Lobsterback" over the relative merits of a land or a sea campaign against Spain.[7] This lavish attention to the war in its early stages continued throughout King George's War, climaxing with extensive coverage of the victory of New England troops at Louisbourg in 1745, complete with various legislative resolutions, gubernatorial proclamations, and letters from soldiers at the scene piling detail upon detail about the siege and the French surrender.[8]

The third great issue of the hour, religious revivalism, had the most transforming effect of all upon American newspapers. It is not just that the young Whitefield's American tour provided yet another occasion for the use of newspaper print for pressing American events. The attention resulted in this case, as Frank Lambert has recently shown, from the manipulations of a skilled press agent—Whitefield himself.[9] The application of marketing and promotional techniques to the orchestration of what amounted to a modern evangelical crusade obviously was a development of profound importance at this stage of the provincial experience, and no element of provincial society tumbled more readily into spectacular compliance than the printers of newspapers—no single printer more readily or cooperatively, perhaps, than the notably unevangelical Benjamin Franklin.[10]

There was, however, one dissenter from the otherwise nearly universal adoration of Whitefield in newspaper print. He was Boston's non-establishment printer Thomas Fleet, whose experience in injecting only a small note of controversy into a highly charged atmosphere was instrumental in settling the role that newspapers would play in some of the similarly charged situations that lay ahead.

The American tour of 1739-40 earned Whitefield a generally sympathetic response, especially in its early phases in the Philadelphia area and in the South, in no small measure because of advance publicity and favorable reporting. Upon his first arrival in New England in September 1740, even Harvard and the Boston clergy for the most part responded cheerfully, though on repeated visits to that region his welcome would wear thin. But because Fleet was willing to print anti-Whitefield letters in his *Boston Evening-Post* and even engage in the controversy in a limited way over his own name, Whitefield became the subject of a paper war in Boston paralleling the debate over currency. There was printed controversy in New York and Philadelphia as well, but that consisted primarily of a series of spirited defenses of the evangelist against attacks that had not appeared in the newspapers.[11] The *New-York Weekly Journal* even printed all the texts upon which Whitefield preached during his four-day visit to the city in November 1739, and the *Pennsylvania Gazette*, in true Franklinian form, estimated the crowds present at half a dozen or more of Whitefield's outdoor sermons in Philadelphia and elsewhere. In addition, Franklin hospitably provided the front of the *Gazette* for two letters from Whitefield, one "*proving* that Archbishop *Tillotson* knew no more of *True* Christianity than *Mahomet.*"[12]

Such warm unanimity did not prevail on the occasion of Whitefield's first visit to Boston, which prompted a dispute among publishers mildly reminiscent of the much less restrained printed warfare over inoculation that had strained the civility of the town nearly two decades earlier. Thomas Fleet, it will be remembered, had been one of the Couranteers before he had acquired his own newspaper. As a Couranteer, however, he had enjoyed both the cloak of anonymity and the clubby comfort of his sophomoric young colleagues. Moreover, the decidedly precocious *Courant* had made its brief appearance before the norms of a printer's role in controversy, discussed in an earlier chapter and articulated as well as anyone by Fleet himself, had been fully developed. On this occasion, he learned to his obvious discomfort that even a subtle challenge to prevailing political correctness could bring forth the wrath of the community, with its implicit threat to his livelihood.

Fleet always professed himself impartial, simply offering his paper to all parties on any question. By subtle arrangement and selection, however, he made his opinion of Whitefield obvious. On Monday, September 22, 1740, for example, five of the hundreds of Bostonians who had jammed into the New South meetinghouse to hear Whitefield were killed in a panic-driven crush. At the same time, Boston was serving as the marshaling point for five companies of New England volunteers being mustered for Admiral Vernon's ill-fated expedition against Cartagena.[13] Fleet's *Evening-Post* of the following Monday reported the meetinghouse tragedy somewhat more sensationally than John Draper's noticeably pro-Whitefield *Weekly News-Letter*, and then followed that account with:

> Last Saturday all the Troops raised here for the Expedition to the West Indies, except Capt. *Winslow*'s Company (who are on board and just upon departing) sail'd from *Nantasket* for *New-York*.
>   And this Morning, the Rev. Mr. *Whitefield* set out on his Progress to the Eastward, so that the town is in a hopeful Way of being restor'd to its former State of Order, Peace and Industry.

Another paragraph of Whitefield news reported without comment or apparent coloration two preaching services at which the evangelist raised over a thousand pounds for his Georgia orphanage.

Even though Fleet's sly editorializing was buried in a substantial column of local news, "several . . . good Friends & Customers" of John Draper sent a quick and acrimonious reply for publication in Thursday's *Weekly News-Letter*. Quoting the offensive paragraph but omitting the introductory "And," the writers asserted that Fleet did not represent "*the Sense of the Town*" and compared Whitefield's detractors to the Biblical opponents of Paul and Jesus. In the next *Evening-Post*, Fleet printed a rather long signed statement wherein he first asserted, somewhat sophistically, that his meaning had been twisted by the omission of the "And" that linked his comment on Whitefield with the departure of the troops, but then defended his position on Whitefield:

> . . . I can with the strictest Truth say, that I never made the least *Opposition* to the Rev. Gentleman, nor have I yet heard of his being *opposed* by any other Person whatsoever. . . . I suppose the Gentleman only means . . . that we have not *followed* him so far as some others . . . ; I have heard the Rev. Gentleman both preach and pray, and am so far from desiring him to *depart out of our Coasts*, that I heartily wish he may stay among us, till we are become a more sober and industrious, a more kind and charitable, a more honest, just and righteous People; and in a Word, *better Neighbours* as well as *better Christians*, and that he may have the Pleasure to leave us a People far more remarkable for *Godliness* and *Honesty* than he found us. . . .
>   . . . I have never been of any *Company*, Clan or Party, either in Church or State, but wherever I have had a Right to speak or act, have always done it with openness and freedom, according to my *own* Judgment, and not that of *others*, which may be one Reason why I have so few hearty Friends at this Time. I have always endeavoured to behave as a good Subject and a good Neighbour, rendering to all their Dues, and hope I have been among those

that *be quiet in the Land*. I have indeed always express'd my self in a free, open and undisguised Manner, as became an *honest* Man, tho' perhaps not as a *prudent* one, as the World now goes. . . .

This remarkable statement, of which only a portion has been quoted here, discloses in the first place the printer's defensiveness in the face of what was obviously a very sensitive situation. Whitefield had polarized the community, causing an alienation and distrust of those who could not share the enthusiasm of the majority. It also makes clear his implicit identification and agreement with others of moderate religious views, presumably including those whose anti-Whitefield letters he had been printing and would continue to print in the *Boston Evening-Post*.

Though Fleet's defense is couched partly in terms of the ideal of the open press, the real debate here is on the issue of Whitefield himself. Fleet's venture into expressing an editorial opinion that is at odds with the views of the majority has been effectively ended. To that extent, the little episode forebodes the era of the American Stamp Act, when neutrality or even silence on the part of a printer would be taken as hostility to the public interest, and therefore unacceptable.

Never again until after American Independence, indeed until 1815, would the Atlantic world experience a relaxation of international tension comparable to the protracted period of peace between 1713 and 1739. It was during that period of peace that, among many other manifestations of growth and maturation in American society, the colonial newspapers underwent their experimental groping toward a solid identity and social role. It was not only war, defense, and diplomacy that now began to command the attention of the newspapers, of course, but other matters of domestic concern and conflict. The contentions over religious revivalism would not run their course at least until 1750. The money question in one form or another would engage the attention of Americans in every section right on through the American Revolution and the debates over the Constitution of 1789. Political factionalism, not only of the bitter personal variety experienced in New York but in the contest for power between governor and assembly in every colony, stimulated the adoption by newspapers of the rhetoric of English opposition politics. The journalistic version of such opposition had flowered especially during the twenty-year ministry of Sir Robert Walpole (1721–42), whose administration, ironically, was an especially good one for the American colonies. During those years, various London periodicals among which the *Craftsman* was preeminent had allocated to themselves the role of government watchdog. It was this journal among others from which Thomas Fleet copied several of the political essays in his *Boston Evening-Post* in 1739, and it was the same journal from which much of Zenger's *New-York Weekly Journal* was borrowed during the height of its attacks on Governor Cosby in 1733 and 1734.[14] The habit of copying and adapting English political essays, and of beginning to conceive of American political situations in the light of the libertarian theory conveyed in such literature, as the *New-England Courant* had done before its time, obviously had profound implications for the years of opposition to British policy that lay not far ahead.

The War of the Austrian Succession and its domestic political implications in Britain, as it happened, also brought about a transition in the press on that side of the Atlantic. In the case of provincial England, it was a movement toward political unanimity, the unanimity of opposition. The war with Spain, because it had been opposed by the Whig ministry of Robert Walpole, was seen by provincial printers, the majority of whom were Tory, as a vindication of opposition politics. Most of the country newspapers, therefore, played up the war, just as the American papers were doing for different reasons. Then after the Walpole ministry fell in 1742, even the editors who had formerly supported Walpole joined with his former critics in condemning the failure of the new government to pursue the "patriotic" fight for civic virtue by bringing the supposedly corrupt former minister to justice. From then until the General Election of 1754, says G. A. Cranfield, the provincial papers almost universally criticized both the present and former governments and expressed a suspicion of official authority in general.[15] With the American Stamp Act, there would follow a period with similar characteristics in the history of the colonial press.

In America, of course, the Stamp Act crisis, followed by the movement for independence, would have obvious transforming effects at least as significant as those of 1739–40. Even before that, a part of the American press began to take on a more highly politicized role than that of its ancestors. Near the outbreak of another international war in 1755, Samuel Kneeland sold the *Boston Gazette* to Benjamin Edes and John Gill, who in the future would become among Boston's most radical and prolific printers of the revolutionary era. Upon acquiring the paper, the two new owners, both more than a generation younger than their predecessor, plunged immediately into the religious and political controversies of their time, and perhaps pointed the way to a new understanding of the newspaper press in provincial society.[16]

These are matters beyond the scope of this book. But by 1740, especially after the transforming events of 1739, a more pointedly political role for the newspaper was in the process of developing. More broadly, the newspaper now occupied a distinct niche in the world of which it was a product and which it served. No longer either an experiment or a miscellany, it had become what it would remain for the rest of the century and beyond, a vehicle of information and discourse primarily about the most pressing public events of its time and place.

Appendix

American Newspapers
Begun before 1740
and Their Publishers

Publick Occurrences, Boston (one number only, 1690). Benjamin Harris (bookseller).

The Boston News-Letter (1704–76; variously titled after 1726). John Campbell (postmaster until 1719), 1704–22; Bartholomew Green (printer), 1722–32; John Draper (Green's son-in-law, printer), 1733–62; Richard Draper (printer), 1762–76.

The Boston Gazette (1719–98; variously titled after 1741). William Brooker (postmaster), 1719–20; Philip Musgrave (postmaster), 1720–25; Thomas Lewis (postmaster), 1725–26; Henry Marshall (postmaster), 1726–32; John Boydell (postmaster until 1735), 1732–39; Hannah Boydell (widow), 1739–41; Samuel Kneeland and Timothy Green (printers), 1741–53; Benjamin Edes and John Gill (printers) and successors (printers), 1753–98. Absorbed *New-England Weekly Journal*, 1741.

The American Weekly Mercury, Philadelphia (1719–c.1746). Andrew Bradford (printer), 1719–39; Andrew and William Bradford (printers), 1739–40; Andrew Bradford (printer), 1740–42; Cornelia Bradford (printer's widow, in partnership with Isaiah Warner 1742–44), 1742–c.1746.

The New-England Courant, Boston (1721–26). James Franklin (printer), aided by literary club of "Couranteers"; as a legal subterfuge, appeared over the name of Benjamin Franklin (printer's apprentice) from Feb. 11, 1723.

The Weekly Jamaica Courant, Kingston (c. 1722–c. 1755). Publisher not known.

The New-York Gazette (1725–41). William Bradford (printer).

The New-England Weekly Journal, Boston (1727–41). Samuel Kneeland (printer; soon in partnership with Timothy Green); content supplied by literary club headed by Mather Byles (writer and future clergyman) until c.1729. Merged with *Boston Gazette* 1741.

The Maryland Gazette, Annapolis (1728–c.1734). William Parks (printer).

The *Pennsylvania Gazette*, Philadelphia (1728–post Revolution). Samuel Keimer
(printer; under original name of *Universal Instructor in all Arts and Sciences;
and Pennsylvania Gazette*), 1728–29; Benjamin Franklin and Hugh Meredith
(printers), 1729–32; Benjamin Franklin (printer), 1732–48; Benjamin Franklin
and David Hall (printers), 1748–65; David Hall (printer), 1766–72, and successors thereafter with suspension during British occupation of Philadelphia.

The *Barbadoes Gazette*, Bridgetown (1731–38). Samuel Keimer (printer).

The *Weekly Rehearsal* (1731–35) and *The Boston Evening-Post* (1735–75). Jeremiah
Gridley (teacher, writer, and future lawyer), 1731–33; Thomas Fleet (printer),
1733–58; Thomas and John Fleet (sons of Thomas Fleet, printers), 1758–75.

The *South-Carolina Gazette*, Charleston (1732). Thomas Whitmarsh (printer).

The *Rhode-Island Gazette*, Newport (1732–33). James Franklin (printer).

The *New-York Weekly Journal* (1733–52). John Peter Zenger (printer, sponsored by
political faction), 1733–46; Catharine Zenger (printer's widow), 1746–48; John
Zenger (printer), 1748–52.

The *South-Carolina Gazette*, Charleston (1734–75, with revivals thereafter). Lewis
Timothy (printer), 1734–38; Elizabeth Timothy (printer's widow), 1738–40;
Peter Timothy (printer), 1740–75.

The *Boston Post-Boy* (1735–54). Ellis Huske (postmaster).

The *Virginia Gazette*, Williamsburg (1736–50, renewed thereafter). William Parks
(printer).

Der *Hoch-Deutsch Pennsylvänische Geschicht-Schrieber*, Germantown (1739–46).
Christopher Sauer, or Sower (printer).

Abbreviations of Newspapers Frequently Cited

AWM	*American Weekly Mercury*
BEP	*Boston Evening-Post*
B.G.	*Boston Gazette*
BNL	*Boston News-Letter*
BPB	*Boston Post-Boy*
L.G.	*London Gazette*
M.G.	*Maryland Gazette*
NEC	*New-England Courant*
NEWJ	*New-England Weekly Journal*
NYG	*New-York Gazette*
NYWJ	*New-York Weekly Journal*
P.G.	*Pennsylvania Gazette*
P.O.	*Publick Occurrences*
SCG	*South-Carolina Gazette*
V.G.	*Virginia Gazette*
WNL	*Weekly News-Letter* (A later title of *BNL*)
W.R.	*Weekly Rehearsal*

Notes

Introduction

1. *The Diary of Samuel Sewall*, ed. M. Halsey Thomas (New York: Farrar, Straus, & Giroux, 1973), I, 501–2.

2. Jürgen Habermas, *The Structural Transformation of the Public Sphere: An Inquiry into a Category of Bourgeois Society*, tr. Thomas Burger (Cambridge, Mass.: MIT Press, 1989), esp. 1–56, 89–102.

3. James W. Carey, *Communication as Culture: Essays on Media and Society* (Cambridge, Mass.: Unwin Hyman, 1988), 14–23.

4. Ibid., 18.

5. Elizabeth Eisenstein, *The Printing Press as an Agent of Change: Communications and Cultural Transformation in Early Modern Europe*, 2 vols. (Cambridge: Cambridge Univ. Press, 1979). Eisenstein's argument was later rendered much more accessible in an abridged and illustrated paperbound version entitled *The Printing Revolution in Early Modern Europe* (Cambridge: Cambridge Univ. Press, 1983). The theoretical writings of Walter J. Ong have also illuminated this topic in important ways, particularly in *Orality and Literacy: The Technologizing of the Word* (London and New York: Methuen, 1982), esp. chap. 5 (pp. 117–38). The chief prophet of the obsolescence of type, whose sensational analyses were among the stimuli that prompted Eisenstein's study, was the late Canadian scholar Marshall McLuhan. See especially *The Gutenberg Galaxy: The Making of Typographical Man* (Toronto: Univ. of Toronto Press, 1962). It is important to notice that new technologies do not simply compete with newspapers. They are also being harnessed to improve newspaper production, presumably serving in this role as a force for the perpetuation of the newspaper rather than its opposite. For one discussion of this development in communications, specifically the application of computers, see

Anthony Smith, *Goodbye Gutenberg: The Newspaper Revolution of the 1980s* (New York: Oxford Univ. Press, 1980).

6. Robert Darnton's much-cited essay, "What Is the History of Books?," which first appeared in *Daedalus* III (1982), 65–83, is usually taken as the cornerstone statement. It is reprinted in Cathy N. Davidson, ed., *Reading in America: Literature and Social History* (Baltimore: Johns Hopkins Univ. Press, 1989), 27–52. Darnton's own major contribution to the field to date has been *The Business of Enlightenment: A Publishing History of the Encylopedie, 1775–1800* (Cambridge, Mass.: Harvard Univ. Press, 1979). One especially important French contributor to the field and to the notion of "print culture" has been Roger Chartier; see *The Cultural Uses of Print in Early Modern France*, tr. Lydia G. Cochrane (Princeton: Princeton Univ. Press, 1987), and Chartier, ed., *The Culture of Print: Power and the Uses of Print in Early Modern Europe*, tr. Lydia G. Cochrane (Princeton: Princeton Univ. Press, 1989).

7. Some of the more important examples are David D. Hall, "The World of Print and Collective Mentality in Seventeenth-Century New England," in John Higham and Paul K. Conkin, eds., *New Directions in American Intellectual History* (Baltimore: Johns Hopkins Univ. Press, 1979), 166–95; Bernard Bailyn and John B. Hench, eds., *The Press and the American Revolution* (Worcester: American Antiquarian Society, 1980); Charles Wetherell, "Brokers of the Word: An Essay in the Social History of the Early American Press, 1639–1783" (Ph.D. diss., University of New Hampshire, 1980); William L. Joyce, David D. Hall, Richard D. Brown, and John B. Hench, eds., *Printing and Society in Early America* (Worcester: American Antiquarian Society, 1983); David D. Hall and John B. Hench, eds., *Needs and Opportunities in the History of the Book: America, 1639–1876* (Worcester: American Antiquarian Society, 1987); Davidson, ed., *Reading in America*; David D. Hall, *Worlds of Wonder, Days of Judgment: Popular Religious Belief in Early New England* (New York: Alfred A. Knopf, 1989); Richard D. Brown, *Knowledge Is Power: The Diffusion of Information in Early America, 1700–1865* (New York: Oxford Univ. Press, 1989); William J. Gilmore, *Reading Becomes a Necessity of Life: Material and Cultural Life in Rural New England, 1780–1835* (Knoxville: Univ. of Tennessee Press, 1989); and Michael Warner, *The Letters of the Republic: Publication and the Public Sphere in Eighteenth-Century America* (Cambridge, Mass.: Harvard Univ. Press, 1990).

8. Some of the chief exceptions: Stephen Botein, "'Meer Mechanics' and an Open Press: The Business and Political Strategies of Colonial American Printers," *Perspectives in American History* IX (1975), 127–55; sections on the newspaper press in Ian K. Steele, *The English Atlantic, 1675–1740: An Exploration of Communication and Community* (New York: Oxford Univ. Press, 1986), 132–67; Brown, *Knowledge Is Power*, passim; Jeffery A. Smith, *Printers and Press Freedom: The Ideology of Early American Journalism* (New York: Oxford Univ. Press, 1988); Charles E. Clark and Charles Wetherell, "The Measure of Maturity: The *Pennsylvania Gazette*, 1728–1765," *WMQ*, 3rd ser., 61 (1989), 279–303; David Paul Nord, "Teleology and News: The Religious Roots of American Journalism, 1630–1730," *JAH* 77 (1990), 9–38; and three recent articles of my own, "'Metropolis' and 'Province' in Eighteenth-Century Press Relations: The Case of Boston," *Journal of Newspaper and Periodical History* V (Autumn 1989), 2–16; "The Newspapers of Provincial America," *Proceedings of the American Antiquarian Society* 100 (1990), 367–89; and

"Boston and the Nurturing of Newspapers: Dimensions of the Cradle," *NEQ* LXIV (1991), 243–71.

9. Michael Harris and Alan Lee, eds., *The Press in English Society from the Seventeenth to the Nineteenth Centuries* (Rutherford, N.J.: Fairleigh Dickinson Univ. Press, 1968); George Boyce, James Curran, and Pauline Wingate, eds., *Newspaper History: From the Seventeenth Century to the Present Day* (London: Constable; Beverly Hills: Sage Publications, 1978); James Sutherland, *The Restoration Newspaper and Its Development* (Cambridge: Cambridge Univ. Press, 1986); Michael Harris, *London Newspapers in the Age of Walpole* (Rutherford, N.J.: Fairleigh Dickinson Univ. Press, 1987); Jeremy Black, *The English Press in the Eighteenth Century* (Philadelphia: Univ. of Pennsylvania Press, 1987); and an important Master of Arts thesis in communications that deals with the period before newspapers, Milton Mueller's "The Currency of the Word: War, Revolution and the Temporal Coordination of Literate Media in England, 1608–1655" (University of Pennsylvania, 1986). Two important earlier works deal with the English provincial press: G. A. Cranfield, *The Development of the Provincial Newspaper, 1700–1760* (Oxford: Oxford Univ. Press, 1962; rpt. Westport, Conn.: Greenwood Press, 1978); and R. M. Wiles, *Freshest Advices: Early Provincial Newspapers in England* (Columbus: Ohio State Univ. Press, 1965). A collection of essays edited by Donovan H. Bond and W. Reynolds McLeod, *Newsletters to Newspapers: Eighteenth-Century Journalism* (Morgantown: School of Journalism, West Virginia University, 1977), treats topics in journalism (as distinct from printing or publishing) on both sides of the English Atlantic.

10. The idea of "anglicization" was introduced by John M. Murrin in "Anglicizing an American Colony: The Transformation of Provincial Massachusetts" (Ph.D. diss., Yale University, 1966). It is now a familiar theme in early American historiography, and will be invoked from time to time in this book. The larger developmental model is that of Jack P. Greene, first articulated in the introductory essay in Greene and J. R. Pole, *Colonial British America: Essays in the New History of the Early Modern Era* (Baltimore: Johns Hopkins Univ. Press, 1984), and more fully developed in *Pursuits of Happiness: The Social Development of Early Modern British Colonies and the Formation of American Culture* (Chapel Hill: Univ. of North Carolina Press, 1988), esp. 164–69.

11. Since this book deals with the newspapers of the eighteenth century, the standards and conventions of that and subsequent eras are taken for granted, as is the terminology of that day. Therefore, I shall consider a "newspaper" to be serially printed and numbered under a consistent title at a regular stated interval, usually not more than a week; printed at least in folio size on a relatively few unbound leaves, easily distinguishable in physical appearance alone from a book or pamphlet; and devoted primarily to the reporting and discussion of recent events and intended for an audience that is normally more general than specialized. The *Oxford* (later *London*) *Gazette* was the first publication answering this description in England, though not in Europe. The pamphlet-like news publications that preceded the *Gazette*, whether published singly or serially, were called "newsbooks" by contemporaries and are best called that today. The definition of "newspaper" offered here, while designed primarily to distinguish the *Gazette* and its imitators from other publications of the seventeenth and eighteenth centuries, is nevertheless compatible with the more involved bibliographic definitions of the newspaper provided by the Library of Congress and the American National Standards Insti-

tute in *Newspaper Cataloging Manual* (Washington: Library of Congress, 1982). For the Dutch origins of English-language printed news, see, e.g., Stanley Morison, *Selected Essays on the History of Letter-Forms in Manuscript and Print*, ed. David McKittrick (Cambridge: Cambridge Univ. Press, 1981), II, 341.

12. The approximate numbers of newspapers are based on my own compilations in the case of the London and colonial newspapers, with the help of the appendix of Solomon Lutnick, *The American Revolution and the British Press, 1775–1783* (Columbia: Univ. of Missouri Press, 1967), and Appendix B (p. 373) of Wiles, *Freshest Advices*, in the case of the English provincial newspapers. Charles Wetherell, in a study of colonial American printers, has counted 48 newspapers begun in the thirteen colonies from the abortive *Publick Occurrences* of 1690 through 1760, and another 46 through 1775. Of these, nine begun before 1760 and three begun after 1760 were in German. Of the English-language newspapers, 11 of those started before 1760 and 19 started after 1760 lasted two years or less.

13. See, e.g., Morris Janowitz, "The Study of Mass Communications," in David L. Sills, ed., *International Encyclopedia of the Social Sciences* (New York: Macmillan, 1968), III, 42–49, and Richard L. Merritt, *Symbols of American Community, 1735–1775* (New Haven: Yale Univ. Press, 1966).

Chapter 1. Genealogy

1. With one minor exception: The gradual increase during the eighteenth century in the maximum size of a whole sheet of paper. Lawrence C. Wroth, *The Colonial Printer*, 2nd ed. (Charlottesville, Va.: Univ. Press of Virginia, 1964), 273–74.

2. The implications of the movement from an "oral" or "aural" culture to a literate one has become for some time a significant theme for historians of early modern Europe and America. Elizabeth Eisenstein's *Printing Press as an Agent of Change* is among the broadest and most obvious expressions of this interest, but other scholars have made important use of this concept in more specific contexts. See, e.g., Michael Kammen, *Colonial New York—A History* (Millwood, N.Y.: KTO Press, 1975), 96–97, 121, 130, 134; Gary B. Nash, *The Urban Crucible: Social Change, Political Consciousness, and the Origins of the American Revolution* (Cambridge, Mass.: Harvard Univ. Press, 1979), 5; and David D. Hall's introductory essay, "The Uses of Literacy in New England, 1600–1850," in Joyce et al., *Printing and Society in Early America*, 1–47.

3. Karl Bücher, *Industrial Evolution*, tr. S. Morely Wickett (New York: H. J. Holt, 1901; New York: A. M. Kelly, 1968), 221–22.

4. Ibid., 23–25. For an eighteenth-century counterpart to these activities of Melanchthon, compare the *Christian History*, published weekly from 1743 to 1745 in Boston by Thomas Prince, Jr., son of the Thomas Prince who figures in Chapter 7 below. Just as Melanchthon had collected and disseminated intelligence in the interests of the Reformation two hundred years earlier, Prince collected and disseminated intelligence in the interests of the American Great Awakening.

5. Bücher, *Industrial Evolution*, 227–33. Jürgen Habermas employs the continental side of these developments, "the *traffic in commodities and news* created by early capitalist long-distance trade," (p. 15) in making his case for the emergence of a "bourgeois public sphere" from the thirteenth through the sixteenth centuries. *Structural Transformation of the Public Sphere*, 14–17.

6. J. B. Williams, "The Newsbooks and Letters of News of the Restoration," *English Historical Review* XXIII (1905), 252.

7. Victor von Klarwill, ed., *The Fugger News-Letters* (London: John Lane, 1924); Peter Fraser, *The Intelligence of the Secretaries of State and Their Monopoly of Licensed News, 1660–1688* (Cambridge: Cambridge Univ. Press, 1956).

8. Henry E. Huntington Library, ms. HM 20583; printed in Julian P. Boyd, ed., *The Papers of Thomas Jefferson*, II (Princeton: Princeton Univ. Press, 1950), 207–8.

9. Some newspapers did appear more frequently than weekly in 1778, but not in America. London had twice-weeklies, thrice-weeklies, and seven dailies, the first of which had appeared in 1702. See appendix of Solomon Lutnick, *The American Revolution and the British Press, 1775–1783* (Columbia: Univ. of Missouri Press, 1967). A German publisher had beaten this English development by 42 years by putting out a daily newspaper in Leipzig in 1660. The first French daily was published in Paris in 1777. Bücher, *Industrial Evolution*, 221–22.

10. Bücher, *Industrial Evolution*, 233–34.

11. Fraser, *Intelligence of the Secretaries of State*.

12. Henry E. Huntington Library, ms. HA 9624.

13. Henry E. Huntington Library, ms. HA 9658.

14. The *Flying Post* of the next day (March 10, 1701/2), however, led with a detailed account of the King's death datelined London, March 10, and filled the rest of page one and part of the back page with a long obituary.

15. Mueller, "The Currency of the Word," 32.

16. Ibid., 33–40.

17. *The Post Man, and the Historical Account*, March 2–4, 1696/7, British Library Burney Collection, Vol. 112. This and other quotations from seventeenth and early eighteenth-century publications in this chapter ignore italics but are otherwise given accurately.

18. *F.P.*, July 8–10, 1703, Brit. Lib. Burney Collection, Vol. 125b.

19. See *Dawks's News-Letter* for Jan. 7, Oct. 1, 13, 15, and 20, 1698, in Brit. Lib. Burney Collection, Vol. 117, and for May 29, June 26 and 28, 1705, in Burney Collection, Vol. 130b. There is one other known instance of a newsletter printed in script type, *Jones's Evening NewsLetter*, also of London, which as far as can be determined lasted only from October 29 to November 23, 1716. The last known number of Dawks's paper appeared on December 22, 1716. (Stanley Morison, *Ichabod Dawks and His News-Letter, with an Account of the Dawks Family of Booksellers and Stationers, 1635–1731* (Cambridge: Cambridge Univ. Press, 1931), 38 and facsimiles on following pages.) R. M. Wiles discusses Dawks's paper briefly in *Freshest Advices: Early Provincial Newspapers in England* (Columbus: Ohio State Univ. Press, 1965), 8, 10.

20. For many such examples, see *National Union Catalogue Pre-1965 Imprints*, Vol. 329, pp. 21–22, 26. For reference to *Gentleman's Journal*, see Wiles, *Freshest Advices*, 11.

21. See Chapter 4 below.

22. The English Secretaries of State of the Restoration acted as collectors and disseminators of intelligence in discharging one of their state functions, but as propagandists in discharging their other function as monopolistic purveyors of licensed news. Fraser, *Intelligence of the Secretaries of State*.

23. Joseph Frank, *The Beginnings of the English Newspaper* (Cambridge, Mass.:

Harvard Univ. Press, 1961), 21–28, 33–34, 48–51; H. R. Fox Bourne, *English Newspapers: Chapters in the History of Journalism* (New York: Russell & Russell, 1966 (rpt. of 1887 ed.), I, 29–34.

24. *The Intelligencer*, Aug. 31, 1663, Brit. Lib. Burney Collection, Vol. 61.

25. William Waller Hening, *The Statutes at Large; Being a Collection of All the Laws of Virginia (1619–1792)* (Charlottesville: Univ. Press of Virginia, 1969; facsimile rpt.of New York 1823 ed.), II, 517.

26. *The Intelligencer*, Aug. 31, 1663.

27. Besides the *Intelligencer* and *Newes* of the dates indicated, see Fredrick Seaton Siebert, *Freedom of the Press in England, 1476–1776: The Rise and Decline of Government Control* (Urbana: Univ. of Illinois Press, 1965), 265–68.

28. *The Newes*, April 21, 1664, Brit. Lib. Burney Collection, Vol. 61.

29. *OED*, s.v. "gazette." The French government was apparently the first in Europe to develop a means of systematically publishing official news to serve the interests of the state. According to Habermas, a French *Gazette* patronized by Richelieu and begun in 1631 was the model for the *London Gazette. Structural Transformation of the Public Sphere*, 22.

30. Morison, *Selected Essays*, II, 341–42. News sheets called "corontos" were printed in Amsterdam not only in Dutch but also in English for circulation in England early in the seventeenth century, and there was a brief run of London-based "corontos" in 1621. The "coronto" format was abandoned by successive English news-publishers until 1665, and does not seem to have served as a precedent for the *Gazette*.

31. Brit. Lib. Burney Collection, Vol. 12.

32. Brit. Lib. Burney Collection, Vol. 48. One can find many variations on these examples by perusing the newsbooks in the Burney Collection. See esp. vols. 12–17, 23, 47–48, 53.

33. P. M. Handover, *A History of the London Gazette* (London: HMSO, 1965), 9–10.

34. Siebert, *Freedom of the Press*, 41–87, 127–46, 179–91.

35. See discussion of the impact of printing manuals by Lawrence C. Wroth in *Typographical Heritage: Selected Essays by Lawrence C. Wroth* (n.p., 1949), 32–6. The earliest such manual and probably the most influential was Joseph Moxon's *Mechanical Exercises*, 3 vols. (London, 1677–96). There is much of interest on seventeenth-century printing practices, a good part of it dependent upon Moxon, in Charles Henry Timperly, *Encyclopedia of Literary and Typographical Anecdote*, 2nd ed. (London, 1842), 514–18.

Chapter 2. The Metropolis

1. Useful secondary sources for growth and change in London and Westminster at the end of the seventeenth century include George Rudé, *Hanoverian London, 1714–1808* (Berkeley: Univ. of California Press, 1971), chap. 1, and Harold Priestley, *London: The Years of Change* (New York: Barnes & Noble, 1966). For a brief specific discussion of the "West End," see Priestley, 221–23. Rudé's book, between pp. 8 and 9, contains helpful maps, as do John Summerson, *Georgian London* (Harmondson, Middlesex: Penguin Books, 1969), passim; Malpas Pearse, *Discovering London 5: Stuart London*, 56–57, and Derek Brechin, *Discovering London 6: Georgian London*, 22–23 (both London: Macdonald, 1969).

2. The mortality figure of 70,000 is of course a rough estimate. According to Priestley, "The total shown on the Bills of Mortality was 97,306 dead from all causes, and from the plague 63,596. Probably the actual totals were very much higher, for many deaths were concealed or returned with the wrong causes given and many people from London and the out-parishes must have died in other parts of the country, being entered on other parish registers or on none at all" (*Years of Change*, 117). L. C. B. Seaman, whose comprehensive survey, *A New History of England* (London: Papermac, 1982), is based, like much of this chapter, on secondary sources, accepts 69,000 as a minimum figure (p. 348). For the exodus from Westminster and the mortality figure for that part of London (4700), see Priestley, *Years of Change*, 84–92.

3. Priestley, *Years of Change*, 76, 81–82.

4. Ibid., 177–78. See also John E. N. Hearsey, *London and the Great Fire* (London: John Murray, 1965).

5. Rudé, *Hanoverian London*, 136; Priestley, *Years of Change*, 206–8; Summerson, *Georgian London*, chap. 4.

6. R. Campbell, *The London Tradesman* (London, 1747), 306–8.

7. Rudé, *Hanoverian London*, chap. 2.

8. Walter Phelps Hall and Robert Greenhalgh Albion, *A History of England and the British Empire*, 2nd ed. (Boston: Ginn, 1946), 405–11.

9. Morison, *Ichabod Dawks and His News-Letter*, 9.

10. M. Dorothy George, *London Life in the Eighteenth Century* (New York: Capricorn Books, 1965), 172–73; Campbell, *London Tradesman*, 301–2. See George, *London Life*, chap. 4, and Peter Earle, *The World of Defoe* (New York: Atheneum, 1977), chap. 6, for discussions of the economic and social structure of London in the eighteenth century. Earle, because he concentrates on the very early part of the century, is somewhat more sensitive than George to the recent changes that had taken place in the late seventeenth century.

11. Rudé, *Hanoverian London*, 8.

12. E. A. Wrigley, "A Simple Model of London's Importance in Changing English Society and Economy 1650–1750," in John Patten, ed., *Pre-Industrial England: Geographical Essays* (Folkstone, Kent: William Dawson & Sons, 1979), 191. Wrigley's footnote on that page contains an extensive discussion of the population estimates for London between 1600 and 1800.

13. Quoted in Rudé, *Hanoverian London*, 4.

14. R. B. Walker, "Advertising in London Newspapers, 1650–1750," *Business History* XV (1973), 113–14; Siebert, *Freedom of the Press in England*, 295. According to Walker (p. 113), the earliest of these advertising sheets, *Publick Advertisements*, appeared under license by L'Estrange even before the fire, in June 1666. Only that number, however, is extant.

15. On the particular importance of John Houghton and his *Collection*, see Walker, "Advertising in London Newspapers," 115–16. Walker quotes with approval Henry Sampson, in *A History of Advertising from the Earliest Times* (London, 1874), who called Houghton "the father of English advertising." Unlike the *City Mercury*, however, Houghton's paper was soon dominated by its publisher's own varied trade interests at the expense of paid advertising.

16. *The City Mercury*, July 4, 1692.

17. Ibid.

18. The Dec. 10, 1694, number, the last in the Burney Collection, is No. 142.

19. Walker, "Advertising in London Newspapers," 117.

20. Bryan Lillywhite, *London Coffee Houses: A Reference Book of Coffee Houses of the Seventeenth, Eighteenth and Nineteenth Centuries* (London: George Allen and Unwin, 1963), 20; Summerson, *Georgian London*, 266–67. The use of public space for the conduct of business survived even into nineteenth-century America in urban "reading rooms" such as the Boston Mercantile Library (Brown, *Knowledge Is Power*, 276) and the two that were sponsored by rival insurance companies in Portsmouth, New Hampshire. The latter are the subject of "Newspaper Subscription Reading Rooms: Centers of Commerce," a seminar paper by Susan Leonard Toll, written at the University of New Hampshire in 1991. A copy is held by the Portsmouth Athenaeum.

21. Wrigley, "A Simple Model," 198.

22. Lillywhite, *London Coffee Houses*, 19–20.

23. *The English Lucien*, Jan. 13–18, 1698[/9?].

24. For Pepys, see Percival Hunt, *Samuel Pepys in the Diary* (Pittsburgh: Univ. of Pittsburgh Press, 1958), 71–72. Sewall's book-buying habits in Boston may only be surmised from his diary, but it contains so many instances of his making gifts of newly printed books and pamphlets that a regular, even systematic survey of the very few bookshops in the Boston of his day must have been a part of his weekly routine. See *Diary of Samuel Sewall*, ed. by Thomas, passim.

25. *The Weekly Miscellany*, Feb. 15–22, 1701.

26. This particular arrangement of the hierarchy in the medical profession is from Richard B. Schwartz, *Daily Life in Johnson's London* (Madison: Univ. of Wisconsin Press, 1983), 133; see 132–37 for a general discussion of eighteenth-century medicine. According to the historian of medicine Roy Porter, in *Disease, Medicine and Society in England 1550–1860* (London: Macmillan, 1987), neither the College of Physicians nor the Company of Surgeons very effectively improved the practice of English medicine during the eighteenth century (pp. 32–33). On this general topic, see also Porter, *Health for Sale: Quackery in England, 1650–1850* (Manchester: Manchester Univ. Press, 1989).

27. *The English Lucien*, Jan. 19–26, 1698[/9?]

28. *The Post Boy*, Dec. 2–4, 1701; *The London Post*, Jan. 6–8, 1700/01, *et seq*; *The Weekly Journal or British Gazetteer*, April 6, 1717. For other examples, see *The Post Boy*, Oct. 3–5, 1695; *The Flying Post*, Jan. 14–17, 1698/9; and *The London Post*, Feb. 7–10, 1700/1.

29. *Weekly Journal*, April 6, 1717.

30. Carl Bridenbaugh, *Vexed and Troubled Englishmen 1590–1642* (New York: Oxford Univ. Press, 1968), 225; Thomas Babington Macauley, *The History of England from the Accession of James II*, 3rd ed. (London: Longman, Brown, Green, and Longmans, 1849), I, 386–88; Lillywhite, *London Coffee Houses*, 19.

31. Lillywhite, *London Coffee Houses*, 20. For a compact and useful discussion of the development of the English postal service, see Steele, *The English Atlantic*, 113–19.

32. Lillywhite, *London Coffee Houses*, 21–23.

33. On the symbiotic relationship between the coffee houses and journalists such as Addison and Steele, see, e.g., Habermas, *Structural Transformation of the Public Sphere*, 42 and 259–60, notes 33–38.

34. Wrigley, "A Simple Model," 217.

35. Ibid., 197.

36. Most sources identify Ridpath as founder of the *Flying Post*, but according to E. S. DeBeer, the actual owner was the bookseller John Salisbury, who hired Ridpath as "newswriter" in charge of the paper. Ridpath, according to this account, acquired ownership in 1697. See "The English Newspapers from 1695 to 1702," in Ragnhild Hatton and S. S. Bromley, eds., *William III and Louis XIV: Essays 1680–1720 by and for Mark A. Thompson* (Liverpool: Liverpool Univ. Press, 1968), 122–23. The transfer of ownership may have come after Salisbury was brought before the Houses of Lords and Commons on two separate occasions that year for printing objectional material (Siebert, *Freedom of the Press in England*, 277–78). In any case, Salisbury and Ridpath shared the same Whig and dissenting views.

37. H. R. Fox Bourne, *English Newspapers: Chapters in the History of Journalism*, 2 vols. (London: Chatto and Windus, 1887), I, 55–57; *DNB*, s.v. George Ridpath (d. 1726) and Abel Roper (1665–1726).

38. Michael Harris, "The Structure, Ownership and Control of the Press, 1620–1780," in George Boyce, James Curran, and Pauline Wingate, eds., *Newspaper History from the Seventeenth Century to the Present Day* (London: Constable; Beverly Hills: Sage Publications, 1978), 84. See also David Harrison Stevens, *Party Politics and English Journalism, 1702–1742* (New York: Russell and Russell, 1967), which emphasizes the role of political sponsorship in financing both the newspapers and the essay journals of the Queen Anne period, esp. 1–14. This is also one theme of William Bragg Ewald, *The Newsmen of Queen Anne* (Oxford: Basil Blackwell, 1956; pub. in the U.S. as *Rogues, Royalty and Reporters: The Age of Queen Anne Through Its Newspapers* (Boston: Houghton Mifflin, 1956)).

39. Philip Pinkus, *Grub St. Stripped Bare: The Scandalous Lives & Pornographic Works of the Original Grub St. Writers* . . . (London: Constable, 1968), 13–16; Michael Harris, "Journalism as a Profession or Trade in the Eighteenth Century," in Robin Myers and Michael Harris, eds., *Author/Publisher Relations during the Eighteenth and Nineteenth Centuries*, Publishing Pathways Series, Vol. 5 (Oxford: Oxford Polytechnic Press, 1983), 38.

40. Harris, "Journalism as a Profession," 38; Pinkus, *Grub St. Stripped Bare*, 118–19, 240–50; Bourne, *English Newspapers*, I, 62. Defoe's punishment resulted from his prosecution by a Tory administration for having published one of his best pieces of satire, "The Shortest Way with Dissenters."

41. Ewald, *The Newsmen of Queen Anne*, 9, 232, 256.

42. Pinkus, *Grub St. Stripped Bare*, 50, 242–43.

43. DeBeer, "English Newspapers," 122.

44. See Chapter 1 above for a discussion of Ichabod Dawks and his eccentric (but nevertheless respected) *News-Letter*.

45. Our understanding of the ownership and operation of the London newspapers of the eighteenth century is due chiefly to Michael Harris. See, e.g., his chapter, "The Structure, Ownership and Control of the Press, 1620–1780" in Boyce, Curran and Wingate, eds., *Newspaper History*, 82–97; his article, "Journalism as a Profession or Trade in the Eighteenth Century," in Myers and Harris, *Author/Publisher Relations*, 37–62; and his monograph, *London Newspapers in the Age of Walpole*, 65–112 passim.

46. Although advertising revenues rose in importance as a means of financing most London newspapers, even in the 1720s and 1730s, this source was only "a useful adjunct to sales revenue," and before that advertising played an even smaller

role in the revenue picture of most newspapers. See Michael Harris's discussion of this point, and of the difficulties in arriving at exact estimates, in *London Newspapers in the Age of Walpole*, 58–64.

47. *P.B.*, Oct. 9–11, 11–14, 16–18, 25–28, and Dec. 2–4, 1701. See also examples of mostly undated handwritten supplements to the *P.B.* interleaved in Vol. 112 of Brit. Lib. Burney Collection, following the numbers of April 29–May 1, June 24–26, Dec. 4–7 and 11–14, 1697; Jan. 1–4, 1698; March 22–24, 1698; and scattered other numbers, ending with that of Dec. 19–21, 1700. They are written in several different hands, and all follow the traditional newsletter format, beginning much like Dawks's printed newsletter.

48. *P.M.*, March 2–4, 1696[/7]; June 10–12, 1703.

49. *F.P.*, July 8–10, 1703.

50. The posts left London for most parts of England on Tuesday, Thursday, and Saturday evenings. The thrice-weekly pattern of publication for papers intended for national distribution, which formed the principal sources for the provincial press, continued throughout the century even though post departures from London became more frequent. As early as 1741, posts for several important provincial centers began leaving London six days a week instead of three. Black, *English Press in the Eighteenth Century*, 97.

51. See prospectus for *St. James's Evening Post* in the May 30–June 1, 1715, number of *St. James's Post*. As for the blank space in the *Evening Post*, Jeremy Black suggests that there was so much of it in 1711 that "it is difficult to escape the impression that there simply was not enough material for the paper." *English Press in the Eighteenth Century*, 52.

52. Harris, "Structure, Ownership and Control of the Press, 1620–1780," 87.

53. J. M. Price, "A Note on the Circulation of the London Press, 1704–1714," *Bulletin of the Institute of Historical Research* 31 (1958), 217; Henry L. Snyder, "The Circulation of Newspapers in the Reign of Queen Anne," *The Library*, 5th Ser., XXIII (1969), 211.

54. *D.C.*, March 11, 1702. The apparent discrepancy between the March 18 date of the sources and the publication date of the *Courant* itself is explained by the 11-day difference between the calendars then in use in Britain and on the Continent.

55. See file of *D.C.* for 1702 in Brit. Lib. Burney Collection, Vol. 121b. On Buckley, see Harris, *London Newspapers in the Age of Walpole*, 117, 139–40, 156.

56. See volumes of *The State of Europe: Or the Historical and Political Mercury* (originally published at The Hague in November 1688) and its successor *The Present State of Europe: Or, the Historical and Political Monthly Mercury* in Beineke Library, Yale University. Another monthly news magazine, *The Political State of Great Britain with the Most Material Occurrences in Europe*, an extensive file of which is also to be found in the Beineke Library, began in 1711.

57. *The New State of Europe, Both as to Publick Transactions and Learning*, May 23, 1701.

58. *L.G.*, June 2, 5, and Juy 3, 1701. The new monthly magazines were *A General View of the World; or, The Marrow of History in 2 Parts. The First, Containing the History of the World, from the Creation, to be Continued to the Year 1700 . . . The Second, an Account of the State of Affairs for the Month of June, 1701*, and *The History of the Works of the Learned; or, An Impartial Account of Books Lately Printed in All Parts of Europe, with a Particular Relation of the State of Learning in*

Each Country. The *State of Europe* had by now changed its title to the *Present State of Europe.*

59. *A Weekly Review of the Affairs of France, Purged from the Errors and Partiality of News-Writers and Petty Statesmen of All Sides; A Review of the Affairs of France, with Some Observations on Transactions at Home;* and *A Review of the State of the English Nation.* See Bourne, *English Newspapers,* I, 62–65. On the circulation of the *Review,* see Black, *English Press in the Eighteenth Century,* 47.

60. See *The New State of Europe,* May 23–July 29, 1701, and Sept. 20, 1701–Jan. 1, 1702 (Burney Collection, Vol. 117b), and Jan. 3–22, 1702 (Burney Collection, Vol. 121b).

61. *English Lucien,* Jan. 18, 1698.

62. *English Lucien,* "from Candlemas Day [Feb. 2] to the Wednesday following, 1698."

63. *Jesting Astrologer,* Feb. 24-March 3, 1701.

64. Ibid.

65. *S.J.E.P.,* April 22–24, Feb. 15–18, 1718.

66. *Weekly Journal, or British Gazetteer,* April 19, 1718.

67. A few of the newsbooks of the Interregnum far surpassed any of the post-1695 newspapers in downright obscenity. G. A. Cranfield has labeled *Mercurius Fumigosus, or the Smoking Nocturnall,* which flourished in 1654 and 1655, "one of the smuttiest papers in the history of the British Press," and provided the evidence to back his assertion. This and others like it were finally suppressed by Cromwell in 1655. See Cranfield, *The Press and Society: From Caxton to Northcliffe* (London: Longman, 1978), 16–18.

68. It is true, for example, that Francis Clifton, publisher of the *Weekly Medley: or, The Gentleman's Recreation,* attacked his rival Nathaniel Mist's *Weekly Journal* in 1719 as appealing to the "lower class of readers" (Black, *English Press in the Eighteenth Century,* 44). Evidence such as this admittedly works against the point I am urging here since it suggests a readership divided by whatever Clifton meant by "class." My view, however, is that such evidence is relatively scanty when compared with both the evidence and the logic in favor of a readership that was relatively small compared with the larger population and was with virtual unanimity at least familiar with just about the entire print culture.

69. Or at least almost everything. Jeremy Black notes that coffee houses tried to keep costs down by declining to put in an automatic subscription for every new paper that came out. *English Press in the Eighteenth Century,* 19.

70. This is a chapter heading in Seaman's delightful *New History of England,* 302–18.

71. Brit. Lib. Burney Collection, Vol. 117a.

72. *Spectator,* No. 452, quoted in Cranfield, *Press and Society,* 32.

73. Brit. Lib. Burney Collection, Vol. 116a.

74. Black, *English Press in the Eighteenth Century,* 14; Harris, *London Newspapers,* 1.

75. Harris, *London Newspapers,* 20–28.

76. Black, *English Press in the Eighteenth Century,* 146.

77. Good treatments of the London newspapers' coverage of foreign news can be found in Black, *English Press in the Eighteenth Century,* chap. 7 (pp. 197–243),

and, by the same author, "Russia and the British Press 1720–1740," *British Journal for Eighteenth-Century Studies* 5 (Spring 1982), 85–92.

Chapter 3. The Provinces

1. Steele, *The English Atlantic*, 116–18.

2. C. W. Chalklin, *The Provincial Towns of Georgian England: A Study of the Building Process, 1740–1820* (London: Edward Arnold, 1974), 4–16. The round figure of five million for the population of England in 1700 is based on the table on pp. 208–9 of E. A. Wrigley and R. S. Schofield, *The Population History of England 1541–1871: A Reconstruction* (London: Edward Arnold, 1981), where the 1701 population of England alone is given as 5,057,790. Applying the factor suggested in a note elsewhere in the text (p. 577) yields the figure of 5,416,180 for England and Wales.

3. These estimates are based on a round figure of five million for the English population as a whole, a population of 575,000 for London, and a figure of 110,000 for the combined populations of Norwich, Bristol, Exeter, Newcastle, Yarmouth, Colchester, and York. The latter sum is derived from Chalklin, *Provincial Towns*, 13–15.

4. Michael Hechter, *Internal Colonialism: The Celtic Fringe in British National Development, 1536–1966* (London: Routledge & Kegan Paul, 1975), 67. The population figure of 400,000 is approximate and more likely to be overstated than understated. It is based on a rough extrapolation of the estimates of 371,000 in 1670 and 489,000 in 1750, offered with great caution by Geraint H. Jenkins in *The Foundations of Modern Wales: Wales, 1642–1780* (Oxford: Oxford Univ. Press, 1987), 88. Great fluctuations in mortality, warns Jenkins, make it impossible to assume a steady growth in population during that span of time. The figure, however, does coincide roughly with that derived from Wrigley and Schofield, *Population History of England*. Cf. note 2, above.

5. Gordon Donaldson, *Scotland: The Shaping of a Nation* (London: David & Charles, 1974), 48–49. Linda Colley, in *Britons: Forging the Nation 1707–1837* (New Haven: Yale Univ. Press, 1992), stresses the bond of Protestantism as the essential element of British nationalism that alone made possible the invention of the United Kingdom in 1707. For that point, see pp. 11–54, and for subsequent strains between the English and the Celtic "peripheries" and their resolution, see pp. 101–45.

6. The figure of about one million Scots at 1700 is the common rough estimate, impossible to corroborate. See R. A. Houston and L. D. Whyte, eds., *Scottish Society, 1500–1800* (Cambridge: Cambridge Univ. Press, 1989), 3, and discussion in Michael Flinn, ed., *Scottish Population History from the 17th Century to the 1930s* (Cambridge: Cambridge Univ. Press, 1977), 4. Houston and Whyte give the population of Edinburgh in 1700 as 30,000 to 50,000 (p. 5).

7. Steele, *The English Atlantic*, 143–44. The standard work on the Edinburgh press before 1800 is W. J. Couper, *The Edinburgh Periodical Press*, 2 vols. (Stirling, Scotland: Eneas Mackay, 1908). The *Edinburgh Gazette* in its several incarnations, the first 1699–1706, and its many immediate successors are treated somewhat comprehensively in I, 202–54, and II, 11–65.

8. Interpolated roughly from population table in K. H. Connell, *The Popula-*

tion of Ireland, 1750–1845 (Westport, Conn.: Greenwood Press, 1975; rpt. of Oxford: Clarendon Press, 1950, ed.), 25.

9. Robert Munter, *The History of the Irish Newspaper, 1685–1760* (Cambridge: Cambridge Univ. Press, 1967), 5–15; Richard Robert Madden, *The History of Irish Periodical Literature*, 2 vols. (London: T. C. Newby, 1867; New York: Johnson Reprint, 1968), I, 19–239; Steele, *The English Atlantic*, 142–43.

10. The term "core" is borrowed from Bernard Bailyn's slightly different description of the American colonies in about 1700 as "a borderland, a part of the expanding periphery of Britain's core culture." While his use of the term emphasizes the regressive nature of the "ragged outer margin" that was America by comparison with Britain as a whole, my emphasis here is upon the common relationship with London that the provincial capitals of British America shared with their counterparts in the home islands. My meaning is perhaps closer to, though not identical with, that of Michael Hechter, who notes that most modern states developed from the extension of political influence and control outward from the "core" regions in which strong central governments were first established. In the process, writes Hechter, "the several local and regional cultures are gradually replaced by the establishment of one *national* culture which cuts across the previous distinctions. The core and peripheral cultures must ultimately merge into one all-encompassing cultural system to which all members of the society have primary identification and loyalty." See Bailyn, *The Peopling of British North America: An Introduction* (New York: Alfred A. Knopf, 1986), 112–13; Hechter, *Internal Colonialism*, 4–5.

11. J. M. Price, "A Note on the Circulation of the London Press, 1704–1714," *Bulletin of the Institute of Historical Research* 31 (1958), 217; Henry L. Snyder, "The Circulation of Newspapers in the Reign of Queen Anne," *The Library*, 5th Ser., XXIII (1969), 211. These same points are made in Chapter 3 above.

12. Roy McKeen Wiles, "The Relish for Reading in Provincial England Two Centuries Ago," in Paul J. Korshin, ed., *The Widening Circle: Essays on the Circulation of Literature in Eighteenth-Century Europe* (Philadelphia: Univ. of Pennsylvania Press, 1976), 87. On literacy, see David Cressy, "Levels of Illiteracy in England, 1640–1730," *Historical Journal* 20 (1977), 1–23.

13. Cranfield, *Development of the Provincial Newspaper*, 12.

14. The first number of *Sam Farley's Exeter Post-Man* that any modern historian has seen is numbered 556 and dated August 10, 1711. If the number is right, and if the paper appeared once every week from its beginning, its first number would have come out in December 1700, before any other provincial paper. Not only, however, do we lack any earlier numbers or other evidence to confirm this possibility, but there is positive evidence, slim to be sure, to the contrary. A publisher's announcement by John Campbell in the April 9, 1705, number of the *Boston News-Letter*, which had started in April 1704, referred to the Exeter paper, which Campbell said was established "much about the same time that we began here." On those grounds, Cranfield has accepted 1704 as the starting date of the *Exeter Post-Man*, both in *The Development of the Provincial Newspaper*, 16, and in *A Hand-List of English Provincial Newspapers and Periodicals 1700–1760* (Cambridge, 1952), 7. On the strength of the same evidence, R. M. Wiles also accepts 1704 as the beginning date for the *Exeter Post-Man*. See Wiles, *Freshest Advices*, Appendix C, p. 413.

15. Steele, *The English Atlantic*, 138–39; Penelope Corfield, "A Provincial Capi-

tal in the Late Seventeenth Century: The Case of Norwich," in Peter Clark and Paul Slack, eds., *Crisis and Order in English Towns, 1500–1700: Essays in Urban History* (London: Routledge & Kegan Paul, 1972), 282.

16. Corfield, "A Provincial Capital," 269–90 passim; for more on Norwich, see John T. Evans, *Seventeenth-Century Norwich: Politics, Religion, and Government, 1620–1690* (Oxford: Oxford Univ. Press, 1979).

17. Dates of Burges's arrival in Norwich, the presumed establishment of the *Post*, and his death and transfer of the business to his widow are in Henry Robert Plomer, *A Dictionary of the Printers and Booksellers Who Were at Work in England, Scotland and Ireland from 1726 to 1775* ([London]: Bibliographical Society, 1968 (rpt. of 1932 ed.)), 248–49.

18. Though provincial newspapers soon adopted other methods of distribution, the Norwich printers at this time were relying on hawkers to sell their one or two hundred copies. Cranfield, *Development of the Provincial Newspaper*, 169, 190–91.

19. Ibid., 34–35.

20. Ibid., 209.

21. The quotation is from *Norwich Post*, May 3, 1707. Other numbers examined in the photostat file in the Colindale Newspaper Library of the British Library were those of May 8, 22, and 29, 1708; Feb. 19, May 21, and July 23, 1709; and July 5, 1712.

22. Steele, *The English Atlantic*, 139.

23. Ronald H. Quilici, "Turmoil in a City and an Empire: Bristol's Factions, 1700–1775" (Ph.D. diss., University of New Hampshire, 1976), 105–7, 125–26.

24. William Barrett, *The History and Antiquities of the City of Bristol* (Bristol: William Pine, 1788; facs. rpt. Gloucester: A. Sutton, 1982), 164.

25. J. H. Bettey, *Wessex from AD 1000* (London: Longman, 1986), 206–7; Quilici, "Turmoil in a City and an Empire," 107–24 passim.

26. Quilici, "Turmoil in a City and an Empire," 53–55, 107–8.

27. Barrett, *History and Antiquities of Bristol*, 181.

28. Ibid., 120.

29. Quilici, "Turmoil in a City and an Empire," 33–34.

30. A. P. Woolrich, *Printing in Bristol* (Bristol: Bristol Branch of the Historical Association, 1986), 2.

31. The *Bristol Weekly Mercury* of Dec. 1, 1716 (No. 61) is the only extant number. This discussion of the *Mercury* is founded on a facsimile of that number in the Bristol Reference Library. It contains four small pages in a pamphlet format, complete with title page, and is probably incomplete. There must have been either two or four pages more. For newsletters as a source for provincial printers, see Cranfield, *The Development of the Provincial Newspaper*, 31–32. The item from Boston is at the bottom of page 4, and is so torn that neither the source nor more than the first few words can be read. The dateline of the item, however, is "*Boston in New England, October* 15," and it is clear from comparing the opening phrase of this item and the brief article on Shute in the October 15 *News-Letter* that the American paper was Greep's source.

32. *Sam Farley's Bristol Post Man*, Dec. 24 and 31, 1715; Jan. 7, 14, 21, and 28, 1716. Collection in Bristol Reference Library. The three items originally communicated from New York to John Campbell's *Boston News-Letter*, all of which appeared in the January 28 *Post Man*, were printed first in the *Boston News-Letter* of October 10, 17, and 31, 1715. The first two concerned ship arrivals in New York, one

reporting storms in the West Indies and the other Spanish pirates. The third was relayed to Campbell by a New York correspondent who had heard in turn from Philadelphia of a "very remarkable story" from Newcastle, Pennsylvania: an extraordinarily localized rain had fallen continually for several days on an old oak tree, only to stop when the tree was cut down. Eighteenth-century gentleman "philosophers" loved this sort of thing.

33. Wiles, *Freshest Advices*, 23.

34. Cranfield, *The Development of the Provincial Newspaper*, 18–21.

35. Ibid., 190–99; Wiles, *Freshest Advices*, 118–42.

36. Carl Bridenbaugh, *Cities in the Wilderness: The First Century of Urban Life in America, 1625–1742* (New York: Ronald Press, 1938), 170–72; Walter Muir Whitehill, *Boston: A Topographical History*, 2nd ed. (Cambridge, Mass.: Harvard Univ. Press, 1968), 4–9, 13–14, 19–21. The quoted passage is from Robert Keayne's bequest to build the Town House, quoted in Bernard Bailyn, *The New England Merchants in the Seventeenth Century* (Cambridge, Mass.: Harvard Univ. Press, 1955), 97.

37. Samuel G. Drake, *The History and Antiquities of Boston* (Boston: Luther Stevens, 1856), 517n.

38. Whitehill, *Topographical History*, 17–18.

39. Bridenbaugh, *Cities in the Wilderness*, 108–9.

40. Thomas Hutchinson, *History of the Colony and Province of Massachusetts Bay* (Cambridge, Mass.: Harvard Univ. Press, 1936), I, 297–351. See also David Lovejoy, *The Glorious Revolution in America* (New York: Harper & Row, 1972); pp. 370–71 describe the return of Mather and Phips with the new charter.

41. Michael G. Hall emphasizes the transforming effect of the military and naval presence upon Boston between 1696 and 1711 in *The Last American Puritan: The Life of Increase Mather, 1639–1723* (Middletown: Wesleyan Univ. Press, 1988), 326–31. In *The Governors-General: The English Army and the Definition of Empire, 1569–1681* (Chapel Hill: Univ. of North Carolina Press, 1979), Stephen Saunders Webb argues that "garrison government" had become the norm in British America by late in the seventeenth century.

42. *Diary of Samuel Sewall*, Thomas, ed., I, 456.

43. Isaiah Thomas, *History of Printing in America*, Marcus A. McCorison, ed. (Barre, Mass.: Imprint Society, 1970), 50–81; Steele, *The English Atlantic*, 145–46; Hall, *The Last American Puritan*, 135–36. The question whether it was actually Stephen Day (or Daye) or his son Matthew who probably operated the first Cambridge press—which in any case was apparently owned not by either but by the widow of the man who died en route while bringing it to America, the Reverend Jose Glover—is discussed inconclusively in Benjamin Franklin V, ed., *Boston Printers, Publishers and Booksellers: 1640–1800* (Boston: G. K. Hall, 1980), 87–91.

44. Wetherell, "Brokers of the Word," 79; Franklin, ed., *Boston Printers*, 11–15, 213–19, 239–44, 301–8, 323–29.

45. It is not clear whether Green issued this piece before or after he received, in 1685, an official license to print. There was apparently a lapse between Sewall's relinquishing of his license and the issuance of one to Green. See Thomas, *History of Printing*, 82, and Franklin, ed., *Boston Printers*, 236. The *Gazette* (dated Feb. 5–9, 1684 O.S.) must have arrived on the ship reported by Samuel Sewall on April 14. Sewall mentions arrival of the news and "a couple of printed Proclamations relating to that affair" on the ship, but not the *Gazette* specifically (*Diary of Samuel Sewall*,

Thomas, ed., I, 60). These observations concerning the novel use of broadside publications beginning in 1685 to disseminate "news" are based on the chronologically arranged broadside shelf list at the American Antiquarian Society.

46. Reference to the reprinting of the *Gazette* of Dec. 2, 1700, of which there is apparently no extant copy, appears in *Diary of Samuel Sewall*, Thomas, ed., I, 446.

47. Although Clarence S. Brigham lists *The Present State of the New-English Affairs* in his *History and Bibliography of American Newspapers, 1690–1820* (2 vols., Westport, Conn.: Greenwood Press, 1975 (rpt. of 1947 ed.)), he notes that bibliographers consider it a broadside rather than a newspaper. By most definitions, of course, newspapers are serial publications and *New-English Affairs* clearly was not. Brigham places its probable publication in November 1689 based on an assumed lapse of about two months between September 3, the latest date on one of its items, and its appearance in Boston print. Michael G. Hall says it came out "that winter" (*The Last Puritan*, 220). Some readers may wish to know of a long and, from a distance of almost 90 years, rather profitless discussion in *Publications of the Col. Soc. of Mass.* X (1907) of whether *New-English Affairs* was or was not a "newspaper." In this discussion, Albert Matthews takes the negative (310–20).

48. Franklin, ed., *Boston Printers*, 277–80; Frank Luther Mott, *American Journalism: A History of Newspapers in the United States Through 250 Years, 1690 to 1940* (New York: Macmillan, 1949), 9–10. For more on Harris, see Judith Serrin, "U.S. Newspapers' 300th Year," *Editor and Publisher*, April 21, 1990, pp. 66–69.

49. Franklin, ed., *Boston Printers*, 412–14.

50. *Publick Occurrences*, Sept. 25, 1690. I have used the American Antiquarian Society's facsimile of the only known surviving copy in the Public Record Office, London.

51. Clyde A. Duniway, *The Development of Freedom of the Press in Massachusetts* (Cambridge, Mass.: Harvard Univ. Press, 1906), has long provided the most comprehensive account of the *Publick Occurrences* episode, but there is a quick and useful summary in Steele, *The English Atlantic*, 145–47. For a fuller discussion of the episode and its context, see my "The Newspapers of Provincial America," *Proceedings of the American Antiquarian Society* 100 (1991), 367–89, and for important details surrounding the decisions both to publish and to suppress, Victor Hugo Paltsis, "New Light on 'Publick Occurrences': America's First Newspaper," *Proceedings of the American Antiquarian Society* 59 (1949), 75–88.

Chapter 4. John Campbell, 1704–1719

1. The collection, which has now been dispersed among other papers in the Society's holdings, is printed in two volumes of Massachusetts Historical Society *Proceedings*. Ten letters dated from April 4, 1666, to Oct. 4, 1703, appear in Vol. XII (1871–75), pp. 419–27; 12 letters, all from John Campbell to Fitz John Winthrop, dated from April 12 to Oct. 1703, appear in Vol. IX (1866–67), pp. 485–501. The total is actually 21 letters rather than 22, because each volume contains a part of John Campbell's long letter of May 3, 1703.

2. For biographical information on both Campbells, see *DAB*, III, 456; Isaiah Thomas, *History of Printing in America*, Marcus A. McCorison, ed. (Barre, Mass.: Imprint Society, 1970), 188; Benjamin Franklin V, ed., *Boston Printers, Publishers and Booksellers, 1640–1800* (Boston: G. K. Hall, 1980), 69–70; Arthur M. Schlesinger, *Prelude to Independence: The Newspaper War on Britain, 1764–1776* (New

York: Alfred A. Knopf, 1958), 51–52; and Carl Wilhelm Ernst, *Postal Service in Boston 1639–1893* (Boston: Trustees of the Boston Public Library, 1975 (rpt. with foreword by John Alden from *The Professional and Industrial History of Suffolk County, Massachusetts* (Boston, 1894), II, 443–504)), 9–11. Two of these sources, Franklin and Ernst (the latter only "probably") identify John Campbell as a bookseller, but the evidence for that is scanty. Only Franklin states definitively that he was Duncan Campbell's son; Thomas says, on what seem obvious grounds, that Duncan was "probably" John's father. Ernst mentions no relationship between Duncan and John, but says John helped settle Duncan's estate. For the reorganization of the colonial postal service in 1693 see, besides Ernst, William Smith, *The History of the Post Office in British North America, 1693–1870* (Cambridge: Cambridge Univ. Press, 1920), 9–12.

3. Schlesinger, in *Prelude to Independence*, 1, in general following Clyde A. Duniway, *The Development of Freedom of the Press in Massachusetts* (Cambridge, Mass.: Harvard Univ. Press, 1906), 76–77, suggests that Campbell sent newsletters to "leading men of the region." The evidence for the suggestion, beyond the letters to Winthrop, is not clear, but it does not seem an unreasonable assumption. The sketch of Campbell in *DAB* (1929) gives essentially the same account, calling his recipients "regular patrons." The only source cited, however, is the collection of letters to Winthrop. Douglas C. McMurtrie's account of the antecedents and origins of the *News-Letter* in *The Beginnings of the American Newspaper* (Chicago: Black Cat Press, 1935) is more detailed than any of these three, but again the evidence for his elaborations is not disclosed. What is disclosed instead is the author's imperfect reading of the only evidence that any of these authors acknowledge, namely the printed version of the letters to Winthrop.

4. The most explicit evidence for this kind of correspondence is in the letter to Winthrop of July 12, 1703, in which Campbell quotes, apparently in its entirety, an unusually rich letter from New York, including those parts that in turn were obviously lifted from the London newspapers. MHS *Proceedings*, IX, 496–97.

5. Schlesinger, *Prelude to Independence*, 51.

6. Steele, *The English Atlantic*, 360n.

7. See, e.g., *DAB*, III, 456.

8. See again Habermas, *Transformation of the Public Sphere*. Michael Warner's application of this concept to eighteenth-century America is especially relevant here. See *The Letters of the Republic*, esp. chap. 20.

9. Botein, "'Meer Mechanics' and an Open Press," 193–96, and "Printers and the American Revolution," in Bailyn and Hench, eds., *The Press and the American Revolution*, 22 and n.

10. David Cressy, *Coming Over: Migration and Communication between England and New England in the Seventeenth Century* (Cambridge: Cambridge Univ. Press, 1987).

11. See again Carey, *Communication as Culture*, chap. 1.

12. This was the case even after 1710, when the status of the American post office was shifted from that of a private monopoly granted by patent to that of a government enterprise operating under the general post office in England. See Smith, *History of the Post Office*, 17, and Ernst, *Postal Service in Boston*, 11–12.

13. *BNL*, April 9, 1705.

14. See, e.g., *BNL*, May 7, 1705, through Jan. 14, 1706. Every one of those 35

numbers carries some version of a publisher's announcement using that phraseology.

15. *BNL*, April 30, 1705.

16. David Paul Nord, "Teleology and News: The Religious Roots of American Journalism, 1630–1730," *JAH* 77 (1990), 9–38.

17. See Peter Fraser, *The Intelligence of the Secretaries of State and Their Monopoly on Licensed News, 1660–1688* (Cambridge: Cambridge Univ. Press, 1956), and Fredrick Seaton Siebert, *Freedom of the Press in England 1476–1776* (Urbana: Univ. of Illinois Press, 1965), 290–94.

18. For eighteenth-century papermaking, see R. Campbell, *The London Tradesman: Being a Compendious View of all the Trades, Professions, Arts, both Liberal and Mechanic, Now Practised in the Cities of London and Westminster* (London, 1725), 125, and Wroth, *The Colonial Printer*, 123–25.

19. Thomas, *History of Printing*, 215.

20. A phrase (and method) I learned from Willie P. Parker and his associates at the printing office at Colonial Williamsburg. It was also called "work-and-turn."

21. The colophon was also a standard fixture at the bottom of every broadside of the period. From the point of view of the printer, it appears, a newspaper or broadside was analogous to the title page of a book, with title and other front matter at the top and printer's or publisher's imprint at the bottom.

22. Nicholas Boone's connection with the *BNL* did not end as abruptly as the change in colophon makes it appear. His name reappears either there or in a publisher's announcement from time to time after that during the first year, and of course the absence of his name is no certain indication that he did not continue to sell the paper or, as announced in the first number, take in advertising. Boone was a bookseller who had apprenticed with Duncan Campbell and taken over his old shop when Campbell changed locations in 1697. His association with the *BNL*, however brief, provides further circumstantial evidence that Duncan Campbell was John Campbell's father. Not only did Boone serve his apprenticeship with the elder Campbell and take over his shop, but he moved again in 1704 to the coffee shop and tavern operated by Duncan Campbell's widow, presumably John Campbell's mother. There he expanded his business to include other retail items as well as books, which may be the reason for the early confusion in his advertised arrangement with Campbell and his eventual disappearance from the printed record altogether. He moved again in 1706. (Franklin, ed., *Boston Printers, Publishers, and Booksellers*, 46–47.)

23. *BNL*, Feb. 4, 1723.

24. *W.R.*, Aug. 11, 1735; *BEP*, Aug. 18, 1735.

25. May 15, June 19, Oct. 2, Nov. 20 and 27, Dec. 4.

26. *BNL*, Feb. 23, 1719.

27. On market-day publishing in England, see Cranfield, *Development of the Provincial Newspaper*, 33. Obviously, market day in many towns was one of the three post days as well.

28. This raises the question of whether the drying time that was necessary for most print jobs applied to newspapers. Books and pamphlets normally were printed on paper that had been moistened by dipping in water to prepare them to take a sharper and more textured imprint. The sheets were then hung to dry. According to experts at Colonial Williamsburg, drying could take as much as fourteen hours. I have not been able to discover a consensus among those familiar

with eighteenth-century printing techniques on the likelihood that newspapers may have been printed on unmoistened sheets, thus eliminating the necessity for drying. However, *Sam Farley's Bristol Post Man* announced in its standing matter that the paper would be published every Saturday morning "Two Hours after the London Post comes in" (Dec. 31, 1715; Jan. 7, 14, 21, and 28, 1716), and the accounts of several celebratory parades on the occasion of the ratification of the U.S. Constitution much later in the century report that printers "struck off" copies of the document or of ballads while riding on elaborate floats and threw them to the crowds hot off the press. Obviously, no drying time was involved in either case. Moreover, as Dale Dippre of Colonial Williamsburg demonstrated by a simple experiment in my presence in the summer of 1986, wetting is destructive of the cheapest paper of the period, namely that made, as some was, with no sizing. He also demonstrated that printing on dry paper, while the imprint is not as good as that on moistened paper, can give satisfactory results. My conclusion is that it was entirely possible to dispense with the moistening-and-drying procedure, and that in the case of newspapers those steps were probably most often omitted to save time.

29. *BNL*, Nov. 10 and 17, 1718.

30. *BNL*, Feb. 23, 1719.

31. Carl Bridenbaugh, *Cities in the Wilderness: The First Century of Urban Life in America, 1625–1742* (New York: Oxford Univ. Press, 1971), 171–72. See also Samuel G. Drake, *The History and Antiquities of Boston* (Boston: Luther Stevens, 1856), 536–37, and Esther Forbes, *Paul Revere and the World He Lived In* (Boston: Houghton Mifflin, 1942), 6, 48. One eighteenth-century term for warehouse was "store."

32. *BNL*, March 12 and April 9, 1705.

33. See Michael Schudson, *Discovering the News: A Social History of American Newspapers* (New York: Basic Books, 1978), and Dan Schiller, *Objectivity in the News* (Philadelphia: Univ. of Pennsylvania Press, 1981), esp. Schudson's introduction, 3–11.

34. The Massachusetts law of 1665 imposing stringent controls on the press had died with the loss of the first charter. All royal governors until 1730, however, were instructed by the Crown to permit printing only by prior consent. (Duniway, *Freedom of the Press in Massachusetts*, 63–82.)

35. *BNL*, June 10, 1706. A quarter of a century later, Benjamin Franklin indulged in a similar bit of callous reckoning of monetary loss from the death of blacks in his *Pennsylvania Gazette* of July 8, 1731. See discussion in Chapter 10 below.

36. Drake, *History and Antiquities*, 525.

37. *Acts and Resolves, Public and Private, of the Province of the Massachusetts Bay*, I (Boston: Wright and Potter, 1869), 606–7, 634.

38. Mather's *Deplorable State* was first published in London in 1708 without the author's name, and reprinted in 1721 in Boston, probably by Samuel Kneeland, again anonymously, under the title *The Deplorable State of New-England, by Reason of a Covetous and Treacherous Governour, and Pusillanimous Counsellors.* . . . By that time, however, Dudley had long since been succeeded by Samuel Shute.

39. Ernst, *Postal Service in Boston*, 11.

40. *Journals of the House of Representatives of Massachusetts*, I, 28, 34, 92, 98, 253;

II, 50, 57; III, 183. Subscription prices during these earliest years seem to have been a matter of individual negotiation between publisher and subscriber.

41. Of the 36 numbers of 1704, all had but two pages except two, one of which (the second) had four pages and another three pages. In 1705, there were 49 two-page and three four-page numbers. Of the 49 numbers now available from 1706, 27 have four pages, 20 two pages, and two six pages. Campbell kept publishing larger numbers into January 1707, but after January 20 there were none with more than two pages for the rest of that year. In 1709 he suspended publication for eight months for lack of "encouragement." In 1713, he published two-page numbers exclusively, but in 1719 he alternated two-page with four-page numbers most of the year. He dropped this practice in 1720, the first year he was not postmaster, but did publish at least four half-sheet "Post Scripts" or supplements, and nineteen of the regular numbers in 1720 were of four pages, most clustered toward the end of the year.

42. The quoted phrase is from *BNL*, April 30, 1705.

43. See, e.g., *BNL*, May 6 and Oct. 28, 1706; April 30 and May 21, 1711; and Jan. 12, 1713.

44. *L.G.*, Aug. 3, 1714; *BNL*, Sept. 27, 1714.

45. Since the letters from Cork were dated August 12 and the ship from Cork arrived in Boston September 15, the voyage from the southern Irish coast had taken not more than 34 days. The other ship that arrived September 15 had sailed from Cowes on the Isle of Wight not earlier than August 1 (the day the Queen died), more likely August 2, a Monday. That would have made a passage from the English Channel of 44 days. The ship that arrived September 17 had cleared London not earlier than August 3, since she carried the *L.G.* of that date, resulting in a passage of 43 days from London, including the descent of the Thames and the wait for proper wind and tide at Deal. Compare these sailing times with those calculated and discussed by I. K. Steele in "Time, Communications and Society: The English Atlantic, 1702," *Journal of American Studies* 8 (1974), 1–21. Based on the transmission of the news to America of the death of William III and accession of Anne, and of the declaration of war, both in the spring of 1702, Steele arrives at a minimum sailing time from London to Boston of 48 days, the quickest "colonial instant," as he calls it, of any other except that between London and Barbardos, which was 45 days (p. 19). Steele discusses ocean routes and sailing times more fully in chapters 5 and 6 of *The English Atlantic*, 78–110. There is also a discussion of transatlantic sailing times in Clarence S. Brigham, *Journals and Journeymen: A Contribution to the History of Early American Newspapers* (Philadelphia: Univ. of Pennsylvania Press, 1950), 55–57. For treatments of the same topic with specific attention to two southern colonies, see Hennig Cohen, *The South Carolina Gazette, 1732–1775* (Columbia: Univ. of South Carolina Press, 1953), 10–11, 15; and Charles Christopher Crittenden, *North Carolina Newspapers before 1790* (Chapel Hill: Univ. of North Carolina Press, 1928), 27.

46. *BNL*, Aug. 10, 1719.

Chapter 5. Competition, 1719–1732

1. Cranfield, *Development of the Provincial Newspaper*, 26.

2. Ernst, *Postal Service in Boston*, 13; *B.G.*, Jan. 11, 1719[/20]. Brooker announced in a paid advertisement in the *BNL* of Sept. 15, 1719, "On Saturday last

the 13th Currant the Post-Office in Boston was removed to the fifth Door to the Southward of the old Office . . . ." In the imprint of that number, Campbell, previously identified as postmaster, now became simply "John Campbell in Corn Hill."

3. Ernst, *Postal Service in Boston*, 13. In the *B.G.* of Jan. 11, 1719[/20], Brooker dates his *appointment* at September 13, 1718, but since he actually took office on that day, Hamilton must have named him to the job somewhat earlier, though not before Musgrave's appointment on June 27. The sources are vague on the exact point at which Musgrave succeeded Brooker. Ernst implies that it was during the summer of 1720, but an advertisement in a supplement to the *Gazette* identified Musgrave as postmaster as early as March 22. Whatever the date in 1720 that Musgrave assumed the postmastership in person, he apparently did not take over the *Gazette* until September 26. See Albert Matthews, "Bibliographical Notes" to Mary Farwell Ayer, "Check-List of Boston Newspapers," *Pub. Col. Soc. Mass.* IX (1907), 441; Clarence S. Brigham, *History and Bibliography of American Newspapers, 1620–1820* (Westport, Conn.: Greenwood Press, 1975), I, 297.

4. Franklin shared with Samuel Kneeland, the Green relative who took over the printing of the *Gazette* when Musgrave stepped in as postmaster and publisher, the distinction of being both the youngest and the newest of the six master printers then in Boston. Kneeland was just four days older than Franklin (Kneeland was born Jan. 31, 1696/7 and Franklin the following Feb. 4), but Franklin had set up his shop in 1717, Kneeland in 1718 (Franklin, *Boston Printers*, 193–96, 323–29; AAS Printers' File; Stillman F. Kneeland, *Seven Centuries in the Kneeland Family* (New York: Pub. by author, 1897); Kneeland's obituary, *Massachusetts Gazette*, Dec. 18, 1769).

5. Cranfield, *Development of the Provincial Newspaper*, 58–61.

6. Anna Janney DeArmand, *Andrew Bradford, Colonial Journalist* (Newark: Univ. of Delaware Press, 1949), 7–11.

7. *DAB*, s.v. William Bradford (May 20, 1663-May 23, 1752).

8. DeArmand, *Andrew Bradford*, 44–45. Franklin, referring in his *Autobiography* to the period immediately after he and Hugh Meredith acquired Samuel Keimer's printing business, including the *Pennsylvania Gazette*, in 1729, commented that because Bradford "kept the post-office, it was imagined he had better opportunities of obtaining news; his paper was thought a better distributer of advertising than mine, and therefore had many more, which was a profitable thing to him, and a disadvantage to me" (quoted in DeArmand, p. 44).

9. *AWM*, March 8 and 17, 1720.

10. Brevier and nonpareil were the two smallest type sizes ordinarily used by American printers, the former approximately equivalent to modern 8 point type and the latter to 6 point type. Some of the London newspapers of the period used large amounts of still smaller type, called pearl (about 5 points), but few American printers could afford the variety of fonts kept by the best-stocked London houses, and pearl was one of the sizes not often found in America. See Wroth, *Colonial Printer*, 90–93, especially the table of equivalents on 92, and, for a comprehensive display of eighteenth-century type specimens, Philip Luckombe, *The History and Art of Printing* (London: W. Adlard and J. Browne for J. Johnson, 1771), 133–53.

11. No. 1 of the *Tatler* (April 12, 1709) is reproduced in Richmond P. Bond, *The Tatler: The Making of a Literary Journal* (Cambridge, Mass.: Harvard Univ. Press, 1971), following p. 98.

12. The file of extant *Gazettes* is not as complete as that of the *News-Letter*, which accounts for the tentativeness of some of these conclusions. The supplements, or "post scripts," like broadsides of the period, are notoriously fugitive and impossible to account for without surviving copies; there may have been more supplements of both papers than have actually been placed in any file. (See Matthews, "Check List," *Pub. Col. Soc. Mass.* IX (1907), 403–6.) The calculations of pages take into account only the four known two-page supplements of the *News-Letter* and the one known two-page supplement of the *Gazette*, and assume that all of the twelve missing numbers of the *Gazette* for 1720 had two pages rather than three or four. The assumption that all the missing numbers were of only two pages, however, probably errs on the side of modesty, since of the 40 extant numbers of the *Gazette* of 1720, 21 (slightly more than half) were full-sheet numbers of either three or four pages. If the twelve missing numbers included a similar proportion of full sheets, there would have been up to twelve or fourteen pages in addition to the minimum of 290 published by the *News-Letter* and *Gazette* in 1720—still assuming no supplements other than the ones we know about. "Year" in both cases means January through December.

13. Brown, *Knowledge Is Power*, 38.

14. *BNL*, Jan. 4, 1720. Campbell's offer to print two pages of the *News-Letter* on a full sheet in order to allow the sending of printed news and a handwritten letter for "single postage" would not have required a special arrangement with the postmaster, assuming the newspaper was not barred from the mails altogether. The rate of postage depended upon both distance and size of the letter: "Single, double, treble, and ounce." The smallest charge was for a "single" letter, which meant one sheet or part of a sheet of paper. Therefore, it would cost no more to mail a full sheet, so long as it weighed less than an ounce, than a half sheet. It would cost twice as much, however, to mail two half-sheets together, even though the weight was no different than if the sheet had not been cut. See Smith, *History of the Post Office*, 20, and a bill for postage from Benjamin Franklin as deputy postmaster-general to the office in Boston, May 22, 1746 (photostat in Norcross Collection, Massachusetts Historical Society).

15. *B.G.*, Jan. 11, 1719[/20]. The *B.G.*, unlike the *BNL*, retained the old year designation until March 25, in 1719/20.

16. *NEC*, Oct. 29, 1722.

17. In a note re-explaining his method of presentation in the *BNL* of April 14, 1720, Campbell gives the dates of arrival of the last ships from Britain for the winter as December 14 and 21. It is evident from the announcement that the first transatlantic ships of the spring have recently begun arriving. A March 17 "Postscript" to the *BNL* reports two arrivals from Portugal, one March 14, the other March 15. The *BNL* for March 26, 1722, noted that "for six Winter Months of the Year, from the last of September to the first of April, seldom any Vessels arrive from Great Britain, and consequently no News in that time from Europe." The December arrivals in 1719 were unusually late in the season.

18. See *L.G.*, Nov. 24, 1719; *AWM*, March 8, 1719/20; *Supplement to B.G.*, March 22, 1719[/20]; and *Postscript to BNL*, March 23, 1720. The means by which the London paper made its way to Philadelphia is not quite clear. The *Mercury* did not list any arrivals in Philadelphia either in its March 8 number or for several weeks prior to that. It did, however, on Feb. 16, 1720, report advice received "By a

Ship from England lately arrived in *Maryland*" of the arrival of the King in London "about the beginning of December," an approximate date obviously slightly inaccurate in view of his speech on November 23. This suggests an oral communication. Conceivably, a parcel of newspapers on board that ship was carried from Annapolis to Philadelphia at some time after the arrival of the message reported in mid-February.

19. DeArmond, *Andrew Bradford*, 39–40.

20. *AWM*, Feb. 16 and 23, March 1, 1719/20.

21. DeArmand, *Andrew Bradford*, 40–42, 40n., 42n. From near the end of 1733, the *Mercury*, like its rival *Pennsylvania Gazette*, even came out with an occasional six-page number.

22. *AWM*, Feb. 16 and 23, March 1, 1719/20.

23. *AWM*, Dec. 22, 1719.

24. We do, however, have such lists for the *Pennsylvania Journal*, published later in the century by the third William Bradford, who was trained and adopted by his uncle Andrew Bradford. In 1766 and 1767, copies of the *Journal* were sent as far north as Portsmouth and Albany and as far south as Charleston, as well as to several West Indian islands, London, and Bristol. Many of these obviously were exchange papers sent to fellow printers. On the other hand, the lists show impressive exploitation of readers' markets throughout the settled parts of Pennsylvania, New Jersey, Maryland, and Delaware, in Princess Ann County, Virginia, and even in Barbados and St. Kitts, especially considering the paper's marginal total circulation for its time. Of 572 subscribers (not total papers, since many subscribers took multiple copies) in 1764, 284, or just under half, lived outside—some far outside—Philadelphia. Record books in Bradford Papers, mss., Historical Society of Pennsylvania.

25. *AWM*, Dec. 29, 1719; Jan. 19, March 24 and 31, April 14, 21, and 28, May 5 and 12, 1720.

26. DeArmand, *Andrew Bradford*, 43 and n.

27. *Papers of Benjamin Franklin*, IV, 131–33.

28. There is no certain record dating Musgrave's replacement of Brooker in the postmastership. From the first number of the *Gazette*, December 19, 1719, through the thirty-third, August 1, 1720, James Franklin's name as printer appears in the colophon without the name of a publisher. At least until March 22, when Musgrave is identified as postmaster in an advertisement, the publisher was Brooker. There are no known copies of either the August 8 or the August 15 *Gazette*, but No. 36, August 22, identifies the printer as Kneeland—without the name of the publisher. The first time the name of Musgrave, or any publisher, appears in that capacity in the colophon is with No. 41, September 26. This has led some bibliographers to conclude that Musgrave's first number was that one and not an earlier one, but it is hard to see why the evidence at hand is that conclusive. Musgrave could quite easily have taken over the paper at any time during the summer without making any changes at all in the colophon, since Brooker's name was never there, and decided only in September to embellish it with his own name. For me the best guess is that Musgrave assumed his new postal duties either just prior to March 22 or during the first two weeks of August, that he took over the *Gazette* during the first half of August, that it was he and not Brooker who fired Franklin and hired Kneeland, and that he decided some five to seven weeks later to start

printing his name in the colophon. For earlier readings of the same evidence, see
Matthews, "Bibliographical Notes," *Pub. Col. Soc. Mass.* IX (1907), 440–46, and
Brigham, *Hist. and Bibl. Am. Newspapers*, I, 297–98.

29. Brigham, *Hist. and Bibl. Am. Newspapers*, I, 297.

30. *BNL*, Jan. 26, 1707. This was America's first newspaper illustration.

31. *Journals of the House of Rep. of Mass.*, IV, 10–12. This assembly was part of
the same 1722 General Court that jailed James Franklin for a sarcastic jibe at the
effectiveness of the province government in the *NEC*.

32. The most direct and defamatory attack on Musgrave as postmaster appeared
in the *NEC* of Jan. 8, 1721[/2]; there were follow-up jibes and criticisms in the *NEC*
of Jan. 15, 22, and 29.

33. The best detailed narrative of the political controversies and personalities of
pre-revolutionary Massachusetts remains Thomas Hutchinson's *History of the Colony and Province of Masschusetts-Bay*, ed. Lawrence Shaw Mayo (Cambridge,
Mass.: Harvard Univ. Press, 1936). The Shute years are covered in Vol. II, pp.
163–257. The Hutchinson account can be usefully supplemented by consulting
Journals of the House of Rep. of Mass., Vols. I–VII. The principal modern interpreta-
tions are Richard L. Bushman, *The King and the People in Provincial Massachusetts*
(Chapel Hill: Univ. of North Carolina Press, 1985), and T. H. Breen, *The Character of a Good Ruler: Puritan Political Ideas in New England, 1630–1730* (New Haven:
Yale Univ. Press, 1970), but see also Leonard W. Labaree, *Royal Government in
America: A Study of the British Colonial System before 1783* (New York: Frederick
Unger, 1958); Perry Miller, *The New England Mind: From Colony to Province* (Cambridge, Mass.: Harvard Univ. Press, 1953; Boston: Beacon Press, 1961); and Benjamin W. Labaree, *Colonial Massachusetts: A History* (Millwood, N.Y.: KTO Press,
1979).

34. Ernst, *Postal Service in Boston*, 14; *BNL*, May 20, 1725 (this is No. 1112;
either the date on the paper or the day of the week, given as the normal publication
day of Monday, is in error, since May 20 was a Thursday). There is no known
extant copy of the *B.G.* for May 24.

35. This grave change can be seen at once by comparing two documents in
Campbell's handwriting, photostats of which are in the Massachusetts Historical
Society. The first, dated in March 1720/1, is a receipt for payment for the *News-
Letter* by John Winthrop; the second is Campbell's certificate as justice of the
peace, dated Dec. 3, 1723, on a legal release. MHS, Photostats 1710–29.

36. The point at which Lewis dropped the official legend may have been when
he ended his postmastership. He is never identified as postmaster in the colophon
of the *Gazette* during the period July 19, 1725, to April 18, 1726, when his name
appears as sole publisher (there is a gap in the extant file between Musgrave's death
in May and July 19), but his obituary of January 1727 refers to him as "sometime
Post-Master and Publisher of the Boston Gazette." From April 25, 1726, to the
time of Lewis's death, the paper was published jointly by Lewis and Henry
Marshall, the postmaster. The record is sparse, but it appears that Lewis, formerly
a young customs officer, was named to the postmastership upon Musgrave's death,
but retained it only until a successor could be found in the person of Marshall.
Lewis evidently took upon himself the publication of the *Gazette*, and perhaps
continued it for a while even after he had been succeeded by Marshall. By April 5,
1726 (the date Marshall's name began to appear with Lewis's in the colophon),

Marshall had taken on the *Gazette*, but with Lewis's help. Marshall continued publishing the *Gazette* on his own after Lewis's sudden death at the beginning of 1727, getting around only on September 2, 1727, to restore "Published by Authority," a reflection of the postal connection, to the nameplate. None of the Boston newspapers carrying Lewis's obituary is extant, but it was copied, under a Boston dateline of January 16, in the *American Weekly Mercury*, Feb. 7, 1727. He was one of two young Bostonians whose unexpected deaths in January 1727 occasioned Thomas Prince's sermon *Morning Health No Security Against the Sudden Arrest of Death Before Night* and Mather Byles's poem *The Bloom of Life, Fading in a Happy Death*, which was appended to the second edition of that sermon (Boston: Printed for Daniel Henchman, 1727).

Chapter 6. The Couranteers, 1721–1726

1. For separate analyses of the contention between parties in provincial Massachusetts, see Breen, *The Character of a Good Ruler*, and Bushman, *The King and People in Provincial Massachusetts*.

2. The story has often been told and can be found with varying emphases in many places, including Benjamin Franklin's *Autobiography*, Leonard W. Labaree et al., eds. (New Haven: Yale Univ. Press, 1964), 66–70; Thomas's *History of Printing*, 234–42; Harold Lester Dean, "The *New-England Courant*, 1721–1726: A Chapter in the History of American Culture" (Ph.D. diss., Brown University, 1943), esp. chap. 3; John B. Blake, "The Inoculation Controversy in Boston, 1721–1722," *NEQ* XXV (1952), 489–506; Miller, *The New England Mind: From Colony to Province*, esp. chap. XXI (pp. 354–66; Genevieve Miller, "Smallpox Inoculation in England and America: A Reappraisal," *WMQ*, 3d Ser., XIII (1956), 476–92; Clyde Augustus Duniway, *The Development of Freedom of the Press in Massachusetts* (Cambridge, Mass.: Harvard Univ. Press, 1906); Otho T. Beall and Richard H. Shryock, *Cotton Mather: First Significant Figure in American Medicine* (Baltimore: Johns Hopkins Univ. Press, 1954); Kenneth Silverman, *The Life and Times of Cotton Mather* (New York: Harper & Row, 1984), esp. chap. XII (pp. 336–63); and Maxine de Wetering, "A Reconsideration of the Inoculation Controversy," *NEQ* LVIII (1985), 46–67.

3. The *Courant* has recently been made the subject of a significant study with yet a different emphasis, namely its role in expressing the political and social aspirations of its publishers' generation, in part through the introduction and application to Massachusetts culture of Real Whig rhetoric and ideology. See Preston Shea, "The Rhetoric of Authority in the *New-England Courant*" (Ph.D. diss., University of New Hampshire, 1992). Michael Warner discusses the *Courant*, with special attention to Benjamin Franklin's Dogood papers, as an expression of the Country ideal of civic virtue. *Letters of the Republic*, 66–67, 82–87.

4. Miller, *From Colony to Province*, 346. The author of the "Philanthropos" letter in the *BNL* of July 24, 1721, surely Dr. William Douglass, lays out the sequence of events with a thinly veiled, not altogether unkind reference to Cotton Mather.

5. Cotton Mather, *An Account of the Method and Success of Inoculating the Small-Pox, in Boston, in New-England* (London, 1722), 14; Zabdiel Boylston, *An Historical Account of the Small-Pox Inoculated in New England . . .* (Boston, 1730), 51–53.

6. *B.G.*, July 31, 1721.

7. Hutchinson, *History of Mass. Bay*, II, 155.

8. Breen, *Character of a Good Ruler*, 220–22. Quotation is on p. 221.

9. Hutchinson, *History of Mass. Bay*, II, 100–121. See also Cotton Mather's *Memorial of the Present Deplorable State of New-England . . . by the Male-Administration of Their Present Governour* (Boston, 1707).

10. Harold Lester Dean has offered as one explanation for the political orientation of most of the clergy in this period the fear that the province charter and the freedom of Massachusetts churches were being jeopardized by the constant flouting of the prerogative by "irresponsible elements in the House." The clergy opposed the Country party, according to this argument, out of fear that Cooke and his followers would eventually provoke Parliamentary retaliation. "*The New-England Courant*, 1721–1726," 67.

11. Hutchinson, *History of Mass. Bay*, II, 224–25; *Journals of the House of Representatives of Mass.*, VI, 257–58, 289, 303–4.

12. Breen, *Character of a Good Ruler*, 261.

13. Identification of the various contributors rests on the discovery in 1922 of Benjamin Franklin's annotated file of the first 111 numbers of the *Courant* in the British Museum. Franklin had marked the articles in the first 43 numbers, through May 28, 1723, with the names of their authors. The discovery is reported and explicated in a paper by Worthington Chauncey Ford entitled "Franklin's New England Courant," in MHS *Proceedings* LVII (1934), 336–53. The most extensive work on the identity of the writers is in Dean, "*The New-England Courant*, 1721–1726." See esp. 83–84, 92n., 106n., 132–34. On Checkley, see Edmund F. Slafter, *John Checkley; or the Evolution of Religious Tolerance in Massachusets Bay*, 2 vols. (Boston: Prince Society, 1897), esp. I, 1–39, 281–92. On Thomas Fleet, see Thomas, *History of Printing*, 93–99; Franklin, ed., *Boston Printers*, 162–67.

14. Thomas says publication ceased "in the beginning of the year 1727" (*History of Printing*, 242), and a letter to Bartholomew Green, who had taken over the *BNL* from Campbell, refers in the March 9, 1727, number of the *News-Letter* to "the late *Courant*." See also Brigham, *History and Bibliography of American Newspapers*, I, 322–23.

15. Thomas, *History of Printing*, 232, 234.

16. *The Spectator. With Sketches of the Lives of the Authors, and Explanatory Notes*, 8 vols. (Edinburgh, 1802), I, 1.

17. Ibid., 3. See also Bond, *The Tatler*, 1, 11; and Mark Lipper, "Benjamin Franklin's 'Silence Dogood' as an Eighteenth-Century 'Censor Morum,'" in Bond and McLeod, eds., *Newsletters to Newspapers*, 73.

18. A copy of the *Little-Compton Scourge* is included in the MHS file of the *NEC* for 1721, a photostat copy of which, complete with the *Scourge* in its proper sequence, is held by the American Antiquarian Society. This interpretation of Walter's role in this episode follows that of Perry Miller in *From Colony to Province*, 334–35. For more on Walter's early association with Checkley, see Slafter, *John Checkley*, 3.

19. *NEC*, Aug. 21, 1721.

20. *NEC*, Sept. 4, 1721. See also discussion in Ford, "Franklin's New-England Courant," 344–45.

21. The first of the Dogood letters began near the bottom of the right-hand column of page one in the *Courant* of April 2, 1722; nearly all the other thirteen,

from the second on April 16, 1722, to the last (No. 14) on Dec. 3, 1722, ran in the first column of page one. Kenneth Silverman suggests that Silence Dogood's name derived from Cotton Mather's Boston lecture for September 28, 1721, published shortly thereafter. If the lecture, given in memory of Mather's daughter and her infant during the epidemic, was in fact Franklin's inspiration for Mrs. Dogood, comments Silverman, "it was a bad, indeed a sick, joke." *Selected Letters of Cotton Mather*, ed. Silverman (Baton Rouge: Louisiana State Univ. Press), 339n.

22. Mrs. Dogood introduces herself in Nos. 1 and 2 (April 2 and 16, 1722) very much as Mr. Spectator did in his own No. 1, but in greater detail, and the "club" that surrounded Dr. Janus is modeled after that described by Richard Steele in *Spectator*, No. 2. (See *Spectator*, I, 3–10.) For *The Spectator*'s influence on Franklin, see his *Autobiography*, 61–62; Lipper, "Benjamin Franklin's 'Silence Dogood'"; Robert V. Hudson, "Non-Indigenous Influences on Benjamin Franklin's Journalism," in Bond and McLeod, *Newsletters to Newspapers*, 73–83; James A. Sappenfield, *A Sweet Instruction: Franklin's Journalism as a Literary Apprenticeship* (Carbondale: Southern Illinois Univ. Press, 1973); and one of the earliest and most specific discussions of the topic, Elizabeth C. Cooks's *Literary Influences in Colonial Newspapers, 1704–1750* (New York: Columbia Univ. Press, 1912), 8–30. George F. Horner, in "Franklin's *Dogood Papers* Re-examined," *Studies in Philology* XXXVII (1940), 501–23, treats the same subject but stresses the local setting of the essays and warns against regarding them as a "slavish imitation" of *The Spectator*. Michael Warner discusses the influence of *Spectator* with emphasis upon ideology in *Letters of the Republic*, 81–87.

23. *NEC*, Dec. 11, 1721.

24. *NEC*, April 9, 1722.

25. *NEC*, Jan. 15, 1722.

26. *NEC*, April 9, 1722.

27. Franklin, *Autobiography*, 68–70, 70n.

28. For references to *The English Lucien*, see Chapter 2 above. The March 3, 1701, number of *The Jesting Astrologer: Or, the Merry Observator* contains some "astrologer's predictions" very much in the style and spirit of a long line of astrological spoofs going back at least to Rabelais and culminating in *Poor Richard*: "The beards of Coffee-house Politicians, will Wag mightily, during this Session of P————————————; and every flying Gull, and foolish Imposition, inserted in the News Papers, will go down as glib, with the Sipers of Ninny-broth [coffee], as a *White-Fryers* Falsity, Publish'd by sham Authority, does oftentimes with the too credulous Multitude. . . . The Plague of Poverty in a little time will creep into many a Cuckold's Family, where the Wife wears the Breeches . . . : Therefore the best Preservative against this Distemper is, for him to keep the staff in his own Hand . . . : and let every Shopkeeper remember this, whoever has his Wife by the Heart, if it be in her Power, may, if he pleases, have the Money-box by the Handle."

29. *NEC*, Jan. 29, March 5 and 12, 1722.

30. Slafter, *John Checkley*, I, 105–6.

31. No discussion of the *Courant* is now complete without a more thorough consideration than has been possible here of its writers' dramatic and precocious attempt to work social and cultural change in early eighteenth-century Boston. See again Shea, "The Rhetoric of Authority."

Chapter 7. The Literary Newspaper, 1727–1735

1. Thomas, *History of Printing*, 203–4; Franklin, ed., *Boston Printers*, 162–66; *B.G.*, May 8 and 15, 1732; *W.R.*, May 1 and 15, 1732.

2. *B.G.*, June 5 and 19, 1732.

3. A Boston edition of Stephen Duck's *Poems on Several Subjects* was printed for Fry in 1732, just as he advertised, but none of the standard bibliographies lists an American edition of *The Spectator*. For Cox, see advertisements in *B.G.*, Oct. 7, 1732; Franklin, ed., *Boston Printers*, 83; Thomas, *History of Printing*, 204; and Cox's *Catalogue of Books, in all Arts and Sciences* . . . (Boston, [1734]).

4. Lawrence Klein, "The Third Earl of Shaftesbury and the Progress of Politeness," *Eighteenth-Century Studies* 18 (1984–85), 201–2.

5. Samuel Eliot Morison, *Three Centuries of Harvard, 1636–1936* (Cambridge, Mass.: Harvard Univ. Press, 1936), 60, 62.

6. David H. Watters, *"With Bodilie Eyes": Eschatalogical Themes in Puritan Literature and Gravestone Art* (Ann Arbor: UMI Research Press, 1981), 72–73.

7. *B.G.*, Jan. 5, 1730; reprinted under the title "To PICTORIO, on the Sight of His Pictures" in Mather Byles, *Poems on Several Occasions* (Boston: Printed by Kneeland & Green, 1744), 89–93.

8. See, e.g., *M.G.*, Dec. 10, 17, 24, and 31, 1728; Jan. 7, 1729. The most celebrated vehicle by which the gentry of Annapolis participated in Augustan culture was the Tuesday Club, founded in explicit imitation of metropolitan British models by Dr. Alexander Hamilton in 1745. Shortly after Hamilton arrived from his native Edinburgh in 1738, he joined an existing society called the Ugly Club, named after the original in the *Spectator*. Hamilton, a physician and Scottish émigré like William Douglass, contributed to the anglicization of Annapolis in a role analogous to that of Douglass in Boston. See Hamilton, *The History of the Ancient and Honorable Tuesday Club*, ed. Robert M. Micklus, 3 vols. (Chapel Hill: Univ. of North Carolina Press, 1990). On Hamilton's arrival in Annapolis and the beginnings of his club life there, see I, xv–xvii.

9. *SCG*, Jan. 8, 1732. Whitmarsh's poetic opening statement portrays in fairly well-polished (which is to say "polite") verse the moderation, loyalty, and rational piety of the idealized British Christian gentleman of the era that we may take to be the "voice" to which not only he but nearly all colonial publishers aspired for their newspapers. It was later appropriated by Benjamin Franklin:

> I'm not High-Church, nor Low-Church, nor Tory, nor Whig,
> Nor flatt'ring young coxcomb, nor formal old Prig.
> Not eternally talking, nor silently quaint,
> Nor profligate Sinner, nor pragmatical Saint,
> I'm not vain of my Judgment, nor pinn'd on a Sleeve,
> Nor implicitly any Thing can I believe.
> To sift Truth from all Rubbish, I do what I can,
> And, God knows, if I err—I'm a fallible Man.
>
>   . . .
>
> Where Merit appears, tho' in Rags, I respect it,
> And plead Virtue's Course, shou'd the whole World reject it.
> Cool Reason I bow to, wherever 'tis found,
> And rejoice when sound Learning with Favour is crown'd.

To no Party a Slave, in no Squabble I join,
Nor damn the opinion, that differs from mine.
Evil Tongues I contemn, no mob Treasons I sing;
I dote on my Country, and am Liege to my King.
Tho' length of Days I desire, yet with my last Breath,
I'm in hopes to betray no mean Dreadings of Death.
And as to the Path, after Death to be trod,
I rely on the Will of a MERCIFUL GOD.

10. Thomas, *History of Printing*, 232–34, 242.

11. Ibid., 323–29.

12. Thomas, *History of Printing*, 244–45. The partnership of Kneeland & Green became the leading printing firm in Boston during the second quarter of the eighteenth century. (Franklin, ed., *Boston Printers*, 239–40, 245–46.) For a provocative treatment of the significance of family associations in the early American printing trade, see Wetherell, "Brokers of the Word," esp. chap. 5, and for a particular discussion of the printing families of New England, chap. 3.

13. There had been much printed byplay for a few months in 1721 and 1722 over the *News-Letter*'s and *Gazette*'s application of the name "Hell-Fire Club," taken from a notorious deliberately blasphemous society in London, to the Couranteers. See, e.g., *News-Letter*, Aug. 28, 1721; *Gazette*, Jan. 15, 1721[/2]; and *Courant*, Jan. 22 and Feb. 5, 1722. Only in Boston could true and overt blasphemy against Christian doctrines, such as was fearlessly practiced by the English original, be equated with opposition to the Mathers.

14. Arthur W. H. Eaton, *The Famous Mather Byles, the Noted Boston Tory Preacher, Poet, and Wit, 1707–1788* (Boston: W. A. Butterfield, 1914), 15–23, 101–6, 232–33; *Sibley's Harvard Graduates*, VII, 464–65.

15. Thomas, *History of Printing*, 245; Cook, *Literary Influences*, 36; Sidney Kobre, *The Development of the Colonial Newspaper* (Gloucester, Mass.: Peter Smith, 1960 (rpt. of 1944 ed.)), 46; Franklin, ed., *Boston Printers*, 328.

16. *Sibley's Harvard Graduates*, VI, 80–86. In a subsequent smallpox epidemic in 1730, Danforth performed several inoculations himself, to the distress of his fellow Cambridge townsmen. (Ibid., VI, 82.) In 1729, Byles was an unsuccessful candidate for appointment as colleague pastor to Danforth's father, John Danforth, in the Dorchester church. (Eaton, *The Famous Mather Byles*, 37.)

17. Thomas, *History of Printing*, 245. "Correcting the press" was the eighteenth-century term for what we now call proofreading. When the compositor had finished setting his pages and locked them up in the form, the form was carried to the press, where the pressman ran off a proof copy. The "corrector"—normally either a person hired for the job or the master printer himself—read the proof, comparing it with the copy and ascertaining that all the typographical conventions of the day were adhered to, and made corrections in the margins of the proof. The form, meanwhile, was carried from the press back to the compositor's imposing stone, where the compositor followed the corrector's directions by changing the metal type as necessary. It was then carried back to the press for another proof, which was read again by the corrector for final approval or further corrections before the run began. (John Smith, ed., *The Printer's Grammar* (London: Printed for the editor and sold by W. Owen and M. Cooper, 1755), 122–23; Philip Luckombe, *The History and Art of Printing* (London: Printed by W. Adlard and J.

Browne for J. Johnson, 1771), 440–45.) No doubt the formal division of labor described by these two writers for the large, guild-regulated printing houses of London was less scrupulously followed in the smaller shops of America. In *The Corrector of the Press in the Early Days of Printing* (Greenwich, Conn.: Conde Nast Press, 1922), Douglas C. McMurtrie quotes a Latin text published in Leipzig in 1608 as follows: "He who purposes to become a corrector of the press should have a full knowledge of the languages in which are to be printed the works which he is to read. He should also have considerable facility in deciphering the handwriting of the learned, which is often extremely bad" (p. 6).

18. *Sibley's Harvard Graduates*, V, 341–68; on Prince's return from London, p. 346.

19. Miller, *From Colony to Province*, 451–52. Prince's difficulty later in the century in adapting Enlightenment science to his rather inflexible theology is discussed by John E. Van Wetering in "God, Science, and the Puritan Dilemma," *NEQ* XXXVIII (1965), 494–507.

20. *NEWJ*, March 20, 1727. This issue was unnumbered. The *NEWJ* of March 27 was No. I.

21. Ibid.

22. *NEWJ*, Aug. 28, 1727.

23. Identification of the likely authorship of the various essays in the "Proteus Echo" series, of which this was one, becomes possible through the literary sleuthing of C. Lennart Carlson, who published a note on the subject entitled "John Adams, Matthew Adams, Mather Byles, and the *New England Weekly Journal*" in *American Literature* 12 (1940–41), 347–48. This essay was signed "X," one of the letters apparently used as a signature by John Adams. For Adams's life, see *Sibley's Harvard Graduates*, VI, 425.

24. *Sibley's Harvard Graduates*, VII, 466.

25. Klein, "The Third Earl of Shaftesbury and the Progress of Politeness," 211–14. See also Warner, *The Letters of the Republic*, 132–38.

26. Watts to Byles, Nov. 27, 1728, and Feb. 27, 1728/9, microfilm transcript of Byles Family Papers 1728–1835 (copies of mss. in Provincial Library, Halifax, N.S.), Massachusetts Historical Society. The collection contains five more letters from Watts to Byles, most of them written after Byles's ordination in December 1733. All bear down on the same theme. In his letter of Jan. 31, 1732, Watts responds to Byles's scheme to illustrate scripture with parallels "from Heathen authors": It "must be agreeable to polite readers especially . . . . But while you are engaged in this Work pray Sir, watch lest the Pagan Elegancies attract your Soul with stronger force than the sacred Institutions of Moses or Christ. . . . May Christ form you more and more to a love and relish of experimental Godliness above all polite Temptations." On April 2, 1737, he wrote: "As fast as your Elegance in Poesy increases will you permit me to wish your increase in Experimental Godliness, in the holy skill of winning souls to God & in your Zeal for the honor of our blessed Savr. & the Enlargement of his Kingdom." And on April 20, 1742: "May the God of all Grace employ our Hearts and our Pens and our Tongues in that which may tend to the honor of our Dear Redeemer & the Salvation of the Souls of Men." See also letters of May 1, 1735, and Feb. 28, 1735/6.

27. Although it was the fourth *Weekly Journal*, it was numbered III, since the first had been unnumbered.

28. See *Spectator*, No. 2 (I, 5–10).

29. See, e.g., *NEWJ*, June 12, July 10 and 17, and Oct. 16, 1727. I am indebted to Kathy Bellerose for making this observation among others in a seminar paper on Proteus Echo written in 1986 at the University of New Hampshire. Elizabeth Cook discusses Proteus Echo in *Literary Influences*, 48.

30. *NEWJ*, July 10 and Oct. 16, 1727; *Spectator*, No. 17 (I, 63–66); Cook, *Literary Influences*, 48.

31. *NEWJ*, June 12, 1727.

32. *NEC*, June 25, 1722.

33. *NEWJ*, July 31, 1727. For more on the deaths in the well, see *NEWJ*, July 24, Aug. 27 and 14, 1727, and *NYG*, Aug. 7, 14, and 21, 1727. Identification of Byles as author of this Proteus Echo essay rests on the letter C with which it is signed. See again Carlson, "John Adams, Matthew Adams, Mather Byles, and the *New England Weekly Journal*," 347. Addison's *Spectator*, No. 26 (March 30, 1711), consisted of reflections on the tombs in Westminster Abbey, where the author says he "very often walk[s] by myself" (*Spectator*, I, 94–97). Byles may have drawn his general inspiration from this or a similar essay, but there is no reference here to the specific statue discussed by Proteus Echo.

34. *NEWJ*, Aug. 14, 1727.

35. *NEWJ*, Sept. 4, 1727, and Feb. 12, 1728; Carlson, "John Adams, Matthew Adams, Mather Byles, and the *New England Weekly Journal*," 348.

36. *WNL*, Nov. 3, 1727; *B.G.*, Nov. 6, 1727. The *News-Letter*'s regular publication day had been switched from Monday to Thursday in 1723, but this and the following week it was published on Friday instead.

37. *NEWJ*, Oct. 30, 1727.

38. Charles E. Clark, "Science, Reason, and an Angry God: The Literature of an Earthquake," *NEQ* XXXVIII (1965), 345, and "The Literature of the New England Earthquake of 1755," *Papers of the Bibl. Soc. of America* LIX (1965), 297–98.

39. *NEWJ*, Nov. 6, 1727. The pamphlet, which appeared under the name of Cotton Mather, was entitled *The Terror of the Lord. Some Account of the Earthquake That Shook New-England, in the Night, Between the 29 and 30 of October. 1727. With a Speech, Made Unto the Inhabitants of Boston, Who Assembled the Next Morning, for the Proper Exercises of Religion, on So Uncommon, and So Tremendous an Occasion.* (Boston: Printed by T. Fleet for S. Kneeland, 1727).

40. *Sibley's Harvard Graduates*, VI, 425–26.

41. Curiously and perhaps not wholly by coincidence, a weekly periodical somewhat along the lines of the *Weekly Journal* and containing both "Echo" and "Weekly Journal" in its title appeared between 1729 and 1734 in Edinburgh. *The Echo, or Edinburgh Weekly Journal*, which made its debut January 10, 1729 (22 months after the birth of the *New-England Weekly Journal*), combined a section of *Spectator*-like essays and letters with a section of news, primarily foreign news. According to W. J. Couper, ". . . the two parts of the paper were under different management. The literary portion was ostensibly conducted as the transactions of a club, letters by whom and to whom formed the chief contents. There was a sprightliness and dash *at first* [my emphasis] in much that appeared in this section." If, as seems more than possible, this Edinburgh namesake of Boston's *Weekly Journal* and "Proteus Echo" was inspired by its American equivalent, this may be the first instance—and a very early one at that—of an eastward flow of journalistic influences amidst the preponderance of influence in the other direction. Couper's

qualification "at first," combined with the relatively short life of the Edinburgh paper, suggests that original literary journalism may have been as difficult to sustain in Scotland as in New England. (W. J. Couper, *The Edinburgh Periodical Press* (2 vols., Stirling, Scotland: Eneas Mackay, 1908), II, 62–65; quotation on 64.)

42. *NEWJ*, April 8, 1728.

43. See publisher's advertisement, *NEWJ*, June 24, 1728. The standard bibliographies contain no indication that the volume was ever published.

44. *Sibley's Harvard Graduates*, VII, 471.

45. Ibid., 472; Eaton, *The Famous Mather Byles*, 40–41.

46. The theory that this series was by more than one author arises from the numbering of the essays. Each is numbered at the top, but the numbers are not always in sequence; each of the writers apparently used his own numbering sequence. Isaiah Thomas suggested that many of these essays may have been by Governor William Burnett, whose death on Sept. 7, 1729, occurred shortly after the series stopped. (*History of Printing*, 243.)

47. Byles's bound file of the *NEWJ*, now in the American Antiquarian Society, begins with the unnumbered issue of March 20, 1727, and includes Nos. I (March 27, 1727) through LIV (April 1, 1728). The papers in the file are annotated, primarily with corrections. Franklin P. Cole has suggested that these are corrections for later printings of Byles's works. (*Mather Books and Portraits through Six Early American Generations, 1630–1831* (Portland, Me.: Casco, 1978), 184.)

48. The essay last mentioned is in *NEWJ*, Nov. 16, 1733. The others are in *NEWJ*, Dec. 25, 1732 (which contains no mention of Christmas), and Jan. 29, May 21, July 16, 23, and 30, 1733.

49. *NEWJ*, March 26, Aug. 6, and Jan. 8, 1733.

50. *NEWJ*, June 11, Aug. 13, Oct. 1, 8, 15, and 22, 1733. For a reconstruction and interpretation of this case, see Charles E. Clark, "A Test of Religious Liberty: The Ministry Land Case in Narragansett," *Journal of Church and State* XI (1969), 295–319.

51. *NEWJ*, July 24, Oct. 16 and 23, Nov. 6, 13, and 20, Dec. 4 and 11, 1739; Jan. 8, March 18, April 22 and 29, Sept. 2 and 9, and Nov. 18, 1740.

52. *Sibley's Harvard Graduates*, VII, 477–78.

53. *NEWJ*, Dec. 16, 1740. Quotation is from Mal. 2:2.

54. It is clear from the printers' announcement of Boydell's death that Hannah Boydell was not expected to take an active role in the *Gazette*'s publication. It said the *Gazette* would be "carried on as usual, for the Benefit of the Family of the late Publisher . . . ." However, there was some separation in the operation of the two papers. Kneeland and Green, it appears from the *Gazette*'s colophon after Boydell's death, were at least spared the necessity of selling *Gazette* advertising and subscriptions in their own office and in competition with their own newspaper. Subscribers and advertisers were directed to "the Office of the late Mr. *Boydell*, in King street." Some former employees of Boydell's must have carried on in that and perhaps other capacities in the widow's interest. (*B.G.*, Dec. 17, 1739 *et seq.*)

55. The last number of *NEWJ* appeared on Tuesday, Oct. 13, 1741. The first number of the combined paper, the *Boston Gazette, or New England Weekly Journal*, which contained the notice of Hannah Boydell's death, was dated Tuesday, Oct. 20, 1741, and numbered 942—evidently a misprint, since 1042 would have been the correct number for the next issue of the *Gazette*. The next number, mistakenly numbered 943, that of Oct. 27, appeared under the revised title, the *Boston Gazette;*

or, Weekly Journal. The words "New-England" appear above the title, as they had appeared above the title of the *Gazette.*

56. *Sibley's Harvard Graduates,* VII, 518–30; R. G. F. Candage, *Jeremy Gridley,* Publications of the Brookline Historical Soc. No. 1 (Brookline, Mass., 1903). Gridley submitted to the Boston town meeting of May 5, 1731, four months before he started the *Rehearsal,* a request for an increase in his £80 salary at the Grammar School, which he said was "very insufficient for the necessary Charges of life" and less than a private shopkeeper usually paid his bookkeeper. He asked the town to consider paying him enough that it will "not only defray his necessary Expences, but admit of some decent Figure in life" (Photostat ms., MHS). The town's response is not recorded.

57. Franklin, ed., *Boston Printers,* 100–101.

58. Thomas, *History of Printing,* 123, 246 and n.

59. *W.R.,* Sept. 17, 1731. Until Aug. 21, 1732, the individual issues of the *Rehearsal* were unnumbered.

60. *W.R.,* Nov. 29, Dec. 6, 13, 20, and 27, 1731; March 6, 1732.

61. *W.R.,* Nov. 1 and 22, 1731.

62. Franklin, however, was eventually convicted, fined, and sent to prison for a year. (Siebert, *Freedom of the Press in England,* 382.)

63. *W.R.,* Nov. 8, 1731.

64. Candage, *Jeremy Gridley,* 15; *Sibley's Harvard Graduates,* VII, 520.

65. Frank Luther Mott, *A History of American Magazines, 1741–1850* (New York: D. Appleton, 1930), 78–79. Two magazines had preceded this one, both in Philadelphia, Andrew Bradford's *American Magazine* and Benjamin Franklin's *General Magazine.* Neither lasted more than a few months in 1740 (pp. 71–77).

66. *W.R.,* Jan. 31, 1732.

67. *W.R.,* Feb. 14, 1732.

68. *W.R.,* Feb. 18, March 4, 18, and 25, and April 1, 1734.

69. *W.R.,* Aug. 19, 1734.

70. Cranfield, *Development of the Provincial Newspaper,* 99–103.

Chapter 8. Three Cities, 1728–1740

1. For biographical data, see obituaries in *B.G.,* Dec. 17, 1739, and *BWNL,* Dec. 13, 1739. Boydell's Boston affairs and his quest for patronage are disclosed in revealing detail in his letters to John Yeamans spanning the period June 15, 1727, to Aug. 12, 1734, mss., David Greenough Collection, Box 1, Massachusetts Historical Society.

2. Boydell to Yeamans, Aug. 12, 1734, Greenough Collection, Box. 1; Matthews, "Bibliographical Notes," *Pub. Col. Soc. Mass.* IX (1907), 466.

3. Boydell to Yeamans, Aug. 12, 1734, Greenough Collection, Box 1.

4. See, e.g., *B.G.,* Nov. 29, Dec. 27, 1731; March 27, 1732.

5. *B.G.,* Jan. 1, July 30, Dec. 4, 1733; Feb. 25, March 25, April 1, June 24, Aug. 19, 1734.

6. A "typical" pre-Boydell *B.G.* is assumed here to be a half-sheet or two-page number, which the majority were, whereas all of Boydell's papers contained at least four pages, and on rare occasions six. The calculation of available space is as follows: For the *B.G.* before Boydell: the length of the body of type on each page was twelve inches; since there were four columns in a "typical" paper (two on each

page), there were 48 column inches of type. From that must be subtracted five column inches for the nameplate, since it was two and a half inches deep, and two column inches for the colophon. For Boydell's *B.G.*: the length of the body of type was nine inches, which multiplied by the eight columns in a "typical" paper comes to 72 inches, less four inches for the two-inch nameplate and two inches for the colophon. Even before Boydell, however, there were occasional four-page numbers every year, in some years not far from half of the total. Each of those numbers contained 89 column inches of available space.

7. Population estimates are based on Evarts B. Greene and Virginia D. Harrington, *American Population before the Federal Census of 1790* (New York: Columbia Univ. Press, 1932; Gloucester, Mass.: Peter Smith, 1966). A footnote on p. 22 quotes a non-contemporary report giving the whole population of Boston in 1700 at 6700. Adult males ("polls") were commonly calculated at about one-fourth the whole population (p. xxiii), but from that result must be deducted the adult male portion of Boston's slaves and free (but suppressed) blacks, of whom there were about 400 of all ages and both sexes in 1708. (Bridenbaugh, *Cities in the Wilderness,* 249.) Population figures for these years must be considered tentative at best, since even contemporary estimates vary wildly. Greene and Harrington cite another source, for example, reporting 3000 "men" in Boston in 1701. If their recommended calculation for "polls" is applied to this number, it would result in a whole population of 12,000, and if "men" meant those eligible for militia duty, the usually accepted ratio of 5 to 1 would yield a population of 15,000, more than double the figure I have used.

8. Greene and Harrington, *American Population*, 22n. The same source that estimated 6700 in 1700 gives the whole population in 1730 and 1735 as 13,000 and 16,000 respectively.

9. See Wroth, *Typographical Heritage*, 38–39, on the importance of Franklin's London experience.

10. Franklin, *Autobiography*, 78–79.

11. Ibid., 80–81, 86–87, 92–95, 106.

12. See Chapter 5 above. Here is part of Bradford's comment: "In these Western Parts, . . . it is the Desire of our Legislators . . . [that] all possible Care is taken to cultivate and encourage Morality and Industry, that our Sovereign King *George* may find a plentiful Territory and ample Strength and Happiness from our Colonies . . . . But by these Ways of transporting villains amongst such a flourishing People, is to less[en] our Improvements and Industry, by filling the Vacancies of honest Men with tricking, thieving and designing rogues, who will hardly be brought to get their Livelihood by such labourious and settled Means; the ill Consequences of which would without doubt be remedied in Great Britain, were they as sensible of 'em as we who are made so by living amongst them." *AWM,* Feb. 14, 1721.

13. *Advertisement* (broadside, Philadelphia: Samuel Keimer, 1728).

14. Clark and Wetherell, "The Measure of Maturity," 284.

15. Franklin, *Autobiography*, 108–13, 115–16, 119–20.

16. Ibid., 120.

17. Ibid. Actually, Franklin's recollection of the details of this episode seems to be flawed. He reports in the *Autobiography* that his contributions to the *Mercury* were in response to Keimer's *proposals* for a new paper, not to the newspaper itself. Yet although Keimer's prospectus was dated October 1, 1728, the *Mercury* took no

notice of its rival until January 28, 1729, more than a month after the *Gazette*'s actual appearance on December 12.

18. *P.G.*, Jan. 21, 1728[/9]. Keimer, either in obedience to his own strange and not always consistent combination of religious scruples or in deference to Philadelphia's Quaker readership, dated it "21st of the 11th month."

19. This is the position, phrased somewhat more carefully, of the editors of *The Papers of Benjamin Franklin*. See Vol. I (New Haven: Yale Univ. Press, 1959), 111–12.

20. *AWM*, Feb. 4, 1729.

21. *Papers of Benjamin Franklin*, I, 114.

22. Not directly, that is. Keimer apparently recognized himself as Cretico, the "sowre Philosopher" who was one of the cast of fictional characters in Busy-Body No. 3 (*AWM*, Feb. 18, 1729), and wrote a gentle reproof in *P.G.*, Feb. 25, 1729. Busy-Body responded in No. 5 (*AWM*, March 4, 1729). These, however, were very rare and discreet jabs, not at all like the broad jests at the competition that the *New-England Courant* featured prominently and fearlessly in its early days.

23. *Papers of Benjamin Franklin*, I, 114n.

24. Keimer's concern over the new success that Busy-Body was bringing to the *Mercury* is evident in his various attacks on the writers that appeared from time to time in the *Universal Instructor*. It is quite clear that he was aware that Franklin was one of the writers. *Papers of Benjamin Franklin*, I, 133–34n., 139n.

25. Franklin, *Autobiography*, 120.

26. Ibid., 122–23, 123n.

27. *Papers of Benjamin Franklin*, II, 380–83.

28. Ibid. When Meredith's father could not come up with part of the money he had promised, Franklin accepted the backing of two of his friends who were anxious to keep him in business on the condition that he part company with Meredith. The parting, nevertheless, was amiable.

29. Clark and Wetherell, "Measure of Maturity," 281–82, 291.

30. Ibid., Table I, p. 286; Table II, p. 288.

31. For the *Gazette*'s advertising, see ibid., 285–89. Those figures are more precise and can be accepted with somewhat greater confidence than those I have provided for the *Mercury*, which are based on a less systematic perusal of scattered numbers over the years 1735–40 than was conducted for the *Gazette* for those five years. However, with only rare exceptions, the random numbers of the *Mercury* I have copied (for various reasons) over that five-year period show little variation from roughly two and a half to slightly less than three columns of advertising in a four-page—or eight-column—number. That figures out to 31 to 37 percent of total space.

32. *P.G.*, July 10 and 24, Sept. 12, 1732. These are all printed in *Papers of Benjamin Franklin*, I, 237–48, with the notation that Franklin's ms. drafts of these and other letters are located in the Historical Society of Pennsylvania.

33. *AWM*, Oct. 18, 1733. How Franklin may have responded to this admonition is unknown, but this is not far from the time that he was devising his famous (and audacious) scheme to achieve "moral Perfection." He originally included only twelve "virtues" in his list, "But a Quaker Friend having kindly inform'd me that I was generally thought proud; . . . that I was not content with being in the right when discussing my Point, but was overbearing and rather insolent; of which he convinc'd me by mentioning several Instances; I determined endeavouring to cure

myself if I could of this Vice or Folly among the rest, and I added *Humility* to my
List. . . . I cannot boast of much Success in acquiring the *Reality* of this Virtue;
but I had a good deal with regard to the *Appearance* of it" (*Autobiography*, 158–59).
He also asserts in his *Autobiography* (p. 165), referring generally to this period of his
life, that "In the conduct of my Newspaper I carefully excluded all Libelling and
Personal Abuse."

34. *AWM*, Dec. 18, 1735; Jan. 6, 1736. *P.G.*, Dec. 24, 1735; Jan. 22 and 29,
1736. This exchange may have been related, at least indirectly, to the attempt by
Governor William Cosby of New York to set up the provincial Supreme Court as
an equity court in 1732, which was what initiated the train of events that culminated in the trial of John Peter Zenger. During that controversy, of course,
William Bradford's *New-York Gazette* took the side of Cosby, and Zenger's *New-
York Weekly Journal* the side of his opponents.

35. *AWM*, Nov. 6, 20, and 27, Dec. 4 and 18, 1740; *P.G.*, Nov. 13, Dec. 11,
1740; *Papers of Benjamin Franklin*, II, 263–69, 270–81; Frank Luther Mott, *A
History of American Magazines, 1741–1850* (New York: D. Appleton, 1930), 24, 71–
77.

36. Patricia U. Bonomi, *A Factious People: Politics and Society in Colonial New
York* (New York: Columbia Univ. Press, 1971), 16.

37. Account of life of William Bradford by his son, William Bradford II, Society Collection, ms., Hist. Soc. Pa. This account also gives the year of Bradford's
birth as 1660 and the date of his arrival in Philadelphia as 1682. I have accepted the
more scholarly findings in the *DAB*, which dates his birth May 20, 1663, and his
arrival in America in 1685, sometime after his marriage in London on April 28.

38. DeArmand, *Andrew Bradford*, 2–3; *DAB*, s.v. William Bradford (May 20,
1663–May 23, 1752).

39. The other three: James Franklin of the *New-England Courant*, 29; Thomas
Lewis, who had just succeeded to the Boston postmastership and the *Gazette*,
probably in his 20s; and William Bradford's son Andrew of the *American Weekly
Mercury*, 39.

40. Douglas C. McMurtrie, *Pioneer Printing in New York* (Springfield, Ill.,
1933; reprinted from *National Printer Journalist* of 1933). Copy in Widener Library,
Harvard University.

41. Dec. 5 and 12, 1726.

42. Counting repeats. In addition, there was one illegible advertisement because the paper in the extant file is torn.

43. The *Gazette*, however, did devote substantial space in the early and middle
months of 1733 to news from London about the parliamentary debates over various
excise bills, including the one we call the Molasses Act. This coverage included
reports of popular demonstrations against some of that legislation in England, and
of the condemnatory reaction of the House of Commons to a memorial from
Massachusetts against the Molasses Act. See esp. *NYG*, Aug. 16 and Sept. 10,
1733.

44. For earlier factional disputes in New York, see Bonomi, *Factious People*, 56–
102.

45. This follows the account of Stanley Nider Katz in his introduction to James
Alexander, *A Brief Narrative of the Case and Trial of John Peter Zenger*, ed. Katz
(Cambridge, Mass.: Harvard Univ. Press, 1963), 2–4.

46. Stephen Botein, *"Mr. Zenger's Malice and Falshood": Six Issues of the New-*

York Weekly Journal, 1733–34 (Worcester: American Antiquarian Society, 1985), 6–7.

47. *DAB*, s.v. John Peter Zenger (1697–July 28, 1746).

48. Charles Evans, *American Bibliography*, Vols. I and II, and Printer's Index.

49. Ibid., Nos. 3511–14, 3530, 3540, 3585, 3595, 3608.

50. Ibid., Nos. 3700–3702, 3727.

51. "Difficult" rather than necessarily "impossible" because Bradford wanted to be impartial and tried, however unsuccessfully, to please both sides. In 1734 he announced that he had refused to run in the *Gazette* an especially virulent pro-Cosby piece, and later in the year he printed and advertised a pamphlet against equity jurisdiction by William Smith, a member of the Morrisite camp. (Botein, "*Mr. Zenger's Malice and Falshood*," 11.)

52. This is close to, and suggested by, Botein's argument in "*Mr. Zenger's Malice and Falshood*," 7. See there and passim his linkage of the Zenger episode to opposition to the Walpole regime in England, especially by the *Craftsman*.

53. Because the trial and acquittal of Zenger in 1735 is one of the most thoroughly discussed episodes in the early history of both American law and American journalism, I have made no effort to offer a reading of that event here. The most thorough treatment is to be found in Katz, *Brief Narrative*, but Botein's more recent "*Mr. Zenger's Malice and Falshood*" is also extremely useful and offers a sensible interpretation of both the printed dispute and the outcome of the case. Another interesting interpretation can be found in Warner, *Letters of the Republic*, 49–58. Among other important treatments is that of Leonard W. Levy, *Emergence of a Free Press* (New York: Oxford Univ. Press, 1985), 35–45. For good discussions of the political context, see, besides Bonomi's *Factious People*, Stanley Nider Katz, *Newcastle's New York: Anglo-American Politics, 1732–1753* (Cambridge, Mass.: Harvard Univ. Press, 1968), and Michael G. Kammen, *Colonial New York—A History* (New York: Charles Scribner's Sons, 1975), 202–7.

54. Carl Bridenbaugh, *Cities in the Wilderness: The First Century of Urban Life in America, 1625–1742* (New York: Oxford Univ. Press, 1971), 435–39.

55. Michael Kammen's discussion of Bradford's contribution to "anglicization" as well as to the movement from an "aural" to a literary culture in New York is especially relevant here. See *Colonial New York*, 133–34.

56. *NYG*, Dec. 11, 1732. A newspaper dateline of the same date as the paper was, by convention, used with items generated internally—even if it meant using some such phrase as "Thursday last" to indicate the day of an actual occurrence. Another indication that this piece was placed by the publisher rather than received from another source is its lack of any of the paraphernalia of a letter, such as a salutation or a closing, or of an explanatory note at the beginning.

57. Bridenbaugh, *Cities in the Wilderness*, 437.

58. *B.G.*, Jan. 8, 1732[/3]. Save for the shipping list, this was the only piece of New York news in *B.G.* that week.

59. *NYG*, Dec. 18, 1732. The issue of "assemblies" and similar diversions was debated in Philadelphia a little more than seven years later, during the visit of George Whitefield. The exchange between "Obadiah Plainman" and "Tom Trueman" in the *P.G.* from May 1 through May 29, 1740, which spilled over into the *AWM* of May 22, makes "the Dancing School, Assembly and Concert Room" an issue of both religion and class. The obvious hand of Benjamin Franklin in promoting that lively exchange, and perhaps contributing to it pseudonymously, leads one

to wonder somewhat wistfully how Silence Dogood might have altered the terms of discourse had she and the *NEC* still been on the Boston scene in 1732.

60. As far as I can determine from the relatively scanty files that survive, the *Post-Boy* contributed little to the development of the newspaper genre in America. Huske, whose primary political interests were in New Hampshire rather than in Massachusetts, was really Boston postmaster in name only, carrying out his duties there through a deputy. Since that is the case, his decision to start up a newspaper after agreeing to let Boydell have the *Gazette* is somewhat puzzling. It may be that he and Governor Jonathan Belcher wished to have an organ that could be used when necessary in the interests of the governor's party against the rising Wentworth party in New Hampshire and as a safeguard, perhaps, against the influence in Massachusetts of Boydell's *Gazette*, whose proprietor was hardly on friendly terms with Belcher. The evidence, however, is too scanty to make a conclusive judgment. For that reason among others, I have elected to omit a full discussion of the *Boston Post-Boy*.

61. Carl Van Doren, *Benjamin Franklin* (New York: Viking, 1957), 4.

Chapter 9. The Printer as Publisher

1. *P.G.*, Oct. 2, 1729; reprinted in Leonard W. Labaree et al., eds., *The Papers of Benjamin Franklin* (New Haven: Yale Univ. Press, 1959–), I, 158–59.

2. See Stephen Botein, "'Meer Mechanics' and an Open Press: The Business and Political Strategies of Colonial American Printers," *Perspectives in American History* IX (1975), 127–225.

3. Charles E. Clark and Charles Wetherell, "The Measure of Maturity: The *Pennsylvania Gazette*, 1728–1765," *WMQ*, 3rd ser., XLVI (April 1989), 279–303.

4. R. Campbell, *The London Tradesman; Being a Compendious View of all the Trades, Professions, Arts, Both Liberal and Mechanic, Now Practised in the Cities of London and Westminster* (London, 1747), 123; Philip Luckombe, *The History and Art of Printing* (London: Printed by W. Adlard and J. Browne for J. Johnson, 1771), 377.

5. Franklin, *Autobiography*, 58.

6. For a brief account of Greeley's early career, see W. J. Rorabaugh, *The Craft Apprentice from Franklin to the Machine Age in America* (New York: Oxford Univ. Press, 1986), 78–85. Another rich source for insights into a printer's apprenticeship is Joseph T. Buckingham, *Personal Memoirs and Recollections of Editorial Life*, 2 vols. (Boston: Ticknor, Reed, and Fields, 1852), I, 21–30. Buckingham (1779–1861) apprenticed in Windham, Conn., Walpole, N.H., and Greenfield, Mass., in the 1790s, and later published the *New-England Galaxy* and *Boston Courier*, both in Boston.

7. Wroth, *Colonial Printer*, 79–80.

8. Ibid., 126–30, 137–39.

9. Donald F. Durnbaugh, "Christopher Sauer, Pennsylvania-German Printer: His Youth in Germany and Later Relationships with Europe," *Pa. Mag. of Hist. and Biog.* LXXXII (1958), 316–40.

10. Philip Gaskell, *A New Introduction to Bibliography* (Oxford: Oxford Univ. Press, 1972), 175–76, cited by C. William Miller in "The Variable Dimension, or the Usefulness in Understanding Printing and Publishing for the American Colonial Historian" (unpub. paper delivered at the American Antiquarian So-

ciety Conference, "Printing and Society in Early America," Oct. 24–25, 1980), 33.

11. On numbers of presses, see Miller, "The Variable Dimension," 33; on the labor shortage in colonial American printing, see Wroth, *Colonial Printer*, 158–59.

12. Mary R. M. Goodwin, "The Printing House, Block 18, Colonial Lot #48. A House History," Colonial Williamsburg Research Dept. Report, Sept. 1952 (typescript at Colonial Williamsburg), 12 and 12n.; Miller, "The Variable Dimension," 34.

13. For one analysis of these and similar associations among American printers, see Wetherell, "Brokers of the Word," 73–83, 113–18.

14. Franklin's ms. "Prices of Printing Work in Philadelphia 1754," which includes journeymen's wages because they were part of the calculation in pricing a printing job, is in the Isaiah Thomas Papers at the American Antiquarian Society. It is reproduced in Wroth, *Colonial Printer*, 181. Wroth uses a facsimile of a Philadelphia printer's hours and wage scale of 1802, contained in Ethelbert Stewart, *A Documentary History of the Early Organization of Printers* (Bull. of Bureau of Labor No. 61, U.S. Dept. of Commerce), 857–1033, as the basis of his assertion that "A fairly competent compositor on book and pamphlet work could set 600 ems an hour . . . ." He adds that he could work faster than that setting the narrow columns of newspapers (which were not quite as narrow in 1740 as in 1802). Since the tools and technology of typesetting were essentially the same in 1740 as in 1802, I have assumed that the speed at which a compositor could work was not greatly different in the two eras. I have selected pages from two different numbers of the *Gazette* in order to combine a characteristically spacious page one with a typically dense inside page, a combination not easily found in a single number.

15. Mary R. M. Goodwin, "The Printing Office. Its Activities, Furnishings, and Articles for Sale," Colonial Williamsburg Research Dept. Report, March 20, 1958.

16. For a discussion of drying, another time-consuming aspect of many print jobs but which I have concluded was probably omitted in the case of most newspapers, see Chapter 4, n. 28.

17. The actual printing schedule of most weekly newspapers was almost certainly not confined to only one day each week. In the case of a paper aimed for morning distribution, as most were, the printer most likely put in a stint of several hours printing one side of the sheet a day or more before publication (perhaps Saturday morning in the case of a Monday morning newspaper) and another in the early morning of publication day printing the other side, usually pages two and three, which customarily contained the news copied from the newspapers that had arrived in the Saturday post and the local items composed in the print shop. This second stint might have been performed more rapidly than the first if it was squeezed in before the regular day's business, with its interruptions, began. In winter, presswork could have been performed before daybreak by candlelight, though it was much better to set type in daylight. Whatever the schedule, a press would have been committed to the newspaper and thus unavailable for other uses for at least a sixth of the printer's weekly working time. For the theoretical press production of a token (240 sheets) per hour, see Wroth, *Colonial Printer*, 80; for pressmen's wages, see Franklin, "Prices of Printing Work in Philadelphia 1754," or Wroth, *Colonial Printer*, 181.

18. Goodwin, "Printing Office. Activities . . . ," 2–3.

19. It was Bartholomew Green's daughter who delivered to Samuel Sewall the

proof of an article he had written for the *Boston News-Letter* on December 24, 1705 (*Diary of Samuel Sewall*, Thomas, ed., I, 537). For "Prime" Fowle, see Thomas, *History of Printing*, 128n. His status as a slave seems clear from subsequent recollections of Fowle's career after he moved from Boston to Portsmouth in 1756 (Charles W. Brewster, *Rambles about Portsmouth*, First Series (Portsmouth, 1873; rpt. Somersworth, N.H.: New Hampshire Publishing, 1971, 210–11). Whether Andrew Cain of Philadelphia, the other black pressman Thomas mentions, was enslaved or free is less clear.

20. Harris, "Structure, Ownership and Control of the Press," 84–86; Wiles, *Freshest Advices*, 45–49.

21. Wroth, *Colonial Printer*, 151.

22. Goodwin, "Printing Office. Activities . . . ," 2–3.

23. Ibid.

24. Franklin, "Prices of Printing Work in Philadelphia 1754," or Wroth, *Colonial Printer*, 181.

25. In 1743, Kneeland & Green charged the Province 12s, 6d per sheet for paper and printing the votes of the House of Representatives, and in 1758 Samuel Kneeland was charging 19s per sheet for the same work. See ms. records in Book Trades Collection, AAS.

26. *BNL*, Feb. 4 and 21, 1723.

27. *W.R.*, Aug. 11, 1735.

28. Copies of these annual broadsides can sometimes be found bound at the appropriate place in files of eighteenth-century newspapers. Two such examples are bound in the AAS files of the (Philadelphia) *AWM* just before the number for Jan. 7, 1734/5, and of the *New-York Weekly Post-Boy* between Dec. 31, 1744, and Jan. 7, 1745. Clarence S. Brigham devotes an entire chapter to this subject in *Journals and Journeymen: A Contribution to the History of Early American Newspapers* (Philadelphia: Univ. of Pennsylvania Press, 1950), 84–98. Buckingham describes his experiences with the "time-indefinite custom" of distributing "a New Year's Address, with which to salute my customers" on New Year's Day 1797 in Greenfield (*Personal Memoirs*, I, 27).

29. ". . . Those Gentlemen who are the Supporters thereof, whose First Quarter is now up, and have not yet paid the same, are desired (if they see cause) to send it in to the Printer hereof . . . or pay it to the Bearer." *BNL*, April 4, 1723.

30. See colophon of *B.G.* throughout 1740, and the April 28, 1740, *B.G.* for the resumption of its post-free status and change of subscription price; for postal charges, see Chapter 6 above, n. 16. The order of 1758 by Benjamin Franklin and William Hunter not only spells out the new regulations for posting newspapers but sheds light on how it had been done previously. The order is printed in the *New-York Mercury* of May 29, 1758.

31. *WNL*, Jan. 5, 1727.

32. Goodwin, "Printing Office. Activities . . . ," 2–3.

33. *BEP*, April 2, 1739; April 21, 1740.

34. Andrew Ward, Jr., to Mrs. Hannah Boydell, May 21, 1740, photocopy, Misc. Bound Collection, MHS.

35. Boydell announced in the *B.G.* of Jan. 1 and 8, 1739, not only that he would grant no further credit to anyone who owed for more than fifteen months, but also

that he would accept no subscriptions that were not paid at least a quarter in advance. At the same time he raised the annual subscription cost by four shillings, but applied the new rates only to new subscribers.

36. Quoted in Brigham, *Journals and Journeymen*, 23.

37. Beverly McAnear, "James Parker versus New York Province," *New York History* XXII (1941), quoted in Schlesinger, *Prelude to Independence*, 52.

38. Mss. in Book Trades Collection, AAS.

39. "Prices of Printing Work in Philadelphia 1754," ms., Isaiah Thomas Collection, AAS.

40. The annual in-town rate for the *News-Letter* was 12s., for the *Weekly Journal* and *Evening-Post* both 16s., and for the *Boston Gazette* 24s., reduced during the year to 20s. The latter two are high compared with the subscription rates one finds later in the century, even though advertising rates appear to have remained about the same for the next twenty years.

41. Clark and Wetherell, "Measure of Maturity," 280n.

42. Ibid., 290.

43. *Papers of Benjamin Franklin*, XII, 87–99. Items 31, 32, 37, 38, 39, 40, 44, and 45 report income from the *Gazette* totaling £16,630; of these, items 31, 32, and 45, amounting to £3,639, identify income from advertising.

44. Based on an analysis by Lawrence C. Wroth in *Typographical Heritage*, 109–11. As for the Boston newspapers a bit earlier in the century, an annual income of £100 in advertising and £360 in subscriptions, as suggested in the previous paragraph, would mean revenues totaling £460, of which £460 is 21.7 percent, almost exactly the 21.9 percent to which the Franklin-Hall figures attribute advertising revenues.

45. *Papers of Benjamin Franklin*, XIII, 97.

46. The relative financial importance of various aspects of the early American printer's business has been much debated. Mary Ann Yodelis, in *Who Paid the Piper? Publishing Economics in Boston, 1763–1775*, Journalism Monographs No. 38 (Lexington, Ky.: Association for Education in Journalism, 1975), emphasizes the importance of "general printing" such as political and religious pamphlets and of newspaper advertising in an effort to show that government printing was not essential to a printer's success in the volatile period of her study. Georgia B. Bumgardner, drawing upon the findings of Peter J. Parker and C. William Miller's analysis of Franklin's and Hall's imprints and accounts, has argued for the relative importance of ephemeral job printing, including broadsides. Part of her study, however, includes an analysis of the *Rutland* (Vt.) *Herald* in the early national period. The Rutland printer's daybook for 1798–1802 attributes 59% of his receipts to newspaper advertising, less than 1% to newspaper sales, and 10% to job printing. ("Vignettes of the Past: American Historical Broadsides Through the War of 1812," *Printing History* IV (1982), 37–48.) One can begin to conclude that the financial structure of a printer's operations varied widely according to individual circumstances throughout the eighteenth century. There may be no satisfactory rule of thumb at all.

47. See Stephen Botein's argument concerning the deliberate political neutrality of pre-revolutionary printers in "'Meer Mechanics' and an Open Press."

48. *W.R.*, April 2, 1733.

49. Stated policies of openness and non-partisanship such as those of Fleet,

while very much the norm among printers of this era, were not always carried out in practice, though (except in New York) printers were usually quite subtle about the way in which they took sides. See Chapter 12 below for an episode during the controversy over George Whitefield in which Fleet's incautious, even though subtle, disclosure of his own point of view on a sensitive issue forced him into a defensive, not entirely ingenuous reassertion of impartiality.

50. Botein, "'Meer Mechanics' and an Open Press"; Thomas Leonard, *The Power of the Press: The Birth of American Political Reporting* (New York: Oxford Univ. Press, 1986).

51. *W.R.*, Jan. 27, 1735.

52. Thomas, *History of Printing*, 370.

53. Hennig Cohen, *The South-Carolina Gazette, 1732–1775* (Columbia: Univ. of South Carolina Press, 1953), 10.

54. Klein, "The Third Earl of Shaftesbury and the Progress of Politeness," 206–8.

55. *V.G.*, June 20, 1766.

56. Franklin, *Autobiography*, 165.

57. *V.G.*, June 20, 1766. This was part of the introduction to his announcement that he was rejecting some pieces that had been offered for publication, along with "cash sent with them to pay for their insertion." The announcement states, "I neither expect, or desire, any fee for publishing such pieces . . . ." It does not say that he would refuse a fee for publishing an acceptable piece if the fee were offered, but it takes no more than a reasonably charitable reading of the announcement to reach that conclusion.

58. *W.R.*, Jan. 27, 1735.

59. Franklin's rejection of the "scurrilous and defamatory" piece offered to the *Pennsylvania Gazette* in 1729 consisted of a characteristically anecdotal reply that was premised upon the recognition that he would have been paid, perhaps handsomely, for printing it: ". . . To determine whether I should publish it or not, I went home in the evening, purchased a two penny loaf at the baker's, and with water from the pump made my supper; I then wrapped myself up in my great coat, and laid down on the floor and slept till morning, when, on another loaf and mug of water, I made my breakfast. From this regimen I feel no inconvenience whatever. Finding I can live in this manner, I have formed a determination never to prostitute my press to the purposes of corruption, and abuse of this kind, for the sake of gaining a more comfortable subsistence." Thomas, *History of Printing*, 370.

60. Cohen, *The South Carolina Gazette*, 10.

61. *WNL*, Jan. 5, 1727.

62. *W.R.*, April 2, 1733. Italics have been disregarded.

63. *Autobiography*, 78. Franklin, it is true, considered Keimer's method of composing from his head unusual, as it may have been at this early date (1723), and did not think of it as particularly praiseworthy. It is hard to imagine, however, that as printers became more experienced in the production of newspapers, and more pressured for time, many did not write at least brief passages right from the case as a matter of course.

64. *W.R.*, Aug. 11, 1735.

Chapter 10. The Ritual: The Reader's World

1. Clark and Wetherell, "Measure of Maturity," Table IV, p. 293.

2. In carrying out a much more limited analysis of the use of space in London's *St. James's Post* between February 1715 and March 1722, I arrived at the following breakdown of all the items and space in the paper, not just the news events: Continental Europe, 42.5% of items and 38.7% of space; British Isles (including London), 51.5% of items and 33.6% of space; Asia Minor or North Africa, 3.3% of items and 24.3% of space; other, 2.7% of items and 2.4% of space. The count includes two very long installments of an atypical essay on the King of Morocco, resulting in a deceptively high proportion of space reported for "Asia Minor or North Africa."

3. The essential work on the eighteenth-century novel is Ian Watt, *The Rise of the Novel: Studies in Defoe, Richardson and Fielding* (Berkeley: Univ. of California Press, 1957). While Watt does not discuss "narrative" as such, the idea is implicit in his emphasis on the importance to literary realism of "the modern sense of time." See pp. 21–25.

4. The reader will recognize here an allusion to one of the main points in Marshall McLuhan's *Gutenberg Galaxy*, but I do not intend my own cautious statement of the possible influence of the medium on the *writer* to be taken as any more than that. Much the same, after all, could be said more broadly of any of the western languages in their written form, whether before or after Gutenberg. I also recognize, thanks in large measure to Preston Shea, who steered me to some of the relevant scholarship, that many contemporary studies of how the *reader* extracts meaning from the printed (or written) word rests on the understanding that the act of reading is not "linear" at all. See Wolfgang Iser, *The Implied Reader: Patterns of Communication in Prose Fiction from Bunyan to Beckett* (Baltimore: Johns Hopkins Univ. Press, 1974) and *The Act of Reading: A Theory of Aesthetic Response* (Baltimore: Johns Hopkins Univ. Press, 1978), and Jane P. Tomkins, ed., *Reader-Response Criticism: From Formalism to Post-Structuralism* (Baltimore: Johns Hopkins Univ. Press, 1980).

5. Quoted in Donald J. Wilcox, *The Measure of Times Past: Pre-Newtonian Chronologies and the Rhetoric of Relative Time* (Chicago: Univ. of Chicago Press, 1987), 22. Wilcox's discussion of "absolute" or "Newtonian" time, its novelty, and its limitations (pp. 16–50, 187–220) is especially pertinent to the point I am trying to make here.

6. The time as stream metaphor was Watts's eighteenth-century embellishment of the line "Thou [God] carriest them away as with a flood" (v. 5) in Psalm 90, of which his hymn "Our God, Our Help in Ages Past" is a paraphrase. The original, though it is very much about time, contains no explicit time imagery.

7. See again Milton Mueller, "The Currency of the Word," in which the "periodicity" of seventeenth-century English news periodicals forms an important part of the argument.

8. *NYG*, March 11, 1733 [/4].

9. *BNL*, Nov. 10, 1718.

10. See, e.g., *AWM*, Nov. 6, 1740, for a letter from a captain whose ship had been taken off the English Channel by a Spanish vessel the previous June.

11. Clark and Wetherell, "Measure of Maturity," Table III, p. 292. Again this use of the news columns of the *Pennsylvania Gazette* bears comparison with that of

St. James's Post, which in the numbers analyzed (see n. 2) devoted 41.6% of its news items and 54.9% of its news space to military and diplomatic subjects. Royalty and nobility, as in the *Pennsylvania Gazette*, ran a distant second, with 12.6% of the items and 8.9% of the space.

12. Except in the columns of the *New-England Courant*, 1721–27, and in the occasional ambiguities of Benjamin Franklin's *Pennsylvania Gazette*.

13. For another example of the apparent newsworthiness of an extraordinary eating performance, see the account of the London razor-grinder copied by the *New-England Courant* on November 27, 1721, Chapter 6.

14. *B.G.*, Jan. 8, 1739. The same item appeared in *BEP* of the same date.

15. *OED*, s.v. "fellow."

16. *BNL*, April 11, 1720.

17. *BEPB*, May 12, 1735; *AWM*, May 22, 1735.

18. *WNL*, Feb. 15 and 22, 1728; *NEWJ*, Feb. 19 and 26, 1728; *B.G.*, Feb. 26, 1728.

19. BEP, Jan. 1, 1739; *WNL*, Jan. 4 and March 8, 1739; *NEWJ*, Oct. 16, 1739.

20. *BNL*, May 13, 1725. For a different, but equally important point to be made about treatments of death in the Boston newspapers to 1730, see Stephen C. Messer, "Loud Sermons in the Press: The Reporting of Death in Early Massachusetts Newspapers," *Historical Journal of Massachusetts* 17 (1989), 38–51.

21. These findings corroborate in general those of Stephen Botein, Jack R. Censer, and Harriet Ritvo, whose analysis of a sample of eighteenth-century French-language and English-language periodicals discloses, for example, that "The poor figured frequently in the English press, as a kind of separate breed with a different moral nature from the sober majority of the population. . . . Criminality was the characteristic of the lower classes most elaborately illustrated in the stories of English-language newspapers." Almost 70 percent of the criminals described in the sample were identifiable as lower-class whites, and more than 10 percent, mostly in American colonial periodicals, were blacks. In noting the difference between the French and the English press of the period, Botein, Censer, and Ritvo report having found a middle-class orientation in the English and Anglo-American newspapers as opposed to the aristocratic orientation of the French-language press. I would not disagree, but neither have I found, as they have, a notable deemphasis or criticism of royalty or the aristocratic classes in the English-language press. Their chief sample, however, was from the years 1755–64, and consisted of three newspapers from London, two from the English provinces, and three from the American colonies. "The Periodical Press in Eighteenth-Century English and French Society: A Cross-Cultural Approach," *Comparative Studies in Society and History* 23 (1981), 464–90.

22. Tales of the privy must have appealed to English as well as to American audiences, since the *Cambridge Journal* of Aug. 27, 1748, reported that "one Day last Week, a pretty lusty Gentlewoman going to a Necessary House at the Bottom of her Garden at Clapton, the Boards gave way, and she fell up to her Chin in the Soil." Cranfield, *The Development of the Provincial Newspaper*, 74.

23. *AWM*, Dec. 29, 1733; Oct. 9, 1740; May 29, 1735. A compilation of advertisements for runaway slaves and indentured servants from the *Pennsylvania Gazette*, with a useful introduction, may be found in Billy G. Smith and Richard Wojtowicz, *Blacks Who Stole Themselves: Advertisements for Runaways in the* Pennsylvania Gazette, *1728–1790* (Philadelphia: Univ. of Pennsylvania Press, 1989).

24. *BEP*, Nov. 19, 1739.

25. *B.G.*, Aug. 4, 1735. For other examples among many of the newspapers' treatment of racial and ethnic minorities, see *B.G.*, July 18, 1726, and *BEP*, April 7 and 28, 1740.

26. *P.G.*, July 8, 1731. Copied in *Papers of Benjamin Franklin*, 1, 217.

27. See Laurel Thatcher Ulrich, "Vertuous Women Found: New England Ministerial Literature, 1668–1735," *American Quarterly* XXVIII (1976), 20–40.

28. See again Ulrich, "Vertuous Women Found," 33–37, 40.

29. *NEWJ*, July 30, 1733. Writing by women in this era was specifically countenanced by New England ministers such as Cotton Mather and Benjamin Colman (Ulrich, "Vertuous Women Found," 34–37), and although this instance of a published woman's poem is rare for the newspapers of the day, other women's poetry occasionally made its way into print in other forms.

30. *SCG.*, Jan. 15, 1731[/2]. Michael Warner makes much of the "Female Pen" phrase in this and similar instances in discussing the metaphorical significance of writing as a "gendered" activity (*Letters of the Republic*, 15–16). This dimension of the issue is not a concern of this book.

31. *SCG*, Jan. 22, 1731/2.

32. *SCG*, Jan. 29, 1731/2.

33. *SCG*, March 11 and 18, 1731/2.

34. *W.R.*, Jan. 10 and 17, 1732. For more on the male response to hoop skirts, see Shea, "The Rhetoric of Authority," 291–95.

35. *AWM*, April 6, 1727.

36. *NEWJ*, April 1, 1728; see Chapter 7 above.

37. *B.G.*, April 15, 1728.

38. *NYWJ*, Sept. 30, 1734.

39. The whole exchange was picked up by the *BWPB* on Dec. 8, 1735.

40. *BEP*, Oct. 13, 1735.

41. *NEWJ*, July 24, 1739.

42. *BEP*, Dec. 10, 1739.

43. *AWM*, Feb. 11, 1734/5.

44. *AWM*, Jan. 23 and Feb. 13, 1721[/2]. The use of the term "Moabite" in the first item apparently refers to the combative nature of the descendants of Moab, who were often at war with the Israelites. See, e.g., II Kings 3:21–27.

45. *B.G.*, Nov. 20, 1732.

46. *NYG*, Dec. 18, 1735. For a full account of this exchange, see Chapter 8 above.

47. *NYWJ*, Nov. 19, 1739.

48. *AWM*, Dec. 18, 1740. For the founding of the *Champion*, see Harris and Lee, eds., *The Press in English Society*, 49. The Salique, or Salic, law, which was part of French and Spanish but not English law, excluded women from succession to the throne.

49. Quoted in Cranfield, *The Development of the English Newspaper*, 75.

50. *NEWJ*, March 20, 1727. See Chapter 7 above.

51. *NEWJ*, July 24 and 31, Aug. 14 and 21, Sept. 4, 11, and 18, 1727; *NYG*, Aug. 7 and 14, 1727.

52. *B.G.*, Aug. 14, 1727; April 1, 1734; April 16, 1739; *BWNL.*, Oct. 29, 1730. Facs. of *NYWJ*, Oct. 7, 1734, and excerpt from *NYG*, Oct. 14, 1734, in Botein, "*Mr. Zenger's Malice and Falshood*," 45, 47.

53. Printed under a London, May 4, dateline in *BWNL*, June 23, 1737.
54. *B.G.*, July 18, 1726.

Chapter 11. The Newspaper in Culture

1. See David D. Hall, "The Mental World of Samuel Sewall," MHS *Proceedings* 92 (1980), 21–44, esp. 31–33, and, more broadly, David Paul Nord, "Teleology and News: The Religious Roots of American Journalism, 1630–1730," *JAH* 77 (1990), 9–38.

2. Nord, "Teleology and News," esp. 338.

3. *Diary of Samuel Sewall*, Thomas, ed., II, 462, 492. For a full and perceptive discussion of Sewall's information world, see Brown, *Knowledge Is Power*, 16–41.

4. Brown, *Knowledge Is Power*, 37–38.

5. *Diary of Samuel Sewall*, Thomas, ed., 531–32, 537. *BNL*, Nov. 26 and Dec. 24, 1705. This mission to Quebec by Samuel Vetch and William Dudley, the governor's son, intended to secure the redemption of English captives, became one of the particulars in Cotton Mather's savage indictment of the Dudley administration in *The Deplorable State of New-England* (1707).

6. Benedict Anderson, *Imagined Communities: Reflections on the Origin and Spread of Nationalism* (New York: Verso, 1983), 62.

7. Mather Family Papers, Box 4, AAS, typescript. See, e.g., diary entries for April 3, May 16, July 24, Aug. 4 and 22, 1696, and Feb. 20, 1696/7 in Folder 1; April 14 and Dec. 10, 1697, in Folder 2; April 20 and 21, Sept. 23, Oct. 1, 1698, and Feb. 3, 1698/9 in Folder 3; March 6 and 13, April 10, 13, and 14, May 23 and 24, June 8, July 1, Aug. 23 and 24, 1702 in Folder 4; and similar entries through 1721, Folder 8. Even after the beginning of the *News-Letter*, Mather continued to make entries from his reading of the *London Gazette* and the *Postman*, and at the end of most years recorded advertisements that interested him from the London newspapers. His diary never mentions the local newspapers by name. Surely this reveals an elaborate conceit around which he apparently built a metropolitan self-image, just as it also probably reflects his well-known contempt of the *New-England Courant*, to which he took pains to renounce his subscription. (*B.G.*, Jan. 29, 1722; *NEC*, Feb. 5, 1722.) But hostility to the *Courant* alone does not account for the absence from his diary of local titles, which he must certainly have read, between 1704 and 1721. For another Bostonian's private use of newspapers, see the commonplace book kept by Benjamin Franklin's Uncle Benjamin (1650–1727), *Publications of Col. Soc. of Mass.* X (1907), 191–205.

8. Photostats of *BNL*, April 26 and Aug. 2, 1739; *NEWJ*, Aug. 14, 1739, Jan. 1, 1740; and *B.G.*, July 2, 1739, in AAS.

9. *Peter Kalm's Travels in North America*, ed. Adolph B. Benson (New York: Wilson-Erickson, 1937), II, 645–48, 656–80, 687.

10. Ibid., II, 681.

11. Papers of Peter Force, 8D, 42:4, ms. Library of Congress. The rather long description of the famous experiment, obviously supplied to David Hall by Benjamin Franklin, did not mention Franklin's name. (*P.G.*, Oct. 19, 1752.) Though Franklin remained a partner of Hall in the ownership of their joint printing business and the *Gazette*, he had turned over the active operation of the business to Hall in 1748.

12. Papers of Peter Force, 8D, 42:5, ms. LOC.

13. *Letters of John Adams, Addressed to His Wife,* ed. Charles Francis Adams (Boston: Charles C. Little and James Brown, 1891), I, 151–52. For Du Simitiere, see *DAB,* V, 553–55, where he is called "one of the first good portrait painters to come to America," and George C. Groce and David H. Wallace, *The New-York Historical Society's Dictionary of Artists in America, 1564–1860* (New Haven: Yale Univ. Press, 1957), 199. Whereas the notebooks discussed here were seen in the Library of Congress, the scrapbooks described by Adams, according to *DAB,* were acquired by the Library Company of Philadelphia.

14. Hall and Hench, eds., *Needs and Opportunities in the History of the Book: America, 1639–1876,* 230.

15. Wolfgang Iser, *The Implied Reader: Patterns of Communication in Prose Fiction from Bunyan to Beckett* (Baltimore: Johns Hopkins Univ. Press, 1974).

16. *NEWJ,* April 10, 1727; April 1, 1728. See Chapter 7 above.

17. *NEWJ,* July 30, 1733; see Chapter 10, above.

18. *SCG,* Jan. 15 and 22, 1731/2. See Chapter 10 above.

19. See James Carey's discussion of the "transmission" view of communication (to which he opposes the "ritual" view) in *Communication as Culture,* 14–18.

20. Careful reconstructions of the conditions of eighteenth-century life such as that at Colonial Williamsburg help the historian as well as the tourist imagine the sort of human interaction that is suggested here.

21. For one survey of recent attempts to deal with the "influence" of the French, English, and American press of the eighteenth century, see Jack R. Censer, "Recent Approaches to the Eighteenth Century Press," *Comparative Studies in Society and History* 31 (1989), 775–83.

22. Jeremy Black, *The English Press in the Eighteenth Century* (Philadelphia: Univ. of Pennsylvania Press, 1987); Botein, "'Mere Mechanicks' and an Open Press" and "Printers and the American Revolution," in Bailyn and Hench, eds., *The Press and the American Revolution,* 11–58.

23. The earliest and perhaps still best-known study of the role of the press in the American Revolution in recent times is Arthur M. Schlesinger, *Prelude to Independence: The Newspaper War on Britain, 1764–1776* (New York: Alfred A. Knopf, 1958). Jeffery A. Smith has recently supplied an extensive exploration of the development of an ideology of press freedom among colonial and revolutionary-era American newspaper publishers (and their English predecessors) in *Printers and Press Freedom* (1988). Other contributions to the debate over the development of freedom of the press have included, most conspicuously, the widely discussed corpus of Leonard W. Levy, especially his *Legacy of Suppression: Freedom of Speech and Press in Early American History* (Cambridge, Mass.: Harvard Univ. Press, 1960) and its revision, *Emergence of a Free Press* (New York: Oxford Univ. Press, 1985), to which Smith's book is in part a response. See also, among many other possible titles, Lawrence H. Leder, "The Role of Newspapers in Early America 'In Defense of Their Own Liberty,'" *Huntington Library Quarterly* 30 (Nov. 1966), 1–16.

24. For one useful discussion of this point, see Joseph M. Torsella, "American National Identity, 1750–1790: Samples from the Popular Press," *Pa. Mag. Hist. & Biog.* 112 (1988), 167–88, esp. 170–71. Anderson's *Imagined Communities* is also relevant, esp. chaps. 2–4.

25. *P.G.,* June 6, 1745.

26. The distinction between "high" and "low" culture, a development of the nineteenth century, is the theme of Lawrence W. Levine, *Highbrow/Lowbrow: The*

Emergence of Cultural Hierarchy in America (Cambridge, Mass.: Harvard Univ. Press, 1988).

27. Anderson, *Imagined Communities*, 33.

28. For the concept of "collective mentality" applied to a slightly earlier period, see David D. Hall, "The World of Print and Collective Mentality in Seventeenth-Century New England," in John Higham and Paul K. Conkin, eds., *New Directions in American Intellectual History* (Baltimore: Johns Hopkins Univ. Press, 1979), 166–80.

Chapter 12. The Transition

1. Estimates for numbers of newspapers in 1740 are derived from lists in R. S. Crane and F. B. Kaye, *A Census of British Newspapers and Periodicals, 1620–1800* (London: Holland, 1966); R. M. Wiles, *Freshest Advices: Early Provincial Newspapers in England* (Columbus: Ohio State Univ. Press, 1965), 373; Edward Connery Latham, comp., *Chronological Tables of American Newspapers 1690–1820* (Barre, Mass.: American Antiquarian Society and Barre Publishers, [1972]), 4–5; and Thomas, *History of Printing*, 604. Circulation estimates are from Harris, "The Structure, Ownership and Control of the Press, 1620–1780," in Boyce, Curran, and Wingate, eds., *Newspaper History*, 86–88; Wiles, *Freshest Advices*, 96–97, 99; Thomas, *History of Printing*, 14; Wroth, *Typographical Heritage*, 109–12; and Schlesinger, *Prelude to Independence*, 303–4.

2. Circulation figures for the first half of the eighteenth century are extremely difficult to come by, despite the records that ought to have been provided and preserved as a result of the Stamp Acts of 1712 and 1725, which affected English but not American newspapers. (See Harris, "Structure, Ownership and Control of the Press, 1620–1780," 82–85.) The rough estimates in this paragraph use 2000 as an average circulation for each of London's six dailies, 4000 for each of the six thrice weeklies and five London weeklies, slightly over 1000 for each of the twenty-nine English provincial papers (recognizing that while most were probably somewhat under that number, a few were substantially over it), and 600 for each American weekly (based on the estimates reported by Thomas for New England and by Schlesinger for New England and New York), rounding the total upward to account for some notably successful newspapers of the period such as the *Pennsylvania Gazette*. (On the other hand, we can guess that *Der Hoch-Deutsch Pennsylvänische Geschicht-Schrieber*, of which no known surviving copies exist, and the *Weekly Jamaica Courant*, to name two, had circulations well below the American average.) Compare these estimates with those in Stephen Botein, Jack R. Censer, and Harriet Ritvo, "The Periodical Press in Eighteenth-Century English and French Society: A Cross-Cultural Approach," *Comparative Studies in Society and History* XXIII (1981), 471. The estimates do not include the newspapers of Ireland, where *Pue's Occurrences* and perhaps two or three other newspapers were published in Dublin; at some time after 1715, there was one fairly long-lived newspaper each in Belfast, Cork, and Limerick. The remaining evidence for precise years of publication, however, is sparse. Moreover, since the Irish newspapers circulated for the most part only among the minority Protestant population, any comparisons of the Irish population with circulation figures would be misleading. See Robert Munter, *The History of the Irish Newspaper, 1685–1760* (Cambridge: Cambridge Univ. Press, 1967), 14–18; and Richard Robert Madden, *The History of Irish Periodi-*

cal Literature, 2 vols. (London: F. C. Newby, 1867; New York: Johnson Reprint, 1968), I, 209–93.

3. Based on an estimate of 6,820,000 in 1740 for England, Scotland, and Wales, compiled from E. A. Wrigley and R. S. Schofield, *The Population History of England 1541–1871: A Reconstruction* (Cambridge, Mass.: Harvard Univ. Press, 1981), table, p. 577 (England 5,576,000, England and Wales 5,971,000); and Michael Flinn, ed., *Scottish Population History from the 17th Century to the 1930's* (Cambridge: Cambridge Univ. Press, 1977), table, pp. 198–99 (849,000 for Scotland after applying 0.4% annual reduction from 1750 to 1755 in accordance with discussion on p. 13. The Boston estimate accepts Thomas's 600 copies for each newspaper (which is also the estimate for Boston of Botein et al.) and uses a population estimate of 17,000. For Massachusetts, the population estimate is 200,000. See Greene and Harrington, *American Population Before the Federal Census of 1790*, 15 and 22, note c.

4. Green and Harrington suggest an average family size of 5.7 to 6 in the American colonies, and at least 7 persons per household. *American Population before the Federal Census of 1790*, p. xxiii. On literacy, the standard work for colonial New England has been Kenneth A. Lockridge, *Literacy in Colonial New England: An Enquiry into the Social Context of Literacy in the Early Modern West* (New York: W. W. Norton, 1974), but see David D. Hall's criticism in "Education and the Social Order in Colonial America," *Reviews in American History* 3 (1975), 178–83, and for a more up-to-date discussion of literacy in early America see Richard D. Brown's summary of current scholarship in *Knowledge Is Power*, 11–12. In the course of the eighteenth century, male literacy moved from 80 to 90 percent in New England and in all sections the gap between male and female literacy almost disappeared. E. Jennifer Monaghan has stressed the distinction between reading and writing abilities in the colonial era. Inability to write, particularly among women, did not also signify an inability to read. See "Literacy Instruction and Gender in Colonial New England," in Cathy N. Davidson, ed., *Reading in America: Literature and Social History* (Baltimore: Johns Hopkins Univ. Press, 1989), 53–80.

5. *NEWJ*, Jan. 14 and 21, Feb. 18, March 11, 1734; *B.G.*, Feb. 25 and March 25, 1734. For a brief but lucid explanation of the problem and the issues surrounding it, see Curtis P. Nettels, *The Roots of American Civilization: A History of American Colonial Life* (New York: Appleton-Century Crofts, 1938), 530–37.

6. *NEWJ*, Jan. 1, 1740.

7. *BEP*, June 16 and July 14, 1740.

8. I am grateful to Neill DePaoli and Mark Russell for their separate investigations, using different methods, of American newspaper content after 1740. Their findings were reported in seminar papers at the University of New Hampshire in 1991 and 1992 respectively.

9. Frank Lambert, "'Pedlar in Divinity': George Whitefield and the Great Awakening, 1737–1745," *JAH* 77 (1990), 812–37.

10. As we should expect, however, Franklin himself did not fail to profit from the Whitefield connection, primarily by printing and selling Whitefield's printed works, proposals for which he advertised weekly in *P.G.* from November 22, 1739, well into early 1740. Lambert notes that Whitefield's printed works generated more revenue for Franklin in some cities than *Poor Richard's Almanac* (p. 821).

11. See, e.g., *AWM*, Nov. 29, Dec. 6, 13, 20, and 27, 1739; Jan. 8, 1740. Both

the *NYWJ* (Dec. 10 and 17, 1739) and the *P.G.* (Dec. 13, 1739) used their front pages for reprinting an anonymous pamphlet entitled *The Conduct and Doctrine of the Rev. Mr. Whitefield Vindicated from the Aspersions and Malicious Invective of His Enemies.*

12. *NYWJ*, Nov. 26, 1739; *P.G.*, Nov. 15 and 29, Dec. 6, 1739; April 17 and 24, 1740.

13. In addition to *BEP* of Sept. 29, 1740, see *WNL*, Oct. 2, 1740.

14. Botein, *"Mr. Zenger's Malice and Falshood,"* 6.

15. Cranfield, *Development of the Provincial Newspaper*, 135–36.

16. The significance of this change of ownership in the *Gazette* is suggested by Richard Bushman in *King and People in Provincial Massachusetts*, 261. See also Franklin, ed., *Boston Printers*, 117–35.

Index

Adams, John, 247
Adams, John, "Proteus Echo" writer, 144, 147, 149, 151, 155
Adams, Matthew, Couranteer, 128
Adams, Matthew, "Proteus Echo" writer, 144, 150–51, 155
Addison, Joseph, 42, 50–51; as model for American writers, 130–31, 148–49; on "politeness," 142. See also *Spectator*
Advertising, 7–8, 10, 16, 23, 30–31, 197; in London, 35–40, 43, 45, 48–49; of books, 36–38, 142, 151, 240; medical, 36, 38–40, 124–25; obscenity in, 48–49; in English provincial newspapers, 61–62, 65; in early Boston, 69; in Boston newspapers, 85, 88, 94–96, 112, 118, 120–22, 124–25, 129, 134, 139, 142, 151, 154, 158–59, 167–69, 213–14, 227, 240; in Philadelphia newspapers, 117–18, 172–73, 176; sham, 137–38; of real estate, 168, 213–14; in New York, 179–80; as factor in newspaper business, 203–6, 209;

fees, 205; cultural significance of, 251, 255, 257–58
Allen, John, 69–71
Almanacs, 69, 176, 217
American Antiquarian Society, 5
American Magazine, 161, 177
American Philosophical Society, 176
American Weekly Mercury, 103, 113, 120, 134; timing of, 105; naming of, 114–15; appearance of, 115; content, 115–19, 171–72, 226–27, 229, 234, 236–38, 241; breadth of coverage, 117–18; political content, 118–19, 172, 177, 262; Franklin contributes to, 173–75; rivalry with *P.G.*, 175, 177–78; use by Peter Kalm, 246; illustration, 116. See also Bradford, Andrew
Americanization of colonial newspapers, 6, 10, 134, 168–71, 211–13, 252–53, 258
Anderson, Benedict, 244, 255–56
Andros, Sir Edmund, 67, 68, 70
Anglicans, 105, 128, 140, 156. See also Church of England